THE
AFRICAN AMERICAN
EXPERIENCE
A HISTORY

CONSULTANTS

Sharon Harley
University of Maryland

Stephen Middleton
North Carolina State University

Charlotte M. Stokes
Alexandria, Virginia, Public Schools

 GLOBE BOOK COMPANY
A Division of Simon & Schuster
Englewood Cliffs, New Jersey

ABOUT THE COVER ARTIST

Ed Butler, an African American, is a graduate of the Philadelphia College of Art and a prominent graphic artist and illustrator. Among his various honors are the Society of Illustrators Merit Award and the American Institute of Graphic Artists 50 Best Books Award.

ABOUT THE COVER

For the cover design, Butler has juxtaposed two symbols—African kente cloth and the American flag. Kente cloth is a traditional West African fabric created by stitching narrow, handwoven strips of material together. These two symbols illustrate the dual heritage of African roots and American culture in the lives of African Americans.

Interior Electronic Design   Siren Design, Inc.

Photo Research   Omni-Photo Communications, Inc.

Cover Art   Ed Butler, Butler/Udell

Maps   Mapping Specialists Limited

Printed in the United States of America.   10   9   8

ISBN: 0-8359-0410-5

GLOBE BOOK COMPANY
A Division of Simon & Schuster
Englewood Cliffs, New Jersey

Distributed by   **PRENTICE-HALL, INC.**
A Simon & Schuster Company
Englewood Cliffs, NJ

ISBN: 0-1301-9969-9

CONSULTANTS

Sharon Harley is Associate Professor of Afro-American Studies and History at the University of Maryland. She received her Ph.D. from Howard University. She has conducted extensive research in African American women's history, focusing on the history of women workers.

Stephen Middleton is Assistant Professor of History at North Carolina State University. He received his Ph.D. from Miami University, Ohio. His particular field of interest is the history of African Americans in pre–Civil War Ohio, an area in which he has written and edited many articles and books.

Charlotte M. Stokes is Teacher Specialist for Social Studies in the Alexandria, Virginia, City Public Schools. She received degrees in history at the University of Chicago and North Carolina A&T State University. Stokes has helped develop and implement new social studies curricula in the Alexandria schools.

REVIEWERS

Dr. Chapman W. Bouldin, Jr.
Instructional Teacher
Leader
Social Studies Department
Brashear High School
Pittsburgh, Pennsylvania

Lawrence D. Broughton
Instructor, African
American History
North Chicago Community
High School
North Chicago, Illinois

Booker T. Coleman, Jr.
Director, Social Studies/
Multicultural Education
Community School District 9
Bronx, New York

Mildred Fryer
Department Head,
Humanities
Snowden International High
School
Boston, Massachusetts

Cleotha Jordan
Consultant, African/African
American History
High School Development
Center
Detroit, Michigan

Subira Kifano
Teacher Advisor
Language Development
Program for African
American Students
Los Angeles Unified School
District
Los Angeles, California

Barbara G. Moses
Curriculum Coordinator
School District of
Philadelphia
Philadelphia, Pennsylvania

Thandiwe M.C. Peebles
New York City Board of
Education
Brooklyn, New York

Margaret Pulley-Johnson
Supervisor of Social Studies
(K-12)
New Orleans Public Schools
New Orleans, Louisiana

Gladys M. Twyman
Coordinator, Social Studies
Coordinator, African
American Curriculum
Infusion Project
Atlanta Public Schools
Atlanta, Georgia

Edna J. Whitfield
Social Studies Supervisor
St. Louis Public Schools
St. Louis, Missouri

Charles A. Williams II
Assistant Director of Social
Studies
Newark Board of Education
Newark, New Jersey

TABLE OF CONTENTS

▼ Unit 6

Hope for a New Way of Life (1820–1880)   160

▼ Unit 7

Freedom Without Equality (1877–1910)   206

▼ Unit 8

Protest and Hope in a New Century (1900–1941)

The Artist's View follows page 260.

Galleries

Incorporated Biographies

Focus On

Building Skills

Maps

Charts and Graphs

LETTER FROM THE PRESIDENT
OF
GLOBE BOOK COMPANY

When I was a high school student in the late 1950s, there were no books that recorded the African or African American experience. The history books that were used in my classes only mentioned Africans and African Americans as slaves. Even more surprisingly, I discovered, as a college student, that there were no courses available on the history of people of African descent. What I did learn about African Americans I learned in anthropology and sociology courses where black people were considered a minority group and/or part of a subculture living in tribes or in poverty. At the time the general view about Africans and African Americans was quite negative—they had no place in the history of the world, and they were portrayed as intellectually, genetically, and socially inferior to all white people. Now, as an African American adult, I am very proud to be a part of publishing a textbook that seeks to get the story of African Americans straight.

This textbook begins the story about African Americans on the African continent, the original homeland for the human race. As you read and study the material in this book, you will discover, as I have, an amazing body of information. Much of what you will learn was either not known or not acknowledged when I was a student. There is a lot more to know and learn about the homeland of the human race and African Americans than could possibly be put into one textbook. This book is simply a good starting place and will lead you to other stories about the human experience.

Please notice that I describe this textbook as a *story* about the African American experience. This story is told, as much as possible, through the voices and experiences of actual people. As you read these stories of African Americans in the United States, you will notice a central theme that echoes throughout the history. That theme is the struggle against persecution, oppression, and injustice. Like a good story, the narrative contains examples of gritty perseverance, magnificent achievements and contributions, and stunning acts of heroism. That these things occurred under the racist conditions in which African Americans were forced to live makes the story even more remarkable. Unlike most good stories, however, the one in this book has no ending. Much of this story remains to be written, and you, the readers of this book, will add to that story.

As the book was being developed for your use, I experienced a new beginning. While reading the pages that follow, I felt great pain and anger and pride and joy. This is as it should be; this is the experience of African Americans in the United States. Equally important was my discovery that Africans and African Americans are at the core of the human experience. The world and the United States have been changed permanently because of the struggle by black people to end racist injustice and persecution. Other people have participated in the struggle, but from the very beginning black people have been in its forefront. The scope of the successes that have been achieved will take your breath away.

Art, music, dance, science, politics, economics, law, government, education, technology, military, agriculture—virtually every aspect of life in the United States reflects the influence of people of African descent. The story you are about to read is glorious. It speaks to the strength of the human spirit and lifts from the ashes of the past a lost legacy.

Irving Hamer, Jr.

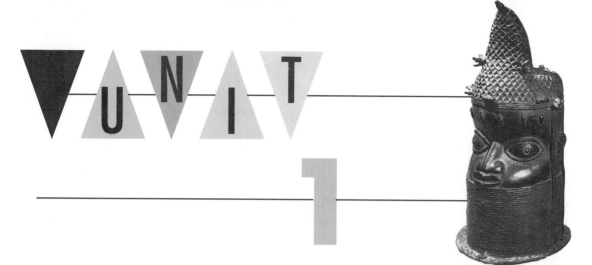

UNIT 1

Bronze head from Benin

THE AFRICAN HOMELAND

(Prehistory–A.D. 1600)

Mosque in Djenné, Mali

Egyptian porters carrying foodstuffs

2

Unit 1 describes the geography of the African continent and traces the development of ancient Egyptian ways of life that became a great **civilization.** The chapters also describe other African peoples who had contact with Egypt over time and later African civilization.

Human history began in Africa millions of years ago. The remains of the first known humans on earth have been found on the African continent in what are now Kenya and Tanzania. In Africa, humans made some of their first tools, grew some of their first gardens, tamed some of their first animals, and rode in some of their first carts. When Columbus stumbled across the Americas in 1492, Africa had a longer cultural history than Europe.

The African Landscape. Africa is the second largest continent in the world. Only Asia is larger. No one knows what ancient peoples called their land, but the name *Africa* may have come from the Greek word *aphrike,* meaning "without cold," or from the Latin word *aprica* for "sunny." Both descriptions are certainly true of Africa.

The climates and land surfaces of Africa vary dramatically. Many people mistakenly think of Africa as a land of thick, hot, steamy **rain forests.** But Africa is more desert than green trees and plants. The Sahara, in northern Africa, occupies one quarter of the continent and is the world's largest desert. The remaining three quarters of the continent south of the Sahara is often referred to as **sub-Saharan Africa.** In the southern part of sub-Saharan Africa, there is another desert,

An African American Speaks

African ancestors were among the major benefactors of the human race. Such evidence as survives clearly shows that Africans were on the scene and acting when the human drama opened. For a long time, in fact, the only people on the scene were Africans.

—Lerone Bennett, Jr.,
Journalist

the Kalahari, which is the world's seventh largest.

The rain forests lie on either side of the equator, which slices through the middle of the continent. These green belts give way to sweeping, flat grasslands with few trees, called **savannas.** The savannas are the homes of most of Africa's large animals, such as lions and elephants. Most African farms and pasture lands are found on the savannas, as they have been for thousands of years.

How much of Africa is made up of desert? How much is made up of rain forest?

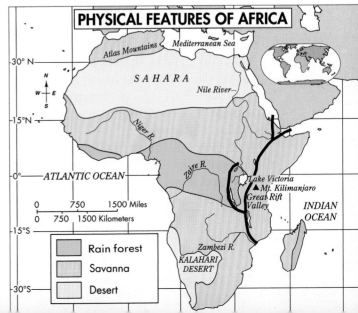

PHYSICAL FEATURES OF AFRICA

Atlas Mountains Mediterranean Sea
30° N
SAHARA
Nile River
15° N
Niger R.
0° ATLANTIC OCEAN
Zaire R.
Lake Victoria
▲ Mt. Kilimanjaro
Great Rift Valley
INDIAN OCEAN
0   750   1500 Miles
0   750   1500 Kilometers
15° S
Zambezi R.
KALAHARI DESERT
30° S

Rain forest
Savanna
Desert

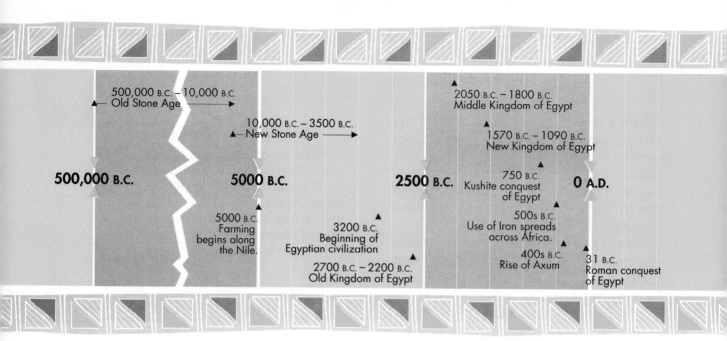

A prominent feature of the continent is the **Great Rift Valley.** This deep cut in the earth's surface extends for more than 6,000 miles (9,600 kilometers), from the Red Sea to Mozambique (moh-zuhm-BEEK). It varies in width from 20 miles (32 kilometers) to 60 miles (96 kilometers) and branches into eastern and western sections. A series of long fingerlike lakes lies in the rift valley. Between the branches of the rift valley is Lake Victoria, Africa's largest lake and the major source of the Nile River. The Nile is the world's longest river, flowing north for over 4,000 miles (6,400 kilometers).

A narrow plain runs along the coasts. Few natural harbors interrupt these flat coastal lands. Not far inland, the land rises sharply up an **escarpment,** or steep cliff. The greater part of sub-Saharan Africa rises from this escarpment as a high flat land called a **plateau.**

Most rivers in Africa rise in the interior of the continent. Those that flow to the oceans and seas that surround Africa plunge over the escarpment in waterfalls and rapids. Because of these wild, tumbling waters it is difficult to navigate these rivers very far inland. This is as true today as it was hundreds of years ago.

Birthplace of Humans. In 1959, anthropologists Louis and Mary Leakey made a startling discovery. In Olduvai (OHL-duh-way) Gorge, in what is now Tanzania (tan-zuh-NEE-uh), they found the remains of a human skull and stone tools that were nearly two million years old. These and later findings led scientists to conclude that the first human beings lived in East Africa. Over a period of millions of years, some early peoples left Africa and crossed into Asia. From there, their descendants, or offspring, fanned out to populate the world.

During the Old Stone Age, which lasted from about 500,000 years ago to about 10,000 years ago, they shaped knives, axes, and spear points out of stone and fashioned needles and fishhooks out of bone. They lived as hunters and food gatherers, moving from place to place, as

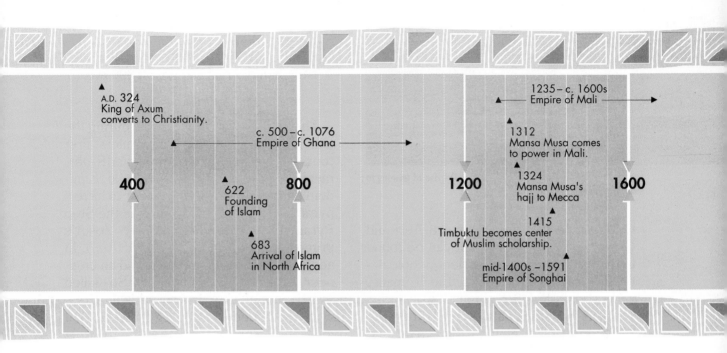

A.D. 324
King of Axum
converts to Christianity.

c. 500–c. 1076
Empire of Ghana

1235–c. 1600s
Empire of Mali

1312
Mansa Musa comes
to power in Mali.

1324
Mansa Musa's
hajj to Mecca

400   622
Founding
of Islam   **800**   **1200**   **1600**

1415
Timbuktu becomes center
of Muslim scholarship.

683
Arrival of Islam
in North Africa

mid-1400s –1591
Empire of Songhai

they followed herds of animals across grassy plains in Africa and elsewhere.

Invention of Farming.   Between 10,000 B.C. and 3500 B.C., in what is called the New Stone Age, one of the great revolutions in human history took place. In parts of Africa, Asia, the Middle East, and the Americas, humans invented farming. They learned to cultivate the seeds and roots of wild plants and to domesticate animals, or tame them, for human use. Some of the earliest farming villages began to appear along Africa's Nile River in about 5000 B.C.

The land along the Nile was particularly well suited to farming. Each year, the river overflowed its banks and deposited rich soil on the broad plain on either side of the river. This soil, and the plentiful waters of the Nile, encouraged the rise of farming at a much earlier date than in many parts of the world.

Now that farming provided their food supply, people were able to settle in one place and devote time to things other than providing food. Egyptian civilization arose along the Nile about 3500 B.C. The Greek historian Herodotus (huh-RAHD-uh-tuhs), writing in the 400s B.C., recognized the importance of the Nile to Egypt by calling Egypt "the gift of the Nile."

The Ancient Civilization of Egypt.
"African Egypt," wrote African American historian W. E. B. Du Bois (doo BOIS) in the mid-1900s, "was the first great experiment in human civilization." Starting more than 5,000 years ago, ancient Egyptians developed systems of mathematics, writing, astronomy, and religion. They also constructed monumental architecture, such as the **pyramids** that served as tombs for their rulers, and huge stone temples.

Egypt, in the northeastern corner of Africa, lay at a crossroads of the ancient world. Through this region, peoples from the continents of Asia and Europe first traveled. The people who lived along the Nile formed important links between Africa and other parts of the ancient

How did the Nile River help to encourage the rise of farming in ancient times?

world, especially southwestern Asia and Greece. Accounts of Egypt can be found in the writings of many ancient peoples— the Hebrews, the Greeks, the Romans, and others. Egypt's population included Africans from the south, peoples from the Mediterranean region to the north, and Asian peoples from the east.

The Nile might seem like a natural link between the peoples who lived along it. However, a series of **cataracts**, or strong rapids, made river travel difficult. Even so, the Egyptians managed to follow the Nile into Nubia. Egyptian **culture**— skills, beliefs, customs, and arts— influenced many aspects of life there, while southern Africans enriched Egypt with their own culture.

The region along the northern portion of the Nile was known as Lower Egypt, while that of the southern portion was called Upper Egypt. For hundreds of years, these two regions were separate kingdoms. Then, in about 3100 B.C. a ruler named Menes (MEE-neez) united the two kingdoms. Menes established the first **dynasty**, or ruling family. Over 30 dynasties ruled Egypt from 3100 B.C. to 340 B.C. The earliest dynasties ruled from about 3100 B.C. to 2686 B.C. The last ten dynasties ruled from about 1085 B.C. to 340 B.C. Egyptian history between these early and late dynasties is divided into three major periods called kingdoms:

Old Kingdom, 2700 B.C.–2200 B.C.
Middle Kingdom, 2050 B.C.–1800 B.C.
New Kingdom, 1570 B.C.–1090 B.C.

The Old Kingdom. It was during the Old Kingdom that Egyptian rulers first took the name **pharaoh** (FAIR-oh), meaning "great house." The Old Kingdom pharaoh Zoser was the first to have a pyramid built for him. Known as the Step Pyramid, it was designed by Zoser's prime minister Imhotep (im-HOH-tep). In addition to being an architect and an engineer, Imhotep was a physician. So skilled was he in medicine that after his death he was worshiped as the Egyptian god of medicine. The pyramid he had built in about 2650 B.C. for Zoser at Saqqara, in Lower Egypt, rises to a height of about 200 feet (60 meters) and is the oldest standing building in the world.

The Old Kingdom is often described as Egypt's Golden Age. The greatest pyramids were built during this time, as were great stone statues of the pharaohs. Also in this period, the Egyptians made advances in their system of writing, known as **hieroglyphics** (hy-ruh-GLIF-iks).

The Middle Kingdom. During the Middle Kingdom, trade with Nubia, Egypt's neighbor to the south, and with areas outside Africa, such as western Asia and Crete, expanded. But after this period, Egypt was invaded by a people from Asia known as the Hyksos (HIK-sohs), who ruled the country for 200 years. The Hyksos had the advantage of iron weapons and horse-drawn chariots, which the Egyptians lacked. But in time the Egyptians adopted the Hyksos' weapons of war and used them in expanding their empire by conquest.

The New Kingdom. During the New Kingdom, Egypt reached the height of its power as an empire. The New Kingdom saw Egypt's first woman ruler, Queen Hatshepsut (haht-SHEP-soot). Her 21-year reign, from 1503 B.C. to 1482 B.C., is noted for her devotion to peace and trade rather than conquest.

One of the greatest pharaohs, Akhenaton (ah-kuh-NAH-tuhn), ruled from about 1375 B.C. to about 1358 B.C. He introduced a new form of religion that centered on the belief in one god, rather than in the many gods and goddesses the Egyptians had worshiped.

After 1090 B.C., civil wars left Egypt too weak to drive away invaders from Nubia, western Asia, and Europe. Alexander the Great, the Greek conqueror, occupied Egypt in 331 B.C. The rule of the pharaohs came to an end some 300 years later when the Romans defeated Queen Cleopatra.

African Civilizations to the South and West. In the thousands of years during which Egyptian civilization was developing, peoples in other parts of Africa were establishing their own ways of life. To the south of Egypt, in Nubia, the kingdom of Kush was established about 1000 B.C. South of Kush, in what is now Ethiopia, the kingdom of Axum developed in the 400s B.C. Both Kush and Axum carried on extensive trade with countries along the Mediterranean and with Asia.

From about A.D. 500 to about 1600, in West Africa, three great kingdoms—Ghana, then Mali, and finally Songhai—also developed. They had extensive trade networks with Arab merchants from North Africa.

The Europeans who finally met the West Africans in the 1500s and later had

▶▶ SOME ACHIEVEMENTS OF THE ANCIENT EGYPTIANS

Achievement	Description
Writing and Recording	
hieroglyphics	writing based on pictures
papyrus	paper made from reeds
Measuring and Mathematics	
calendar	first accurate calendar
clocks	sundial for daytime; water clock for night
mathematics	Pythagorean theorem used to set boundaries
Engineering and Architecture	
pyramids	giant stone tombs
irrigation	canals carried Nile water to fields
Medical Knowledge	
embalming	dead preserved as mummies
medicines	over 260 prescriptions

How do you experience African influence in the things you do or see every day?

only a vague idea of these great empires. They dealt with African traders, exchanging guns, cloth, and manufactured goods for gold, ivory, and **slaves**. It would be West Africans as slaves, who would one day be forced to cross the Atlantic Ocean, and in the process, bring their customs and beliefs to the Americas.

Taking Another Look

1. Describe three physical features of the geography of Africa.

2. How do we know that Africa was the birthplace of the earliest humans?

3. Why was Egypt referred to as "the gift of the Nile?"

4. **Critical Thinking** Egyptian civilization lasted for thousands of years. What qualities must this civilization have had to last so long?

The Sphinx and the pyramids at Giza, Egypt

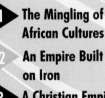
Egypt, Kush, and Axum

(c. 3200 B.C.–A.D. 800)

THINKING ABOUT THE CHAPTER

How did the ancient civilizations of northeastern Africa interact with one another?

They called themselves by such names as the "Vigorous Gang" and the "Craftworker Gang." Starting in about 2600 B.C., thousands of them worked in the blazing sun to carve out huge blocks of stone weighing an average of 2.5 tons (about 1,350 kilograms). The stone-cutting crews competed with one another and took pride in being part of a great building project to honor their pharaoh.

Having cut millions of stone slabs, the workers began the job of moving them to a site at Giza near what is today the city of Cairo, Egypt. Twenty years later, the product of their labor, the Great Pyramid, was completed. It covers over 13 acres (5.26 hectares) and soars 481 feet (147 meters) above the desert.

More than 2,000 years later, Greek tourists swarmed into Egypt to gaze at the Great Pyramid and other nearby smaller pyramids. The structures so awed the Greeks that they listed them among the "Seven Wonders of the Ancient World." Of the seven, only the pyramids still stand. They are only the most visible evidence of the extraordinary contributions that the Egyptians made to world culture.

1 THE MINGLING OF AFRICAN CULTURES

▼ Who were the Africans in the lands south of Egypt?

The exact location of what was called the land of Yam, south of Egypt, is still uncertain today. But in 2275 B.C., stories of its wealth fascinated Egypt's Pharaoh Merenra—so much so, that he ordered an expedition into the region. To lead the expedition, he chose a trusted official named Herkhuf. Herkhuf kept careful records of his adventures so that they might be written on his tomb. Wrote Herkhuf of his journey:

> The majesty of Merenra, my lord, sent me . . . to Yam to explore a road to this country. I did it in only seven months, and I brought all [kinds of] gifts from it . . . I was greatly praised.

Herkhuf went back to Yam three more times. Each trip was more successful than the last. On the fourth and final trip, he returned to Egypt with 300 donkeys loaded with incense, ebony, ivory, panther skins, and curiosities such as "throw sticks," or boomerangs.

Herkhuf's journey was the first of many trips by Egyptians into the lands to the south. As a result of such trading expeditions and of raiding parties, Egypt's wealth grew. In the process, many Africans who lived to the south became part of the life of Egypt. They brought to Egyptian civilization many valuable goods and skills. At the same time, their own lands were influenced by Egyptian civilization.

The People of Ancient Egypt. The great diversity of people in ancient Egypt stemmed from the contact Egypt had with neighboring regions. Lower Egypt had an extensive trading network with people from lands along the Mediterranean, Mesopotamia in western Asia, and Libya in northern Africa. Many of these people later retired in Lower Egypt and married Egyptians. Many of the people from the lands south of Egypt became Egyptians through conquest or through **migration** into Egypt.

Egypt and the Kushite Peoples of Nubia. Over many years, Egyptians pushed into the interior of Africa, trading with the Nubians. Copper tools of Egyptian origin found in Nubian graves are evidence of this trade. During the Middle

How did the locations of the ancient kingdoms of eastern Africa encourage cultures to mix?

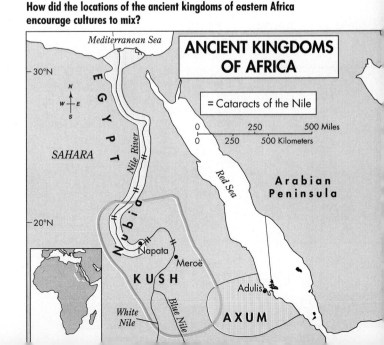

ANCIENT KINGDOMS OF AFRICA

⟜ = Cataracts of the Nile

2275 B.C.	Egyptians begin to explore the interior of Africa.
1785 B.C.	Hyksos invade Egypt.
750 B.C.	Kush conquers Egypt.
c.591 B.C.	Meroë is founded.
A.D. 350	Axum conquers Kush.
324	King of Axum converts to Christianity.

Kingdom (2050 B.C.–1800 B.C.), ambitious pharaohs built a series of forts along the Nile as far as the Second Cataract (see map, page 9). They then boasted that Egypt controlled the "Gateway to the South," or the trade routes leading southward from Egypt.

The Egyptians' sweep to the south was interrupted in 1785 B.C. by an invasion of Egypt by the Hyksos, a people from Asia, who were aided by the Kushites of Nubia. After regaining its strength, Egypt drove the Hyksos out in 1580 B.C. and punished Kush. The Egyptians killed the Kushite king and seized thousands of Kushites as slaves. Thus began the New Kingdom

In this Egyptian wall painting from about 1400 B.C., Nubians bring offerings to Egyptian gods and goddesses.

(1570 B.C.–1090 B.C.), a period that saw Egypt and Nubia united.

Horns of the World. During the New Kingdom, Egypt advanced its borders to the "Horns of the World," or the Fourth Cataract of the Nile. Egypt now controlled most of Nubia and its great wealth. Nubian mines produced about 48 tons (40,000 kilograms) of gold a year, a level of world production not reached again until the A.D. 1800s. Egypt became wealthier and more powerful than ever.

Goods and people flowed freely between Nubia and Egypt. The Nubian kingdom of Kush accepted many Egyptian ways. As time passed and Kush grew stronger, the Kushites began to envy Egypt's power. By the 700s B.C., a Kushite king named Kashta led armies northward. "I will take it [Egypt] like a flood of water," declared Kashta. In 750 B.C., Egypt fell to the Kushites.

Kushite Pharaohs. For the next 80 years, Kushite pharaohs sat on the Egyptian throne. For a brief time, Napata (NAP-uh-tuh), the capital of Kush, was one of the centers of the ancient world. The Kushite pharaohs ruled much the same way the Egyptian pharaohs had, and the Egyptians accepted their authority.

Kushite rule of Egypt ended in the 600s B.C. when a group of Asian invaders, the Assyrians (uh-SIR-ee-uhns), pushed into Egypt. Although the Kushites and the Egyptians fought bravely, their bronze weapons proved no match for the Assyrians' iron swords and armor. The Kushites retreated south, and Egypt fell to the Assyrians in 663 B.C.

In the centuries that followed, Egypt was invaded by several other foreign powers and never returned to a position of leadership in Africa. The Kushites, however, realized how superior iron was to bronze. As you will read in the next section, they set about building their own empire, based on iron and ironworking.

Taking Another Look

1. Why did the Egyptians seek to control Nubia?

2. Why did the Egyptians accept Kushite rule?

3. **Critical Thinking** If you had been a Kushite, why do you think you might have both admired and hated Egypt?

2 AN EMPIRE BUILT ON IRON
▼ Why was iron important to the
▼ Kushites?

About 100 miles (160 kilometers) south of Khartoum (kahr-TOOM), capital of the present-day country of Sudan, lie the ruins of a city that flourished about 350 B.C. Egyptian pharaohs knew of the city, as did the ancient Greeks and Romans. But few people from the north visited Meroë, center of the Kushite empire. The cataracts of the Nile made the trip difficult for tourists.

Crumbling temples and weatherworn pyramids today mark the spot where Meroë stood in its glory. Writings carved in stone exist there, too, but scholars have been unable to decipher them. They have had to piece together the story of the city from its ruins.

Iron and Trade. The Kushites probably founded Meroë sometime after 591 B.C., when invaders from Egypt destroyed their capital at Napata. The location of Meroë had several advan-

Why are the pyramids at Meroë especially important to scholars studying Kush?

tages. First, it was beyond easy reach of Egypt. Second, the city lay near rich deposits of iron ore. Third, because the land was so fertile, fewer people had to spend their time raising food. Some people were freed to work in the iron industry. Fourth, caravans carrying goods for trade could travel between Meroë and ports on the Red Sea in just a few weeks.

In about 500 B.C., the Kushites began to follow the example of the Assyrians and turned to iron-making. Meroë became the first African center of iron manufacture. The metal was so precious that one ruler had iron spearheads wrapped in gold foil and placed in his tomb.

With iron ploughs, the Kushites were able to produce ample quantities of food. With iron spears, they were able to protect their trade routes to the Red Sea and to conquer neighboring peoples. At trading posts on the Red Sea, they exchanged goods they had gathered from a wide region of Africa—ivory, gold, ostrich feathers, elephants, and slaves—for luxuries from India, the Arabian peninsula, Greece, and Rome. Remains uncovered at Meroë prove that the city grew rich from this trade.

11

This statue of Aspelta, a Kushite king, was found in the ruins of a temple.

Kushite murals, or wall paintings. At the same time, human figures in paintings began to look less like Egyptians and more like Africans of the south. These changes in the culture of the Kushites indicated that their contacts with their neighbors to the south were growing stronger and becoming more important.

The Kushite empire flourished for over 800 years, until about A.D. 350. It was succeeded by an empire that did not take up Kush's iron-making skills. It took over its trade network.

Taking Another Look

1. Why did the Kushites build Meroë?

2. How did iron-making help Meroë grow?

3. **Critical Thinking** Describe how the relationship between Kush and Egypt changed over time.

3 A CHRISTIAN EMPIRE IN AFRICA

▼ How did Axum become a powerful empire?

About A.D. 350, armies of its southern neighbor, Axum, stormed into Kush, set fire to its cities, and brought the Kushite empire to an end. Axum's ruler, King Ezana celebrated his victory by inscribing the story on a huge stone pillar. Boasted the triumphant Ezana:

I pursued them [the Kushites] for 23 days, killing some and capturing others. . . . I burnt their towns, . . . and my army carried off their food and copper and iron and destroyed their statues, their granaries and cotton trees and cast them into the river Seda [Nile].

Cultural Influences. The influence of Egyptian culture was strong in Meroë. Kushites worshiped Egyptian gods and goddesses. They created sculptures in the Egyptian style and built Egyptian-style pyramids.

However, as time went on, the spirit of southern Africa grew stronger in Meroë and replaced the Egyptian influence. Lions and elephants, animals rarely seen in Egyptian art, began to appear in

12

The church of Saint George in Lalibela, Ethiopia, is an example of the presence of Christianity in Axum. The church is carved out of a single piece of rock.

As a result of King Ezana's invasion, Kush nearly disappeared from history, leaving only shadowy records such as the ruins at Meroë. Axum, on the other hand, continued its history unbroken into the 20th century. Today, the people of Ethiopia trace their beginnings to Axum.

An Ancient Shopping Center. Within 50 years of its conquest of Kush, Axum grew into an important trading empire and became the second great civilization south of Egypt. It controlled most of the caravan routes from the interior of Africa to the Red Sea. Its Red Sea port of Adulis (ah-DOO-lis) was one of the gateways into Africa for merchants from India and the Mediterranean world. A Greek sailor wrote a shopping guide to the city, telling of such rare finds as "ivory and tortoise-shell and rhinoceros horn."

The Coming of Christianity. By about A.D. 300, **Christianity,** a religion based on the teachings of Jesus, had become well established in the Mediterranean regions of Europe. A Christian friend of Ezana who became the archbishop of Axum succeeded in converting Ezana to Christianity in 324. Ezana then proclaimed Christianity the official religion of Axum.

In the 600s, the religion of **Islam,** based on the teachings of Muhammad, swept over northern Africa. But the people of Axum refused to give up their Christianity. Axum became a Christian island in a sea of Islamic nations. The sight of Christian worshipers in Ethiopia amazed European explorers when they arrived there some 600 years later.

Taking Another Look

1. On what was Axum's power based?

2. What did Ezana contribute to Axum?

3. **Critical Thinking** How did Axum's geographic location affect its power?

LOOKING AHEAD

The empires of northeastern Africa— Egypt, Kush, and Axum—had a longtime relationship, not always peaceful, with one another. In the process, each learned from its neighbors and strengthened its own civilization. While these kingdoms were rising and falling, other empires were developing far across the continent in the west.

> *Imagine my joy when I saw the tops of a crowd of pyramids raised a little on the horizon. . . . I saw a second group of pyramids off to the west, and not far from the river, a huge field of ruins . . . the site of an ancient city.*

So wrote a French explorer in 1822. Driven by a desire to find the source of the Nile, Europeans plunged into the interior of Africa. They knew about Meroë from the works of ancient scholars. But in the late 1700s and early 1800s, they glimpsed this great city with their own eyes for the first time.

The pyramids of Meroë sit on a small plain surrounded by huge, dark hills. Pieces of sparkling white plaster still cling to the rock slabs that make up the tombs. No other buildings exist on the plain except a small house. Some experts think that priests may have lived there to offer prayers for the departed spirits of kings and queens.

First robbers and then archaeologists have long since emptied the tombs. But the items that are preserved in museums show the grandeur of an ancient African people—a people that once ruled over Egypt.

CLOSE UP: Chapter 1

The Who, What, Where of History

1. **Where** do scientists believe the first humans lived?
2. **What** is an escarpment?
3. **What** is a plateau?
4. **What** does the word *migrate* mean?
5. **What** is a dynasty?
6. **Who** were the pharaohs?
7. **What** is sub-Saharan Africa?
8. **Who** were the Hyksos?
9. **Where** was the center of the Kushite empire?
10. **What** kingdom conquered Kush?
11. **Who** proclaimed Christianity the official religion of Axum?

Making the Connection

1. What is the connection between the variety of peoples in ancient Egypt and the mural on page 10?
2. What events led to the uniting of Egypt and Nubia?
3. How were iron-making and the Assyrian conquest of Egypt related?

Time Check

1. Which of these people invaded Egypt *first:* the Assyrians, the Hyksos, or the Kushites?
2. When did Axum conquer Kush?

What Would You Have Done?

1. If you had lived in Meroë, would you rather have been a farmer or an ironworker? Explain.
2. Suppose you could choose to accompany one of these expeditions: the

team of anthropologists with Louis and Mary Leakey who found evidence of the earliest human life in Tanzania or a team of archaeologists working to decipher Kushite writing. Which would you choose? Explain.

Thinking and Writing About History

1. Write an advertisement for iron ploughs as if you were a Kushite blacksmith. Explain why every farmer needs an iron plough.

2. Imagine that you are a travel agent in the year A.D. 50. Write a travel brochure about the attractions of Meroë. Include information about its art, markets, monuments, and rulers.

3. One Egyptian pharaoh gave the following advice to his son:

   Advance thy great men, so that they may carry out thy laws. . . . Great is a great man when his great men are great. . . . Do not distinguish the son of a noble man from a poor man, but take to thyself a man because of the work of his hands.

   a. What did the pharaoh mean? Rewrite the pharaoh's advice to his son in your own words.
   b. On what did the pharaoh suggest his son base his judgment of people? Why do you suppose the pharaoh gave his son this advice?
   c. What does this advice tell you about how the Egyptians evaluated other people? Using this advice as evidence, predict how the Egyptians would judge people of different cultures.

   d. Imagine you are the ruler of an African empire. What advice about choosing people to help govern would you give your children? Write your advice in a letter.

Building Skills: Comparing Maps

When you look at photographs of a person taken over a period of many years, you notice that although his or her basic looks—bone structure, facial features—stay the same, many other things change. The same is true of maps showing the same place at different times. Some things are the same from one map to another and some things are different.

There are several maps of Africa in this book. Some show all of the continent; some show only an area. There is more than one map of Africa because different kinds of maps have different purposes.

A *physical* map shows the natural features of an area, such as rivers, oceans, mountains, and deserts.

A *political* map shows the human-made boundaries of kingdoms or empires. A political map may also indicate capitals and other cities, and roads, routes, and places of interest.

A *historical* map shows an area as it used to be many years ago.

Find and examine the maps of Africa on pages 3, 9, 17, and 396. Then answer the following questions.

1. Which map or maps can you use to locate the following natural features: a. rain forest? b. Great Rift Valley? c. savannas? d. Nile cataracts?

2. On which map or maps can you find sub-Saharan Africa?

3. Which map or maps show(s) the city of Meroë?

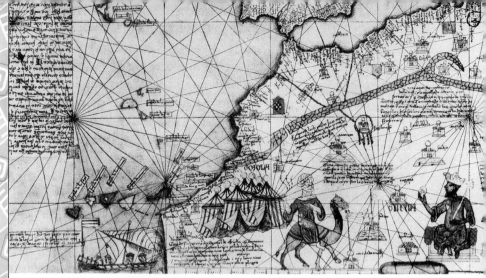

Map of Ghana showing Mansa Musa on his throne

CHAPTER 2

Great Empires of West Africa

(500s–1600)

SECTIONS

THINKING ABOUT THE CHAPTER

How did trade give rise to the great empires of West Africa?

Mansa Musa (MAHN-suh MOO-suh), the ruler of the West African empire of Mali (MAH-lee), was a devout **Muslim,** a believer in the religion of Islam. In 1324, he set out on a **hajj,** a pilgrimage to the Muslim holy city of Mecca, in Arabia. But this was no ordinary hajj. Legend has it that his caravan consisted of 60,000 people. Among them were Mansa Musa's rivals. By taking them along on the pilgrimage, he kept them from threatening his power at home while he was gone. Also in Mansa Musa's party were 500 slaves, each one carrying a gold-adorned staff weighing 6 pounds (2.7 kilograms). Mansa Musa was well supplied with money, for 80 camels were heaped with 300-pound (136-kilogram) bags of gold dust.

In midsummer, Mansa Musa and his party arrived at Cairo, Egypt. The vastness and richness of the party made an enormous impression on the Egyptians, especially when Mansa Musa began handing out gifts of gold.

Stories of Mansa Musa's fabulous hajj spread far and wide. Mali became known as one of West Africa's great kingdoms—kingdoms that rivaled those of Europe at the time. As a result of this journey, Mansa Musa's empire appeared on the first European map of West Africa. In this chapter, you will read about Mali and two other important West African empires.

1 THE EMPIRE OF GHANA

▼ What made the kingdom of Ghana a great trading state?

If there was one word that meant more than any other in Ghana, it was *gold*. In fact, the name Ghana, which originally meant warrior king, eventually came to mean gold. At Ghana's height in the mid-1000s, the ruler was called "king of gold." When the king walked in the capital of Kumbi, he wore a tall golden cap. At his side walked dogs with gold-and-silver collars. Princes who accompanied the king had strands of gold in their hair.

The Founding of the Empire of Gold. Ghana was founded between 300 and 500 by the Soninke (soh-NIN-kuh) people of West Africa. Like the Kushites, whom you read about in Chapter 1, the Soninke knew how to make iron tools and weapons. With their iron swords, they were able to conquer their neighbors, who were equipped only with wooden weapons, and build a great empire.

So great were the Soninke conquests that people began to call them by the name they called their leader—Ghana. In time, Ghana became the name of the entire empire. Ancient Ghana was located

north and west of the modern nation of Ghana, in an area now occupied by parts of the nations of Mauritania and Mali.

Trade in Salt and Gold. Ghana's power rested on trade. Ghana lay across the trade routes between the sources of salt in the Sahara and the gold region south of Ghana known as Wangara.

For the people of Ghana, salt was a necessity. Like other people in desert climates, they sweated away body salts and had to replace them through salt in their food. They also used salt to preserve foods. Therefore, they traded the gold from the south for the salt from North Africa. Salt, Ghanaians (GAH-nee-uhns) said, was worth its weight in gold.

Because of the lack of a common language, the exchange of gold and salt took place through **silent trade.** Not a word was spoken between the traders. The salt traders left their blocks of salt on the ground at some distance from the gold

Which ancient West African kingdoms controlled parts of the same territory?

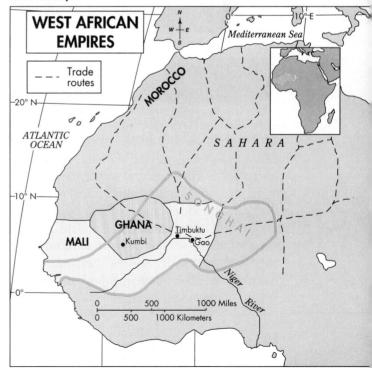

300s–500s	Rise of Ghana
1076	Almoravid invaders conquer Ghana.
1235	Sundiata defeats Sumanguru and establishes Mali empire.
1324	Mansa Musa makes pilgrimage to Mecca.
Mid-1400s	Rise of Songhai
1464–1492	Reign of Sunni Ali
1493–1528	Reign of Askia Muhammad
1591	Moroccans invade Songhai.

traders and then retreated a little way. The gold traders then approached to examine the amount of salt. After leaving what they believed was a fair amount of gold in payment for the salt, they too withdrew. The salt traders came back to examine the amount of gold. If they accepted it, the transaction was complete. If they did not, the process was repeated until agreement was reached.

The rulers of Ghana maintained tight control over the production and supply of gold. They charged taxes on all gold and salt that went through their empire. The traders paid these taxes in gold. With their income, the kings supported large armies to protect the trade routes.

A Market for Slaves. By the mid-1000s, caravans of more than a thousand camels were entering Ghana from the north across the Sahara. In the capital city of Kumbi were many busy marketplaces that offered foods and clothing of all kinds for sale. The Ghanaians also sold human merchandise—slaves. North African merchants eager for slaves helped make Kumbi into the slave-trading center of West Africa at the time.

Slavery, the system of owning people, had existed in Africa for hundreds of years, as it had in other places in the world, including Greece and Rome. For the most part, before the coming of Europeans, Africans enslaved other Africans, whom they captured during wars. These slaves often worked as servants or as farm laborers. Some became members of the families to whom they were enslaved. Most could earn or buy their freedom after a period of time.

The Coming of Islam. The North Africans with whom Ghana traded were followers of Islam. Islam was a religion founded by an Arabian merchant named Muhammad (moo-HAM-uhd) in 622. Muslims, followers of Muhammad, believed they had a duty to spread Islam, peacefully if possible or by a holy war, called a **jihad,** if necessary.

Desert Conquerors. The rulers of Ghana for many years allowed Islam to be practiced in the empire. But most Ghanaians remained faithful to their own religions, which you will read about in Chapter 3. In the 1000s, however, Muslims from North Africa called Almoravids (ahl-MOH-rah-vidz) launched a jihad against Ghana. The Almoravid leader, Abu Bakr (AH-boo BAH-kuhr), vowed to force the Ghanaians to accept Islam at sword point.

In 1062, Abu Bakr led an invasion to the gates of Kumbi itself. The Ghanaians held out for nearly ten years. In the end, however, the Almoravids destroyed the capital and killed any Ghanaians who refused to accept Islam.

Almoravid control of Ghana ended with the death of Abu Bakr in 1087. However, Ghana never regained its former power. In 1235, other conquerors swept through Ghana—invaders from Mali.

Taking Another Look

1. How did Ghana's geographic location help build its trading empire?

2. What was the impact of Islam on the empire of Ghana?

3. **Critical Thinking** Why did the rulers of Ghana insist on controlling the supply of gold in their empire?

2 THE EMPIRE OF MALI
▼ How did Mali differ from Ghana?

From generation to generation, **griots** (GREE-ohz), storytellers who memorize and pass down the history of their people, told of the legendary founding of Mali. This West African empire succeeded Ghana in power and glory.

The story begins with Sundiata (soon-dee-AH-tah), a crippled prince. His life was spared by the cruel conqueror Sumanguru (soo-man-GOO-roo) when Sumanguru enslaved Sundiata's people. Over time, Sundiata grew stronger, and in 1235, he led a revolt against Sumanguru. The two met in a final battle, according to West African griots:

His eyes red with anger, Sundiata struck out right and left. Sumanguru retreated far behind his men. . . . His eyes met Sundiata's. Now trembling like a man in the grip of a fever, the vanquished [defeated] Sumanguru looked up towards the sun. A great black bird flew over the fray [battle] and he understood. It was the bird of misfortune.

Sundiata was the victor. As the new ruler, he set about adding other states, including Ghana, to his kingdom, which he called Mali.

A Muslim State. Unlike the Ghanaians, the people of Mali had converted to Islam under the Almoravids. As Mali prospered and grew, it became a key state in the Muslim world.

Mali followed the trade pattern set by Ghana, but it ruled a much larger territory, an area roughly the size of Western Europe. Mali took over the gold and salt trade from Ghana. Through a system of local officals, the kings of Mali, called mansas, collected vast sums in taxes in the form of gold.

Timbuktu. While Mansa Musa, the Mali king whom you read about on page 16, was in Mecca, he persuaded some of Islam's finest architects, scholars, and other professionals to return with him to Mali. They helped enlarge and enrich the city of Timbuktu (tim-buk-TOO).

Handsome new buildings were erected. Islamic schools were opened, and the city became the home of several great universities. The University of Sankore housed an impressive collection of Greek, Roman, and Arabic manuscripts. Scholars taught religion, poetry, law, astronomy, and medicine. Their students came from across Africa. The city also

Asante craftworkers made these brass weights, used to weigh gold on scales.

A European artist did this drawing of Timbuktu in 1830. Who was responsible for making Timbuktu a great city?

Taking Another Look

1. In what ways did Timbuktu become a great city?

2. What caused the downfall of Mali?

3. **Critical Thinking** If you were a griot of Mali, what events in Mali's history would you tell your listeners?

3 THE EMPIRE OF SONGHAI

▼ Who were Songhai's chief rulers?

Muslim scholars called him a "master tyrant." His people called him a hero. All agreed, however, that Sunni Ali (SOO-nee AH-lee), the emperor of Songhai from 1464 to 1492, was one of the fiercest warriors that West Africa had ever seen.

Sunni Ali's Rule. Like Ghana and Mali, the empire of Songhai grew rich from trade. Its main trade goods were gold and ivory. Unlike the two earlier empires, however, Songhai expanded its trade network to Europe and Southwest Asia. Some of Songhai's gold was sent by desert caravan to Egypt, which then shipped it to other areas. In turn, Egypt shipped to Songhai goods made on the east coast of Africa, such as cloth, copper, and beads.

During his reign, Sunni Ali enlarged Songhai so that it spanned most of West Africa. One of his conquests was Timbuktu in 1468.

Although Sunni Ali was a Muslim, he came into conflict with Muslim religious leaders. They resented the fact that he also practiced the traditional Songhai religion. Similarly, they did not approve of his willingness to allow conquered peoples to retain their old religious beliefs and practices rather than become Muslims.

became a lively center of West African trade. Timbuktu's period of greatness lasted until the 1500s.

The End of Mali. After Mansa Musa's death in 1332, the Mali empire began to fall apart. Raiders from neighboring lands attacked its cities. In addition, power-hungry local rulers broke away from the empire to set up their own kingdoms. In the mid-1400s, sons of the king of the city of Gao (GAH-oh) led a revolt and set about building the empire of Songhai (sahng-HY).

Askia Muhammad. When Sunni Ali died in 1492, a power struggle broke out that brought a devoted Muslim, Askia Muhammad (AHS-kee-uh moo-HAM-uhd) to the throne. In 1493, the year after Columbus came upon the Americas, Askia began a 35-year reign that brought Songhai to the height of its powers. Through military conquests, he greatly expanded the empire. He also reformed the system of laws and taxation.

Askia became blind in his final years, and his sons battled for control of the empire. For a short time, they exiled their father to an island "infested with mosquitoes and toads." None of Askia's sons shared their father's wisdom, and rivalry and arguments plagued the empire. But the final challenge to Songhai came from invaders.

New Technology in Warfare. In 1591, an army from Morocco, in North Africa, marched into West Africa in search of gold. Although the army had only 4,000 soldiers, it possessed a fearsome new weapon, the harquebus (HAHR-kwuh-buhs). This was an early type of gun. With this weapon, the Moroccans were able to defeat a Songhai force of some 18,000 cavalry and 9,700 foot soldiers. "From that moment on," wrote one scholar, "everything changed. Danger took the place of security; wealth gave way to poverty. Instead of peace came distress, disasters, and violence."

Taking Another Look

1. What problems did Sunni Ali have with Muslim religious leaders?

2. Describe two of Askia Muhammad's contributions to Songhai.

3. **Critical Thinking** Using the conquest of Songhai by the Moroccans as an example, explain the effect of new technology on warfare.

LOOKING AHEAD

With the fall of Songhai in 1591, the thousand-year rule of the three great West African empires came to an end. By that time, European merchants had built a string of trading posts south along the West African coast. These merchants continued the profitable trade in gold and ivory, but as you will read in Unit 2, they added another trade good—Africans, for sale in the Americas.

Ghana was halfway between salt mines in the Sahara to the north and gold mines to the south. Huge caravans with as many as a thousand camels carried salt and gold through Ghana.

They file into the mosque, greeting each other, "As-salaam alaikum." Before entering the *musallah*—the large room where Muslims pray—both men and women remove their shoes. The men kneel on prayer rugs in the front. The veiled women kneel behind the men. Arabic fills the room as the *imam*, or Muslim priest, begins the midday prayers. To a non-Islamic listener, the prayers sound like songs.

The scene above did not take place in the Middle East or in Africa, but in the New York neighborhood of Harlem, at the Malcolm Shabazz mosque. Similar scenes are repeated daily in cities such as Los Angeles and Perrysburg, Ohio, as growing numbers of African Americans practice Islam.

The history of African Americans and Islam begins with the African Muslims who were brought to the Americas as slaves. Islam nearly disappeared among their descendants. But ever since slavery ended, especially in the 1900s, Islam has been on the rise among African Americans. For many, a return to Islam goes hand in hand with a new pride in their African heritage.

Today, about 1 million African Americans are Muslim. Many take Arabic names—Khalil, Rasheeda, Muhammad, for example. The most devout wear veils and turbans of African cloth and worship at mosques, such as Malcolm Shabazz.

CLOSE UP: Chapter 2

The Who, What, Where of History

1. **Who** was Mansa Musa?
2. **What** is a Muslim?
3. **What** is a hajj?
4. **What** is a jihad?
5. **What** was silent trade?
6. **Who** was Muhammad?
7. **What** do griots do?
8. **Who** was Sundiata?
9. **Who** was Sunni Ali?
10. **Where** was Timbuktu located?

Making the Connection

1. How were gold and salt connected in ancient Ghana?
2. What was the connection between the spread of Islam and the fall of the Empire of Ghana?

Time Check

1. Which of the following events happened *last*? Askia rules in Songhai; the Soninke people found Ghana; Sundiata leads a revolt against Sumanguru.
2. In what century did Mansa Musa make his hajj?

What Would You Have Done?

1. If you had lived between A.D. 300 and A.D. 1000, would you rather have been a salt trader or a gold trader? Explain.
2. If you had had the choice of becoming a trader or a griot in Mali, which career would you have chosen? Explain.

Thinking and Writing About History

1. Imagine that you live in Cairo, Egypt in the A.D. 1300s. Write a news report about the caravan of Mansa Musa passing by on its way to Mecca. Remember to answer the questions *who, what, when, where, and why.*

2. Imagine that you are a student who has traveled to Timbuktu in the A.D. 1300s to study. Write a letter telling a relative about your studies and about all the resources in Timbuktu.

Building Skills: Making Comparisons

Do you make comparisons? When you go shopping for a new shirt, you may find 15 shirts on the rack in your size. You may choose to try on 3. You buy only 1. How did you get your selection from 15 to 1?

By comparing. What did you compare? Several things, probably—price, fabric, color, fit. When you tried on three shirts, you probably concentrated on fit and color. Whether you are shopping or studying, making comparisons is a way of making sense of a great deal of information.

This chapter gives you information about three great African empires. How can you keep information on those three empires organized? Making comparisons is one way.

1. Use the information in your textbook to complete the following chart.

2. Use the information in the chart to answer the following question: What was one thing that the three West African empires had in common?

COMPARING WEST AFRICAN EMPIRES

Empire	Dates	Founder	Major Religion	Source of Wealth
Ghana			local religions until 1000s	
Mali				
Songhai				

Tanzanian schoolchildren listening to a village storyteller

The West African Heritage

(500s–1500s)

THINKING ABOUT THE CHAPTER

What was the West African way of life like before the Atlantic slave trade began?

Many of today's African Americans ask, "Where did my ancestors come from?" Most often, it is a question that is impossible to answer—except to say West Africa.

Yet, one African American was able to find exactly where his family came from. Alex Haley was so determined to learn who his ancestors were and where they came from that he spent years searching for his roots. The trail finally led Haley to a small village in Gambia, West Africa, where he found a griot who was able to recite the history of Haley's people.

Haley turned his search into a best-selling book called *Roots* (see page 62). In this chapter, you will learn about the lives of West Africans like Haley's ancestors and those of millions of other African Americans.

1 WEST AFRICAN FAMILIES

▼ What was family life like in West Africa?

A child is like a rare bird.
A child is precious like coral.
A child is precious like brass.
You cannot buy a child in
     the market.
Not for all the money in the world.
The child that you can buy for
     money is a slave.
You may have twenty slaves.
You may have thirty laborers.
Only a child brings us joy.
One's child is one's child.

This poem comes from the Yoruba (YOH-roo-buh) people, from the area that is now Nigeria and Benin. Like other West Africans, the Yoruba valued family ties, which formed the basis of society for them. Some West African peoples believed that a family's children represented the reborn spirits of their deceased ancestors. Thus their children were the link between the generations—present and past—of a family.

Extended Families. Like people in many cultures, West Africans lived in **extended families.** These were made up of parents, unmarried children, married sons and their families, and, sometimes, grandparents, aunts, uncles, and cousins.

Men dominated most families, but women played important roles. They made the clothes, farmed alongside the men, and in a few societies, even served as warriors. The care of children was also among the duties of women. Olaudah Equiano (oh-LOW-duh ek-wee-AH-noh), who was brought to the Americas as a slave in the 1700s, recalled how his mother treated him as a child:

As I was the youngest of the sons, I became . . . the greatest favorite with my mother, and was always with her; and she used to take particular pains to form my mind. I was trained up from my earliest years in the arts of agriculture and war: my daily exercise was shooting and throwing javelins [spears]; and my mother adorned me with emblems [designs], after the manner of our greatest warriors.

Olaudah Equiano

Marriage. Like other cultures, many West African peoples arranged their children's marriages when the children were still young. The actual marriages, however, did not take place until the children were grown. Usually, after the marriage, the bride went to live with her husband's family. The groom's family was expected to give her parents a **bridewealth,** gifts of money or goods to pay them for the loss of her labor.

Almost all West African societies permitted **polygyny** (puh-LIJ-uh-nee), that is, a man could have more than one wife at a time. In practice, however, few men could afford to support more than one wife. Having several wives showed that a man was wealthy.

Men who had several wives built separate houses for each wife and her children within the family compound, or living area. Sometimes, jealousies arose among the women. But because the women did most of the family's day-to-day work, they also welcomed one another's help. The first wife often supervised the work of the others.

Work. Outside the trading centers of the great West African empires, most people lived in villages. They were farmers who worked on land that their ancestors had cleared. The land belonged to the community, not to individual farmers. Almost all were **subsistence farmers**— that is, they grew only enough for their own use. Among the crops they grew were pineapples, cotton, plantains, yams, beans, corn, and spices.

Society. Village society was organized in social and economic classes, or groups. The top rank consisted of elders, men who had gained the respect of others through age and experience. Groups of elders formed the local village governments. Farmers and craftworkers, who made up the majority of people, were in the middle class of society.

Africans put this figure in front of a house to guard against thieves. Why might the figure have many heads?

Captives taken during wars and enslaved were on the lowest rung of society.

The treatment of slaves varied from people to people. In some West African societies, most slaves lived on a nearly equal footing with others. Equiano recalled that among his people, slaves did

> no more work than other members of the community, than even their master; their food, clothing, and lodging were nearly the same as theirs, except that they were not permitted to eat with the free-born.

Taking Another Look

1. What was the reason for bride-wealth?

2. What social classes existed in West Africa?

3. **Critical Thinking** Does Equiano's description of African slavery mean that if a slave was well treated by his or her owner, then slavery was acceptable? Explain.

2 WEST AFRICAN RELIGIOUS PRACTICES

What were the religious beliefs and practices of West Africans?

West Africans had their own religious beliefs. In the countryside away from the cities, these religions continued even after the arrival of Islam and Christianity. Nearly every African people believed in an all-powerful Creator. Equiano described the Creator that his people of Benin believed in as one who lived in the sun, wore a tight belt around his stomach so that he might never need to eat or drink, and smoked a pipe, the favorite luxury of Equiano's people.

Gods and Goddesses. West Africans also believed in a number of other gods and goddesses. Each represented some aspect of life. The people of Dahomey, for example, organized their gods and goddesses into the categories of sky, earth, and thunder. The two most important were Mawu, the moon goddess, and her husband, Lisa, the sun god. They were the parents of all other gods and goddesses.

At the same time, most West Africans believed that spirits lived in all things—in plants, trees, animals, and even stones, as well as in people. All things on earth were connected by a life force that tied people to people, and people to things.

Importance of Ancestors. West Africans practiced **ancestor worship**. They believed that a person's soul survived after death and that they could be in touch with the souls of their long-dead ancestors. People prayed to ancestors for protection against evil spirits or for help in solving the problems of everyday life. They uttered the names of their ancestors frequently to make sure that they would always be connected to them.

West Africans engaged in elaborate ceremonies to honor their departed relatives. Mourning of the dead sometimes went on for months, ending with a burst of celebration when the mourners believed the soul had reached "home."

To West Africans, religion was not something apart from other aspects of life. It was life itself to them. The social group in which people lived was also a religious community. Farming, hunting, or fishing was as much a religious activity as it was the act of obtaining food.

This mask from Côte d'Ivoire was used in the burial of a woman. It is made from wood.

Taking Another Look

1. What religious beliefs did most West Africans share?

2. Why did West Africans honor their ancestors?

3. **Critical Thinking** What do you think might have been some effects of West Africans' belief that religion was part of all human activities?

3 OTHER WEST AFRICAN TRADITIONS

What other customs and practices helped shape West African life?

In the mid-1800s, a U.S. missionary named R. H. Stone journeyed to West Africa to spread Christianity. As he neared the Yoruba city of Abeokuta, Stone climbed a high rock to catch his first glimpse of the people. Like many non-Africans of his time, Stone expected to see a people who did little to support themselves. Instead, he found a city alive with activity and creativity. Wrote Stone:

What I saw disabused [rid] my mind of many errors in regard to . . .

Women from Mali dance to celebrate the end of a drought. What other kinds of events might be marked by dancing?

Africa. . . . The men are builders, blacksmiths, iron-smelters, carpenters, calabash [wood] carvers, weavers, basket makers, hat makers, traders, barbers, tanners, tailors, farmers, and workers in leather. . . . Women . . . spin, weave, trade, cook, and dye cotton fabrics.

Stone wrote these words some 300 years after Europeans had begun to enslave West Africans. But the activities he described had been going on for centuries. West Africans had developed lively and varied cultures long before the 1500s. In time, artistic styles born in Africa would influence a wide range of arts outside the continent—from the modern paintings of the Spanish artist Pablo Picasso to the musical rhythms of jazz and blues in the United States.

Musicians and Dancers. "We are almost a nation of dancers, musicians, and poets," remarked Olaudah Equiano. Because religion played a central role in the lives of West Africans, so did the music, dance, and other arts that were part of religious activities.

Musicians were admired for the skill with which they played their drums, whistles, horns, guitars, flutes, and other instruments in complicated rhythms. A favorite kind of music had a **call-and-response** pattern. The leader sang out a short bit of music and the people sang it back to him, accompanied by drums and other percussion instruments.

Dances were elaborate, with women and men in separate lines swaying, leaping, and clapping their hands to the sound of beating drums. Dances were used to mark important occasions such as birth, marriage, and death. Sometimes, dances went on for several days and nights.

Storytellers. **Folktales**, traditional stories that were handed down, were favorites of West African peoples, especially stories of animals with human qualities. Folktales often had morals that taught lessons to the listeners. Storytellers told their tales to the accompaniment of drums and responses from their listeners. Many of these stories have survived to this day. Some deal with a trickster in the form of a spider, a tortoise, or a rabbit who defeats bigger and stronger animals.

Proverbs were also used to teach lessons. The Ibo (EE-boh) people of West Africa described proverbs as the "palm oil with which words are eaten." A Yoruba proverb goes, "If the earthworm does not dance in front of the rooster, he will still be eaten, but at least the rooster cannot claim that he was provoked into eating it."

Other Art Forms. Craftworkers of West Africa worked in leather, ivory, wood, and metals such as gold, silver, copper, and bronze. Each people developed its own special crafts. The Asante (uh-SAHN-tee) of what is now Ghana, for example, produced a brilliantly colored cotton cloth called **kente** (KEN-tee) that is still woven today. A piece of kente cloth is shown on the cover

of this book. The bronzesmiths of Benin crafted statues and other objects that are considered to be models of metalworking. You can see pictures of these and other works of art in the special full-color section of this book called "The Artist's View."

Taking Another Look

1. What role did music play in West African life?

2. What were some of the crafts that West Africans practiced?

3. **Critical Thinking** Why do you think West African arts were closely related to religion?

LOOKING AHEAD

West Africans of the 500s–1500s had a rich, varied way of life. Family ties were strong, and religion played a central part in their lives. In the arts, they produced works of such creativity and skill that they influenced the paintings and music of people in other countries centuries later.

As Africans experienced the agonies of slavery in the Americas, they held on to their traditions. The folktales they told in the Americas mirrored those of Africa. In North America, the African musical instrument the mbanza, which is made from a hollowed-out gourd, became the banjo. The rhythms of their work songs and spirituals and the call-and-response pattern of their singing recalled African music.

The Nupe people of Nigeria crafted this jar made from clay and iron.

29

FOCUS ON: AFRICAN FOLKTALE

In many cultures, folktales are passed from generation to generation by word of mouth. This oral storytelling tradition reflects, and thus teaches, the values and wisdom of a culture. Folktales can also entertain. What does the following folktale from the Asante (uh-SAHN-tee) people of Ghana tell you about Asante culture?

Turtle came to the house of Anansi the Spider, drawn by the fragrant smells of Anansi's cooking. Anansi was annoyed that Turtle had come to share his dinner, but he offered Turtle food anyway.

As Turtle reached out to take the food Anansi reminded him that it was rude to eat dinner without washing. Turtle waddled down to the stream to wash his dusty feet and face. By the time Turtle returned, Anansi had gobbled down all the food.

A few months later, Turtle invited Anansi to dine at his house at the bottom of the river. Anansi dove into the water, but before reaching the bottom, he floated back to the surface. Next, Anansi filled his pockets with stones and sank down to Turtle's table. Turtle reminded Anansi that it was rude to eat with a coat on. Anansi removed his coat. Without the stones to hold him down, he floated right back to the surface of the river again.

CLOSE UP: Chapter 3

The Who, What, Where of History

1. **Where** do the Yoruba people live?
2. **Who** belongs to an extended family?
3. **What** is bridewealth?
4. **Who** was Mawu?
5. **What** does the term *subsistence farmer* mean?
6. **What** does ancestor worship mean?
7. **What** is a call-and-response pattern?
8. **What** is kente cloth?

Making the Connection

1. What is the relationship between bridewealth and the value of a woman's work in her family?
2. What was the connection between religion and daily life among West Africans?

What Would You Have Done?

1. If you had been a Ghanaian craftworker, what kinds of materials would you have chosen to work with? Explain.
2. To which class of society do you think you would have preferred to belong—farmers or craftworkers? Explain.

Thinking and Writing About History

1. Explain why one writer says that dancing combined the two most important parts of West African life: religion and community relationships.
2. Look at the bronze head from Benin on page 2. Why do you think the work of the bronzesmiths of Benin is considered a model of metalworking?

3. How did West African music and art influence the music you hear and the art you see today? Explain.

4. Do you think that it was a good or a bad idea for land to belong to a community rather than an individual? Explain.

Building Skills: Making Comparisons

In this chapter, you have read about the customs and traditions of West Africans before Europeans came to Africa in any number. As you read the chapter, you might have noticed that some customs and traditions of the West Africans were similar to African American customs and traditions of today. Some customs and traditions were very different.

Compare the customs and traditions of West Africans with those of African Americans by completing the chart below on a separate sheet of paper. Then, write a sentence summarizing the chart.

Tradition	West African	African American
Families	*extended* *children important*	*children important*
Marriage		*monogamy*
Work		
Society		
Religion		
Music		
Stories		
Art		

UNIT 2

Enslaved Africans and an overseer

AFRICANS IN THE AMERICAS
(1500s–1760s)

Processing sugar in the West Indies

European slave trader and African captive

An African American Speaks

At the time we came into this ship, she was full of black people, who were all confined in a dark and low place, in irons. . . . [M]any of us died every day. . . . When our prison could hold no more, the ship sailed.

—Slave story about the Middle Passage

Unit 2 tells the story of Africans who were brought to the Americas as slaves, first by Europeans and then by Americans. The first European settlers came to the Americas in search of freedom and a better life. Africans were brought to the Americas in chains.

For nearly 400 years, slave traders shoved, pushed, and threw Africans aboard slave ships in the largest forced movement of people in history. According to some historians, the slave trade cost Africa nearly 40 million people. Millions never made it to the Americas. They died at the hands of slave traders or as a result of conditions in the filthy cargo holds of slave ships during what came to be called the **Middle Passage** across the Atlantic.

The nearly 20 million Africans who survived the trip to the Americas came in chains. Although deprived of even the most basic human rights, these people helped shape the course of history in the Western Hemisphere.

Expanding the Horizons of Europe.

The Atlantic slave trade, which began in 1502, had its roots in the centuries-old craving of Europeans for goods that came from Asia. During the Crusades from 1095 to the late 1200s, which were undertaken to wrest the Holy Land from Muslims, Europeans saw for the first time the thriving trade between Arabs and Indians and Chinese. Europeans wanted some of the goods for themselves and competed to gain them—exotic spices to preserve and flavor their foods, fine porcelain to serve the foods in, and shimmering silks to dress the wealthy. However, Europeans were not able to take from the Muslims either the Holy Land or the land routes to Asia. As a result, Europeans began to look for all-water routes to Asia.

One such route would take European ships around the southern tip of Africa, into the Indian Ocean, and then to India, China, and the Spice Islands. No ship had ever sailed more than a few hundred miles south along the west coast of Africa. Sailors feared the Atlantic Ocean, calling it a "green sea of darkness." But in the early 1400s, a Portuguese prince, nicknamed Henry the Navigator, ordered his sailors into the unknown waters. Slowly they edged southward, hugging the west coast of Africa.

As the Portuguese went farther and farther south, they took Africans with them as guides and interpreters. Six Africans sailed with Bartholomeu Dias when he rounded the southern tip of Africa in 1488. Africans also traveled with Vasco da Gama when, in 1498, he sailed around Africa and across the Indian Ocean to India.

Da Gama and other Portuguese set up trading posts along this route, and Portugal became one of the great trading countries of Europe. Portugal traded not only

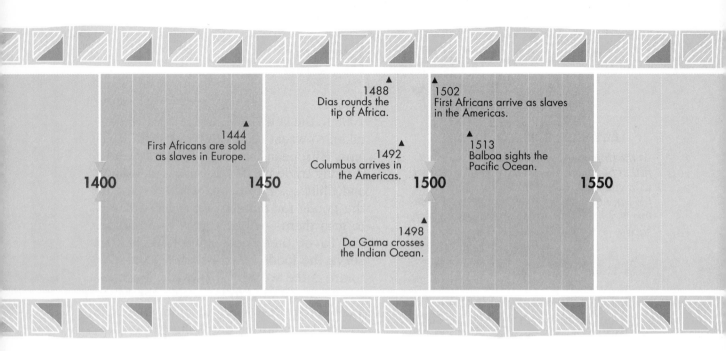

1488
Dias rounds the
tip of Africa.

1502
First Africans arrive as slaves
in the Americas.

1444
First Africans are sold
as slaves in Europe.

1492
Columbus arrives in
the Americas.

1513
Balboa sights the
Pacific Ocean.

1400   **1450**   **1500**   **1550**

1498
Da Gama crosses
the Indian Ocean.

with countries in Asia, but also with kingdoms of West Africa and city-states of East Africa.

Face to Face in Africa. Only a narrow waterway separated Portugal from North Africa. However, Portugal's first-hand knowledge of Africa stopped at the northern edge of the Sahara until Portuguese explorers began to move south along the coast.

The first Portuguese encounter with a large group of Africans came in 1444. That fateful year, Portuguese sailors crept inland from their ship and attacked a West African village. They carried about 200 men, women, and children back to Portugal and sold them at a public auction.

Start of the African Slave Trade. The Portuguese saw possibilities for trade in Africa. As they pushed along the west coast, they renamed parts of the continent after the leading product from each region: the Grain Coast (named after

pepper, the "grains of paradise"), the Ivory Coast, and the Gold Coast. One region was the Slave Coast, making clear that European–West African trade included trade in human beings.

African rulers saw an economic advantage in the slave trade. Slavery—the practice of owning human beings as property—had existed in Africa, as it had in other places in the world, for hundreds of years. Although slavery differed across the continent, until this time, most slaves in Africa were people who had been captured during wars. These slaves were either servants or worked the land, and most could earn or buy their freedom after a period of time. Some also received their freedom through service. Now, however, deciding that slaves were good business, African **slave-raiders** rounded up thousands of captives for sale to the Portuguese at slave-collecting forts along the coast of West Africa.

The Portuguese generally accepted the Africans as trading partners. For their

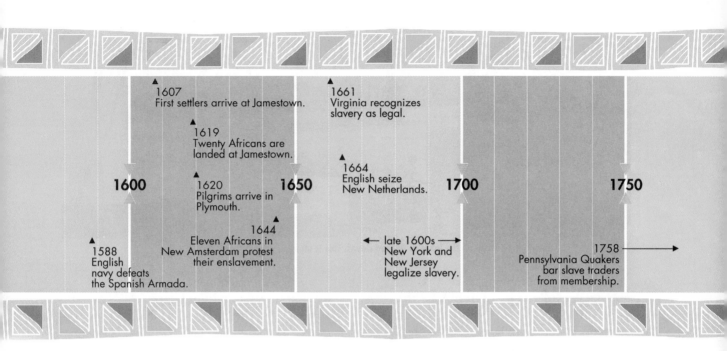

1600 **1650** **1700** **1750**

1607
First settlers arrive at Jamestown.

1619
Twenty Africans are landed at Jamestown.

1620
Pilgrims arrive in Plymouth.

1644
Eleven Africans in New Amsterdam protest their enslavement.

1588
English navy defeats the Spanish Armada.

1661
Virginia recognizes slavery as legal.

1664
English seize New Netherlands.

← late 1600s →
New York and New Jersey legalize slavery.

1758 →
Pennsylvania Quakers bar slave traders from membership.

part, African nobles from such great centers as Benin saw themselves as being on equal footing with, or even a step above, the Europeans. African rulers traveled to Lisbon, Portugal, or Rome, Italy, to study. In 1518, a king from the Kongo (present-day Zaire) visited the Vatican and spoke to the pope in Latin. The pope, in turn, appointed him bishop of Kongo. While traders bought enslaved Africans, missionaries set out to convert Africans to Christianity.

Black Gold for the Americas.   By the time da Gama reached India, Christopher Columbus had already made three trips to the Americas, returning with news that turned world history upside down. Spain and Portugal quickly realized the wealth that was to be had in the new lands across the Atlantic. Spain sent **conquistadors** (kahn-KEES-tuh-dawrs), or conquerors, to establish outposts in the Americas. One conquistador was frank in stating his reasons for going to the Ameri-

cas: "We came here to serve God and the king, and also to get rich."

From the start, descendants of the first African slaves in Portugal and Spain took part in the expeditions that opened the Americas. At least 30 Africans stood with Vasco Núñez de Balboa (bal-BOH-uh) when he sighted the Pacific Ocean in 1513. Still others accompanied the Spanish conquistadors into what are now Peru, Mexico, Florida, and the southwestern United States.

However, European discovery of the Americas created a whole new demand for labor. The number of Europeans who came as workers did not meet the growing demand. The Spanish tried enslaving Native Americans to work in the mines of Peru and Mexico and the sugar **plantations,** or large farms, of the Caribbean islands. After the Native American slaves died by the thousands, Europeans bought enslaved Africans to take their place. From the Caribbean islands, slavery spread to the American mainland. In the

35

The West Indian economy was based on the labor of African slaves. This is an indigo plantation.

300 years following Columbus's first voyage, the trade in enslaved Africans swelled into the millions. Slave ships carried the flags of many countries—first, Portugal and Spain; later, England, Holland, France, Denmark, Prussia, Sweden, Brazil, and the United States. The Atlantic slave trade yielded such high profits that Europeans came to call Africans "black gold."

The English Colonies in North America. In 1588, an event occurred that opened the way for the spread of African slavery to the mainland of North America. In that year, the English navy smashed the Spanish Armada in the English Channel, ending Spain's control of the Atlantic. In the next century, England planted 13 **colonies** up and down the Atlantic seaboard of North America. A colony is a settlement in another land that remains under the control of the home country.

Most of the settlers in these colonies came from England, many in search of religious freedom for themselves. From Germany, Holland, and Sweden came settlers who sought simply to escape poverty. The white **immigrants,** as settlers who move to another country are called,

set about establishing farms, villages, and towns. As they did this, Native Americans, who were the original settlers, were pushed aside, often with great brutality.

In all 13 colonies, farming was the basic way of life. In New England, the name for the northernmost colonies, winters were long and the growing season short. The soil was rocky. Subsistence farming was the main occupation. Like the farmers of West Africa, New England farmers grew only enough for their own families. The entire farm family worked the land, only occasionally hiring one or two extra laborers. In time, the New England colonies also developed sizable manufacturing, shipbuilding, and fishing industries. Colonists carried on trade with England and the West Indies. After 1698, New England's ships, loaded with captured Africans, traveled the Middle Passage between West Africa and the Americas.

In the Middle Colonies, with a more temperate climate and more fertile soil than New England, many farmers produced **cash crops,** crops raised for sale rather than for a farmer's personal use. The Middle Colonies, with large crops of wheat, corn, and rye, were called the "breadbasket colonies." Some farms were large enough to hire farm laborers on a regular basis. Some farms, especially in the Hudson River Valley of New York, were very large estates, requiring many additional laborers. Most of these were African slaves. Commerce, or trade, and manufacturing over time also became important in the Middle Colonies.

In the Southern Colonies, the plantation that raised tobacco, rice, or indigo (a blue dye) became the symbol of farming, although in reality most farms were small. Trade and industry played little part in the Southern **economy,** the system of producing, distributing, and using goods and services. Crops were shipped to England in New England vessels, and manufactured goods were bought from England.

Plantations had heavy demands for labor. At first, landowners tried **indentured servants,** people who exchanged a period of work for payment of their passage to the Americas. But every few years, when the servants received their freedom, a new group had to be trained. Eventually, plantation owners found it more practical and profitable to use slaves as their main source of labor. At first, they enslaved Native Americans and then, later, Africans.

From their arrival in the first colony, at Jamestown, in 1619, as indentured servants, Africans played a part in the English settlement of what would one day become the United States of America. Soon, enslaved Africans would be used as workers in both New England and the Middle Colonies. However, the largest number of African slaves were taken to the colonies that ran from Delaware south to Georgia.

The Issue of Slavery. With slavery in existence in all regions of English America, few colonists gave much thought to the question of whether one person should own another. Some colonies imposed heavy taxes on enslaved Africans brought into the colony, and some religious groups, such as the Quakers of Pennsylvania, protested the whole idea of slavery. In 1758, they barred slave traders from membership. But for the most part, colonists did not trouble themselves with considering the morality of slavery. Making a living was enough of a problem for most colonists. Further, as time went on, difficulties with Great Britain came to occupy their attention.

In addition to those considerations, whites looked upon Africans as less than human. Europeans and then colonists did this in order to justify the mass enslavement of Africans. Explained one British critic of slavery in the 1700s, "If they believe them [Africans] to be of human kind, they cannot regard them . . . as no better than dogs or horses."

Such attitudes bound Africans tighter and tighter in a web of slavery. At the same time, white colonists were demanding greater and greater freedom from Great Britain. It was not until the second half of the 1700s, that slavery began to seem inconsistent with the idea of liberty to some colonial leaders.

Taking Another Look

1. Why did Europeans seek a sea route to Asia?

2. Why were Africans called "black gold" by Europeans?

3. Why did most white colonists not worry about whether or not slavery was wrong?

4. **Critical Thinking** Explain why there were more slaves in the Southern Colonies than in New England or the Middle Colonies.

Africans on a slave ship

The Atlantic Slave Trade

(1500–1760s)

THINKING ABOUT THE CHAPTER

How did the Atlantic slave trade rob Africans of their most basic human rights?

In 1493, a strange parade made its way through Seville, Spain. Christopher Columbus proudly marched through the city's streets displaying objects from his first voyage across the Atlantic—colorful parrots, exotic plants, and people he called Indians. A 19-year-old student, Bartolomé de Las Casas (bahr-toh-loh-MAY de lahs KAH-sahs), watched the procession with great interest.

In 1502, Las Casas himself traveled to the Americas as a conquistador. His bloody conquests in the Caribbean won him a huge estate and the labor of many Native American slaves. Ten years later, he became the first Roman Catholic to be ordained a priest in the Americas. In 1514, Las Casas read a passage in the Bible that convinced him "that everything done to the Indians thus far was unjust." He spent the rest of his life trying to end the enslavement of Native Americans.

However, Las Casas did not oppose the idea of slavery completely. In 1517, in order to help Native Americans, he persuaded the king of Spain to substitute African labor for Native American labor in the Americas.

When Las Casas died at 92 in 1566, he left behind a book called *History of the Indies*. It remained unpublished for more than 300 years. When people finally read it, they learned that Las Casas had repented his decision to enslave Africans. By that time, however, the Atlantic slave trade had changed the history of three continents.

1 ▼ SLAVE RAIDS IN WEST AFRICA

▼ How were West Africans rounded up for sale as slaves?

Just before dawn broke, wooden drums sounded the alarm. Enemies had surrounded the village. Warriors grabbed their weapons, but it was too late. Intruders armed with heavy wooden clubs, spears, and bows and arrows overran the compound. Some villagers fled. Others fought back. Most fell stunned by well-aimed blows to the head. When the battle ended, the invaders joined the captured villagers together neck to neck with heavy logs and ropes.

The villagers had fallen victim to African slave-traders from the Atlantic coast. The traders marched them barefoot over mountains, through forests, and along rivers. Those who rebelled were killed. Those who fell ill were left to die along the trail. Near the end of the journey, the slave traders fattened the survivors with yams, melons, and dried fish. They covered bruises on the captives with powder and rubbed palm oil into their skin until it glistened.

The African slave-traders marched their captives to a slave-trading station along the coast. Here a silent trade began. White slave-traders examined the captives and piled up bundles of red and blue cotton cloth in payment. The African traders pushed these goods away. The white traders added a few guns, some gunpowder, and a keg of rum. When there was enough, the deal was sealed.

The Slave "Factories" of West Africa. Beginning in about 1500, such cooperation between African and Euro-

Africans from the interior were led in coffles to the coast for sale to European slave traders.

SNAPSHOT OF THE TIMES

1492–1493 Columbus makes his first voyage to the Americas.

1502 Atlantic slave trade begins.

1517 Bartolomé de Las Casas asks Spain to replace Native American labor with African labor.

1624 Queen Nzinga begins battle against Portuguese slave-raiders.

1700–1800 Atlantic slave trade reaches its peak.

pean slave-traders took place time and time again in the Atlantic slave trade. At first, the Portuguese and Spanish controlled much of the European side of the trade. But as time passed, other nations wanted a share of the profits. Soon the English, the Dutch, the French, and other Europeans entered the race for Africa's "black gold".

By the 1600s, merchants in these European countries had formed slave-trading companies. Their agents built what became known as **slave factories** in harbors along the West African coast. The factories were made up of supply warehouses, living quarters for the Europeans, and pens for the captured Africans.

Africans from thousands of villages passed through these factories, sold by fellow Africans. They came from the Yorubas, Mandingos (man-DING-gohs), Hausas (HOW-suhs), Fantis (FAHN-tees), Asantes (uh-SAHN-tees), Dahomeans (duh-HOH-mee-uhns), Binis (BEE-nees), and many other peoples.

By the 1600s, the silent trade had given way to very vocal trade as Europeans had learned African languages. Bargaining might go on for several weeks.

To prevent their captives from plotting to escape, the merchants were careful not to put too many Africans who spoke the same language into the same holding pen. Whip-carrying guards kept the slaves in constant fear until they were loaded onto ships for the next leg of their journey to the Americas—the Middle Passage.

Taking Another Look

1. How were West Africans captured for the Atlantic slave trade?

2. What happened to African captives at the factories along the Atlantic coast?

3. **Critical Thinking** The Atlantic slave trade helped cause wars both between European nations and between African peoples. Explain why this might have been so.

2 THE MIDDLE PASSAGE

What were some of the cruelties experienced by Africans during the Middle Passage?

The men who fastened irons on the mothers took the children out of their hands and threw them over the side of the ship into the water. Two of the women leaped overboard after the children. . . . One of the two women . . . was carried down by the weight of her irons before she could be rescued; but the other was taken up by some men in a boat and brought on board. This woman threw herself overboard one night when we were at sea.

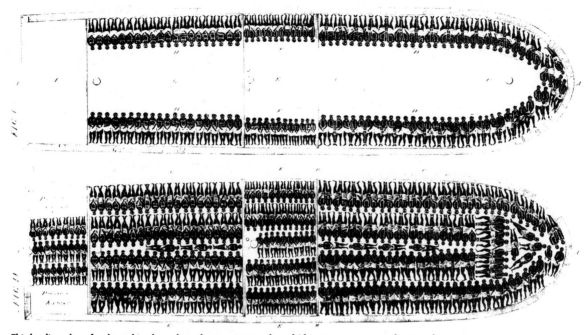

This loading plan of a slave ship shows how the greatest number of Africans were squeezed onto a ship to make the transatlantic voyage as profitable as possible.

This was only one of the horrors described by an African who survived the Middle Passage—the long, nightmarish trip across the Atlantic. Other Africans recalled equally terrible scenes: brutal whippings, forced feedings, and the smell of death and filth in disease-ridden cargo holds. Hundreds of Africans lay wedged together, bound by chains, and praying that death would come to them, too.

The Cruelty of the Voyage. The holds of most slave ships measured only about 5 feet (1.5 meters) high. But this space was cut in half by a shelf that extended about 6 feet (1.8 meters). The Africans were chained by the neck and legs to the shelf or to the deck below and had only about 20 to 25 inches (50 to 64 centimeters) to sit up. On storm-tossed seas, they banged into one another, and the chains cut deeply into their flesh.

Sanitary facilities were crude. The foul odor of a slave ship could be smelled for miles downwind.

Diseases—hookworm, dysentery, malaria, smallpox, yellow fever, and the like—swept through the ships. Some slave ships lost half of their human cargo during the Middle Passage. The death rate averaged between 13 and 20 percent. Amid the suffering, many Africans went mad. Some killed each other fighting and clawing for breathing space.

To run a successful business, ship captains needed to be able to deliver a majority of live captives to buyers in the Caribbean islands and the mainland Americas. Accordingly, the crews brought the Africans on deck in shifts for fresh air and food. They fed them cornmeal, bean pulp, or stewed yams. Next, came the "dancing of the slaves." A piper or fiddler played a tune, while sailors with whips forced the

Africans to dance around so they would get some exercise.

Resistance and Rebellion. Africans did not submit easily to such brutality. From the start of the voyage to the end, they fought back, preferring death to the inhumanity of the Middle Passage. Some threw themselves overboard when they came up to be fed. Others refused food and medicine. Sailors pried open clenched jaws or broke teeth to pour food down the throats of resisting Africans. But some of them still managed to starve themselves to death.

The crew aboard most slave ships lived in constant fear of rebellion. "If care not be taken," wrote one sailor, "they [the Africans] will mutiny and destroy the ship's crew." Ship diaries document 55 uprisings aboard ship by Africans between 1699 and 1845 and mention hundreds of attempted uprisings.

Taking Another Look

1. How did the Middle Passage brutalize Africans?

2. How did Africans resist the Middle Passage?

3. **Critical Thinking** What lasting effect do you think the experience of the Middle Passage had on Africans after they came to the Americas?

3 WEST AFRICA AFTER THE
▼ SLAVE TRADE
▼   How did the Atlantic slave trade affect the development of West Africa?

The Portuguese slave-traders described her as an Amazon—a member of a mythological ancient race of female warriors. The people of Matamba saw her as a hero. Her name was **Queen Nzinga.** She came to power in 1624 and ruled the state of Matamba, in what is now Angola, until 1663. She used her power to launch a war against the Portuguese for enslaving her brother. She battled slave-traders for nearly 30 years and greatly disrupted the inland slave trade. In 1656, the Portuguese negotiated a treaty with her. It remained in effect until Nzinga's death at 83.

Other West African leaders tried to fight slavery, too. But European guns and the greed of African slave-raiders defeated them in the end. By the 1700s, most West Africans found themselves victims of a system that spelled tragedy for West Africa's future.

The Weakening of Society. For more than 300 years, the slave trade plundered West Africa. The area suffered an enormous loss of population. At least one African died for every one who reached the coast alive. Estimates for the total number of Africans lost to the slave trade range from 25 to 50 million. Slave-traders showed no respect for rank or skills. Noble and peasant, artisan and laborer—all might find themselves lashed together in a slave ship.

African slave-raiders eager for European manufactured goods captured more and more people over the years. Local warfare spread, and professional armies arose. Wars were fought only for the purpose of gaining captives to sell as slaves. By the mid-1700s, gunsmiths in Birmingham, England, were making over 100,000 guns a year for the trade with Guinea

European goods were brought to West Africa through slave factories and trading forts like this one.

(GIN-ee) alone. The splendor that was Africa under the empires of Ghana, Mali, and Songhai had been destroyed.

Effects on the West African Economy. The exchange of humans for manufactured goods created a vicious cycle of economic dependence in Africa. Europeans used their profits from African slave labor to invest in trade and industry in their own countries. The cheap goods that Europeans exchanged for slaves made it unnecessary for West Africans to develop further any manufacturing or any commerce other than the slave trade. The result was that when European interest in slaves declined in the 1800s, West Africans did not have the economic strength to resist European exploitation of Africa for its natural resources. Consequently, European domination of the African continent met with little resistance. African economic development was delayed for over 300 years.

Taking Another Look

1. What were the effects of the slave trade on West African society?

2. How did the Atlantic slave trade disrupt the West African economy?

3. **Critical Thinking** Why do you think Europeans in the slave trade might want to consider their victims as "something less than human"?

LOOKING AHEAD

The white view that Africans were something less than human grew out of the whites' need to justify the African slave trade. Wrote one British author in the 1700s: "The Africans are . . . little better than the lions, tigers, leopards, and other wild beasts, which that country produces in great numbers." Such racist ideas about Africans were among the most evil legacy of the slave trade.

A woman applies a paste made of red clay and water to repair the wall of her family compound in a Soninke village in Mauritania. Another woman rushes to work in a modern office building in downtown Accra, capital of Ghana. Young boys in a rural village in Togo learn to make spearheads. A student takes a physics course at Lagos University in Nigeria. Such scenes—a mixture of past and present—typify the West Africa of today.

West Africa bears the cultural marks of its thousands of years of history. Once the home of ancient African kingdoms, West Africa fell prey to European conquerors in the 1800s. After World War II, West African colonies shook off European rule and formed 16 independent nations (see map, page 396). Official languages include French, English, and Portuguese. But hundreds of African dialects can be heard across the continent—Twi, Hausa, and Fanti, for example. People practice Christianity, Islam, and many African religions.

Today, about 200 million people live in West Africa. Once stripped of its people by the slave trade, the region now faces the problem of overpopulation. It also faces the struggle of trying to modernize while not giving up its traditions.

CLOSE UP: Chapter 4

The Who, What, Where of History

1. **Who** was Prince Henry the Navigator?
2. **Where** was the Slave Coast?
3. **Who** were the conquistadors?
4. **What** does the term *indentured servant* mean?
5. **Who** was Bartolomé de Las Casas?
6. **Where** were the European slave factories located?
7. **What** was the Middle Passage?
8. **Who** was Queen Nzinga?

Making the Connection

1. What was the connection between the efforts of Las Casas to protect Native Americans and the Atlantic slave trade?
2. What was the connection between the slave trade and later European domination of Africa?

Time Check

1. When did the Atlantic slave trade begin?
2. During what years did the Atlantic slave trade flourish?

What Would You Have Done?

1. If you had been an African trader, how would you have responded to a request by a European merchant to become partners in the slave trade?
2. If you had been Queen Nzinga, what terms would you have demanded from the Portuguese in a treaty?

3. Imagine you are an English sailor in 1701. You have agreed to sail on a ship going to Africa and then the Americas. Just before the ship sails, you learn it will carry African slaves. What do you do? Explain.

Thinking and Writing About History

1. Imagine that you are an African noble visiting Spain in 1517. Write a letter to the Spanish king giving your reaction to Bartolomé de Las Casas's idea of using more African labor in the Americas.

2. Imagine that you are a Pennsylvania Quaker in 1758. Write a letter to a relative in England explaining why your group has barred slave traders from membership.

3. Imagine that you are an African who was captured and brought to the Americas as a child. After many years, you have gained your freedom. A newspaper that opposes slavery asks you to describe your voyage across the Atlantic. Write a brief account of your Middle Passage.

Building Skills: Understanding Cause and Effect

Most things that happen to you in your life happen for a reason or reasons. Sometimes it's very easy to see why an event happens. The fire alarm goes off *because* someone pulls it. The pulling of the handle is the *cause;* the alarm is the *effect.*

When events take place over a long period of time, it is sometimes harder to identify causes and effects. One day you notice that a classmate looks different.

What are the *causes* for the *effect* of your classmate's appearance? He explains that it has been a gradual process. For about four months, he's been eating only healthful foods, drinking lots of water, and exercising every day. He's also gotten a new haircut. These several causes created the effect of his appearance.

Some effects in history had very obvious causes. Bartolomé de Las Casas suddenly began to work against the use of Native Americans as slaves. The *cause* was a passage he read in the Bible; the *effect* was a change of opinion.

Other events in history occur because of several causes working together. Below is a list of possible causes for this effect: West Africans were unable to resist European domination. On a separate sheet of paper write the numbers of the items that were *not* causes of this effect.

1. West Africans did not have guns.

2. Some Africans threw themselves from slave ships.

3. West Africa suffered enormous population loss because of the slave trade.

4. The slave trade destroyed the order of society in West Africa.

5. Queen Nzinga battled the Portuguese and their slave traders for nearly 30 years.

6. Africans fought each other to acquire more captives to sell as slaves.

7. In the 1500s, Europeans searched for an all-water route to Asia.

8. West Africans became dependent on European goods.

African slaves taking sugar to market

The West Indies, First Stop for Africans

(1500–1760s)

THINKING ABOUT THE CHAPTER

Why did the plantation system make slavery profitable in the Caribbean?

In northwest Jamaica, one of the West Indian islands, lies a rugged region called the Cockpit Country, after the Jamaican word for pothole. In the 1600s and 1700s, Cockpit Country was home to runaway African slaves, known as **Maroons.** The first Maroons fled Spanish owners on the island in the 1500s. After the English took Jamaica in 1655, they tried to subdue the Maroons for more than 75 years. Finally, in 1739, they signed a peace treaty granting the Maroons independence.

As a result of the West Indian colonists' experience with Maroons, they took brutal measures against Africans.

This chapter describes the system of slavery that emerged in the English-speaking islands of the West Indies. This same system spread in the late 1600s to the English colonies in North America.

1 EMPIRES BUILT ON SUGAR

▼ How did sugar become "king" in the
▼ West Indies?

On a Sunday morning in July 1631, Sir Henry Colt joined his crew in early morning prayer aboard the *Alexander.* As sailors knelt on the deck, a cannon shot rang out. Off in the distance, the crew saw 20 Spanish ships bearing down on them under full sail.

Colt ordered his crew to fight. When the smoke cleared, the English had triumphed, and the Spanish were sailing away. But the danger had not passed. Colt raced back to alert the colonists on St. Christopher Island (St. Kitts), which the English had colonized in 1623, that the Spanish were coming to push the English out of the Caribbean.

A Taste for Sugar.   The Spanish had taken possession of the West Indies in the early 1500s, colonizing Puerto Rico in 1508, Jamaica in 1509, and Cuba in 1511. But once other European countries—France, England, the Netherlands, and Denmark—learned of the riches there, they challenged Spain's hold on the islands. For over 200 years, from the late 1500s to the early 1800s, the waters of the Caribbean were an almost constant battleground.

The West Indies offered many cash crops for sale—dyewoods, cotton, and spices. But what Europeans wanted the most was sugar and molasses. The latter was shipped to New England where it was made into rum.

Sugar and Slavery.   The story of sugar in the Caribbean goes hand in hand with the story of slavery. As the demand for sugar grew, so did the demand for slaves. Huge plantations devoted to the production of sugar were set up. Like Spain, other countries tried to enslave Native Americans to work the plantations, but they died by the thousands.

A few European countries tried using the forced labor of white prisoners. England, for example, used Irish prisoners to work in the islands, but they too died. Europeans generally did not use the forced labor of other Europeans because there was opposition to enslaving fellow Christians. West Indian plantation owners, called **planters,** soon turned to enslaved Africans as their major source of labor.

By the mid-1600s, European ships were carrying some 10,000 enslaved Africans a year to the West Indies—and at an extraordinary profit. Company agents in the 1600s paid the equivalent of about $25 each for African slaves in West Africa, and then sold them in the West Indies for more than $150 each. Slave owners expected the labor of African slaves to repay their cost in less than two years. They barely fed the Africans, and they worked them so hard that many died from the cruel treatment within two years. Plantation owners had to keep buying slaves to maintain their supply of workers at the same level.

African slaves fueled almost the entire sugar industry. They planted and harvested the sugar cane. They turned the huge rollers that ground up the stalks and stirred the giant, boiling copper vats that melted sugar into molasses. The sweat of African workers produced two of the West Indies' most valuable products—sugar and molasses.

1508	Spanish colonize Puerto Rico.
1509	Spanish colonize Jamaica.
1511	Spanish colonize Cuba.
1625	English colonize Barbados.
1631	Spain comes to take Caribbean islands from the English.
1655	English take over Jamaica.
1739	English sign treaty with Jamaican Maroons.

Triangular Trades. With Barbados, colonized in 1625, and Jamaica among its West Indian holdings, England became one of the leading nations in the sugar-slave trade of the 1600s and 1700s. This trade rested on a number of three-legged routes known as the **triangular trades.** These routes began in West Africa, crossed to the West Indies, went north to the English colonies on the mainland, and then either returned to Africa or continued to Europe. The slave trade formed a vital part of the English economy until the late 1700s.

How many triangular routes do you see on the map? What was shipped on the Africa-Americas triangle?

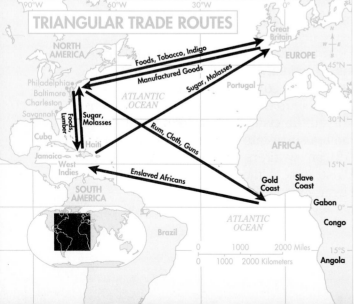

England's interest in the Americas began to shift from the Caribbean to the mainland in the mid-1600s, and the islands started sending Africans to English colonies in North America. As part of this process, African slaves were brought to the islands for an introduction to life under slavery. This process was known as seasoning. Then they were shipped to plantations in the South.

Taking Another Look

1. How did the growing of sugar cane help promote the Atlantic slave trade?

2. What regions were involved in the triangular trades?

3. **Critical Thinking** Do you think sugar could have become so important in the West Indies without the use of African slaves? Explain.

2 PATTERNS OF WEST INDIAN SLAVERY

How were slaves treated in the English West Indies?

In 1756, a British slave ship docked at the West Indian island of Barbados. Among those on board was an 11-year-old African, Olaudah Equiano, whom you met in Unit 1. That evening, a group of white merchants who had financed the voyage examined the human cargo, poking and prodding. "There was much dread and trembling among us," wrote Equiano years later, as a free man, "and nothing but bitter cries."

After the slave merchants set a price for each African, they herded them into the shipyard. At the sound of a drum, the

Why was African slave labor so important to the sugar economy of the West Indies?

who falsely believe that their race is by nature superior to another and who have the political, economic, and military ability to enforce their attitude. A racist attitude allowed the English to deny African slaves their rights as human beings.

Racism existed among other Europeans in the West Indies, as well. But racism was the most severe among the English. The Spanish and the French, for example, sometimes married Africans. The English almost never did. The Spanish often gave former slaves the rights of people who were born free. The English restricted the rights of all Africans—free and slave. In most of the West Indies, a person's standing in society was related to the color of his or her skin. But nowhere was color as important as it was in the English West Indies by the late 1600s.

scramble began. Buyers raced to tag the healthiest Africans for purchase. The sight of a mass of whites swarming toward them left the Africans panic-stricken.

Worse was yet to come. After the buyers paid for the Africans, they dragged them to waiting wagons, often ripping them from the arms of sobbing family members. "In this manner," wrote Equiano, "without scruple [misgiving], are relations and friends separated, most of them never to see each other again."

The Africans who were sold in Barbados faced a severe life. Most were marched off to work in blazing-hot sugar fields or in mills that sometimes ground up people as well as raw sugar.

A System Based on Racism. The cruelty suffered by Africans in the West Indies grew out of **racism.** Racism is the unjust treatment of a people by others

Taking Another Look

1. What awaited Africans after they arrived in the West Indies?

2. What part did racism play in the treatment of Africans in the British West Indies?

3. **Critical Thinking** Reread page 34. Then explain how slavery in Africa differed from slavery in the West Indies.

LOOKING AHEAD

The West Indies introduced Africans to the harsh realities of slavery in the Americas. The racism and hard labor on English sugar plantations set the pattern for the later treatment of Africans in the English colonies. These practices set the stage for the bitter racial divisions that would trouble the United States for some two hundred years.

Salsa, reggae, calypso—hear this music and you're listening to the sounds of the Caribbean. Fufu, fried plantains, cassava pone—eat these foods and you're tasting the cooking of the Caribbean. Each of these sounds and tastes is rooted in the region's African heritage, helping to create what some call an Afro-Caribbean culture.

The culture is as rich and varied as the region's people. Some 22 nations and nearly 30 million people make up the Caribbean Islands. Official languages include Spanish, English, Dutch, and French—languages of the nations that first brought Africans there as slaves. Creole, a dialect rooted in African languages, is widely spoken, too.

With the end of slavery in the islands, during the 1800s, grew feelings of pride in traditional African culture—music, foods, and dialects. Many islands also gained independence at this time.

The transition to independence in most of the islands has been smooth. Today, 11 of the 13 independent island-nations practice democracy. Even islands still tied to a home country have much independence. "The Caribbean people," says one expert, "have undoubtedly proven their capacity to govern themselves."

CLOSE UP: Chapter 5

The Who, What, Where of History

1. **Who** were the Maroons?
2. **What** were cash crops?
3. **What** were the triangular trades?
4. **What** is racism?
5. **Where** were sugar, molasses, and rum produced for England?

Making the Connection

1. What was the relationship between the Maroons and the brutal treatment of slaves in the West Indies?
2. What was the connection between sugar and slavery?

Time Check

1. Which of these Caribbean islands did Spain colonize *first:* Cuba, Puerto Rico, Jamaica?
2. When did the English take over the island of Jamaica?

What Would You Have Done?

1. If you had been an enslaved African in Jamaica, would you have tried to join the Maroons? Explain.
2. Imagine that you are an African on board a slave ship in the Caribbean. You and a young Englishman are washed overboard in a storm and have survived by clinging to debris. You wash ashore in Jamaica. The Englishman says he will get a boat and sail you to safety on any island in the Caribbean you choose. Which island would you choose? Explain your reasons.

Thinking and Writing About History

1. Write a newspaper account of the naval battle described on page 47. Remember to answer the questions *who, what, when, where,* and *why.*

2. Imagine that you are a British ship-owner in the early 1700s. Write an advertisement aimed at attracting people to invest in your ship's next voyage to the West Indies.

3. Imagine that you are the owner of a plantation in the English West Indies. You have just received a letter from an old friend back in England who asks why you use African slaves on your plantation. Write a short letter giving your explanation.

Building Skills: Identifying Cause and Effect

Finding out what were the causes and what were the effects in history often answers the important question *why?* To be sure you understand the *whys* of this chapter, complete the following exercise. Match each of the effects with its cause, by writing the correct letter after the number of each effect.

Effects

1. Many nations claimed islands in the West Indies.

2. West Indian colonists brutally restricted their African slaves.

3. Demand for slaves increased in the West Indies.

4. The English denied African slaves their rights as human beings.

5. Africans were the main source of labor in the West Indies.

6. Slave owners barely fed and clothed their African slaves.

Causes

A. Native Americans and Irish people died when forced to work in the West Indies.

B. Slave owners expected the labor of African slaves to repay their cost in less than two years.

C. More people wanted to buy more West Indian sugar.

D. The Maroons, runaway slaves in Jamaica, successfully resisted the English and were granted their independence.

E. The English believed that they were by nature superior to the peoples of Africa.

F. There were great riches available in the West Indies.

Of course, when you are reading your textbook, causes and effects are not isolated as they were in the exercise above. Read the following paragraph about the decline of the sugar industry in the West Indies. Then write in a sentence one effect and one cause for it that you find in the paragraph.

By the nineteenth century, West Indian slavery had stopped bringing big profits. In fact, by 1807 the typical British West Indian planter was operating at a loss. Other areas of the world now produced sugar, and there was a glut on the market. The price of West Indian sugar fell lower and lower, and the need for slaves decreased along with it.

Arrival of the first Africans in Jamestown, Virginia

Africans in the Thirteen Colonies

(1619–1760)

THINKING ABOUT THE CHAPTER

How did Africans help settle what would one day become the United States of America?

In 1522, Luis Vasquez de Ayllon, a wealthy Spanish judge on the Caribbean island of Hispaniola (his-puhn-YOH-luh) (where present-day Haiti and the Dominican Republic are located), sailed for Spain. He wanted to convince King Charles I to finance Spain's first permanent colony north of Mexico. Hernando Cortés and his conquistadors had just conquered the rich Aztec empire in Mexico. Charles, thinking there might be more fabulous wealth in the Americas, agreed to the plan.

In July 1526, six Spanish ships left Hispaniola with 500 men and women aboard, including 100 Africans as slaves. The expedition put ashore along the marshy Pee Dee

River near present-day Georgetown, South Carolina. Here Ayllon ordered the Africans to build a settlement.

The colony, San Miguel, lasted a year. Over half the Spanish died, including Ayllon. The Africans rebelled and set fire to the settlement. The 150 Spanish who survived fled back to Hispaniola.

To this day, the fate of the Africans at San Miguel remains a mystery. Perhaps they built a new settlement, or perhaps they went to live among the Native Americans. They were the first non–Native Americans, however, to live permanently in what is today the United States.

Other Africans played a role in the country's early history, too. In the late 1530s, an African named Estevanico (es-tay-vah-NEE-koh) trekked with a handful of Spanish through much of the present-day U.S. Southwest. In 1565, African slaves helped the Spanish build St. Augustine, Florida, the oldest permanent city founded by Europeans in the United States. In the 1600s, the English also used the forced labor of Africans to build their colonies in North America.

1 ARRIVAL IN JAMESTOWN
▼ Who were the first Africans to arrive in the Virginia Colony?

In August 1619, a Dutch ship sailed up the James River to the struggling English settlement at Jamestown, Virginia. The captain of the ship offered to trade 20 Africans for much-needed food. Many of the Africans had Spanish-sounding names— Pedro, Isabella, Antoney, Angelo—so the English suspected that the Dutch had stolen them from a Spanish slave ship headed for the West Indies. The English also suspected that the Africans had been baptized as Christians, as was the Spanish

custom. As a result, the English took them as indentured servants.

The Africans amazed the English colonists with their farming abilities—talents they had learned in their farming villages in Africa. Two of the Africans—Antoney and Isabella—married, and in 1624, Isabella gave birth to a son whom they named William. He was the first child of African descent born in English America. William escaped the fate of later generations of African American children—he was not automatically born a slave.

A Taste of Freedom. By the time the first Africans arrived in Jamestown, the settlement, founded in 1607, had weathered drought, starvation, and disease. The terrible winter of 1609–1610, when nearly nine out of ten colonists starved to death, was only a memory. In 1612, John Rolfe, one of the colonists, had helped change the colony's fortunes by successfully growing tobacco. Virginia now had a profitable cash crop for sale in Europe.

However, the colony faced a severe labor shortage. To promote settlement, the colony offered settlers 50 acres of land (about 20 hectares) for each indentured servant they brought to Virginia. The colony also promised settlers the same rights they enjoyed in England. In 1619, shortly before the arrival of the first Africans, the colony had established the House of Burgesses, the first legislative assembly in the Americas. Here, male property-owners voted on day-to-day affairs in the colony.

During the early years of struggle, Virginia welcomed the labor of all workers— both Africans and Europeans. Indentured servants, both African and European, who finished their contracts could become

1526	West Africans become first non–Native Americans to live permanently in the present-day United States.
1619	First Africans arrive at Jamestown.
1638	First Africans arrive in Massachusetts.
1641	Massachusetts legalizes certain forms of slavery.
1641	Mathias De Sousa elected to Maryland's General Assembly.
1644	Africans in New Netherlands sue for their freedom.
1660s	Virginia passes its first slave laws.
1663	Maryland makes all Africans in the colony slaves for life.
1750	Georgia legalizes slave trade.

settlers. For a time, Africans enjoyed a measure of freedom they would not know again until the mid–20th century. Individual African males acquired property, voted, and testified in court. One such person was Anthony Johnson.

Anthony Johnson arrived in Jamestown in 1621 as an indentured servant. He married a woman named Mary, and the two gained their freedom sometime in the 1630s. In 1651, the Johnsons bought the indentures, or contracts, of five servants—some European, some African—and were granted 250 acres of land. In the following years the Johnsons' children acquired more land. A third-generation Johnson named his plantation "Angola," perhaps in memory of his grandfather's African homeland.

Slavery Amid Freedom. By the mid-1600s, landowners in Virginia and farther south had found steady markets for tobacco, rice, sugar cane, and indigo. For maximum production, the planters were growing their crops on plantations similar to those in the West Indies.

Faced with the need for a large supply of labor, the planters looked increasingly to Africans to fill that need, not as indentured servants, but as slaves. Africans offered several advantages over indentured servants to a landowner. First, the cost of buying and supporting slaves was about the same as supporting indentured servants, but slaves worked for life rather than for a period of time. Second, unlike African slaves, European indentured servants could appeal to the home country for protection against neglect or mistreatment. Third, enslaved Africans would find it difficult to escape because they could be identified by skin color. European indentured servants could fade into the general population. Finally, the supply of Africans seemed endless.

Restrictions on Slaves. In the 1660s, Virginia passed its first laws regulating slavery. In 1660, a Virginia law recognized that African slaves were slaves for life. Even baptism no longer protected Africans from slavery. Declared a 1667 law: "Baptism does not alter the condition of the person as to his bondage or freedom." Another law held that children born in the colony would have the same status as their mothers. In other words, if a mother was a slave, her children would also be slaves.

There were only about 300 Africans in Virginia in the 1660s. By the end of the 1600s, Africans were being brought to the colony at the rate of about 1,000 a year. By 1756, of Virginia's 293,000 people, more than 120,000 were of African descent. Of this number, only about 3,000 lived as free people.

Racism. Less than a century after the arrival of the first Africans in Virginia, racism had come to distinguish how the colonists treated Africans and those of African descent, just as it did in the West Indies. By the late 1600s, English men and women began to refer to themselves as *white* and to Africans as *black*.

The liberty enjoyed by the Anthony Johnsons of the past had disappeared. In 1691, the House of Burgesses—symbol of freedom in English America—banned marriages between English and Africans. It also denied free Africans the vote and the right to testify against whites in court. Most Africans could no longer boast, as an African farmer in the 1640s had, "I will work when I please and play when I please." By the 1700s, most Africans in English America lived according to the will and whip of white owners.

Taking Another Look

1. What rights did free Africans enjoy in Virginia before 1660?

2. Why did plantation owners turn to the system of slavery as a labor source?

3. **Critical Thinking** Why do you think racism developed in Virginia?

2 AFRICANS IN THE SOUTHERN ▼ COLONIES

▼ How did slavery take root in the English colonies of the South?

In 1634, Cecilius Calvert, Lord Baltimore, sent 200 settlers from England to what is now the state of Maryland. Cal-

THE THIRTEEN BRITISH COLONIES

New England Colonies
Middle Colonies
Southern Colonies
State boundaries today

How many Southern colonies were there? Which region had the fewest colonies?

vert hoped to establish a refuge for England's Roman Catholics, persecuted because of their religion. Among those who landed on the Maryland shore were three African indentured servants—John Price, Francisco Peres, and Mathias De Sousa.

After he completed his term of service, De Sousa built a thriving trade with the Native Americans of the region. In 1641, the colonists elected him to serve in the General Assembly, the colony's lawmaking body. Within about 20 years, however, Maryland followed the lead of Virginia. The word *slave* crept into the colony's laws, and Africans lost their voice in colonial affairs.

Durante Vita. Like the Virginians, the colonists of Maryland found the soil and climate around Chesapeake Bay well suited to growing tobacco. They, too, turned to the plantation system—and to Africans as slaves. In 1663, Maryland

Tobacco was colonial Virginia's major crop. These drawings show African slaves preparing the tobacco leaves for drying, curing, and storing. Where did the colony sell most of its crop?

passed a law enslaving Africans and their children *durante vita,* or for life.

Soon enslaved Africans became the backbone of Maryland's labor force. They cleared forests, tended fields, and harvested and processed tobacco. Africans also worked as servants in the elegant homes of planters, doing everything from cooking to caring for children.

The Slave Trade. Maryland and Virginia became known to slave traders as good markets for buying African slaves. To prevent colonists from buying Africans from rival nations such as the Netherlands, England formed the Royal African Company in 1663. The company built eight forts in West Africa, and between 1663 and 1698, carried some 120,000 Africans to English America.

At first, most Africans were shipped to the West Indies to be "seasoned," or broken in, on sugar plantations (see page 48). English slave-traders then sold the Africans to colonists along the Atlantic coast. By the 1700s, however, most Africans were shipped directly from Africa to the mainland.

The Carolinas. In 1663, King Charles II of England granted eight nobles a huge tract of land south of Virginia. The colony's owners asked English philosopher John Locke to draw up a plan of government. Locke believed that government existed to protect the life, liberty, and property of the people. Because slaves were "property" to him, Locke gave them no rights. His plan declared: "Every freeman of Carolina shall have absolute power and authority over his negro slaves."

The owners of Carolina saw the colony as a business. They dreamed of cash crops suitable to warm climates—olives, citrus fruits, tea, and more. Eventually, only rice provided the profits they sought, when farmed with slave labor. Four of Carolina's founders were members of the Royal African Company, and they gave land to all settlers who bought slaves for the colony.

In 1729, Carolina split into two colonies—North Carolina and South Carolina. North Carolina's economy was more varied than South Carolina's and it had a larger number of small farmers. In South Carolina, slavery and rice plantations became a way of life. By 1763, Africans accounted for 70 percent of the colony's population. Almost all were enslaved.

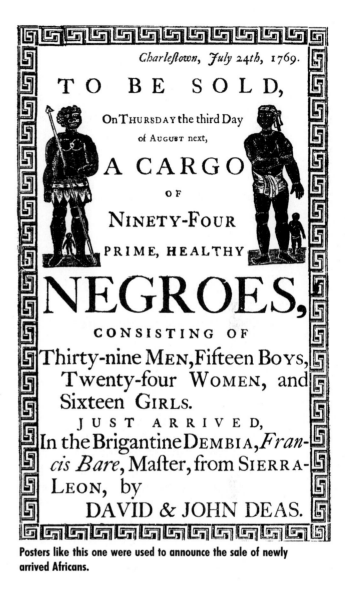

Posters like this one were used to announce the sale of newly arrived Africans.

Georgia. The founders of Georgia pictured a colony without slaves. Led by James Oglethorpe, they wanted to establish a haven for people who had been imprisoned for their debts. All settlers were to start on an equal footing, without great differences in wealth.

In 1733, Great Britain agreed to the plan. It hoped that Georgia would act as a buffer between its colonies and Spanish Florida to the south. Planters in South Carolina favored the plan for the same reason. Georgia's colonists opposed the ban on slavery. "All unanimously agree," wrote one leader, "that without Negroes Georgia can never be a colony of any consequence [importance]." To get around the rule, they "hired" Africans from South Carolinians on 100-year terms. Finally, slavery was allowed in 1750. By 1760, enslaved Africans made up one third of Georgia's population.

Taking Another Look

1. Why was slavery established in Maryland?

2. What did the founding of Carolina reveal about English attitudes toward Africans by the 1660s?

3. **Critical Thinking** Compare the different ways slavery became established in Maryland, the Carolinas, and Georgia.

3 ▼ AFRICANS IN THE MIDDLE COLONIES
▼

What conditions discouraged the widespread use of slavery in the Middle Colonies?

In 1644, 11 African indentured servants petitioned the Council of New Netherlands for their freedom. The Africans had helped the Dutch build the colony's first village—New Amsterdam—18 years before. They had been "promised their freedom on the same footing as other free people in New Netherlands." Yet they remained bound to the Dutch West India Company, the trading firm that had financed New Netherlands.

The council ruled in the Africans' favor. Each person named in the petition—Manuel de Gerrit de Rens, John Francisco, Little Anthony, John Fort Orange, Simon Congo, Big Manuel, Little Manuel, Paul d'Angola, Anthony Portuguese, Gracia, and Peter Santome—received a grant of land in the area that is now New York City's Greenwich Village. Here, they took up life with the same legal rights as the Dutch.

New York and New Jersey. The Dutch never attracted many settlers from the home country to New Netherlands, so they welcomed people from other nations. Even so, the colony suffered from a continual shortage of farm workers. The Dutch West India Company sold thousands of enslaved Africans in the Americas and encouraged their use in New Netherlands. As early as April 1638, the colony's director wrote that the largest farms, or patroonships, were "cultivated by the blacks."

Still New Netherlands grew slowly, and the Dutch West India Company gave little attention to the colony's defense. In 1664, the English easily seized it. King Charles II gave the colony to his brother James, the Duke of York, who renamed it New York. James awarded what is now New Jersey to two friends.

In the late 1600s, both New York and New Jersey legalized slavery. The Royal African Company imported thousands of Africans into the two colonies, but the region's climate proved unsuited to the plantation system. Because farms could not be worked year-round, few people wanted to feed and clothe large numbers of farm laborers all winter. By 1750, the numbers of Africans in New York and New Jersey lagged far behind those in the Southern Colonies.

Pennsylvania and Delaware. In 1681 and 1682, William Penn received grants from the English king for the lands that now make up Pennsylvania and Delaware. Penn founded Pennsylvania as a religious haven for Quakers and other Christians seeking religious freedom. He generally treated Native Americans more fairly than other colonial founders had. But since African slaves already lived along the Delaware River on lands once held by the Swedes and the Dutch, Penn allowed slavery to continue.

Most farms in New Jersey were small. How does this help account for the few African slaves in the colony?

Not all of Pennsylvania's colonists shared Penn's tolerance of slavery. In 1688, members of the German Quakers issued the first antislavery protest in North America. The document declared, "Negroes are brought hither against their will. . . . Have these poor Negroes not as much right to fight for their freedom as you have to keep them as slaves?"

The protest fell on deaf ears. Even so, Africans in Pennsylvania managed gradually to win more rights than Africans in other colonies. By the mid-1700s, Pennsylvania claimed the largest number of free Africans in any of the 13 colonies. It would be these people and their descendants who would give voice to the antislavery movement of the late 1700s and the 1800s (see Units 3, 4, and 5).

Africans in Delaware were less successful. Delaware's location made tobacco production on plantations profita-ble. Some settlers bought African slaves—first from the Dutch, then from the English. When Penn gave Delaware its own legislature in 1703, the lawmakers made it more difficult to free Africans. By the mid-1700s, Delaware had allied itself more closely with slaveholding colonies to the south than with its neighbors to the north.

Taking Another Look

1. How did their location affect slavery in the Middle Colonies?

2. Why did the Royal African Company stand to benefit from the English takeover of New Netherlands?

3. **Critical Thinking** Suppose the Dutch had kept New Netherlands. How might the lives of Africans there have been different?

59

4 AFRICANS IN NEW ENGLAND

▼ How did New Englanders help promote the African slave trade?

In February 1645, the *Rainbow* left Boston, Massachusetts, intending to trade for Africans along the Guinea coast. When the ship reached Guinea, however, James Smith, the captain, found no Africans for sale, and he took matters into his own hands. He ordered his crew to attack several villages. They set one village ablaze, killed perhaps 100 people, and kidnapped a handful of others.

Smith had hoped to sell his human cargo in the West Indies, but a strange twist of events took him back to Boston. Never before had a Massachusetts ship carried West Africans directly to the colony. Colonial leaders charged Smith with "man-stealing" and ordered the Africans to be returned. Little did anyone know that Massachusetts ships would soon be sailing regularly to Africa for human cargoes.

"A Model Community." Massachusetts started as a haven for religious dissenters who were unhappy with the Church of England. The Puritans (from *purify*) wanted to make the church stricter and simplify its services. The first group of Puritans arrived in what is now Plymouth, Massachusetts, in 1620. They called themselves Pilgrims—people on a holy mission. By the end of the 1630s, over 16,000 men and women had arrived in the colony.

In building their model Christian community, the Puritans struggled with the question of whether to allow slavery. The question first arose in 1638 when a Massachusetts ship, the *Desire,* landed a shipment of Africans from the West Indies. Because the captain had bought the Africans, rather than kidnapped them, he was allowed to sell them.

In 1641, the question came up again when the Puritans drafted a code of laws. The code prohibited slavery except for "lawful captives taken in just wars" and those who would "sell themselves or are sold to us." By this wording, the Puritans tried to distance themselves from the "man-stealing" in West Africa.

The New England Slave Trade. Eventually, economics settled the question. The rocky soil and cool climate of Massachusetts made farming difficult, so many settlers turned to the sea for their livelihood. Fishing and trade with England

During which 10-year period were the most Africans brought to the colonies? During which 10-year period did the greatest increase occur?

▶▶ NUMBERS OF AFRICANS BROUGHT AS SLAVES TO THE THIRTEEN COLONIES, 1701–1775

Years	Slaves
1701–1710	9,000
1711–1720	10,800
1721–1730	9,900
1731–1740	40,500
1741–1750	58,500
1751–1760	41,900
1761–1770	69,500
1771–1775	15,000
Total	255,100

Source: R.C. Simmons, *The American Colonies: From Settlement to Independence* (New York: David McKay Company, Inc.). Copyright 1976 by R. C. Simmons. Reprinted by permission of Harold Matson Co., Inc.

became the basis of New England's economy. Then, in 1698, the Royal African Company licensed New England merchants to allow them to participate in the Atlantic slave trade.

New Englanders built, sailed, and financed many of the vessels involved in the Middle Passage. While New Englanders owned few slaves themselves, they sold thousands to planters in the Southern Colonies. The colonial slave trade, in which New England participated, grew so rapidly that the number of Africans in the colonies soared from 59,000 in 1714 to nearly 300,000 by 1754.

Treatment of Africans. There were far fewer African slaves in New England than in either the Southern or Middle colonies. Yet, even here, laws called **slave codes** limited the rights of enslaved Africans, although they were not as harsh as laws elsewhere. Africans in New England were better able to win their freedom than slaves in other colonies. In time, Africans—free and enslaved—in New England would take up the cause of African American liberty.

Eventually New Englanders banned slavery for two reasons. The first was the contributions of African Americans during the American Revolution and the early years of the new nation. The second was the fact that slavery had no important place in the economy of the region.

Taking Another Look

1. How did Puritan laws help ensure the future of slavery in Massachusetts?

2. Why did New Englanders become involved in the Atlantic slave trade?

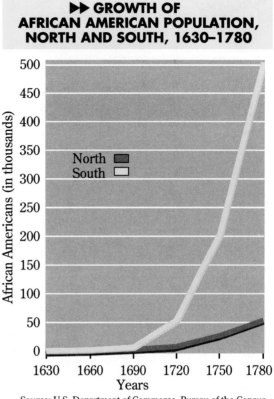

▶▶ GROWTH OF AFRICAN AMERICAN POPULATION, NORTH AND SOUTH, 1630–1780

Source: U.S. Department of Commerce, Bureau of the Census, *Historical Statistics of the United States, Colonial Times to 1970, Part 2* (Series Z 1–19), p. 1168

How many more African Americans were there in the South than the North in 1720? in 1750? in 1780?

3. **Critical Thinking** How did geography influence the existence of slavery in the Southern, Middle, and New England colonies?

LOOKING AHEAD

By the 1700s, the English colonies had two separate populations—one free and one in chains. In colony after colony, lawmakers established ways to keep Africans enslaved. Meanwhile, Africans struggled to find ways to survive the day-to-day humiliations of being owned by another person—and to find a way out of slavery.

Kunta Kinte was the "furthest-back person" Alex Haley's grandmother could remember. As a child in Henning, Tennessee, Haley listened to stories about his family's ancestors. Recalled Haley about his grandmother: "When telling about Kunta Kinte, her voice would fill with awe, like she was talking about a Bible story." Inspired by these stories, Haley set out to find his "roots"—that is, he researched his family's history and discovered their beginnings in West Africa.

Haley told the story of Kinte and the generations that followed him in a best-selling book called *Roots*. The book so captured the public imagination that television producers turned it into a 12-hour mini-series, which ran for eight nights in a row on prime time television.

In February 1977, a record 130 million people watched all or part of "Roots." The last episode drew 80 million, making it the highest-rated program in TV history at that time. The size of its audience surpassed that of 11 Super Bowl games.

For the first time, a TV program told the story of African Americans from the perspective of an African American. The popular show awakened an interest in African American history and led countless numbers of African Americans to search for their own roots.

CLOSE UP: Chapter 6

The Who, What, Where of History

1. **Where** was San Miguel?
2. **Who** was Estevanico?
3. **Where** in the Virginia Colony did the first Africans arrive?
4. **Who** was the first child of African descent born in the Virginia Colony?
5. **What** was the House of Burgesses?
6. **Who** was Anthony Johnson?
7. **Who** was Mathias De Sousa?
8. **What** does the phrase *durante vita* mean?
9. **Who** drew up a plan of government for the Carolinas?
10. **Who** was James Oglethorpe?

Making the Connection

1. What was the connection between the cultivation of tobacco in Virginia and the growth of slavery there?
2. What was the connection between climate and slavery in the 13 colonies?

Time Check

1. When did the first Africans arrive at Jamestown?
2. When did Maryland make all Africans slaves for life?

What Would You Have Done?

1. Imagine that you are an African living in Maryland. You came to the colony as an indentured servant, but have completed your term of service. Now the colony has passed a law enslaving Africans for life. What will you do?

2. If you had been James Oglethorpe, how would you have argued against slavery in Georgia?

Thinking and Writing About History

1. Write a story that explains what happened to the Africans of San Miguel.

2. Write a letter from the daughter of John Fort Orange to the king of England explaining how her father obtained his freedom and protesting the legalization of slavery in New York.

Building Skills: Recognizing Relevant Information

A friend of yours has moved to a new part of town. You ask for directions to her house and she tells you the following:

[1] You go down Washington Street, then turn right at Garvey. [2] Go down Garvey past the video store. [3] They've got the new tape I was telling you about there. [4] Go three blocks on Garvey and take a left on Wheatley. [5] Angie Thomas, who used to be in our class, lives in the first yellow house on the left. [6] I'm in the fourth house on the right.

Which of the sentences in her directions are *not* necessary to help you find her house?

The sentences you listed are examples of *irrelevant* information. They do not have any significant, or relevant, information about what you are trying to find out—how to get to your friend's house. They may contain true or interesting information, but not information directly related to the subject

The skill of recognizing relevant information is an important one to develop. It can help you focus your reading and think more clearly about a topic.

Each of the questions below has three facts listed after it. On a separate sheet of paper, write an *R* next to the letter of the fact if it is relevant to the topic. Write an *I* next to the letter of the fact if it is irrelevant to the topic.

1. What was the economy of colonial Virginia like?
   a. Tobacco was successfully cultivated there in 1612 for sale in England.
   b. William, the son of Antoney and Isabella, was the first child of African descent born in English America.
   c. In its early years, the colony faced a severe labor shortage.

2. What were conditions like for Africans in New York?
   a. In 1644, 11 African indentured servants successfully petitioned for their freedom.
   b. The growing season in New York was shorter than in Virginia.
   c. New York was named for the Duke of York.

3. How did the British colony at Georgia develop?
   a. James Oglethorpe wanted to establish a haven for debtors.
   b. The Royal African Company brought many enslaved Africans to British America.
   c. James Oglethorpe died in 1785.

A Revolutionary War soldier

AFRICAN AMERICANS AND A NEW NATION

(1768–1840s)

Benjamin Banneker

The Constitution of the United States

We the People of the United States
insure domestic Tranquility, provide for the common defence, promote the general
and our Posterity, do ordain and establish this Constitution for the United States of

THE BIG PICTURE

Unit 3 traces one of the great ongoing debates in U.S. history—the debate over the rights of African Americans—from the years of the American Revolution through the establishment of the **nation** under a new form of government. Thousands of African Americans* fought for the nation's liberty in the Revolution. Yet the question of their freedom was pushed aside by the new nation's **Constitution,** the document containing its basic laws and principles. Nonetheless, African Americans—enslaved and free—played important roles in building the new nation. As the nation spread westward, so did slavery. Gradually, as you will read in later units, the debate grew louder.

The Seeds of Conflict. The question of independence, both for the 13 British colonies and for African Americans, became sharper in the years following the French and Indian War. This nine-year conflict between Great Britain and France was fought over control of much of the North American continent. When the war ended in 1763, a victorious Britain took possession of Canada and most of the land from the Atlantic coast west to the Mississippi. The colonists were happy with Britain's victory. But the war had been expensive for the British and they felt it was time for the colonists to help pay the

costs of empire. Beginning in 1764, the British imposed a series of heavy taxes on the 13 colonies. When the British moved to collect the new taxes, howls of protest went up throughout the colonies.

Many colonists claimed that since they were not represented in Parliament, the British law-making body, Great Britain had no right to **levy,** or impose, taxes on them. From Massachusetts to Georgia, these colonists rallied behind a single cry: "No taxation without representation!"

Calls for Independence. The protest over taxes led some colonists to speak openly of independence from Britain. African Americans wondered what liberty would mean to them. Would it mean an end to slavery? Would it mean increased rights?

Some white Americans, such as Benjamin Franklin, Patrick Henry, and Thomas Paine, did call for the **abolition,** or ending, of slavery. However, most colonists considered such views too extreme. Southern slave owners feared revolts if African American slaves heard about freedom. Many white Northerners rejected

---

*Beginning with this unit, the term *African American* is used to indicate people of African descent even though the rights of citizenship were not yet available to them. This was also true at this time for both Native Americans and women.

An African American Speaks

That liberty is a great thing we know from our own feelings, and we may likewise judge so from the conduct of the white people in the late war [Revolution].

—Jupitor Hammon,
African American Slave,
New York, 1787

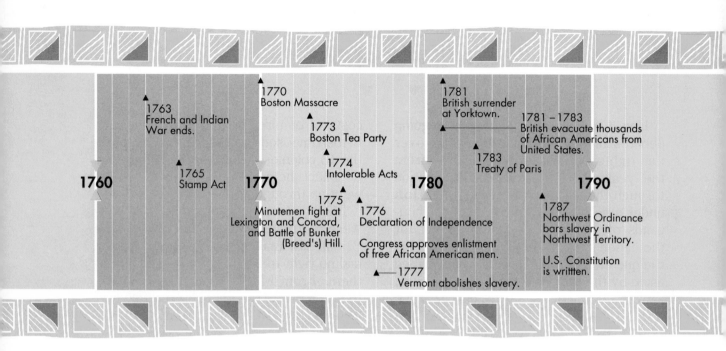

1760

1763
French and Indian
War ends.

1765
Stamp Act

1770

1770
Boston Massacre

1773
Boston Tea Party

1774
Intolerable Acts

1775
Minutemen fight at
Lexington and Concord,
and Battle of Bunker
(Breed's) Hill.

1776
Declaration of Independence

Congress approves enlistment
of free African American men.

1777
Vermont abolishes slavery.

1780

1781
British surrender
at Yorktown.

1781–1783
British evacuate thousands
of African Americans from
United States.

1783
Treaty of Paris

1790

1787
Northwest Ordinance
bars slavery in
Northwest Territory.

U.S. Constitution
is writtten.

the idea of equality for African Americans. Some Northerners were engaged in the profitable slave trade, while others believed African Americans were inferior and did not deserve to be free.

Backing Liberty. However, the spirit of liberty led some free African Americans to become **Patriots,** the name given to colonists who favored independence. Free African Americans, for example, helped force the repeal of the Stamp Act. This act placed a tax on every kind of paper, from marriage licenses to playing cards, and was one of the most hated taxes. Free African Americans joined other colonists in anti-British **boycotts,** refusing to buy goods from Great Britain. They also took part in the riots against the Stamp Act in Boston. African Americans and whites threatened tax collectors and held protest meetings, gathering around huge bonfires, crying, "Liberty and Property!"

As the 1770s unfolded, ties between the colonists and Great Britain weakened. About one third of the colonists remained loyal to Britain, and about one third supported neither side.

Patriots began to arm themselves. Laws generally forbade African Americans from owning guns. Many white colonists, especially in the South, feared that armed African Americans might try to stage slave rebellions. In the North, some free African Americans loaded muskets and trained as **Minutemen**—Patriots ready to fight at a minute's notice.

When war finally came, African Americans took part in every major battle. Some were volunteers; others were drafted, or taken for military service. Most were from the North. On the whole, African Americans fought side by side with white Americans. This practice changed in later wars, when African Americans were forced to serve in separate army units.

66

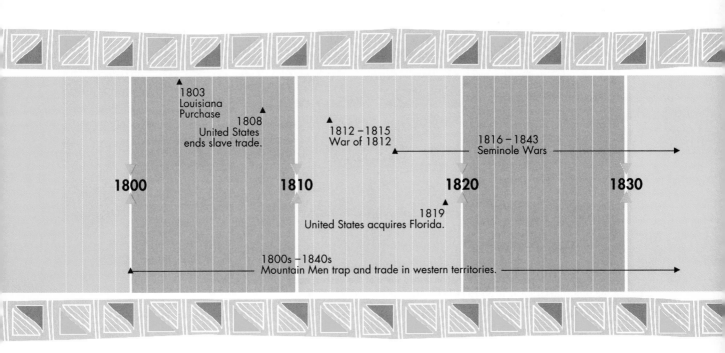

1803
Louisiana
Purchase

1808
United States
ends slave trade.

1812–1815
War of 1812

1816–1843
Seminole Wars

1800   **1810**   **1820**   **1830**

1819
United States acquires Florida.

1800s–1840s
Mountain Men trap and trade in western territories.

Promises of Freedom. At the start of the American Revolution, the British were short of soldiers and eager to undercut the colonial army. They offered freedom to any African American slave who would join them. On November 7, 1775, Lord Dunmore, royal governor of Virginia, declared all African Americans "free, that are able and willing to bear arms . . . [in] his Majesty's troops." African Americans by the thousands joined the British as soldiers, laborers, and even spies.

Countless more African Americans, however, were swayed by the words of the Declaration of Independence. Signed on July 4, 1776, this document captured the Patriots' belief in liberty. "All men are created equal," it boldly proclaimed.

These words inspired many African Americans to place their faith in an independent United States. They believed liberty for the nation could mean liberty for them, too. Throughout the war, African

American soldiers displayed individual acts of valor. Time and again, the officers of the **Continental Army,** as the colonists' military force was called, praised the courage of African Americans.

Debating Slavery. Even while the Revolution raged, some African Americans asked the new state governments created by the Declaration of Independence to end slavery. Typical of such pleas was a petition sent to the New Hampshire assembly in 1779. "From what authority [do our owners] assume to dispose of our lives, freedom and property?" asked a group of 19 African American slaves.

These words echoed the earlier Declaration of Independence. What African Americans did not know, however, was that a debate over slavery had nearly prevented the Continental Congress from approving the document. When Thomas Jefferson first wrote the Declaration, he

67

African American soldiers stood by the nation during some of the darkest hours of the war. Here they are with Washington at Valley Forge in the bleak winter of 1778–1779.

listed British abuses of colonial rights. Among them, he charged, the British king had "waged cruel war against human nature itself, . . . in the persons of a distant people [Africans]; . . . captivating and carrying them into slavery in another hemisphere." Angered at the attack on slavery, Southern delegates, most of whom were slave owners, forced the Congress to drop this clause.

After American troops defeated the British in 1781, the nation faced a dilemma. Asked one white soldier, "What is to be done with these [African American] soldiers who have shed their best blood in its [the nation's] defense?"

One by one, state governments in the North answered the question by ending slavery. However, slavery remained firmly established in the South.

A New Law of the Land. Differences between the North and South over slavery created a crisis in 1787. Delegates from the new states met in Philadelphia and decided to create a new constitution for the United States.

Many delegates to the **Constitutional Convention,** as the meeting was later called, feared for the future of a democratic nation that allowed slavery to continue. However, they feared the danger of a disunited nation even more. Some Southern delegates threatened to walk out if any antislavery measures were adopted. Eventually, each side gave up some demands in order to reach a **compromise.** The Constitution recognized slavery. It did, however, permit Congress to put an end to the Atlantic slave trade beginning in 1808. It took a bloody civil war and a constitutional change, or **amendment,** in the 1860s to end slavery in the United States.

Defending the Nation. In the years following 1787, the United States took steps to strengthen itself in the eyes of the world. In 1812, the nation fought another war against Great Britain. This time they fought to prevent the British from violating U.S. rights at sea and from arming Native Americans in the Northwest Territory. In 1819, the United

States also acquired Florida from Spain to protect its southeastern border.

Expanding the Nation. Even before the colonies won their independence, some colonists were leaving their homes along the East Coast and heading inland. After independence, U.S. territory extended as far as the Mississippi River. Some of the settlers going west and south were slave owners who took their African American slaves with them. However, in one area slavery was forbidden. This was the Northwest Territory, a large region that lay north of the Ohio River and east of the Mississippi. The **Northwest Ordinance** (AWRD-en-uhns), passed by Congress in 1787, barred slavery in the Northwest Territory. Here some free African Americans built homes.

The new territory had rich farmland. Farmers there shipped their products to market down the Mississippi River to New Orleans. From New Orleans, their goods were sent to the East Coast and overseas. However, New Orleans and the whole region from the Mississippi River to the Rocky Mountains was owned by France. The farmers wondered what would happen if France chose to close the port of New Orleans to them. President Thomas Jefferson eased these farmers' concerns by buying the entire French territory in 1803.

This **Louisiana Purchase** doubled the size of the United States and gave its people an enormous new territory in which to make their homes. The fact that Native Americans already lived on the land was of little concern to the thousands of settlers who began pouring into these lands. Among them were Southerners who established plantations and ran them with the forced labor of enslaved African Americans.

THE NORTHWEST TERRITORY, 1787

Some free African Americans made their homes in the Northwest Territory. Which rivers and lakes were included in this territory? What states were made from this territory?

The expansion of the country stepped up the debate over slavery. Expansion brought Americans face to face with a question that had troubled them since the Revolution. Could a democratic nation exist part slave and part free?

Taking Another Look

1. Why did some African Americans choose to side with the British in the American Revolution, while others sided with the Patriots?

2. How did the members of the Constitutional Convention compromise on the question of slavery?

3. How was the Northwest Ordinance favorable to African Americans?

4. **Critical Thinking** List three ways African Americans showed their loyalty to the colonies and then to the United States from 1763 to 1812.

Washington Crossing the Delaware, by Emmanuel Leutze

CHAPTER 7

The American Revolution: Liberty for All?

(1768–1783)

THINKING ABOUT THE CHAPTER

How did the Revolution affect the lives of African Americans?

On Christmas night, 1776, amid a blinding snowstorm, a band of ragged colonial troops dragged rowboats toward the Delaware River. Some men wrapped strips of blankets around their feet to keep their torn boots from falling apart.

George Washington, commander of the Continental Army, hoped to score a desperately needed victory against the British stationed on the opposite shore. As Washington's troops slid the boats into the ice-clogged river, Washington climbed into one of them. An African slave named Prince Whipple was one of those who pulled at the oars of Washington's boat.

Prince Whipple's wealthy African parents had sent him to America at age ten to receive an education. But a treacherous slave trader seized the boy and sold him to William Whipple of New Hampshire. When war came to the 13 colonies, Captain Whipple and his slave Prince served as aides to General Washington.

On the morning of December 26, Prince Whipple took part in a stunning victory over the British at what became known as the Battle of Trenton, in New Jersey. He went on with his owner to fight in other battles of the American Revolution. By summer 1777, Captain Whipple noticed that Prince's spirits had fallen. He asked why. Said Prince: "Master, you are going to fight for your liberty, but I have none to fight for."

Prince was later freed by his owner, but most African American slaves were not so lucky. In this chapter, you will learn why and how African Americans, enslaved and free, took part in the American Revolution.

1 FROM PROTEST TO WAR

▼ What role did African Americans play on the road to war?

In September 1768, drums rolled as two regiments of red-coated British soldiers marched up King Street in Boston. The **Redcoats,** as the British troops were called, set up camp on the Commons, a park in the center of the city. The sight of British troops on the Commons angered the Patriots. Passersby hurled insults. "You lobster-backs! You bloody-backs!" they shouted.

African Americans were among those who resented the presence of British troops in Boston to protect British cus-

Crispus Attucks, who worked as a sailor on a whaling ship, was the first colonist killed by the British army. How did Attucks help advance the cause of liberty?

toms officers. The customs officers were sent to stop smuggling, so that Britain could collect its new taxes.

The Boston Massacre. During the next year, African Americans joined with white Patriots in regularly harassing the Redcoats. Tensions reached a peak in the winter of 1770. On the snowy evening of March 5, violence erupted. A mob ran down King Street, shouting, "Let us drive out these [Redcoats]; they have no business here!"

The leader of the group was a 47-year-old runaway African American slave named Crispus Attucks. Attucks was well known in Boston as a strong opponent of British rule. That night he told the crowd: "Don't be afraid. They dare not fire."

The crowd pelted the troops with snowballs, pieces of ice, and anything else they could find. The British struck back, and a fight broke out. An African American slave named Andrew later described what happened next:

This stout man [Attucks] held [a] bayonet with his left hand, and twitched it and cried kill the dogs. . . . The people then crowded in, and . . . I turned to go off, when I heard the word fire. . . .

British bullets killed five people. The first person to fall in the cause of liberty was Attucks, a man who was himself not free. Patriots named the sad event the **Boston Massacre.**

The Coming of War. News of the Boston Massacre set off a storm of outrage throughout the 13 colonies. The victims' funeral, the largest ever held in Boston, drew thousands of mourners.

The incident moved many people, including a young slave named Phillis Wheatley. She wrote a poem about it entitled "On the Affray [Fighting] in King Street on the Evening of the 5th of March 1770."

At the time **Phillis Wheatley** wrote that poem, she was one of the best-known poets in the colonies. Wheatley arrived in the colonies from Africa aboard a slave ship in 1761. She was only about seven or eight years old. She stood on the slave block clutching a piece of carpet around her. The young girl caught the attention of John Wheatley, a rich merchant. He bought the child and took her home to his wife, Susanah. Within 16 months, Susanah had taught the girl, whom she named Phillis, to read and write. By her teens, Phillis was an accomplished poet. In 1773, a London publisher agreed to print her poems. Phillis Wheatley was the first African American to publish a book, and only the second woman in the colonies to do so. The first was Puritan poet Anne Bradstreet.

The pace of events, however, soon overshadowed the accomplishments of Wheatley. In 1773, the British passed the Tea Act, which included a tax on tea. The Patriots struck back by boldly dumping hundreds of pounds of tea into Boston harbor, an act of defiance that came to be called the **Boston Tea Party**.

Furious at the Patriots' action, the British punished Boston by passing a series of harsh laws, known as the Intolerable Acts. These acts convinced many colonists that Britain was trying to do away with their rights. The time had come, the colonists decided, to stand together.

Taking Another Look

1. List events that increased tension between Britain and the colonies.

2. What role did Crispus Attucks play in the fight against the British?

3. **Critical Thinking** If you had been a free African American in Boston during the 1770s, would you have joined the Patriots? Explain.

2 FIGHTING THE WAR

How did African Americans help win the Revolutionary War?

On the evening of April 18, 1775, some 700 British troops, under the command of Major John Pitcairn, tried to slip out of Boston. Pitcairn had learned through spies that the Patriots had collected a store of guns and powder in Concord, a village about 20 miles (32 kilometers) away. Pitcairn decided to search Concord and make an example of it.

Opening Battles of the War. As the sun rose on April 19, 1775, the British marched into Lexington, a village on the road to Concord. There 77 Minutemen, alerted by Patriots Paul Revere and William Dawes, stood ready to block the British advance. One was an African American, Prince Estabrook. Someone shouted "Fire!" and shots rang out. Eight Minutemen fell, mortally wounded. The rest scrambled for cover.

In a jubilant mood, the British broke into song and began the march to Concord. While they searched the village for arms, Minutemen from nearby towns quietly took up positions behind trees and stone walls. On spotting the Minutemen, British guards on Concord's North Bridge panicked and opened fire. The Minutemen returned the shots. Several African Americans, both slave and free, joined the battle that followed. Among these fighters were Lemuel Haynes, Peter Salem, Pomp Blackman, Cuffe Whitemore, Cato Woods, and Prince Estabrook. By day's end, the British dead and wounded totaled more than 250, while colonial casualties numbered less than 100. The British had little choice but to make a hasty retreat to Boston.

Digging in at Boston. Two months later, on June 17, 1775, the British and the Patriots met again. That day, the British repeatedly stormed the Patriots' stronghold on Breed's Hill, overlooking Boston harbor. On one charge, two veterans of Concord—Peter Salem and Major Pitcairn—faced each other. As Pitcairn cried out, "The day is ours!" Salem cut him down.

The Battle for Bunker Hill, as it was called, was one of the bloodiest battles of the war. Although the colonists lost, they proved they could stand up to the better-trained British troops. African Americans distinguished themselves. Salem Poor, for example, was commended by 14 white officers as a "brave and gallant soldier." Others cited Cuffe Whitemore for "fighting to the last."

Enlisting African Americans. In 1775, hundreds of African Americans stood ready to join the Continental Army. At first, a debate raged in Congress over whether to enlist African Americans. Some members doubted the loyalty of armed African Americans. Slave owners feared the loss of valuable property. "I hope none of our [slaves] enlist," wailed one Southerner. "The price if paid . . . is not equal to their value."

This situation changed, however, when many African Americans accepted the British promise of freedom if they joined the British army. George Washington, commander of the Continental Army, worried that this move might dangerously increase the size of the British army. So he asked the Congress to approve the enlistment of African Americans. This reversed his earlier position against African American enlistment.

REVOLUTIONARY WAR HONOR ROLL

Colonel Middleton—Commanded a company of African American volunteers from Massachusetts

Caesar Tarrant—Served four years in Virginia navy as a pilot on the armed ship *Patriot*

George Latchom—Under British attack, dragged his colonel out of waist-high mud and carried him to safety

Quaco—African American slave sold to a British colonel, fled to Patriots with valuable information

John Peterson—Launched attack that prevented British spy Andre from escaping

Saul Matthews—Spied for Virginia militia

James Armistead—Acted as double agent to spy on British officers, helping Patriots win Battle of Yorktown

James Armistead

In 1776, Congress recruited only free African Americans. But as the fighting dragged on, many white soldiers deserted. Washington entered the winter of 1777–1778 at Valley Forge with only 9,000 soldiers. Faced with defeat, he welcomed any able-bodied soldier into the army—African American or white, free or slave. By the end of the war, of the 300,000 troops who served in the Continental Army at one time or another, 5,000 were African Americans, from all 13 states except South Carolina. Another 2,000 served in the navy.

Liberty and Independence. African Americans entered the service for many reasons. Some believed the words of the Declaration of Independence, signed July 4, 1776, which said, "All men are created equal." Many African American slaves served because their owners took them to war or sent them in their place. Still others hoped to exchange military service for freedom.

No matter what led African Americans into the Revolution, they served with honor. They fought in almost all the important battles of the war, and their presence in some helped to turn the tide. In commenting on one battle, a white soldier said: "Had they [African Americans] been unfaithful, or even given way before the enemy all would have been lost."

In 1781, the Continental Army finally defeated the British at the Battle of Yorktown. The battle meant independence for the United States. But what did the future hold for African Americans?

Taking Another Look

1. How did the Battle of Bunker Hill win respect for African Americans?

2. Why did Washington and Congress finally enlist African Americans?

3. Why did some African Americans decide to join the Continental Army?

4. **Critical Thinking** If you had been a free African American in 1781, what arguments would you have used to convince your state to end slavery?

3 SEEKING LIBERTY

▼ What changes did the Revolution bring to African Americans?

In 1783, the United States and Great Britain signed the Treaty of Paris, officially ending the American Revolution. Nearly 20,000 African Americans who had sided with the British during the Revolution decided to leave the United States. True to their word, the British ferried them to freedom in Jamaica, in England, or in Nova Scotia, Canada. "We cannot," said one British official, "in justice abandon [them] to the merciless resentment [displeasure] of their former masters." The British also returned slaves to their owners in some cases and sold others in the West Indies.

Freedom in the North. Thousands of African Americans who lived in the North also found freedom. Slavery died in the North for many reasons. For one thing, slavery was never widespread, since the geography and climate of the region made large-scale farming using slave labor impractical. Efforts by African American and white Patriots during the war helped speed the end of any slavery that did exist there. In 1777, Vermont became the first Northern state to pass a law ending slavery. New Jersey was the last state, in 1804.

Slavery in the South. A different fate awaited African American slaves in the South. Some slave owners freed their slaves to reward their bravery during the war. In 1783, Virginia passed a law giving freedom to ex-soldiers, but most slave owners did not free them. Many slave owners in the Upper South sold African American veterans to plantation owners farther south, where they were less likely to run away. "I didn't like to sell a man who fought for his country," said the owner of one slave ship. "[But] if I didn't do it, I never could get a bale of cotton, . . . nor anything, to carry from or to any Southern port."

Taking Another Look

1. What happened to slaves who joined the British?

2. How did the Revolution affect slavery in the new United States?

3. **Critical Thinking** In what ways do you think the United States benefited by allowing African Americans to join the Continental Army?

LOOKING AHEAD

The Revolution had mixed results for African Americans. The number of free African Americans in the United States reached 60,000 by 1790. A decade later, the number topped 100,000. Even so, nearly 700,000 African Americans remained enslaved.

Some leaders of the war changed their ideas on slavery. One was George Washington, who owned slaves. In 1786, he wrote: "I can only say that there is not a man living who wishes more sincerely than I do to see some plan adopted for the abolition of [slavery]."

The French called them the Volunteer Chasseurs (sha–SERS)—the Volunteer Infantry. They came from the Caribbean island of Santo Domingo and included 545 free Africans. They had signed up with the French rulers of Santo Domingo to help the Patriots fight for their freedom from Great Britain.

The Volunteer Chasseurs joined a larger French unit sent to drive the British out of Savannah, Georgia. On October 9, 1779, the French troops needed every bit of bravery they could summon. As they charged into battle, the British rained murderous fire upon them.

French commander Count D'Estaing ordered a retreat. The British followed, determined to wipe out the French. Then the Volunteer Chasseurs swung into action and held the French rear line against the British assault. The Volunteer Chasseurs refused to break ranks and run, preventing a breakthrough by the British troops.

After this battle, D'Estaing, who was twice wounded, and his weary troops set sail from Savannah, leaving the war behind. Sailing with the fleet was Henri Christophe, a 12-year-old Volunteer Chasseur. In the battle, Christophe had glimpsed the sacrifices required for freedom. In later years, he would help Haiti to shake off French rule and to emerge as the independent Republic of Haiti in 1804.

CLOSE UP: Chapter 7

The Who, What, Where of History

1. **Who** were the Redcoats?
2. **Who** was Crispus Attucks?
3. **What** were the Intolerable Acts?
4. **Who** was the first African American to publish a book?
5. **Who** were the Patriots?
6. **What** was the Boston Tea Party?
7. **Who** were the Minutemen?
8. **Where** were the opening battles of the Revolution fought?
9. **What** did the British promise to African American slaves who joined the British army?
10. **What** was the Continental Army?
11. **Who** was Salem Poor?
12. **Where** was slavery first officially ended in the North?

Making the Connection

1. What was the connection between the Boston Tea Party and the Intolerable Acts?
2. What was the connection between the Declaration of Independence and the decision of many African Americans to become Patriots?
3. What was the connection between the policies of the British and Continental armies on using African Americans as fighting troops?

Time Check

1. In what year did the Boston Massacre occur?

2. Which event happened *last:* the writing of the Declaration of Independence, the end of the French and Indian War, the battles at Lexington and Concord?

3. In what year did the first Northern state end slavery?

4. Which of the following came *first:* the writing of the Declaration of Independence or the British offer of freedom to African American slaves who joined the fighting on their side?

What Would You Have Done?

1. If you had been an African American who decided to serve in the Continental Army or the navy, what would have been your main reason for deciding to join? Explain.

2. If you had been an African American slave during the American Revolution, would you have fought with the British, with the Patriots, or with neither side? Explain.

Thinking and Writing About History

1. Imagine that you are going to interview Prince Whipple 25 years after the Battle of Trenton. Write at least three questions that you would like to ask him.

2. Imagine that you are an African American who fought with the British during the Revolution. Now you are leaving North America for a new life in Great Britain. Write an entry in your diary explaining why you are leaving the new United States.

Building Skills: Skimming and Scanning

At different times, you may read for different reasons. For example, you may want to get a general idea of the kind of information that is presented in a chapter before you read the chapter carefully. At other times, you may need to find information quickly. Skimming and scanning will help you to do both of these.

When you skim, you skip words in order to read rapidly and get a quick overview of the text. When you scan, you read quickly in order to locate a specific piece of information. Skim and scan Chapter 7 in order to answer the questions below.

1. What is the title of this chapter?

2. Answer the question in the title.

3. List the titles of the three sections in this chapter.

4. By skimming and scanning, find which chapter section contains each of the following:
   a. discussion of the departure of some African Americans with the British after the Revolution;
   b. actions of the British that convinced many colonists to seek independence;
   c. a chart listing the names of some African American heroes of the Revolution.

5. Each section of the chapter begins with a question. Skim each section and write a statement that answers the question.

Richard Allen (left) and Absalom Jones (right)

Forging a New Constitution

(1787–1799)

THINKING ABOUT THE CHAPTER

What did the Constitution say about the rights of African Americans?

Benjamin Banneker's habits seemed strange to many people. This African American astronomer, farmer, mathematician, and surveyor spent nights wrapped in a cloak under a pear tree, watching the stars and planets. At dawn, he slept for a few hours and then took care of his garden or observed his bees. Most afternoons, Banneker huddled over a large oval table, reading through his books and papers and working with mathematical instruments.

Born a free African American in 1731, Banneker lived all his life on a farm near Baltimore, Maryland. He learned to read and write at a small private school for whites and free African Americans. But Banneker taught himself mathematics and astronomy from books that were lent to him by a Quaker neighbor.

In 1791, when the nation's new capital city, Washington, D.C., was being planned, Secretary of State Thomas Jefferson recommended Banneker to help with the survey. The next year, Banneker asked Jefferson to read an **almanac** he had written. An almanac is a book that contains weather forecasts and astronomical information. Banneker also sent a letter to Jefferson, reminding him of the writing of the Declaration of Independence:

> Sir, suffer [allow] me to recall to your mind that time, in which the arms and tyranny [unfair rule] of the British crown were exerted . . . in order to reduce you to a state of servitude [enslavement] . . . This, Sir, was a time when you clearly saw into the injustice of a state of slavery.

Banneker also pointed out that Jefferson had written the words "all men are created equal." He then criticized Jefferson for allowing African Americans to suffer "under groaning captivity and cruel oppression." Banneker and other African Americans realized that liberty still lay beyond their grasp.

1 AFRICAN AMERICANS ORGANIZE

▼ What were the aims of the Free African Society?

By the first census in 1790, some 60,000 free African Americans lived in the United States, about a third in the Northern states. Pennsylvania had a larger African American population than any other Northern state. Most African Americans in Pennsylvania lived in Philadelphia.

The word *Philadelphia* means "City of Brotherly Love," and the city followed its name in the 1700s by welcoming people from many nations and of many religions. It was also the city where the Declaration of Independence had been signed. In 1787, six years after the Revolution, Philadelphia was the site of another important meeting. This one was organized to improve the lives of African Americans and to deal with the questions of **prejudice,** or intolerance, against them.

Promoting Self-Help. Although Philadelphia had the reputation of a friendly city, some white Philadelphians were prejudiced against African Americans. Some schools barred African American children from attending. Most social clubs prohibited African Americans from becoming members. Many churches forced them to sit in separate pews.

Realizing that they had to take matters into their own hands to improve their situation, Richard Allen, Absalom Jones, and six other African American Philadelphians met to form the **Free African Society.** Both Allen and Jones were ex-slaves who had purchased their freedom.

The Free African Society committed members to work for African Americans' freedom and to live "an orderly and sober life . . . to support one another in sickness, and for the benefit of their widows and fatherless children." Education for African Americans was another important goal. Similar societies soon formed in New York City, Boston, and Newport, Rhode Island.

Support for Liberty. In 1793, a yellow fever epidemic struck Philadelphia, claiming the lives of thousands of people. The members of the Free African Society joined in a round-the-clock fight to help victims of the plague, white as well as African American.

79

1787	Free African Society is founded.
	Constitutional Convention is held.
	Northwest Ordinance bars slavery in Northwest Territory.
1788	U.S. Constitution is ratified.
1790	First U.S. Census: African Americans account for 19 percent of U.S. population.
1791	Benjamin Banneker is part of land survey commission for Washington, D.C.
	Benjamin Banneker begins his almanac.

What African Americans did during the epidemic impressed many whites and inspired them to join African Americans in calling for the abolition of slavery. In fact, Philadelphia was to become a stronghold for the powerful abolition movement of the 1800s.

Taking Another Look

1. Why did Richard Allen, Absalom Jones, and six others form the Free African Society?

2. What did the Free African Society hope to accomplish?

3. How did the Free African Society influence white Philadelphians?

4. **Critical Thinking** How might Allen and Jones have reacted to the letter written by Benjamin Banneker to Thomas Jefferson (see page 79)? Explain.

2 COMPROMISES OVER SLAVERY

How did the writers of the Constitution deal with the issue of slavery?

In 1787, one month after the founding of the Free African Society, another important meeting took place in Philadelphia. Fifty-five leading citizens of the United States arrived in the city for what became known as the Constitutional Convention. Some came on horseback, others by stagecoach, and a few by ship. All were white men, and 16 owned slaves. Congress had called the meeting to revise the **Articles of Confederation**, the plan of government drawn up during the Revolutionary War. The delegates soon decided to write an entirely new constitution. The document they wrote set up a democratic government for the nation that has endured for over 200 years. However, that document did nothing to abolish slavery.

Slavery Untouched. The men who met in Philadelphia came to build a strong and united nation. Government under the Articles of Confederation had proved too weak. So they created the **federal system** that we have today—a system that divides power between the national government and state governments. They also divided the government into three branches—executive, legislative, and judicial—each with power to check, or control, the other branches. This is known as the system of **checks and balances.** The legislative was further divided into the Senate and the House of Representatives.

In hammering out this form of government, the delegates compromised on many issues. No issue caused more disagreement than slavery. Sometimes tempers soared as high as the blistering summer heat. The delegates spent hours arguing thorny questions. Should slavery be abolished? Should the national government have the power to regulate the slave trade? Should slaves be taxed as property? Should they be counted in determining a state's number of representatives in the House of Representatives?

To ensure support for the Constitution from Southern slave owners and from slave traders in both the North and the South, delegates agreed to the following:

1. Slavery itself would not be abolished.

2. The Atlantic slave trade would continue until 1808, after which time Congress could abolish it if it wished. Meanwhile, a tax of up to $10 for each African brought into the country could be imposed.

3. Three-fifths of the number of slaves would be counted in determining the number of representatives in the House a state was entitled to.

4. All states would be required to return runaways to their owners.

The word *slave* does not appear in the Constitution. Instead, the delegates used expressions such as "persons held to service or labor."

While the Constitutional Convention was meeting, Congress passed the Northwest Ordinance, banning slavery in the Northwest Territory. This action supported the view of many that slavery would remain limited to the South. "Slavery in time," said one Northern delegate, "will be but a speck in our country."

African American Reaction. African Americans were not content to wait for slavery to become that "speck in our country." On December 30, 1799, 74 members of the Free African Society sent a petition "to the President, Senate, and House of Representatives." It called for an immediate end to the slave trade and for the protection of free African Americans against kidnapping by slave catchers. The petition also asked that African Americans "be allowed to partake of the liberties" to which they were entitled.

The House of Representatives debated the petition briefly, then rejected it by a vote of 85 to 1. This was a chilling glimpse of the struggle facing African Americans.

Taking Another Look

1. How did the Constitution affect the slavery in the United States?

2. Why did antislavery delegates agree to these provisions?

3. **Critical Thinking** In five Northern states, African American men voted in the process that ratified the Constitution. If you had been one of these voters, would you have voted for or against the Constitution? Explain.

LOOKING AHEAD

When the Constitution went into effect in 1789, the United States had a new form of government, but slavery was untouched. As the 1700s drew to a close, slavery began to move beyond the South. In 1803, the United States added the vast Louisiana Territory. Unlike the Northwest Territory, much of this area was suitable for growing cotton, the South's most valuable crop. Southern plantation owners, free under the new Constitution to continue slavery, extended their cotton kingdom into the new lands. As a result, slavery increased, and African Americans and antislavery whites would have an even harder struggle to abolish it.

In 1767, a white Englishman named Granville Sharp came upon a badly injured man lying in a London street. The injured man, Jonathan Strong, told Sharp that he had traveled to London with his owner, a West Indian planter. In a fit of rage, the owner had savagely whipped Strong and left him in the street.

Sharp helped Strong escape his brutal owner, and then Sharp resolved to take the issue of slavery before the British courts. In 1772, Sharp presented his case to Lord Chief Justice Mansfield, who ruled: "Is not a Negro a Man? . . . As soon as any slave sets foot on English soil he shall be free."

Sharp next took aim at the slave trade, helping to organize the British Anti-Slavery Movement. Its members pleaded the antislavery cause before Parliament. In 1807, Parliament voted to halt Britain's slave trade, but it did not end slavery in British colonies.

In all but a few of the British possessions in the Americas, slavery came to an end as the colonies gained their independence from Great Britain. One of the countries that did not follow this pattern was the United States. It took nearly 100 years of independence and a bloody civil war to unlock the chains of slavery here.

CLOSE UP: Chapter 8

The Who, What, Where of History

1. **Who** was Benjamin Banneker?
2. **What** was the Free African Society?
3. **What** is an almanac?
4. **Who** was Absalom Jones?
5. **Who** was Richard Allen?
6. **What** is abolition?
7. **What** was the Constitutional Convention?
8. **Where** was the Free African Society founded?
9. **What** is the federal system of government?
10. **What** was the Northwest Territory?

Making the Connection

1. What was the connection between the yellow fever epidemic of 1793 in Philadelphia and support for the abolition of slavery?
2. What was the connection between the treatment of slavery in the Constitution and the desire of many delegates to the Constitutional Convention to have a new plan of government for the United States?
3. What was the connection between the Northwest Ordinance and slavery in the Northwest Territory?

Time Check

1. Which of these events happened *first*: the founding of the Free African Society, the adoption of the Articles of Confederation, the adoption of the Constitution?
2. When did the U.S. Constitution go into effect?

What Would You Have Done?

1. If you had been a member of the House of Representatives or the Senate in 1799, how would you have voted on the petition from the Free African Society? Explain.

2. If you had been a newly freed African American in 1804, would you have settled in Philadelphia or the Northwest Territory? Explain.

Thinking and Writing About History

1. Write an advertisement for the Free African Society, urging African Americans to join.

2. Imagine that you are an African American veteran of the Revolution. Write a letter to one of your white comrades, explaining your reactions to the new Constitution.

Building Skills: Main Ideas and Details

Just as chapters and chapter sections contain main ideas, paragraphs also have main ideas. Usually there is a single sentence in a paragraph that tells what the paragraph is about. The rest of the sentences in the paragraph give details that support the main idea. Keeping track of the main ideas as you read will help you to understand and remember the points that the author is making.

In the following paragraph, the first sentence gives the main idea:

Benjamin Banneker's habits seemed strange to many people. This African American astronomer, farmer, mathematician, and surveyor spent nights wrapped in a cloak under a pear tree watching the stars and planets. At dawn, he slept for a few hours and then took care of his garden or observed his bees. Most afternoons, Banneker huddled over a large oval table reading through his books and papers and working with mathematical instruments.

1. Read the paragraph that follows and then write the sentence that states the main idea.

Although Philadelphia had the reputation of a friendly city, some white Philadelphians were prejudiced against African Americans. Some schools barred African American children from attending. Most social clubs prohibited African Americans from becoming members. Many churches forced African Americans to sit in separate pews.

2. The main idea is not always contained in the first sentence of a paragraph. Read the paragraph below and then write the sentence that states the main idea.

The men who met in Philadelphia came to build a strong and united nation. Government under the Articles of Confederation had proved too weak. So they created the federal system that we have today—a system that divides power between the national government and state governments.

Toussaint L'Ouverture (right) with French officers

Expanding the Nation
(1779–1840s)

THINKING ABOUT THE CHAPTER

How did African Americans contribute to the new nation's growth?

In 1760, a ship sailing from the West Indian island of Haiti sank in storm-tossed waters off the coast of New Orleans. The ship's captain, Jean Baptiste Point Du Sable (jon ba-TEEST pwan doo SAH-buhl), managed to get ashore with his life. But he lost everything he owned, including papers proving he was a free man. Without such papers, Du Sable knew he faced the constant threat of being seized and sold as a slave. He decided to head up the Mississippi River into safer territory.

Du Sable's parents, a French sailor and an African woman living in Haiti, had sent him to France for an education. The six-foot, elegant Du Sable spoke French, English, and Spanish fluently. He also learned to speak several Native American languages.

In 1779, Du Sable and his Native American wife, Catherine, settled in the Illinois Territory. They chose a spot on

CHAPTER

9

the southwestern edge of one of the Great Lakes and not far from a river that flowed into the Mississippi. Believing that this would be a natural crossroads for trade between Native Americans and fur traders, they built a trading post.

The business flourished after the Revolutionary War. Visitors to the Du Sables' home gazed in amazement at their elegant collection of European paintings, crystal mirrors, and French furniture. In 1800, the Du Sables sold their holdings and moved on. The area they left behind is known today as Chicago, and Chicagoans honor Du Sable as their city's founder.

Du Sable was one of the many people of African descent who helped the new nation expand. Like Du Sable, some explored the interior of the continent. Others fought in a war with Great Britain to defend the United States' freedom at sea. Still others fled slavery and built new lives with Native Americans.

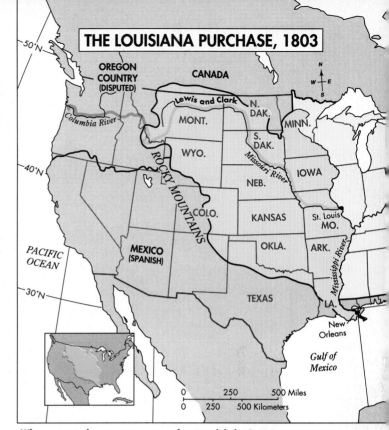

THE LOUISIANA PURCHASE, 1803

What present-day states or parts of states did the Louisiana Purchase include?

1 ▼ INCREASING THE NATION'S SIZE

▼ Why was the purchase of the Louisiana Territory important to the future of the United States?

On a steamy August night in 1791, more than 100,000 African slaves revolted in the French colony of Haiti. Their leader, Toussaint L'Ouverture (too-san loo-ver-TYOOR), vowed to drive the French from Haiti. Napoleon Bonaparte, the powerful emperor of France, sent tens of thousands of French troops into Haiti, but bullets and yellow fever nearly wiped them out.

In 1803, Napoleon tricked Toussaint, who called himself the "Black Napoleon," into surrendering. Toussaint died a year later in a French prison. However, his followers fought on until they won independence for Haiti in 1804.

The Louisiana Purchase. President Thomas Jefferson knew that Napoleon was involved in two costly wars—the one with Haiti and another with Great Britain. Hoping to ensure that New Orleans would remain open to farmers in the Northwest Territory, he asked Napoleon to sell the port city to the United States. Napoleon, worn out by the revolt in Haiti, decided to give up his plans for building an empire in North America. In 1803, he astounded Jefferson by offering to sell to the United States for $15 million the entire Louisiana Territory, which stretched from the Mississippi River to the Rocky Mountains.

1779	Jean Baptiste Point Du Sable founds Chicago.
1791	Toussaint L'Ouverture leads slave revolt on Haiti.
1803	Louisiana Purchase
1803–1806	Lewis and Clark explore Louisiana Territory, with York as guide.
1808	James P. Beckwourth heads west as Mountain Man.
1812–1815	War of 1812
1813	African American sailors fight in Battle of Lake Erie.
1815	African Americans fight in Battle of New Orleans.
1816–1843	African Americans and Native Americans fight the United States in Seminole Wars.
1819	United States acquires Florida.

Jefferson quickly accepted Napoleon's offer. In doing so, he made one of the best bargains in U.S. history. For what amounted to four cents an acre, the United States bought a territory that nearly doubled the nation's size.

Into the Unknown. Jefferson decided to send an expedition into the vast Louisiana Territory to find out who lived there and what the land was like. To head the expedition, he chose two 23-year-old army officers, Meriwether Lewis and William Clark.

The exploring party consisted of about 45 people, among them Clark's African American slave, York. York turned out to be one of the expedition's most valuable members. An excellent hunter and fisher, he provided food for the expedition. Also,

because of his dark skin, the Native Americans in the territory were less suspicious of him than they were of the white members of the party. York easily made friends with the Native Americans and traded with them for supplies. Upon the expedition's return, Clark freed York. York's final days remain a mystery. According to legend, he returned west and died a chief among the Crow people.

Another valuable member of the expedition was a Native American woman named Sacajawea (sak-uh-juh-WEE-uh). She also helped the explorers in their dealings with Native Americans.

Importance of the Expedition. For over two years, the Lewis and Clark expedition surveyed and mapped the Louisiana Territory and the land beyond it. They brought back records of what they had seen, so that these western lands were no longer an unknown country to those living in the eastern United States. The Lewis and Clark expedition was an important factor in opening the Louisiana Territory and beyond to settlement. Before long, this area would also become the center of a debate over slavery that would eventually lead to the Civil War.

Taking Another Look

1. Why did Napoleon sell the Louisiana Territory to the United States?

2. **a.** What did the Lewis and Clark expedition accomplish? **b.** How did York contribute to the success of the expedition?

3. **Critical Thinking** How might events in Haiti have affected the way U.S. slave owners treated African Americans?

2 SECURING INDEPENDENCE
▼ How did African Americans help win the War of 1812?

On January 1, 1813, a British warship opened fire on a small U.S. vessel. Two African American sailors fell. As one of them, John Johnson, lay dying, he called out to the rest of the crew, "Fire away, my boys!" The other sailor, John Davis, asked only that he be moved out of the way. The captain of the ship later wrote, "When America has such tars [sailors], she has little to fear from the tyrants of the ocean."

What did Andrew Jackson say about the African American troops who fought in the Battle of New Orleans?

The War of 1812. The sea battle you have just read about was part of the War of 1812. The war was fought to prevent the British from arming Native Americans in the Northwest Territory and searching U.S. ships at sea for British sailors.

When the war began, African Americans were willing to set aside their own struggle for liberty and fight again for their homeland. In Philadelphia, for example, Richard Allen and Absalom Jones (see page 79) rallied more than 2,000 African Americans to help fortify their city against the British. Other African Americans fought in battles along the frontier and in Canada.

Most African Americans, however, served at sea, where they made up at least one out of every six members of the U.S. Navy. At first, one naval officer, Captain Oliver Hazard Perry, objected to having African Americans assigned to his ship. But his commander assured him, "[They] are not surpassed by any seamen we have in the fleet!" When African American sailors helped Perry win the Battle of Lake Erie in 1813, he agreed. "They are absolutely insensible [indifferent] to danger," said Perry.

The Battle of New Orleans. The most famous battle of the war took place in New Orleans. Hundreds of African Americans, including slaves from nearby plantations, volunteered to fight to save the city from an expected British attack.

On the cold, foggy night of December 23, 1814, Andrew Jackson led his troops against the British as they tried to sneak into the city through the swamplands to the east. The U.S. troops went into battle to the rattling drum of a 14-year-old African American named Jordan Noble. Brutal hand-to-hand fighting forced the British to withdraw.

On January 8, 1815, the British stormed the city directly. Jackson's troops, including two African American units, crouched behind a huge earthen wall. As the British headed directly toward this wall, they were mowed down by U.S. sharpshooters and cannon. More than 1,500 British fell dead or wounded. Only 13 of Jackson's soldiers were killed.

Because of the slow communications of that time, Jackson did not know that two weeks before the battle, Great Britain and the United States had agreed to end the war.

The Battle of New Orleans again showed the ability of African American soldiers to fight. Said Jackson to his African American troops:

> I expected much from you. . . . I knew that you could endure hunger and thirst and all the hardships of war. I knew that you loved the land of your nativity [birth]. . . . But you surpass my hopes. I have found in you. . . that noble enthusiasm which impels [drives one] to great deeds.

Florida and the Slavery Issue. The praise given to African Americans during the War of 1812 was soon forgotten. Slave owners had a new complaint. They demanded loudly that the government stop runaway African American slaves from fleeing into Florida, which was owned by Spain at that time.

The swamps and marshes of Florida were home to Native Americans who called themselves Seminoles, meaning "runaways" in their language. The Seminoles sympathized with runaway African Americans and gave them shelter. The ex-slaves built villages near the Seminoles and often intermarried with them.

Georgia slave owners saw Florida as a threat to the whole slave system. They asked the government to **annex** (uh-NEKS), or take over, Florida and destroy the villages hidden there. As a result, starting in 1816 and continuing to 1843, the United States fought three wars to subdue the Seminoles and re-enslave the African Americans among them.

These Seminole Wars started after about 1,000 African Americans and Seminoles took over an abandoned British fort not far from the Georgia border. Troops led by Andrew Jackson attacked the fort. A cannonball fired by his soldiers landed in an ammunition dump. The entire fort burst into flames, killing more than 300 men, women, and children.

Ignoring Spain's rights, Jackson took more territory. Finally, to avoid war, the United States in 1819 bought Florida from Spain for $5 million. By 1843, the federal government had forced many Seminoles onto reservations west of the Mississippi. Among them were Black Seminoles, people of mixed Seminole and African American descent.

Taking Another Look

1. Describe three events in the War of 1812 in which African Americans played important parts.

2. Why did some African American slaves flee into Florida?

3. **Critical Thinking** Why might the Seminoles have sided with runaway African American slaves?

3 LOOKING WESTWARD

▼ How did African Americans open up new territory?

Writer Washington Irving called him "powerful in frame and fearless in spirit." This is how he described Edward Rose, one of the first **Mountain Men**. Mountain Men were rough-and-tumble fur trappers who helped open the lands beyond the Mississippi. Native Americans simply named Rose "Cut-Nose," for the huge slash that ran across his nose.

Most Mountain Men looked as rugged as the Rocky Mountains they explored. Many of them were more comfortable living with Native Americans than with the city folk back East.

Building the Fur Trade. In the early 1800s, most people who headed across the Mississippi were interested in furs, not settlement. Edward Rose, an African American, led his first group of fur traders west in 1806. He later became the guide and interpreter for three of the largest fur-trading companies in North America.

One of the best-known African American Mountain Men was **James P. Beckwourth**, a former slave. Beckwourth's career as a Mountain Man started in 1808, when he got into a fist fight and punched a white blacksmith in St. Louis, Missouri. The 19-year-old Beckwourth decided to run away rather than face a whipping—or worse.

For the next 50 years, Beckwourth swept across the continent hunting for furs, running a trading post, and serving as an army scout. On a trip through the Sierra Nevada, Beckwourth found a mountain pass that became one of the most important routes into California in the mid-1800s. It bears his name today.

Beckwourth spent most of his adult life with Native Americans. The Crow named him "Morning Star" and made him a chief. According to legend, when Beckwourth tried to leave the Crow in 1866, they poisoned him so that his spirit would remain with them forever.

By the 1840s, the days of fur trading were over. Some of the Mountain Men turned to guiding the many settlers who headed west.

Taking Another Look

1. How does James P. Beckwourth's name live on today?

2. **Critical Thinking** Why do you think the life of a Mountain Man appealed to some African Americans?

LOOKING AHEAD

While Beckwourth and others explored the lands beyond the Mississippi, cotton became "king" in the South. Slave owners looked to the Louisiana Territory as a place where they could start new cotton plantations. Soon more African Americans would arrive in the lands west of the Mississippi, but most of them would come as slaves.

FOCUS ON: NEW ORLEANS TRADITIONS

The French called them the *gens de couleur*. They were free "people of color"—part African and part Spanish or French. The *gens de couleur* came to form an important part of New Orleans' Creole population, the people whose ancestors were the original settlers of what is today Louisiana. The term *Creole* comes from the Spanish *criollo* meaning "native to the place."

The first Africans who came to New Orleans were brought as slaves. Children of these Africans who also had a Spanish or French parent were often set free, becoming the *gens de couleur*. When New Orleans became a center of the U.S. slave trade in the 1800s, the *gens de couleur* experienced prejudice. As a result, they often lived in separate communities, or neighborhoods, in New Orleans.

It was in these communities that many traditions associated with New Orleans took root and grew. These traditions include musical styles such as jazz and zydeco, foods such as gumbo (a hearty soup made of vegetables, and meat or fish), and the Creole dialect. It was the *gens de couleurs* who built many of the Spanish-style churches and lacy iron balconies that tourists have come to admire in the part of New Orleans known as the Old City.

CLOSE UP: Chapter 9

The Who, What, Where of History

1. **Who** is considered the founder of Chicago?
2. **Who** was Toussaint L'Ouverture?
3. **What** was the Louisiana Purchase?
4. **What** did York do?
5. **What** was the most famous battle of the War of 1812?
6. **Where** did the Seminoles live?
7. **What** does it mean to annex a territory?
8. **Who** were the Black Seminoles?
9. **Who** were the Mountain Men?

Making the Connection

1. What was the connection between the revolt in Haiti led by Toussaint L'Ouverture and the Louisiana Purchase?
2. What was the connection between the slave system of the South and the purchase of Florida?

Time Check

1. Which event happened *last:* the purchase of Florida, the Louisiana Purchase, the War of 1812?
2. When was the Battle of New Orleans fought?
3. Which of the following events happened *first:* the Lewis and Clark expedition, Toussaint L'Ouverture's revolt in Haiti, or the beginning of the Seminole wars?

What Would You Have Done?

1. Imagine that you are an African American slave of William Clark. He has asked you to join the expedition

he and Meriwether Lewis will lead into the Louisiana Territory. Clark has explained that the expedition will be dangerous and that you do not have to go. Explain your reasons for deciding to accept or reject Clark's invitation.

2. If you had been an African American slave in New Orleans in 1814, would you have volunteered to fight the British? Explain.

Thinking and Writing About History

1. Imagine that you are part of a committee designing a memorial to Jean Baptiste Point Du Sable. Write the words for a plaque explaining his role in Chicago's history.

2. Imagine you are an African American who has heard about James Beckwourth. Make a list of the pros and cons of becoming a Mountain Man. Think about what life might be like and what you might need to learn.

3. Write a short, two-character play set in Florida in 1816 in which a runaway African American slave from Georgia asks a Seminole leader for shelter.

Building Skills: Distinguishing Fact From Opinion

As you study history, you will often be asked for your opinion about the people and events that you read about. At other times, you will be asked to give the facts about a person or an event. Opinions and facts are different, but they are connected.

A fact is a statement that can be checked or tested to see whether it is true. The statement "James P. Beck-

wourth was an African American slave" is a fact. You can check it in reference books to see whether it's true or not.

An opinion is a person's attitude or thoughts about something. An opinion cannot be checked or tested to see whether it's true. It is what someone believes about a subject. The statement "James P. Beckwourth was the greatest of all the Mountain Men" is an opinion. Someone else might think that Edward Rose was by far the greatest of all Mountain Men.

Facts and opinions are related because we form opinions based on facts. A person might hold the opinion that Beckwourth was the greatest Mountain Man because of the following facts: he lived in the mountains for 50 years, he discovered an important pass through the Sierra Nevada, and he became a Crow chief. Some of the sentences below are facts and some state opinions. On a separate sheet of paper, write the numbers of the sentences that state opinions.

1. Jean Baptiste Point Du Sable was a ship captain who became a trader.

2. Jean Baptiste Point Du Sable had a more exciting life than any of the Mountain Men.

3. Toussaint L'Ouverture called himself the "Black Napoleon."

4. Sacajawea was the most valuable member of the Lewis and Clark expedition to map the Louisiana Territory.

5. The Battle of New Orleans was fought after the treaty ending the War of 1812 had been signed.

6. Andrew Jackson took over territory in Florida that legally belonged to Spain.

VUNIT 4

Eli Whitney's cotton gin

FREE AND ENSLAVED

(1619–1860)

Mary Jane Patterson, first African American graduate of Oberlin College

African American slaves in the cotton fields

THE BIG PICTURE

Unit 4 is the story of how Africans and their descendants lived in the years between 1619 and 1860, first in the 13 English colonies and later in the United States of America. Despite the attempts of slave owners to dehumanize them, Africans and their descendants forged a new culture from their experiences. Much of it was based on African traditions. As life under slavery worsened in the 1800s, enslaved African Americans fought back. Resistance and rebellions occurred more often. The pressure against slavery was mounting, but profits from slave labor blinded Southern leaders to its certain downfall.

From Colonies to Nation. In Unit 2, you read about how Africans were brought to the Americas in chains and forced to work in the colonies. Unit 3 discussed the war for independence that the 13 English colonies waged against Great Britain and the role of African Americans in that war. Six years after the war ended, the Northwest Ordinance forbade slavery in the territories that the new United States had won from Great Britain. One by one, the Northern states abolished slavery. By 1800, however, slavery was solidly established in the Southern states.

As the nation expanded across the continent, three regions developed after 1800—the industrial Northeast, the agricultural Midwest, and the Cotton Kingdom in much of the South. These three areas developed different interests and different needs.

The United States in 1800. As the 1800s dawned, the United States was still a small nation. It had fewer than 5 million people. Most lived in the states along the Atlantic coast, from Maine to Georgia. Much of the land between the Appalachian Mountains and the Mississippi River was inhabited by Native Americans.

As U.S. settlers pushed west of the Appalachians, they asked for government protection against the Native Americans. In reality, they wanted the Native Americans' land. With government support, they took it. In the 1790s, there were enough settlers to petition for statehood for Kentucky and Tennessee. In 1803, Ohio became a state, and soon the rest of the Northwest Territory (see map, page 69) was rapidly settled.

Improved Transportation. Four important improvements sped transportation from region to region and within regions during the first decades of the 1800s. One was the steamboat. Robert Fulton proved that a boat could travel upstream against a river's current by using a steam engine. In 1807, his boat the *Clermont* steamed up the Hudson River from New York to Albany. Soon, steamboats were carrying large cargoes of corn, wheat, and cotton quickly and cheaply along many rivers. Among the most important river routes were the Ohio and the Mississippi.

An African American Speaks

Seen in this perspective [of slavery], theirs [African Americans'] has been one of the great human experiences and one of the great triumphs of the human spirit in modern times, in fact, in the history of the world.

—Ralph Ellison,
author

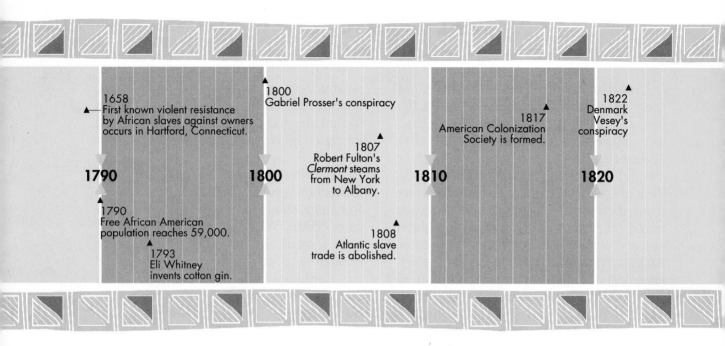

1658
First known violent resistance by African slaves against owners occurs in Hartford, Connecticut.

1800
Gabriel Prosser's conspiracy

1817
American Colonization Society is formed.

1822
Denmark Vesey's conspiracy

1807
Robert Fulton's *Clermont* steams from New York to Albany.

1790

1800

1810

1820

1790
Free African American population reaches 59,000.

1793
Eli Whitney invents cotton gin.

1808
Atlantic slave trade is abolished.

Up to the early 1800s, most roads were dirt tracks. Traveling on them by wagon or carriage was slow, expensive, uncomfortable, and dangerous. In the early 1800s, however, new methods made it possible to build roads that would carry goods and people more quickly, cheaply, and with some comfort.

Like the steamboat, the new roads made it easier for settlers to move west and for products grown or made in one part of the country to be sold in another. One of the most important roads was the National Road across the Appalachians, connecting the Potomac and Ohio rivers.

The building of canals also sped the transportation of people and goods. The first important canal was built across New York State, linking the Hudson River at Albany with Lake Erie, 350 miles (560 kilometers) away. The canal was completed in 1825. By 1840, canals connected the Great Lakes with the Ohio and Mississippi rivers. It was now possible to travel by water from New York City through the Great Lakes to New Orleans.

The first U.S. railroad opened for business in 1830. By 1860, the Northeast and Midwest were covered by a network of railroads. Fewer railroads were built in the South because of the availability of water routes to ship people and goods.

Improved Communication. With improvements in transportation came improved communications. In 1800, a letter took a week to travel the 200 miles (320 kilometers) from New York to Washington, D.C. In 1860, a letter covered the same distance by train in a few hours.

Even faster communication was made possible by the invention of the telegraph by Samuel F. B. Morse in 1844. The telegraph used electricity to send messages over wires. Within 15 years, a network of telegraph lines covered the eastern half of the nation. In 1861, a telegraph line reached all the way to California.

The Growth of Factories in the Northeast. Before 1800, almost everything made in the United States was made

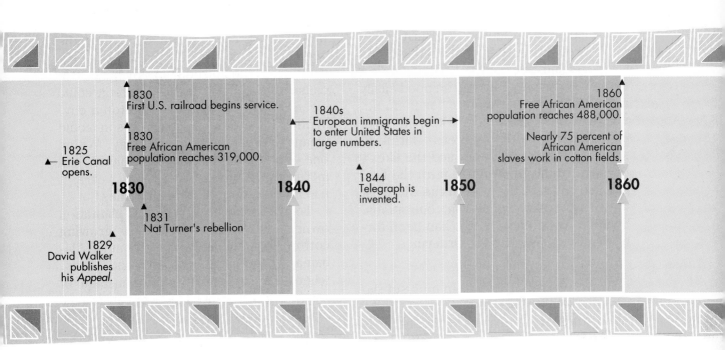

1825
Erie Canal opens.

1829
David Walker publishes his *Appeal.*

1830
First U.S. railroad begins service.

1830
Free African American population reaches 319,000.

1831
Nat Turner's rebellion

1830

1840s
European immigrants begin to enter United States in large numbers.

1844
Telegraph is invented.

1840

1850

1860
Free African American population reaches 488,000.

Nearly 75 percent of African American slaves work in cotton fields.

1860

by hand in small workshops. The first factory appeared in 1790 in Pawtucket, Rhode Island. By the 1820s, factories had become an important part of the nation's economy.

The first factories were spinning and weaving mills that used fibers such as cotton and wool to turn out finished cloth. The majority of factories were built in the Northeast, particularly in New England. There, a number of small villages like Lowell, Massachusetts, grew into industrial cities. Other factories, mainly making farm equipment, were established in the Midwest in the 1830s and 1840s.

The Arrival of European Immigrants. At first, the factories in New England employed girls and young women from nearby farms. By the 1840s, owners had cut wages, and working conditions in the mills had worsened. The women were replaced by immigrants from Europe, who came to settle in the United States and who were willing to work for less money and under poor conditions.

Most of these immigrants were farmers from Ireland, where a disease had destroyed the potato crop, their major source of food. In the terrible famine that followed, millions of Irish were forced either to leave or to starve. Most Irish immigrants settled in the factory cities of the Northeast.

Large numbers of German immigrants also came to the United States in the 1840s and 1850s. Most moved to the cities and farms of the Midwest. Few European immigrants moved to the South because there were few factories. Enslaved African Americans already provided most of the nonplantation labor needed in the South.

Cash Crops in the Midwest. Most of the early settlers in the Midwest were subsistence farmers. They grew only enough for their own needs. They bought few goods and sold few goods. But in the first decades of the 1800s, farmers began to plant cash crops, such as corn and wheat. The improvements in transporta-

95

tion made it possible for the farmers to move crops cheaply from the Midwest to the ports and cities of the Northeast.

Now that crops could be shipped easily and cheaply, a large market for them developed. The growing market, in turn, encouraged more settlers—farmers, shopkeepers, and doctors and the like—to move to the Midwest to farm the land and set up towns. Farms in the Midwest were generally family-run operations. Slavery, as you have read, had been forbidden by the Northwest Ordinance.

Cotton in the South. In much of the South, cotton was the cash crop. It became so profitable that most Southerners felt no need to invest in factories. They could always sell their raw cotton to the factories of the Northeast or to Great Britain. But cotton required large numbers of workers. In the South, that meant enslaved African Americans.

During the 1700s, most African American slaves in the South had worked on plantations that raised tobacco, indigo, sugar, or rice. Beginning in 1793, however, several factors combined to turn cotton into the main crop and slavery into big business. In that year, Eli Whitney invented the **cotton gin**. Until then, the seeds of the cotton plant had to be separated from the cotton fibers by hand. Because it was hard to do, a person could clean only a few pounds of cotton a day. With the cotton gin, one person could clean 50 times as much in a day. Within one year, Southern cotton production had increased 12 times. Within eight years, it had increased more than 250 times.

To produce such large crops, plantation owners devoted more land to growing cotton. They expanded to new land in Alabama, Mississippi, Louisiana, and Texas, where they grew cotton on thousands of acres. Soon Southerners were proclaiming, "Cotton is king."

The Internal Slave Trade. To raise so much cotton, huge numbers of laborers were needed. The nation officially ended the Atlantic slave trade in 1808. But by 1820, a booming trade in enslaved African Americans had developed within the nation. It was centered in the states of the Upper South: Maryland, Virginia, Kentucky, North Carolina, and Tennessee. In these states, tobacco production had worn out the soil, and fewer field hands were needed.

By the 1830s, these states were selling about 80,000 African Americans a year to the **Cotton Belt**. This was the band of cotton-growing states that stretched from Georgia to Texas (see map, page 103). With the Atlantic slave trade legally closed, slave traders in the Upper South packed African Americans aboard ships in voyages similar to those of the Middle Passage (see Chapter 4). They unloaded the African Americans in port cities, such as Charleston, South Carolina, and New Orleans, Louisiana, and marched them inland to plantations.

How was the invention of the cotton gin, shown here, related to the claim, "cotton is king"?

Within earshot of this Georgia planter's mansion were the cabins of the African American slaves who worked the fields and enabled the planter's family to lead a rich and comfortable life.

Southern Slave Owners. When many people think of the South before the Civil War, they think of a huge white house, or mansion, and rows of slave cabins. In reality, few Southern whites owned such estates. Nevertheless, most whites in the South dreamed of joining the handful of people who did. The key to becoming wealthy, they believed, was owning African American slaves. Even if a white family owned only one slave, it considered itself socially better than a family who owned none.

How many Southerners actually owned African American slaves? By 1860, some 8 million white people lived in the South. About 385,000 individuals owned African American slaves. But only 12 percent of these owners had more than 20 slaves, and fewer than 3,000 planters owned over a hundred slaves. Still, this minority of planters dominated the economy, politics,

and society of the Cotton Belt. No one felt their iron-fisted rule more heavily than the 2 million African Americans who labored under King Cotton.

Taking Another Look

1. How did transportation in the United States change after 1800?

2. **a.** What were the cash crops in the Midwest? **b.** in the South? **c.** Who worked the farms in each region?

3. What effects did changes in Southern agriculture have on African American slaves?

4. **Critical Thinking** There were few factories in the South. How would this affect the development of the South in the long run?

Working in the cotton fields

The Tyranny of Slavery

(1619–1860)

CHAPTER

10

THINKING ABOUT THE CHAPTER

How did African Americans survive the cruelty of slavery?

Several inches of snow lay on the ground that February. Harriet Jacobs silently thanked her grandmother, a freed African American slave, for giving her a new pair of shoes. The old ones were so tight that they cut into her feet. But Jacobs's owners, Dr. and Mrs. Flint, had little sympathy for the young teenager.

As Jacobs walked past Mrs. Flint, her new shoes squeaked. The sound annoyed her owner. "Take them off," Mrs. Flint ordered, "and if you put them on again, I'll throw them into the fire."

Jacobs knew that Mrs. Flint would whip her if she disobeyed, so she took off the shoes. When Mrs. Flint sent her on an errand, Jacobs walked barefoot through the snow and got sick. As she lay in bed, she wished for death rather than to spend the rest of her life with the Flints. As Jacobs later recalled, "What was my grief in waking up to find myself quite well."

Eventually, Jacobs escaped to the North and wrote the story of her life as a slave. The story, published in 1861, shocked her readers. She told of African American slaves working in the fields from dawn to sundown. She revealed how African American women were forced to have children fathered by their white owners or by African American slaves whom they did not love. She described children ripped from their mothers' arms to be sold. She recounted the brutal treatment of any slave—man or woman—who dared to say no to an owner.

In this chapter, you will read about how for 250 years African Americans were enslaved. You will also read about how, under a system in which their owners considered them to be no more than property, African Americans still carried on a rich cultural life that reflected their African origins.

1 THE EARLY YEARS OF SLAVERY
▼ What was life like for enslaved Africans from 1619 to the early 1800s?
▼

> For you must both . . . bear in mind that you remain . . . your Master's Property, and therefore it will be justly expected, both by God and Man, that you behave and conduct yourselves as Obedient and faithful Servants toward your respective Masters & Mistresses.

These words form part of a marriage ceremony written by a white New England minister in the early 1700s. Some slave owners allowed their slaves to marry, but they reserved the right to separate husbands from wives and sell either. Children, too, could be sold. This was one of the most brutal aspects of slavery, especially to people like the West Africans

to whom family life was so important. Yet, against all odds, African American slaves, descended from many peoples, created a common culture—including a sense of family—that made life bearable.

The First Generations. The first generations of Africans to arrive in English America in the 1600s and 1700s came from many different West African cultures. Until about the mid-1700s, they spoke the many different **dialects**, or forms of language, of the regions of West Africa from which they came. When Africans from different places had to work together on the same farms or plantations, they often had difficulty communicating with one another at first. Only after two or three generations did English become the common language. Over time, some African words crept into English—tote, okra, mumbo jumbo, goober, yam, and gumbo, to list a few.

Ship captains and planters often gave Africans English names. Renaming Africans was an attempt to strip them of their identities as individuals. But most new arrivals continued to use their African names regardless of what owners called them. An ad in a Georgia newspaper reflected this fact:

> Run aways . . . TWO NEW NEGRO YOUNG FELLOWS; one of them . . . calls himself Golaga, the name given him here Abel; the other . . . calls himself Abbrom, the name given him here Bennet.

Many first-generation Africans gave their children African names. However, slave owners usually respelled the names to make them sound more familiar to English ears. For example, the African names Quashee, Cudjo, Abbe, and Cuffee became Squash, Joe, Abby, and Cuff.

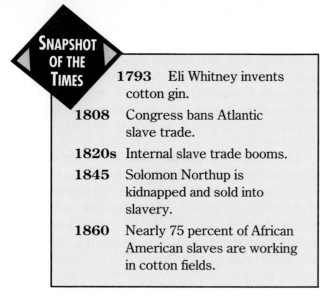

SNAPSHOT OF THE TIMES

1793 Eli Whitney invents cotton gin.

1808 Congress bans Atlantic slave trade.

1820s Internal slave trade booms.

1845 Solomon Northup is kidnapped and sold into slavery.

1860 Nearly 75 percent of African American slaves are working in cotton fields.

As Africans picked up English, they sometimes pretended, when it served their purposes, not to understand the English spoken by whites. They also developed pronunciations and sayings that had meaning only to them.

Daily Life. The living quarters of African slaves were often no worse than those of most European colonists in the 1600s. Most people had little more than a few pieces of furniture, an iron pot or frying pan, and some animal skins or straw for floor covering. But as time passed and the slave system grew, differences between Africans' and Europeans' living conditions widened. By the 1800s, most Europeans lived in board or brick houses, while enslaved Africans continued to live in shacks.

Since slave owners bought Africans to earn profits, they tended to spend as little as possible on their upkeep. They clothed them in the cheapest material available—usually a coarse fabric known as Negro cloth. They fed them rice, corn, beans, salt pork, and molasses.

Africans turned some of these foods into dishes they had enjoyed in Africa. They pounded corn into meal and made hoe cakes or mush similar to African fufu

or kenkey. Some dishes such as spoon bread, a puddinglike dumpling, also made their way to the tables of slave owners.

Working Conditions. Most Africans came from farming villages and adapted quickly to farming in the Americas. But as slaves, they faced grueling hours in the fields. A 1740 South Carolina law passed to "protect" Africans gives a glimpse of their working conditions.

> [I]f any owner of slaves . . . shall work or put such slave or slaves to labor more than fifteen hours in twenty-four hours . . . every such person shall forfeit [give up] a sum not exceeding twenty pounds nor under five pounds of current money.

Officials rarely collected such fines.

Owners of large plantations worked slaves in gangs. Owners did leave enough time in a day for slaves to tend their own garden plots and to have some time for their families. Slave owners soon found that Africans had their own ways of resisting bad working conditions. They worked slowly, broke tools, or, in a few cases, set fire to farm buildings.

Defenses Against Slavery. To forget the pains of slavery, Africans often turned to activities that reminded them of their homeland. In the slave quarters, the area that housed slaves on farms and plantations, they sang African songs. Craftworkers made drums or fashioned three-stringed banjos similar to those used in West Africa. Africans also brought their dances to English America. The dances involved hand-clapping, singing, and moving to complicated rhythms.

Like West Africans' words and foods, their dances slipped into the culture of white colonists. In the mid-1700s, one English visitor was shocked at the sight of

During the limited hours when African American slaves were not working, they created their own dances, songs, and other forms of recreation. Many were based on African traditions.

Southern colonists swaying to "Congo minuets" and dancing African-style "jigs."

Storytellers, similar to West African griots, told folktales that recalled their African homeland. These tales have since become part of the African American heritage. Some tales described the deeds of African ancestors or clever slaves. Many tales involved weak, helpless animals who defeated larger, stronger animals. Especially popular were the Brer Rabbit stories, in which the clever rabbit outsmarted such enemies as Brer Fox (see page 30).

Work Songs. Singing was a way to get through the long day. There were special songs for picking cotton, for doing the laundry, and for many other tasks. Most songs, however, expressed a deep longing for freedom. Said one song:

> Rabbit in de briar patch,
> Squirrel in de tree,
> Wish I could go huntin',
> But I ain't free.

Family Life. By far the strongest defense against the cruelties of slavery was the family. Slaves recognized marriages among themselves even when whites did not. According to tradition, a couple married by "jumping over the broomstick." It was bad luck to stub your toe on the broom, so most couples, said one slave, tried to fly over the broomstick "like a cricket." Slaves created a sense of closeness among themselves by calling one another "brother," "sister," "aunt," "uncle," and so on, even when they had no actual family relationship.

Religion. Time after time, enslaved Africans heard white ministers tell them that slavery was God's will. They sat while ministers pounded home one message—obedience. But they largely ignored the ministers because they had their own preachers and spiritual beliefs.

The early generations of Africans in English America believed that their souls returned to Africa when they died. Some

Africans buried bodies with items needed for the journey—a bow and arrows, a small canoe and paddle, and some food. But by the mid-1700s many began to adopt the Christian idea of heaven.

Some enslaved Africans in the South even viewed death as a positive event. One African, known as Uncle Silas, asked a white preacher, "Us slaves gonna be free in heaven?" The preacher ignored the question, but Silas and most other slaves believed the answer was yes.

Many slave owners read to their slaves from the Bible to try to impress on them that slavery was God's will. But Africans had another view of the Bible stories. In their eyes, they were the Israelites (IZ-ree-uh-lyts), who suffered enslavement at the hands of wicked Egyptian pharaohs. Christianity taught about a gentle Jesus who suffered persecution—and was set free—on the cross. Where they could, Africans gathered together in "invisible churches" to hold their own services. These were places in the woods, away from the eyes of slave owners.

Taking Another Look

1. What elements of African ways entered into the lives of the colonists?

2. In what ways did Africans soften the cruelties of slave life?

3. **Critical Thinking** Why might Christian hymns with titles like "We Are the People of God" have given enslaved Africans hope?

2 ▼ AFRICAN AMERICANS IN THE COTTON KINGDOM

▼ What was life like for African American slaves after 1800?

An African American child named Stephen huddled with his family in the corner of a slave-trading yard. Their owner had just died, and his relatives wanted to sell off Stephen's family. As the slave trader approached, Stephen's mother held tightly to him and his two sisters, Mary and Jane. She begged the trader not to break up the family.

This drawing shows a slave auction in New Orleans in the 1850s. No other aspect of slavery was dreaded more by African American slaves than the possibility of being sold and separated from their families.

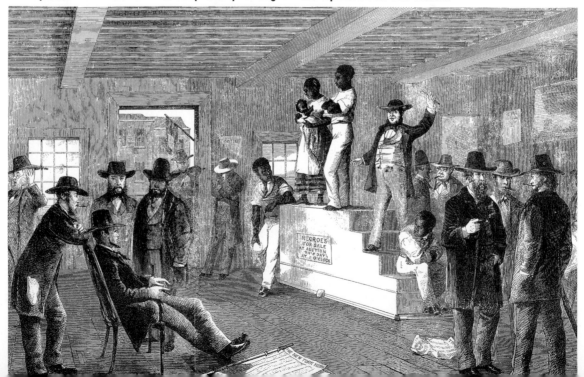

Which states had the highest percentage of African American slaves? How many of these states were in the Cotton Belt? What does this tell you about the relation between slavery and cotton?

But the trader had other ideas. To him, the slave trade was a business. He bought African American slaves from plantation owners who no longer needed them or who needed money more, and sold them at a profit to other owners. He did not care that in the process of buying and selling he broke up families.

Bullwhip in hand, the trader grabbed Mary and shoved her toward a well-dressed plantation owner. The trader's words stuck in Stephen's mind. "Here's jes' the girl you want for a nurse," said the trader.

Stephen never forgot the slave-trading yard. He vividly recalled the scene in his later life.

I was jes' a little chap, . . . but I can remember that place like it happened yesterday—husbands sold away from wives, and children taken away from mothers. A trader, them days, didn't think no more of selling a baby or little child away from its mother than a little calf away from a cow.

Breaking up families by selling members to distant owners was much more common after 1793 than before. With the invention of the cotton gin that year, cotton became the major crop of the South. As a result, cotton plantations needed the labor of more and more enslaved African Americans. Thus, slavery became big business, and the life of African American slaves, never easy, became much harder.

How did it feel to be enslaved on the cotton plantations of the South? In the 1930s, interviewers put this question to former African American slaves, many of whom were 75 to 100 years old. Some still bore deep scars on their backs from the lash of the whip. To be a slave meant to have no rights at all. "Once they whipped my father," said elderly Roberta Mason, " 'cause he looked at a slave they killed and cried."

103

African American slaves who worked on the plantations of the Cotton Kingdom spent their whole working lives planting and picking the crop that brought the South its great wealth in the years before the Civil War. How many people benefitted from the labor of African American slaves in the pre-Civil War South?

Compare the figures for 1820 and 1860 in the graph below. In which year did the average African American slave produce more cotton? African American women and children as well as men worked in the cotton fields.

▶▶ **AFRICAN AMERICAN SLAVE POPULATION AND COTTON PRODUCTION, 1790–1860**

Cotton ▮
Slaves ▯

Slaves or Bales of Cotton (in hundred thousands)

Years: 1790, 1820, 1860

Source: U.S. Department of Commerce, Bureau of the Census, *Historical Statistics of the United States, Colonial Times to 1970, Part 1* (Series A 91–104 and K 550–563), pp. 18, 518

From Sunrise to Sunset. Slavery varied from state to state and from owner to owner. But the worst conditions existed on the "cotton factories" of the Deep South, the lands that extended west from Georgia through Alabama, Mississippi, Arkansas, and Louisiana to Texas. Nearly every enslaved African American dreaded the thought of being "sold down the river" (the Mississippi) to plantations in Louisiana or Texas. One free African American who was sold down the river was Solomon Northup.

Solomon Northup was a free African American from New York. In 1845, while he was visiting Washington, D.C., slave traders grabbed Northup and shipped him to a slave market in New Orleans. There, a cotton planter bought him and forced him to work in the cotton fields for 12 years. After Northup's freedom was secured by a family friend in 1853, he published the story of his years as a plantation slave. The book sold widely and helped whip up antislavery feeling throughout the North.

Northup wrote how, as a typical field hand on a cotton plantation, he worked from sunrise to sunset:

> The hands [workers] are required to be in the cotton field as soon as it is light in the morning, and with the exception of ten or fifteen minutes, which is given them at noon to swallow their allowance of cold bacon, they are not permitted to be a moment idle until it is too dark to see and when the moon is full they often times labor till the middle of the night.

On larger plantations, white **overseers** stood constant watch. Assisting them were **slave drivers**, often African American slaves themselves, who snapped the whip at any worker who lagged. Although they were hated by other slaves, for slave drivers to do otherwise meant facing the anger of the plantation owner. A slave driver could find himself sold away from his family or put to work in the fields. So, as Northup wrote, "The lash flew from morning to night."

Each evening, weary slaves trudged home to put away tools, unload cotton bags, and do the owner's chores—chop wood, feed mules, and so on. Then they built fires in their cabins and threw potatoes or some ash cakes—patties of corn meal and water—onto the coals to cook. After they ate, they tumbled into bed. An hour before dawn, a horn or bell awoke them to another day of labor.

Skilled Workers. By 1860, nearly 75 percent of all African American slaves worked in the cotton fields. A few, however, worked in the planter's mansion, called the "big house." They were skilled craftworkers, tailors, butlers, maids, cooks, and nurses for the owners' children. Some house servants and planters developed close personal ties. But even the kindest owners rarely freed African American slaves until they were old and no longer able to work.

Some owners, both on plantations and in Southern towns and cities, trained their slaves in various skills such as blacksmithing. Then, they hired out the slaves, receiving pay for their work. Some owners gave the workers a part of what they earned. In this way, some African Americans in the South were able to buy their freedom and that of their families.

African American slaves worked at a variety of jobs, ranging from ship pilot to carpenter to factory worker. They preferred city work to working on a plantation because they had more freedom and the hope of earning money. Also, with greater freedom came the opportunity to escape, as you will read in Chapter 14.

Cultural Changes. The closing of the Atlantic slave trade in 1808 and the rise of the Cotton Kingdom brought about great changes among enslaved African Americans in the 1800s. Because slave owners could not buy any more Africans, they created an interregional trade in African American slaves. By now, most had been born in the United States. All or almost all spoke English.

Reliance on the Extended Family. As families were increasingly under the threat of being broken up by slave owners

Family ties were strong among African American slaves. This photograph shows five generations of the same family on a South Carolina plantation.

in the 1800s, the extended family became especially important. Because slave owners could sell off one or both parents, children were thought of as belonging to the whole community. Everyone took part in the care of children. It was the extended family that saw children through their early years. Harriet Jacobs fondly recalled the role of her grandmother in raising her. She wrote:

> It has been painful to me . . . to recall the dreary years I passed in bondage. . . . Yet . . . with those gloomy recollections come tender memories of my good old grandmother, like light, fleecy clouds floating over a dark and troubled sea.

A slave owner who had sold a man's wife to a distant plantation might order the man to take another wife. To refuse such an order took courage, but many men did. Henry "Box" Brown (see page 145) gave this reason for his refusal to obey his owner: "Marriage was a sacred institution binding upon me."

Strengthened Religion. The religious beliefs African Americans had developed in the 1700s grew stronger in the 1800s. Now, almost all African American slaves adopted Christianity, but in a form that included some of their African religious beliefs. They continued to worship at "invisible churches." Despite slave owners' efforts to track them down with savage "slave hounds," the believers refused to give up their meetings. They posted guards to listen for barking dogs. Sometimes, they strung vines through the trees to trip patrols. Other times, they deadened the voices of worshipers with "hush harbors"—shelters built out of tree branches.

As slaves were sold throughout the South, religious songs known as **spirituals** spread from plantation to plantation. The spirituals expressed a defiance toward slavery and a belief in equality, even if only after death. The words of one spiritual led officials in Georgetown, South Carolina, to lock up anyone who sang them. The song declared:

> And it won't be long. And it won't be long,
> And it won't be long, Poor sinner suffer here.
> We'll soon be free
> De Lord will call us home.
> . . . .
> We'll fight for liberty
> When the Lord will call us home.

Taking Another Look

1. Describe in a paragraph the life of a field hand.

2. List two ways in which African American slave life of the 1800s was different from that of the 1700s.

3. **Critical Thinking** Why do you think slave owners tried to crush "invisible churches"?

LOOKING AHEAD

As the plantation economy of the South boomed with the growth of the Cotton Kingdom, the lives of African American slaves grew harsher. Yet, they were able to build on and strengthen their sense of family and to develop ways of coping with slavery. The will to be free, however, burned brightly in slave quarters. The Cotton Kingdom contained within itself the seeds of its own destruction, and its end loomed on the horizon.

We rose and stood for a few moments in breathless silence . . . afraid that someone might have been about the cottage listening. . . . I took my wife by the hand, stepped softly to the door, raised the latch, drew it open, and peeped out. . . . Everything appeared to be as still as death.

At this moment, the two African American slaves fled into the night—runaways, risking their lives for their freedom. Would they make it to freedom? To find out, anxious readers turned page after page of slave narratives. These were books published about the lives of enslaved African Americans.

These stories sold quickly in the North and in Great Britain, France, and Germany in the 1840s and 1850s. For example, the British edition of Frederick Douglass's slave narrative sold 4,500 copies in five months in 1845.

Slave narratives undermined foreign support for the South. Southern slave owners claimed that African American slaves enjoyed better lives than factory workers in Europe, but the slave narratives proved otherwise. They described terrible living conditions, brutal whippings, backbreaking labor, and heartbreaking slave auctions. "This fugitive slave literature," said one American, "is destined to be a powerful lever [tool] [to help end slavery]."

CLOSE UP: Chapter 10

The Who, What, Where of History

1. **Who** was Harriet Jacobs?
2. **What** are dialects?
3. **What** were the slave quarters?
4. **Who** was Solomon Northup?
5. **Who** were the overseers?
6. **What** were "invisible churches"?
7. **Who** were the slave drivers?
8. **Where** was the Cotton Belt?
9. **What** are spirituals?

Making the Connection

1. What was the connection between the system of slavery and the development of a distinct form of the English language?
2. What was the connection among the closing of the Atlantic slave trade, the rise of the Cotton Kingdom, and the importance African American slaves attached to extended families?
3. What was the connection between the Biblical story of the Israelites and the feelings of African American slaves about their condition?

Time Check

1. What event in 1793 changed life for African American slaves?
2. When did Congress end the Atlantic slave trade?

What Would You Have Done?

1. Imagine you are an African American slave whose owner permits some slaves to work and earn wages. What arguments would you use to convince

your owner to allow you to learn a skill such as blacksmithing?

2. Imagine that you are Solomon Northup. You have been captured by slave traders and have just learned that you have been sold to a Louisiana cotton planter. Write a brief passage describing your reaction on hearing where you are being sent.

Thinking and Writing About History

1. Write a paragraph that begins with this sentence: "Of all the cruelties and injustices of the slave system, I think the most brutal feature was _____."

2. Choose one of the following: write a folktale about a small, weak, but clever, animal who outsmarts a large, strong animal, or write a work song that describes a job or chore that you do.

3. Reread the question that Uncle Silas asked the white preacher (see page 102). Write a paragraph explaining why the white preacher might have wanted to ignore his question.

Building Skills: Stating the Main Idea in Your Own Words

Most of us have had a conversation like this one more than once in our lives:

Mother: Did you read your history assignment?
You: I sure did and it was kind of interesting, too.
Mother: What was it about?
You: Slavery.
Mother: What about slavery?

You: Lots of things; I can't explain it really.
Mother: Maybe you had better go read it again.

Sound familiar? One way to be sure that you understand and remember the main ideas of what you've read is to put them into your own words.

Here is an example. Read the following paragraph from Chapter 10:

Since slave owners bought Africans to earn profits, they tended to spend as little as possible on their upkeep. They clothed them in the cheapest material available—usually a coarse fabric known as Negro cloth. They fed them rice, corn, beans, salt pork, and molasses.

1. On a separate sheet of paper, write the sentence that states the main idea of the paragraph. Next, try to rewrite the sentence in your own words.

2. Find the main idea of the following paragraph and write a sentence that states it in your own words.

To forget the pains of slavery, Africans often turned to activities that reminded them of their homeland. In the slave quarters, the area that housed slaves on farms and plantations, they sang African songs. Craftworkers made drums or fashioned three-stringed banjos similar to those used in West Africa. Africans also brought their dances to English America. The dances involved hand-clapping, singing, and moving to complicated rhythms.

The title page from *Walker's Appeal*

CHAPTER 11

Armed Resistance to Slavery

(1658–1860)

THINKING ABOUT THE CHAPTER

What actions did enslaved African Americans take to show their hatred of slavery?

"If I remain in this bloody land," said David Walker of North Carolina, "I will not live long." The son of a freed mother and an enslaved father, Walker knew the pain of slavery from his father's stories. In 1827, Walker left North Carolina for Boston, Massachusetts, where he set up a secondhand clothing store. Within a short time, Walker had taught himself to read and write. Soon he was writing fiery articles for the nation's first African American newspaper, *Freedom's Journal.*

In September 1829, Walker released a booklet entitled *Walker's Appeal, in Four Articles.* In it, Walker urged African Americans to rebel against slavery. "Kill or be killed," wrote Walker. "Had you rather not be killed than to be a slave to a tyrant, who takes the life of your mother, wife, and dear little children?"

Walker also sent a message to white Americans. "While you keep us and our children in bondage," said Walker, "we cannot be your friends." Resisting change, he warned, might mean violence. "Remember, Americans, that we must and shall be free."

Walker's Appeal sent shock waves through the South. Slave owners recalled earlier slave rebellions and feared that African Americans might take Walker's words to heart. Some slave owners offered a reward for his capture—dead or alive. Several Southern state legislatures held special sessions to discuss Walker's words. A number of Southern mayors demanded that Boston officials arrest Walker and burn his books.

In 1830, Walker mysteriously disappeared. Some said he was murdered. Still the fear he had stirred lingered in the South. State after state in the South outlawed the *Appeal* and tightened their restrictions on African American slaves.

1 EARLY SLAVE REBELLIONS

Where did slave rebellions take place in the 1600s and early 1700s?

On April 7, 1712, a group of 23 African slaves met in an orchard near a slave owner's home in New York City. They crept up on the house and set it afire. When a group of white colonists tried to put out the blaze, the Africans fell upon them with axes, knives, and guns. In the fighting that followed, nine whites died, and six others were injured.

English soldiers stationed in New York City tracked down the slaves and arrested them. The incident terrorized the city's white population. New York had more African slaves than any other colonial city except Charleston, South Carolina.

This incident highlighted the fact that chances of success were small.

Unrest in the 1600s and Early 1700s. This New York uprising was not the first time slaves had staged a rebellion in the colonies. In 1658, African and Native American slaves in Hartford, Connecticut, burned the homes of their owners. In 1663, white indentured servants and African slaves in Gloucester County, Virginia, plotted against their owners but were betrayed by a spy. In

Why did so many early rebellions, like the "Great Negro Plot," take place in the North?

How did the building of a fort by African slaves in Florida lead to the Stono Uprising?

1708, two slaves—a Native American and an African—killed their owner's family on Long Island, New York. In 1741, 34 people were killed for supposedly taking part in what New Yorkers called the "Great Negro Plot." A wave of fires and thefts had broken out and rumors placed the blame on the city's Africans.

In each case, colonial officials executed the rebels and passed tough slave codes. These laws limited the personal movements of slaves. Most slave codes prohibited slaves from meeting in groups of two or more. Codes set curfews and required slaves to carry passes from their owners when on business. Violations of these laws resulted in severe whippings. Some slave codes gave officials the right to brand offenders on the forehead with a hot iron. In this way, "troublemakers" could be easily spotted.

The Stono Uprising. Throughout the colonies, slaves also resisted slavery by running away. Some African slaves fled to live with Native Americans. African slaves in South Carolina and Georgia escaped whenever they could to live in Spanish Florida.

In 1733, the Spanish king, eager to strike at his enemy Great Britain, offered **fugitives** from the colonies their freedom. In 1739, a group of African runaways built a fort near St. Augustine, Florida, to protect their families from slave catchers. The Spanish helped arm the Africans and their Native American allies, the Seminoles.

The thought of an armed African fort near the Florida border horrified Southern slave owners. News of the fort reached African slaves in South Carolina through ships arriving in Charleston harbor. The number of escaping Africans increased.

On Sunday, September 9, 1739, a group of about 20 African slaves gathered along the Stono River, 20 miles (32 kilometers) from Charleston. Led by a man named Jemmy, they looted an arsenal for weapons. Then, they headed for St. Augustine and the fort.

Along the way, they burned plantations and killed about 20 to 30 whites. One observer recalled the scene: "They called out liberty, marched on with colours displayed, and two drums beating." A colonial militia finally caught up with the rebels and killed or wounded many of them.

Once again, the authorities turned to slave codes, passing even tighter restrictions. The South Carolina assembly also ordered every white male in the colony to carry a gun or pair of horse pistols. Any African slave caught without a pass was to be shot on sight.

Taking Another Look

1. Where did slave rebellions occur in the 1600s and early 1700s?

2. How did slave owners respond to rebellions?

3. **Critical Thinking** Many of the slave codes passed after 1700 forbade the education of enslaved Africans. Why do you think that white colonists enacted such laws?

2 THE PROSSER CONSPIRACY

▼ What was Gabriel Prosser's daring rebellion plan?

Gabriel, a 24-year-old African American slave who was owned by Thomas Henry Prosser of Henrico County, Virginia, was a skilled craftworker. Prosser hired him out to work at nearby plantations and towns. Little did he know that soon Gabriel's name would strike fear in the hearts of most white Southerners. In the spring and summer of 1800, Gabriel began making plans for a revolt.

A Vision of Freedom. Gabriel Prosser drew his inspiration for rebellion from the Bible. He compared the enslavement of African Americans to the enslavement of the Israelites by Egypt. Like the Moses of the Israelites, Prosser dreamed of leading his people to a promised land— an African American state carved out of the heart of Virginia.

Prosser believed that a successful rebellion was possible. In his visits to

<table>
<tr><td colspan="2">SNAPSHOT OF THE TIMES</td></tr>
<tr><td>1658</td><td>Enslaved Africans and Native Americans burn owners' homes in Hartford, Connecticut.</td></tr>
<tr><td>1663</td><td>Plot by African slaves in Gloucester County, Virginia, is discovered.</td></tr>
<tr><td>1708</td><td>African slave and Native American slave kill owner's family on Long Island, New York.</td></tr>
<tr><td>1712</td><td>African slaves revolt in New York City.</td></tr>
<tr><td>1739</td><td>Stono Uprising occurs.</td></tr>
<tr><td>1741</td><td>"Great Negro Plot" occurs in New York City.</td></tr>
<tr><td>1800</td><td>Gabriel Prosser's conspiracy fails.</td></tr>
<tr><td>1822</td><td>Denmark Vesey's conspiracy is discovered.</td></tr>
<tr><td>1829</td><td>David Walker publishes his Appeal.</td></tr>
<tr><td>1831</td><td>Nat Turner leads rebellion.</td></tr>
</table>

nearby plantations and towns, he learned about the uprising in Haiti under Toussaint L'Ouverture (see page 85). Prosser also listened to white Virginians talk with pride about their own struggle for independence from Great Britain.

Spreading the Word. Prosser convinced his brother Martin and his wife Nanny to join him. At fish fries and barbecues, they asked other slaves throughout Henrico County to rise up against their owners on the night of August 30. To prepare, Prosser advised his followers to whittle handmade swords or to steal axes,

113

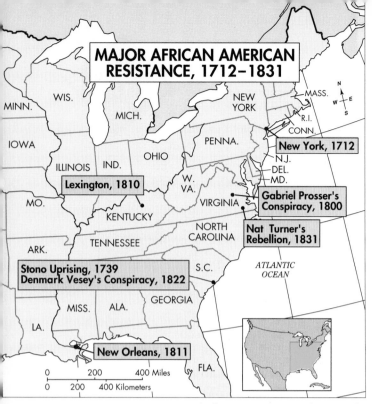

MAJOR AFRICAN AMERICAN RESISTANCE, 1712–1831

New York, 1712

Lexington, 1810

Gabriel Prosser's Conspiracy, 1800

Nat Turner's Rebellion, 1831

Stono Uprising, 1739
Denmark Vesey's Conspiracy, 1822

New Orleans, 1811

ATLANTIC OCEAN

| 0 | 200 | 400 Miles |
| 0 | 200 | 400 Kilometers |

How many instances of African resistance are shown on the map? What other ones does the text describe?

shovels, or anything else that might serve as weapons.

Prosser expected to arm his followers more fully with guns seized from local slave owners. He would then lead his forces in a lightning attack on Richmond, the capital of Virginia. There African American slaves would put all whites to death except Quakers, Methodists, and any French, groups thought to be friendly to African Americans.

A Failed Uprising. On the night of the raid, more than a thousand supporters gathered outside Richmond. Little did they know that two slaves had informed on Prosser. As the rebels advanced, a great thunderstorm struck. It washed out roads and bridges and made it impossible for Prosser's army to march toward Richmond. Their fate was sealed when 600 troops, who had been called out by Governor James Monroe—the future Presi-

dent of the United States—set out after the rebels.

Prosser tried to escape by sea but was captured. He was put on trial with some 35 other rebels. One of the defendants, perhaps even Prosser, made this moving speech at the trial:

> I have nothing more to offer than what General Washington would have had to offer, had he been taken by the British and put to trial by them. I have adventured my life in endeavoring to obtain the liberty of my countrymen, and am a willing sacrifice to their cause.

On October 7, 1800, Prosser was hanged. The fact that the Prosser plot had failed did not discourage African Americans. Within a year, more plots were reported elsewhere in Virginia and in North Carolina. In 1810, an uprising was put down in Lexington, Kentucky. A year later, a free African American named Charles Deslondes led hundreds of African American slaves in an unsuccessful attack on New Orleans. Meanwhile, a much larger uprising was being talked about in South Carolina.

Taking Another Look

1. What was Prosser's goal?

2. What inspired Prosser to act?

3. **Critical Thinking** Why do you think the defendant at the Prosser trial compared himself to George Washington?

3 THE VESEY CONSPIRACY
How did the Vesey conspiracy further prove African Americans' willingness to resist slavery?

114

In 1800, the same year that Gabriel Prosser died, a slave named Denmark Vesey won $1,500 in a lottery. He used $600 to buy his freedom and then opened a carpentry shop in Charleston, South Carolina, with the rest of the money.

Desire for Revolution. In his spare time, Vesey studied the Haitian and French revolutions. His hatred of slavery grew so intense that he vowed to lead slaves in a rebellion to take over Charleston. If threatened with capture, Vesey planned to sail to the island of Haiti—homeland of his hero Toussaint L'Ouverture (see page 85).

For years, Vesey cornered African American slaves on the streets of Charleston to talk about rebellion. He held meetings in his home to try to persuade others to join him in an attack on Charleston.

In May 1822, one of his recruits, Peter Poyas, helped Vesey organize an elaborate plot. They scouted Charleston and set up seven points of attack that would give them control of most of the city's arsenals and the harbor.

Betrayal. Vesey thought he had guarded against betrayal. He and Poyas had been very careful. For example, only they knew the names of everyone involved in the plot. Still, before they could act, an African American slave close to Vesey and Poyas turned in their names and those of several other leaders to the authorities.

Officials arrested some 130 African Americans. Only one of them broke down and confessed. But this confession was enough to sentence Vesey, Poyas, and others to death.

In the end, some 45 of the rebels were executed. Others were sent to islands in the Caribbean. The South Carolina legislature rewarded the informer, named Peter, with a pension of $50 a year. The legislature also passed laws limiting the rights of free African Americans in the state. No African American, vowed white officials in Charleston, would ever again have the freedom of Denmark Vesey. When the abolitionist leader Frederick Douglass was recruiting African Americans for the Union army during the Civil War, he urged them to "remember Denmark Vesey."

Taking Another Look

1. How were Prosser's and Vesey's plans similar?

2. How did the Vesey conspiracy affect the rights of free African Americans in South Carolina?

3. **Critical Thinking** After the Vesey conspiracy, the South Carolina legislature banned all criticism of slavery. How effective do you think this act might have been as a way of preventing slave uprisings? Explain.

4 "OLD NAT'S WAR"

▼ Why was it said that no Southerner before the Civil War could ever forget Nat Turner?

Nat Turner lived as a slave on a plantation in Southampton County, Virginia. People called him the Prophet. From an early age, he had seen visions and heard voices. Turner firmly believed he had a special mission in life. He waited for a message to guide him. In 1825, he felt,

Nat Turner had long dreamed of staging an uprising against slave owners but did not reveal his plans to other African American slaves until he was ready to act. Why did Southerners so fear Turner's rebellion?

the message came. Turner later recalled the vision:

> White spirits and black spirits engaged in battle, and the sun was darkened—the thunder rolled in the Heavens, and blood flowed in streams—and I heard a voice saying, 'Such is your luck, such you are called to see, and let it come rough or smooth, you must surely bare it.'

The vision convinced Turner that the Lord wanted him to take revenge on the white planters who enslaved African Americans. He waited for a sign to tell him when to strike.

Judgment Day. The sign came in February 1831 when a total eclipse darkened the sun. Turner took a few people into his confidence about his goal. However, unlike Prosser and Vesey, he did not form an elaborate plan nor did he try to organize large numbers of African Americans.

After months of delay, Turner made his move on August 21, 1831. Along with eight other African American slaves, he set out on a journey of death. The first stop was the home of Turner's owner, where they killed everyone. They then headed for other plantations, picking up about 50 supporters along the way. In all, they killed some 60 whites.

A hastily formed militia combed the countryside looking for Turner. But he escaped capture until the end of October. Meanwhile, as panic gripped whites in the South, dozens of innocent African Americans were seized and put to death. Turner later described his capture:

> I [hid] under a pile of fence rails in a field, where I concealed myself for six weeks. . . .[Two] Negroes having started to go hunting . . . discovered me. . . .On making myself known, they fled. . . . I immediately left my hiding place, and was pursued almost incessantly [endlessly] until I was taken a fortnight [two weeks] afterwards.

To celebrate Turner's capture, guns were fired all over Southampton County. On November 5, 1831, a judge ordered Turner "hung by the neck until you are dead! dead! dead!"

Reaction to Turner.   Turner became a legend among African American slaves in Southampton County, who passed on stories of "Old Nat's war." White planters saw him as a devil. Turner's rebellion confirmed fears raised by David Walker's *Appeal*. Southern states strengthened the slave codes and enforced them with a new determination.

For any whites who still believed that enslaved African Americans generally were satisfied with their lives, the Turner rebellion was a shock. Such uprisings continued throughout the South up to and even during the Civil War.

After hiding for almost two months, Turner was captured and later executed.

Taking Another Look

1. How did Turner's rebellion differ from the Prosser and Vesey conspiracies?

2. What actions did the South take after Turner's rebellion?

3. **Critical Thinking**   Although none of the slave revolts succeeded, why were they important?

LOOKING AHEAD

The economy of the South was based on slavery. When uprisings and revolts by African American slaves quickened in the 1800s, few Southern whites realized that slavery was in danger of collapse. Instead, they tightened the slave codes and hoped the danger would pass. Meanwhile, free African Americans in the North and South gave the lie to the Southern view that slavery was the "natural" condition for African Americans.

CLOSE UP: Chapter 11

"Captain Cudjoe"—the name of the Jamaican Maroon leader struck fear into the hearts of British soldiers who spent much of the early 1700s trying to capture him. In 1739, the British finally signed a treaty with the Jamaican rebel, guaranteeing the Maroons independence.

Just five years later, Cudjoe died. The wooden board that once marked his grave is lost. But the words carved on the marker remain etched in Maroon memory: "Cudjoe, a Maroon forever free." Freedom for the rest of Jamaica, however, lay off in the future.

After the British ended their slave trade in 1807, Jamaican slaves longed for freedom. In 1831, slaves in Montego Bay led a full-scale rebellion. The British crushed the rebellion, but clashes continued until slavery was ended in 1838.

The end of slavery, however, did not guarantee equality. On October 11, 1865, poverty-stricken former slaves attacked the Morant Bay courthouse, burning it to the ground and killing at least 19 whites. The British governor handled the crisis so badly that he was removed and a new form of government was established.

On August 6, 1962, freedom finally came to Jamaica. It was the first British territory in the Caribbean to win its independence.

The Who, What, Where of History

1. **Who** was David Walker?
2. **What** was *Freedom's Journal?*
3. **What** were the slave codes?
4. **Where** did the "Great Negro Plot" take place?
5. **What** was the Stono Uprising?
6. **Who** was Gabriel Prosser?
7. **Where** did Charles Deslondes and his followers launch their unsuccessful attack?
8. **Who** was Denmark Vesey?
9. **Who** was Nat Turner?

Making the Connection

1. What was the connection between slave revolts and slave codes?
2. Explain the relationship between the king of Spain and the Stono Uprising.
3. What was the connection between Toussaint L'Ouverture and Prosser?

Time Check

1. Which of the following slave revolts or conspiracies happened *last:* the "Great Negro Plot," Turner's rebellion, Vesey's conspiracy?
2. When did the first known slave revolt in the colonies occur?
3. When did David Walker publish his *Appeal?*

What Would You Have Done?

1. If you had been the owner of a bookstore in Charleston in 1831, would

you have carried copies of Walker's *Appeal?* Explain your answer.

2. Imagine that you are a judge who must pass sentence on an African American slave who had planned an uprising similar to that of Gabriel Prosser. You strongly believe that slavery is a great evil. However, as a judge, you must uphold the law. What would you do?

3. Imagine that you are a Northern white who opposes slavery. Details of Nat Turner's unsuccessful revolt have just been published in the newspaper. Write a letter to the editor giving your reaction to the event.

Thinking and Writing About History

1. Write a review of Walker's *Appeal* for the newspaper *Freedom's Journal*. In your review, include information about David Walker himself, about the contents of the book, and give your opinion of the book.

2. Write an editorial for a Charleston newspaper giving the paper's reaction to the discovery of the Vesey conspiracy. In the editorial, offer suggestions for measures that might help prevent further conspiracy.

3. Imagine that you are an African American slave who can read and write. Write a very short account of Nat Turner's rebellion that will be smuggled to other African American slaves throughout the South.

4. What impact do you think Prosser's, Vesey's, and Turner's rebellions had on enslaved African Americans? Write a brief paper explaining why you think such revolts would have inspired or discouraged African Americans in the South.

Building Skills: Main Ideas in a Chapter Section

In previous chapters, you practiced finding the main idea of a paragraph and stating a main idea in your own words. You have also practiced using the titles and section headings of your textbook to keep track of main ideas. Now try putting these skills together by restating the main ideas from a chapter section in your own words.

Section 1 of Chapter 11 begins on page 111. On a separate sheet of paper, write the title of the section. Next write the question that follows the title. Then write one sentence that states the main idea. If you have trouble, see if you can turn the section-opening question into a sentence.

The sentence you have written probably does state the main idea of the section, but it may be a bit vague. Skim the section and review its content. Now rewrite the main idea sentence, making it stronger and more specific. You may add dates, or give an example.

For instance, suppose you wrote for the main idea: "A number of slave rebellions took place in the late 1600s and early 1700s." You could make that sentence much more specific by writing: "As early as 1658, Africans showed their resistance to slavery by rebellion and by running away."

Follow the same steps for sections 2, 3, and 4 of this chapter. Look at the section title and the question that follows it. Write a sentence that gives the main idea of the section. Then skim the section and rewrite your main idea, making it clearer or more specific.

Prosperous free African Americans in the North

Free African Americans in the North and South
(1700s–1860)

THINKING ABOUT THE CHAPTER

How did free African Americans undermine arguments in favor of slavery?

"It is well known that the color of one's skin does not prohibit [prevent] one from any place or station that he or she may be capable of occupying." So wrote Nancy Gardner Prince, an African American in the 1820s. But her words described Russia, not the United States.

Prince traveled to Russia with her husband, Nero, a former sailor who took a job as a personal servant to Czar Alexander I, the ruler of Russia. There, Prince opened a dressmaking business. She made elegant dresses for the empress of Russia and other noblewomen.

The cold Russian weather forced Prince to return home for health reasons. When she reached Boston, a stagecoach driver denied her a seat inside the carriage.

"The weight of prejudice," mourned Prince, "has again oppressed me." This chapter tells the story of the obstacles free African Americans faced and how they overcame them.

1 NEITHER SLAVE NOR FREE

▼ What hardships did free African Americans face in their daily lives?

At the time Prince arrived in Boston, all African Americans in New England were legally free. Slavery existed only in the slave states of the South (see map, page 103). Even so, free African Americans everywhere experienced **discrimination**. This is unjust treatment based on a characteristic such as color or religion.

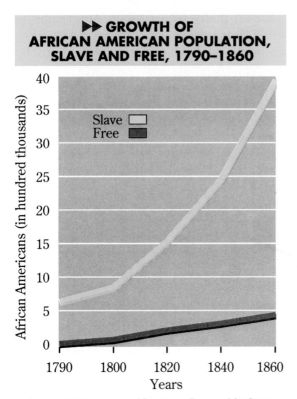

▶▶ GROWTH OF AFRICAN AMERICAN POPULATION, SLAVE AND FREE, 1790–1860

Source: U.S. Department of Commerce, Bureau of the Census, *Historical Statistics of the United States, Colonial Times to 1970, Part 1* (Series A 91–104), p. 14

Compare the rate at which the number of free and enslaved African Americans grew after 1800.

The Free African American Population.   The nation's free African American population had steadily increased in the years following the American Revolution. In 1790, free African Americans totaled about 59,000. In 1830, the number had climbed to 319,000. By 1860, it had reached 488,000, or about 11 percent of the total African American population in the United States.

The banning of slavery in the North helped account for this increase, but the number of free African Americans in the South also grew. In 1860, for example, Maryland, a slave state, had more free African Americans than any other state. About half the African Americans there were free.

Routes to Freedom.   In 1860, nearly half of all free African Americans in the United States lived in the South. Some had bought their freedom. Others were freed by their owners. Many were the descendants of Africans who had won their freedom during the colonial period.

One African American in Mobile, Alabama, Pierre Chastang, was freed by grateful citizens. Whites in the city raised money to buy his freedom because of his service in the War of 1812 and his help during a yellow fever epidemic in 1819.

Thousands of African Americans became free simply by running away. As you will read in Chapter 14, many made their way to freedom in the North on the Underground Railroad.

Limits on Freedom.   Fears that free African Americans would aid or organize a slave rebellion led Southern lawmakers to sharply limit the rights of free African Americans. Laws denied them the right to vote, to have a trial by jury, and to testify against whites. African American children could not attend public schools. Yet, in some places, their parents were expected to pay school taxes.

Free African Americans were not even free to move about in the South. Laws required them to carry passes proving they were free. They were denied the right to reenter a state after they had left it. In some states, free African Americans were not allowed to gather together— even in church—without the presence of a white person.

Free African Americans in the North suffered discrimination, too. In 1840, only four Northern states—Maine, Massachusetts, New Hampshire, and Vermont— granted equal voting rights to African American men. In New York State, all white males over age 21 could vote, but African American men had to own $250 worth of property to vote. All Northern states except Massachusetts barred African Americans from serving on juries. California, Illinois, Indiana, Ohio, and Iowa prohibited them from testifying against whites. Some states did not permit African Americans to sign binding contracts. Often, they had to show a certificate of freedom to obtain work.

Separation of races also existed in the North. Although laws did not keep African Americans and whites apart, custom did. Many white churches in the North required African Americans to sit in separate pews. Public schools were closed to African American children. In many ways, African Americans in the North were neither free nor slave.

Earning a Living. Because of the severe limits on free African Americans in the South, it might seem that earning a living there would have been more difficult. But free African Americans in the South were no worse off than those in the North. In fact, in some Southern cities, they did better financially.

A constant labor shortage in the South allowed many free African Americans to build businesses as craftworkers. For example, in 1850, Charleston had among its free African American workers 122 carpenters, 87 tailors, and 30 shoemakers. The city also had more than half a dozen African American innkeepers. A number of free African Americans became wealthy.

THOMAS DAY,
CABINET MAKER,

RETURNS his thanks for the patronage he has received, and wishes to inform his friends and the public that he has on hand, and intends keeping, a handsome supply of

Mahogony, Walnut and Stained FURNITURE,

the most fashionable, and common BED STEADS, &c. which he would be glad to sell very low. All orders in his line, in Repairing, Varnishing, &c. will be thankfully received and punctuallo attended to.

Jan. 17.   38

Day, a free African American, was a master craftworker. See "The Artist's View" for a picture of his work.

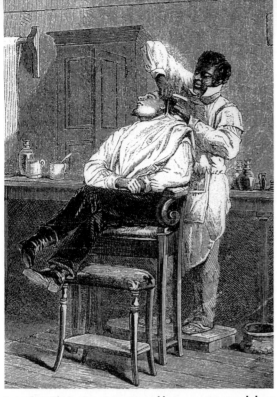

Some free African Americans were able to own stores and shops and served whites and African Americans.

Taking Another Look

1. How did laws limit the liberty of free African Americans in the mid-1800s?

2. How did immigration in the 1800s affect job opportunities for free African Americans in the North?

3. **Critical Thinking** Why might African Americans have been better treated in Europe than they were in the United States?

2 A FRAGILE FREEDOM
How did some free African Americans succeed?

Despite the obstacles that free African Americans faced, there were success stories in both the North and the South. Godfrey Brown of Cincinnati bought the freedom of his family for $2,350, purchased 550 acres [223 hectares] of land, and set up a shoemaking business. Thomy Lafon of New Orleans built a real estate fortune worth $500,000. Aaron Ashworth of Jefferson County, Texas, owned some 2,470 head of cattle and 4,578 acres [1,854 hectares] of land. These are only three of the many free African Americans who became successful business people in the mid-1800s.

Developing Businesses. A number of free African Americans became the managers of restaurants, barbershops, hotels, and other businesses. A few became **entrepreneurs**—people who risk money to earn more money. James Forten, for example, invented a device for handling sails. He then built a sail-making factory in Philadelphia that employed more than 50 African American and white workers. Another successful entrepreneur was Paul Cuffe.

In the North, most free African Americans did not do as well. Some worked as furniture makers, barbers, or tailors, or in other skilled crafts. Many were laborers or servants. But in addition to discrimination, African Americans faced competition from the immigrants who flooded the cities of the North beginning in the 1830s. Many of the new arrivals were poor farmers from Ireland. They usually had fewer skills than free African Americans. However, because they were white, they gradually crowded African Americans out for jobs and housing. Wrote Frederick Douglass in 1853:

> White men are becoming house-servants, cooks and stewards on vessels—at hotels. They are becoming porters, stevedores [dock-workers], . . . brick-makers, . . . barbers, so that the blacks can scarcely find the means of subsistence [support].

Paul Cuffe, who was born in 1759, went to sea at 16. After an adventurous life at sea, he decided to build his own fishing fleet. By 1806, Cuffe owned three ships, several smaller vessels, and a wharf and warehouse on Connecticut's Westport River. He hired African American crews to sail to Great Britain, the West Indies, Russia, and Africa. Cuffe believed that African Americans would be better off in Africa than in the United States, and he paid the costs of transporting a number of them in his ships.

Many African Americans who earned money in business helped finance the abolition movement that took shape in the 1800s. James Forten, for instance, contributed money to start *The Liberator,* a newspaper run by white **abolitionist** William Lloyd Garrison (see page 131). An abolitionist was a person who worked to end slavery.

Getting an Education.

Many free African Americans realized how important education was to success. In both the North and the South, they paid money out of their own pockets to educate themselves and their children.

Some teachers opened schools to educate African Americans. In 1833, townspeople burned down a Connecticut boarding school for girls when Quaker principal Prudence Crandall admitted African Americans. In spite of the dangers, teachers—African Americans and some whites—continued to set up schools, and African Americans continued to attend.

Free African Americans began attending colleges and universities, and several African American colleges were founded in the North (see map, page 233). Out of these schools came doctors, dentists, teachers, ministers, writers, and poets. They were in the forefront of the battle to abolish slavery.

In the years prior to the Civil War, free African Americans established some 32 newspapers, wrote hundreds of pamphlets and books, and delivered thousands of speeches and sermons. Their ranks included some of the great leaders of the abolition movement, such as Frederick Douglass and Frances Ellen Watkins Harper (see Chapter 13).

Mutual Aid.

As you have read, laws passed in the South during the 1800s prevented free African Americans from meeting together. But in Northern cities, free African Americans formed more than 45 mutual-aid societies to provide help to families in case of sickness or death. They established libraries and reading rooms, and offered lectures. Some of these societies later turned to helping runaway slaves resettle in the North.

Threats to Freedom.

As free African Americans became more vocal in their demands for equality, they faced harsh treatment in both North and South. In 1840, white mobs attacked free African American workers in Cincinnati. Frederick Douglass recalled Massachusetts train conductors beating him for sitting in all-white cars. There was also the constant threat of slave catchers waiting to pounce on free African Americans and sell them into slavery in the Deep South.

Migration and Colonization.

Some free African Americans supported migration to Canada. Most African Ameri-

COLORED SCHOOLS BROKEN UP, IN THE FREE STATES.

In places in the North, as this picture shows, some whites were as much opposed to the education of African American children as Southern whites were.

can leaders, however, opposed colonization, a plan to send African Americans back to Africa. In 1817, white Southerners, anxious to remove free African Americans, formed the American Colonization Society to set up a colony in Africa for them. President James Monroe helped negotiate the establishment of Liberia, on Africa's west coast, for this purpose. But few African Americans wanted to resettle in Liberia. The United States was their home.

As soon as the colonization society was founded, a meeting of some 3,000 in Philadelphia denounced these efforts to resettle free African Americans. A statement issued by the meeting mirrored the feelings of many free African Americans at the time.

> Resolved, That we never will separate ourselves voluntarily from the slave population of this country; they are our brethren by the ties of consanguinity [blood], of suffering, and of wrong.

Taking Another Look

1. How did free African Americans support education?

2. Why did most free African Americans oppose colonization in Africa?

3. **Critical Thinking**   Imagine you are a free African American in the early 1800s with a good job. Why might you be concerned about African Americans who are still enslaved?

LOOKING AHEAD

Free African Americans in the 1800s lived in the shadow of slavery and the reality of racism. Yet they kept the dream of freedom alive for enslaved African Americans who could not speak for themselves. The presence of free African Americans was a visible reminder of what African Americans could—and did—achieve outside of slavery. When a reform movement took shape in the United States in the 1840s, free African Americans were more than ready to speak out against slavery.

125

CLOSE UP: Chapter 12

Vela McClam advised the president of Hughes Missile Systems against spending hundreds of millions of dollars to merge with another company. The president listened. Reginald Lewis bought what is now TLC Beatrice International. Today, he controls part of the European snack-food market. Reggie and Bobbye Butts invested nearly $130,000 in a postal service franchise. In two and a half years, they were bringing in $24,000 a month in sales.

Each of these success stories involves an African American business leader. In the 1700s and 1800s, prejudice made it extremely difficult for African Americans to match the business success of a Paul Cuffe or a James Forten. But today, thanks to the Civil Rights Movement of the 1950s and 1960s, African Americans can be found in nearly every major U.S. corporation.

Many African Americans are climbing the corporate ladder—or founding their own multi-million-dollar operations. Yet, inequalities still exist. African American executives earn between 68 percent and 78 percent as much as their white counterparts earn. As a group, African American women earn about 84 cents for every dollar earned by an African American male.

The Who, What, Where of History

1. **Who** was James Forten?
2. **What** is discrimination?
3. **What** is an entrepreneur?
4. **Who** was Paul Cuffe?
5. **Who** were the abolitionists?
6. **Where** was a colony set up for free African Americans?

Making the Connection

1. What was the connection between immigration and the loss of jobs by free African Americans?
2. What was the connection between discrimination and the efforts to resettle African Americans in Africa?

Time Check

1. When was the American Colonization Society formed?
2. The free African American population of the United States increased by how much from 1790 to 1860?

What Would You Have Done?

1. If you had been Nancy Gardner Prince, what would you have done after experiencing the incident of prejudice in Boston? Would you have stayed in the United States or would you have tried to make a home in another country? Explain the reasons for your choice.

2. Imagine you are an African American entrepreneur in the 1850s. You want to help other African Americans.

Explain what you would do to be of the greatest benefit to other African Americans.

3. Imagine that you are a free African American in the early 1800s. You have just met Paul Cuffe, who has explained his plan for settling African Americans in Africa. He asks if you would like to take part in the plan. How would you respond to his offer?

4. Imagine that you are a free African American cabinetmaker in the 1840s. If you were offered the chance to open a new shop in either Charleston, South Carolina, or New York City, which would you choose? Be sure to explain the reason for your selection.

Thinking and Writing About History

1. Write a short play in which Nancy Gardner Prince and her husband, Nero, describe the lives of African Americans to some Russian servants of the czar.

2. Make a poster to advertise a meeting of African Americans to protest the efforts of the American Colonization Society.

Building Skills: Stating an Implied Topic Sentence

Darrell was angry at his friend Yolanda. "You said that I wasn't smart," he said. Yolanda denied it. "I never said that you were not smart." "Yes, you did. You said that there were only four smart kids in school—Martin, Kahlil, Lisa, and Tamara. So you implied that I am not smart."

To *imply* something is to say it indirectly. When you look for the main ideas in your reading, you will find that sometimes writers do not clearly state the main idea in a sentence. Sometimes they imply the main idea.

Read the following paragraph from Chapter 12:

A number of free African Americans became the managers of restaurants, barbershops, hotels, and other businesses. A few became entrepreneurs— people who risk money to earn more money. James Forten, for example, invented a device for handling sails. He then built a sail-making factory in Philadelphia that employed more than 50 African American and white workers. Another successful entrepreneur was Paul Cuffe.

The main idea of this paragraph, although not stated in a sentence, is clear: Some African Americans became successful by working for others; others were entrepreneurs who started their own businesses.

Now read the following paragraph. Write what you think is its implied main idea on a separate sheet of paper.

Laws passed in the South during the 1800s prevented free African Americans from meeting together. But in Northern cities, free African Americans formed more than 45 mutual-aid societies to provide help to families in case of sickness or death. They established libraries and reading rooms, and offered lectures. Some of these societies later turned to helping runaway slaves resettle in the North.

UNIT 5

From *Uncle Tom's Cabin*

CHALLENGES TO SLAVERY

(1800–1860)

$2,500
REWARD!

RANAWAY, from the Subscriber, residing in Mississippi county, Mo., on Monday the 5th inst., my
Negro Man named GEORGE.

Said negro is five feet ten inches high, of dark complexion, he plays well on the Violin and several other instruments. He is a shrewd, smart fellow and of a very affable countenance, and is twenty-five years of age. If said negro is taken and confined in St. Louis Jail, or brought to this county so that I get him, the above reward of $1,000 will be promptly paid.

JOHN MEANS.
Also, from Radford E. Stanley,

A NEGRO MAN SLAVE, NAMED NOAH,

Full 6 feet high; black complexion; full eyes; free spoken and intelligent; will weigh about 180 pounds; 32 years old; had with him 2 or 3 suits of clothes, white hat, short blue blanket coat, a pair of saddle bags, a pocket compass, and supposed to have $350 or $400 with him.

ALSO--A NEGRO MAN NAMED HAMP,

Of dark copper color, big thick lips, about 6 feet high, weighs about 175 pounds, 36 years old, with a scar in the forehead from the kick of a horse; had a lump on one of his wrists and is left-handed. Had with him two suits of clothes, one casinet or cloth coat and grey pants.

Also, Negro Man Slave named BOB,

Copper color, high cheek bones, 5 feet 11 inches high, weighs about 150 pounds, 22 years old, very white teeth and a space between the centre of the upper teeth. Had a blue blanket sack coat with red striped linsey lining. Supposed to have two suits of clothes with him; is a little lame in one ancle.

$1,000 will be given for George—$600 for Noah—$450 for Hamp—$450 for Bob if caught in a free State, or a reasonable compensation if caught in a Slave State, if delivered to the Subscribers in Miss. Co., Mo., or confined in Jail in St. Louis, so that we get them Refer to

**JOHN MEANS &
R. E. STANLEY.**

ST. LOUIS, August 23, 1852 (PLEASE STICK UP.)

Reward poster

William Lloyd Garrison's newspaper

THE LIBERATOR.

Unit 5 describes the abolition movement and how it brought the nation closer to war. Abolitionists, both free African Americans and whites, worked to bring an end to slavery by publicizing its evils. Through their newspapers, books, and speaking tours, they worked to influence **public opinion**—the collective beliefs of the people—against slavery. This strategy was similar to what reformers concerned with other problems in U.S. society were doing.

The Spirit of Reform. The years from 1820 to 1860 brought great changes to the United States. The nation was expanding rapidly across the continent. Immigrants were arriving in ever-increasing numbers from Europe. New roads, railroads, and canals carried goods from new factories to market. The nation was alive with economic progress.

Some Americans, however, saw a gloomier side to these years. In drunkenness, illiteracy, and slavery, they saw the nation's weaknesses. In a spirit born of the belief that Americans could accomplish anything they chose to do, these people set out to reform the nation. They formed organizations to end drunkenness, create asylums for the mentally ill, change prisons, promote **women's rights** as equal citizens, and end slavery.

Reform Movements. The temperance movement was one of the earliest attempts to reform U.S. society. By the 1820s, the nation's consumption of liquor was at an all-time high. In 1826, a group opposed to heavy drinking formed the American Society for the Promotion of Temperance. The organization grew rapidly, with many religious leaders, doctors, and business people among its members. They feared the damage that alcoholism was doing to individuals' health, to the family, and to the nation's economy. In its first 15 years, the temperance movement persuaded many Americans to cut back on their drinking or to stop entirely.

The early successes of the temperance movement inspired other reformers. Teacher and writer Dorothea Dix worked to improve the care of the mentally ill. She visited prisons throughout the nation and reported that the mentally ill were imprisoned as criminals. Through her writings, she advocated the building of asylums to care for and treat the mentally ill.

Prisons became another target of reformers. They pushed for the building of new prisons where they hoped prisoners could reform their lives.

Reformers also brought change to the field of education. Up to this time, an elementary school education was available in most parts of the country, only to those who could pay for it. Now, reformers urged that schools be tax-supported and

---

An African American Speaks

Those who profess to favor freedom, and yet deprecate [disapprove of] agitation [stirring people up], are men who want crops without plowing up the ground, they want rain without thunder and lightning. They want the ocean without the awful roar of its many waters.

—Frederick Douglass,
Abolitionist Leader

129

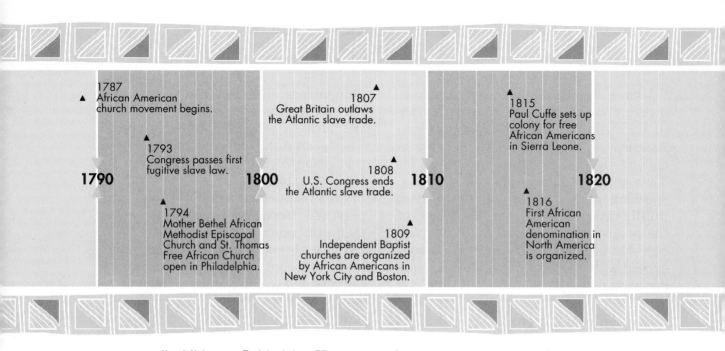

1787
African American church movement begins.

1793
Congress passes first fugitive slave law.

1790

1794
Mother Bethel African Methodist Episcopal Church and St. Thomas Free African Church open in Philadelphia.

1800

1807
Great Britain outlaws the Atlantic slave trade.

1808
U.S. Congress ends the Atlantic slave trade.

1809
Independent Baptist churches are organized by African Americans in New York City and Boston.

1810

1815
Paul Cuffe sets up colony for free African Americans in Sierra Leone.

1816
First African American denomination in North America is organized.

1820

open to all children. Guided by Horace Mann, Massachusetts became the model for other states' reforms. Mann revised the course of study, lengthened the school day, and raised teachers' salaries. Public high schools also appeared during this period.

At the time, these improvements in education, as in other areas of U.S. society, were of little benefit to African Americans. But in years to come, the principle of free public education for all would become central to their fight for justice (see page 323).

Early Antislavery Efforts. Antislavery efforts drew their strength from the reforming spirit of the period. The first antislavery movements did not attack slavery directly. Instead, they hoped to encourage owners to free large numbers of African American slaves.

Before the American Revolution, most white colonists did not object to the idea of holding African Americans as slaves (see page 37). During the Revolution, however, some people's attitudes began to change, in the South as well as in the North. The Northwest Ordinance of 1787 barred slavery from the territories north of the Ohio River. By the early 1800s, the Northern states had ended slavery. In 1808, the U.S. Congress ended the Atlantic slave trade. The year before, Great Britain had abolished its Atlantic slave trade. To many people, slavery seemed a dying institution that would gradually fade away on its own.

Some early reformers did not believe that African Americans and white Americans could live peacefully together in the United States. They looked to Africa as a place to establish colonies for freed African Americans. In 1815, Paul Cuffe, the wealthy African American sea captain (see page 124), spent his own money in an unsuccessful attempt to set up a colony of African Americans in Sierra Leone, on the west coast of Africa. In the 1820s, the American Colonization Society, founded by Southerners as a way of removing free African Americans from the South, set up

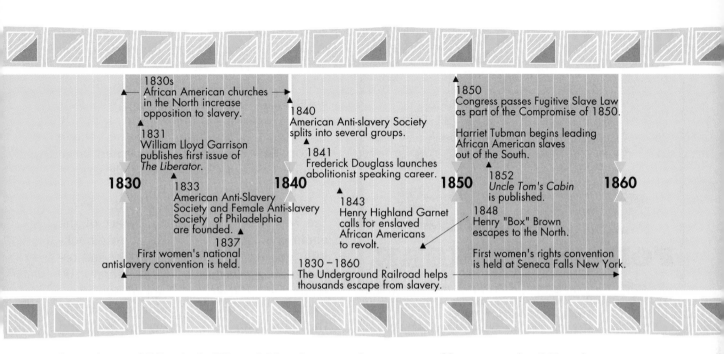

1830s
African American churches in the North increase opposition to slavery.

1831
William Lloyd Garrison publishes first issue of *The Liberator.*

1833
American Anti-Slavery Society and Female Anti-slavery Society of Philadelphia are founded.

1837
First women's national antislavery convention is held.

1840
American Anti-slavery Society splits into several groups.

1841
Frederick Douglass launches abolitionist speaking career.

1843
Henry Highland Garnet calls for enslaved African Americans to revolt.

1830 – 1860
The Underground Railroad helps thousands escape from slavery.

1850
Congress passes Fugitive Slave Law as part of the Compromise of 1850.

Harriet Tubman begins leading African American slaves out of the South.

1852
Uncle Tom's Cabin is published.

1848
Henry "Box" Brown escapes to the North.

First women's rights convention is held at Seneca Falls New York.

1830   1840   1850   1860

the colony of Liberia in West Africa (see page 125).

The trouble with these plans was that hardly any free African Americans wanted to relocate to Africa. By 1830, only about 1,400 African Americans had settled in Liberia. Populated mostly by native Africans, Liberia survived to become one of the few independent African nations of the late 1800s.

William Lloyd Garrison and the Abolitionist Movement. How could slavery be ended? A young white man from Boston thought he had the answer. On January 1, 1831, William Lloyd Garrison published the first issue of a weekly newspaper called *The Liberator.* On the front page of the first issue, Garrison made a promise: "I will not equivocate [beat around the bush]—I will not excuse—I will not retreat a single inch—AND I WILL BE HEARD."

What Garrison wanted was simply stated—the immediate end to slavery. All enslaved African Americans should be set free at once. No money should be given to their "owners" to repay them for their lost property.

Garrison and those who agreed with him were called abolitionists. The main abolitionist organization was the American Anti-Slavery Society. Abolitionists were the most radical arm of the antislavery movement. Other antislavery supporters, called gradualists, opposed slavery and wanted to do away with it. However, they felt a slower, more orderly way should be found.

Most abolitionists were whites, with the greatest number in New England. As the movement gained strength, however, free African Americans joined. Some of them, such as ex-slaves Frederick Douglass and Sojourner Truth, became its most effective spokespersons.

At first, the abolitionists hoped to advance their cause by persuasion, as the temperance movement had done. By 1840, however, it was clear that something more was needed. At this point, the American Anti-Slavery Society divided

131

135,000 SETS, 270,000 VOLUMES SOLD.

UNCLE TOM'S CABIN

FOR SALE HERE.

AN EDITION FOR THE MILLION, COMPLETE IN 1 Vol., PRICE 37 1-2 CENTS.
"   "   IN GERMAN, IN 1 Vol., PRICE 50 CENTS.
"   .   "   IN 2 Vols,. CLOTH, 6 PLATES, PRICE $1.50.
SUPERB ILLUSTRATED EDITION, IN 1 Vol., WITH 153 ENGRAVINGS,
PRICES FROM $2.50 TO $5.00.

The Greatest Book of the Age.

Why was the publication of *Uncle Tom's Cabin* important to the abolitionists?

into several groups. The most radical, led by Garrison, urged that people have nothing to do with a government that allowed slavery. He argued, for example, that people should not vote, hold office, or use the courts.

Other people saw political action as the best way to attack slavery. They joined such antislavery parties as the **Free-Soil party**, and the **Liberty party**, which were able to affect the outcome of elections in some states. These parties tended to focus on preventing the spread of slavery to new territories, rather than on abolishing it entirely.

In 1852, the antislavery movement received a tremendous boost with the publication of *Uncle Tom's Cabin*, a novel by white author Harriet Beecher Stowe.

Stowe described the lives of an enslaved African American family, showing in particular the cruelty of the brutal overseer. The novel was a huge success. It was soon turned into a play that was performed around the country—except in the South. More than any other single factor, *Uncle Tom's Cabin* turned large numbers of Americans against slavery.

The Women's Movement. From the beginning, women were part of the abolitionist movement. They wrote booklets, got signatures on petitions, and organized conventions. More than 100 women's antislavery societies were formed. Yet women could not take part in the American Anti-Slavery Society and the other leading abolitionist organizations. Membership in these groups was limited to men. According to custom, women could not even speak before audiences that included men.

Two South Carolina women challenged these practices. Sarah and Angelina Grimké had been born into a wealthy slave-owning family but moved to the North and became abolitionists. In 1837, when Angelina was attacked for speaking before audiences of men and women, Sarah wrote a booklet defending her sister's action. She went on to address other inequalities in the treatment of women. Women, she argued, should not be treated differently from men.

In 1840, three Americans sent to England to represent the United States at an antislavery convention were turned away because they were women. As women, they had to sit in the spectators' gallery, where the wives of the male delegates also sat.

One of the rejected delegates, Lucretia Mott, met another American woman at the convention, Elizabeth Cady Stanton,

Women in the United States in the 1800s had few rights. For example, married women who worked outside the home had no control over the money they earned.

wife of a delegate. As the two women talked about the treatment of women in the United States, they decided that something had to be done. Eight years later, in 1848, Mott and Stanton organized the first women's rights convention at Seneca Falls, New York.

At that time, women had few legal rights. Although single women could own property, married women could not. When a woman married, her husband gained complete control of her property. If she worked, her wages belonged to her husband. She could not make a contract or sue for damages. In a divorce, the husband usually was given custody of any children. It was very difficult for women to attend college, and impossible for them to become doctors or lawyers.

The convention drew up the Seneca Falls Declaration. It spelled out the rights that women did not have but were entitled to. Soon other groups around the country were working for women's rights, and some laws began to change.

Because they also were active in the antislavery movement, most women's rights supporters felt that slavery was the issue that should be attended to first. However, the spirit of reform was not strong enough to end slavery. Instead, as abolitionists worked to end slavery, tensions increased, and the threat of war grew greater.

Taking Another Look

1. What problems of U.S. society did reformers attack in the first half of the 1800s?

2. What was the goal of the abolitionists versus the gradualists?

3. **Critical Thinking** Besides the antislavery movement, how might the women's rights movement and educational reform have long-term importance for African Americans? Explain.

Pennsylvania Hall set afire by anti-abolitionists

Abolitionists

(1800–1860)

THINKING ABOUT THE CHAPTER

How did African Americans work to end slavery in the United States?

On December 4, 1833, 63 delegates from 11 states walked along Philadelphia's Walnut Street toward Adelphi Hall. Bystanders flung insults at them, and police stood guard to prevent violence. At the request of city officials, the delegates held all their meetings in daylight hours to avoid attacks under the cover of darkness.

Thus began the American Anti-Slavery Society. Its purpose was to coordinate the activities of white and African American abolitionists. For three days, the band of reformers pounded out a program of action. They called for the immediate abolition of slavery and the elevation of the condition of African Americans.

William Lloyd Garrison, the strong-minded, radical white abolitionist leader, dominated the convention. Most of the delegates were white, but African Americans such as James Forten, the Philadelphia businessman and abolitionist; James C. McCrummell, a Philadelphia dentist;

Robert Purvis, a Philadelphia merchant; and James G. Barbadoes, a Boston clothing-store owner, took active roles in the proceedings.

On December 5, a committee of delegates drew up a **Declaration of Sentiments**—a statement of liberation for the more than 2 million African Americans living in slavery. The convention unanimously approved it.

Within a short time, dozens of agents of the American Anti-Slavery Society were spreading the word of abolitionism in the North and South. They helped form local groups and raised money for the cause. With that money, antislavery pamphlets and periodicals poured off the presses. Antislavery sentiments, long simmering, were about to boil over.

1 NEW DIRECTIONS
▼ How did African Americans take part in the early abolition movement?

A handful of women—African American and white—attended the opening sessions of the American Anti-Slavery Society. No one asked them to speak. No one asked them to sign the Declaration of Sentiments. But women were ready to join the abolitionist movement as active members, and they started an antislavery society of their own.

On December 14, 1833, the Female Anti-Slavery Society of Philadelphia was born. Seven African Americans were among the 18 women who signed the society's constitution. They included Sarah Douglass, Quaker principal of a school for African Americans, and Harriett, Sarah, and Margarette Forten, the daughters of James Forten.

The women abolitionists of Philadelphia worked with women around the country to form a network of women's antislavery societies. In 1837, they held their first national convention in Boston. More than 100 women from ten states attended. The next year, they held a second convention in Philadelphia's Pennsylvania Hall.

The sight of African American and white women walking together inflamed racial hatred among some whites. Mobs threatened the women and hurled rocks through the windows of Pennsylvania Hall. When the mobs failed to break the women's courage, they set fire to the hall. The delegates responded with a public statement. It read in part:

> Resolved, That prejudice against color is the very spirit of slavery. . . . That it is, therefore, the duty of abolitionists to identify themselves with these oppressed Americans, by sitting with them in places of worship, by appearing with them in our streets, by . . . visting them at their homes and encouraging them to visit us, receiving them as we do our white fellow citizens.

Moving Toward Action. Some antislavery sentiment had existed in colonial times. Two African American New Englanders, Prince Hall and Abijah Prince, and a white New Englander, Samuel Sewall, were among the leading abolitionists in the colonies. The Quakers (see page 59) were the first religious group in the 13 colonies to speak out against slavery. Most early abolitionists were mild in their protests. They feared that a more **militant,** or aggressive, approach would turn away supporters.

After 1830, however, with the growth of slavery in the Cotton Belt, abolitionism took on a new spirit. African American and white abolitionists loudly demanded

1833 American Anti-Slavery Society is formed.
Female Anti-Slavery Society of Philadelphia is founded.

1834 Homes of New York City African American abolitionists are burned.

1837 First women's national antislavery convention is held.

1841 Frederick Douglass launches abolitionist speaking career.

1843 Henry Highland Garnet calls for a slave revolt.

that Americans face the slavery question now—not some time in the future. David Walker ushered in the new era with his militant *Appeal* in 1829 (see page 110). William Lloyd Garrison followed close behind in 1831 with his fiery newspaper, the *Liberator*. The stage was set for a showdown between proslavery and antislavery forces.

Reactions to Abolitionism. The reactions of proslavery white Americans to abolitionists were sometimes violent. White abolitionists risked public insults, the loss of jobs, and worse. In 1836, in Cincinnati, Ohio, the office of James G. Birney's antislavery newspaper was attacked. The next year mobs in Alton, Illinois, killed Elijah P. Lovejoy, publisher of an antislavery newspaper. Mobs had already destroyed his press three times before. The commitment of white abolitionists like Lovejoy earned them high respect among African Americans.

African American abolitionists also faced great risks. In 1834, for example, mobs in New York City burned the homes of 20 of them to the ground. Everywhere, African American abolitionists might be marked for arrest or even murder—the suspected fate of David Walker.

Differences Among Abolitionists. While all abolitionists agreed that slavery must be ended, they could not agree about how to achieve their goal. One especially important issue was whether the abolitionist movement should be as radical as leaders like Garrison wanted it to be. Although members of the American Anti-Slavery Society called for an immediate end to slavery, Garrison felt they were not militant enough. He attacked the U.S. government for allowing slavery and refused to vote. He criticized churches for not taking a clear stand. He linked abolitionism to the movement for women's rights. He wanted women to hold office in the American Anti-Slavery Society.

By the late 1830s, splits occurred in the abolitionist movement because of these and other differences. Moderates and those who believed in working through political action were at odds with Garrison. On the other hand, abolitionists who advocated the use of force rejected Garrison's emphasis on nonviolent change. Still another group decided to focus on winning certain rights for slaves rather than eliminating slavery itself.

In the 1840s, new patterns emerged in the abolitionist movement. Joining free African Americans were a group of new leaders—former slaves with a powerful message to send to the world.

Taking Another Look

1. How did women contribute to the growth of abolitionism?

2. Why did splits develop within the abolitionist movement?

Why did a mob destroy Elijah P. Lovejoy's newspaper and murder him? Why do you think abolitionists were so hated?

3. **Critical Thinking** Why might many white women have been sympathetic to the struggle to end slavery?

2 NEW VOICES

How did former African American slaves help the cause of abolition?

In January 1842, a strikingly handsome speaker stepped before the annual meeting of the New England Anti-Slavery Society. He stood six feet tall with broad shoulders. In a steady voice, he declared:

I stand before the immense assembly this evening as a thief and a robber. I stole this head, these limbs, this body from my master, and ran off with them.

The speaker was a runaway slave named Frederick Douglass.

Stories to Tell. The tales told by former slaves such as Douglass horrified and fascinated audiences. Fugitive slave laws—laws requiring states to return runaways—threatened their very freedom. Yet they spoke. Henry Highland Garnet explained: "I was born in slavery and have escaped, to tell you, and others, what the monster [slavery] has done, and is still doing."

Henry Highland Garnet fled slavery in Maryland while he was still a child and made his way to New York City. There he received an education at the African Free School. Garnet later graduated from New York's Oneida Institute and began his career as a minister. In 1843, he became the pastor of a mostly white Presbyterian church in Troy, New York. In 1881, the United States government appointed Garnet as its representative to Liberia, a nation that had been set up in West Africa in

137

1822 as a way to relocate African Americans to Africa. He died in the capital city of Monrovia a short time after his arrival.

In 1843, the 28-year-old Garnet delivered a fiery speech to a Buffalo, New York, audience. It matched the passion of Walker's *Appeal*. Addressing enslaved peoples everywhere, Garnet cried out:

Brethren, arise, arise! Strike for your lives and liberties. Now is the day and the hour. Let every slave throughout the land do this and the days of slavery are numbered. Rather die freemen than live to be slaves.

Such strong words shocked and frightened some white audiences. But Garnet spoke for a group of African Americans impatient with the slow pace of change. Not all went as far as Garnet in calling for rebellion. But they wasted no words and spared no feelings in driving home the evils of slavery. "I intend to make full use of you," wrote Frederick Douglass to his former owner, "as a weapon to assail [attack] the system of slavery."

The Orator From Slave Row. When Douglass spoke, people listened. He made them feel the sting of the overseer's whip, the hunger for enough food to eat, and the grief of a mother seeing her child sold away.

Why would the Boston police and anti-abolitionists try to stop Frederick Douglass from speaking?

Frederick Douglass was born Frederick Augustus Washington Bailey, a slave on a Maryland plantation. When his owner refused him an education, he tricked white playmates into teaching him the alphabet. Later, he was sent to a new owner in Baltimore, whose wife helped him with his reading and writing. By age 17, Douglass proved so troublesome that his owner sent him to a slave-breaker named Edward Covey. There, recalled Douglass, "I reached the point at which I was not afraid to die." At that moment he wrestled Covey to the ground. Shamefaced, Covey kept the incident to himself.

At age 21, Douglass was working in a shipyard. He disguised himself as a sailor and ran away to New Bedford, Massachusetts. There, to escape capture, he changed his last name from Bailey to Douglass. In 1841, he began to lecture to audiences about his life as a slave.

Douglass's fame as a speaker grew. He traveled abroad to speak to huge antislavery audiences in London and the West Indies. He called for justice for all oppressed peoples regardless of their race, nationality, or sex. In 1846, he told a London audience: "You may rely upon me as one who will never desert the cause of the poor, no matter whether black or white."

Women Speakers. After the late 1830s, former slave women began speaking out, too. Perhaps the most effective woman abolitionist was Sojourner Truth.

Sojourner Truth was born Isabella Baumfree in New York State about 1797. Freed by a New York law in 1827, she became deeply religious and changed her name to Sojourner Truth. She traveled to abolitionist meetings throughout the North and Midwest. Although she could neither read nor write, she became a spellbinding orator and the most effective of women abolitionists. After the Civil War, she became a champion of women's rights.

Other women joined Truth in speaking out. They included Mary Ann Shadd, Mary Bibb, and Sarah Parker Remond, to name a few. They joined with Frederick Douglass, Henry Highland Garnet, and hundreds of others in seeking to bring a swift end to slavery.

Taking Another Look

1. What were two purposes for the founding of the Female Anti-Slavery Society of Philadelphia?

2. List four of the great African American abolitionists of the mid-1800s.

3. How did Douglass and Truth broaden the struggle beyond slavery?

4. **Critical Thinking** Douglass once remarked "justice to the Negro is safety to the nation." Explain what you think he may have meant by this comment.

THE NORTH STAR.

VOL. 1. NO. 1. ROCHESTER, N. Y. FRIDAY, DECEMBER 3, 1847. WHOLE

Frederick Douglass published the first issue of his newspaper in 1847.

3 TAKING ACTION

▼ What were some other tactics African Americans used to oppose slavery besides public speaking?

Born free in Baltimore, Maryland, Frances Ellen Watkins faced a difficult life. Orphaned at an early age, she was raised by an aunt and uncle. They sent her to a school for free African Americans so that she could support herself. Beginning at 13, Watkins took jobs as a servant, a seamstress, and a teacher. But her first love was writing.

In the 1840s and 1850s, Watkins turned her pen to the antislavery cause. She wrote under the name F. E. W. Harper (Harper was her married name). By the late 1850s, she was one of the most popular African American poets in the United States. Her verses did much to advance abolitionism. "Bury Me in a Free Land" demanded the title of one poem.

> I could not rest if I heard the tread
> Of a coffle-gang . . .
> And the mother's shriek of wild despair
> Rise like a curse on the trembling air.

The Power of the Pen. Other African Americans also battled slavery with their pens. William Wells Brown wrote histories of the African American people and dozens of antislavery pamphlets. Many former slaves, including Frederick Douglass, published their stories in best-selling slave narratives (see page 108).

LADIES' DEPARTMENT.

"Am I not a Woman and a Sister?"

White Lady, happy, proud and free,
Lend awhile thine ear to me ;
Let the Negro Mother's wail
Turn thy pale cheek still more pale.
Can the Negro Mother joy
Over this her captive boy,
Which in bondage and in tears,
For a life of wo she rears ?
Though she bears a Mother's name,
A Mother's rights she may not claim ;
For the white man's will can part,
Her darling from her bursting heart.

From the Genius of Universal Emancipation.
LETTERS ON SLAVERY.—No. III.

William Lloyd Garrison's paper, *The Liberator,* tried to attract women to the abolitionist cause.

Harriet Beecher Stowe, the author of *Uncle Tom's Cabin,* benefited from the narratives. She had an audience more than ready for *Uncle Tom's Cabin.*

In the North, African American journalists built upon the tradition started by

THE FUGITIVE'S SONG,

WORDS
composed and respectfully dedicated in token of confident esteem to

FREDERICK DOUGLASS
A Graduate from the
"PECULIAR INSTITUTION"
For his fearless advocacy, signal ability and wonderful success in behalf of
HIS BROTHERS IN BONDS.
(and to the FUGITIVES FROM SLAVERY in the)
FREE STATES & CANADAS.
by their friend
JESSE HUTCHINSON JUNr

BOSTON. Published by HENRY PRENTISS 33 Court St.

The cover of an abolitionist song sheet shows Frederick Douglass escaping from slavery.

Freedom's Journal (see page 110). In the mid-1800s, antislavery newspapers were being published in 17 African American communities in the North. One of the most famous was *The North Star,* published by Frederick Douglass. Even though most journals failed for lack of funds, while they published, they drove home two themes—equality and freedom for African Americans.

Committees and Raising Money. Following a long tradition of self-help, African American mutual-aid societies formed committees and raised funds to promote antislavery causes. Some organizations sponsored lectures by famous abolitionists. A few groups used the profits from such activities to buy the freedom of family members of escaped African American slaves.

The self-help societies also set up legal committees to defend runaways from being taken under the fugitive slave laws. John Mercer Langston, a lawyer who had been born a slave, took the struggle further. He argued that African Americans should be given the right to vote.

Legal aid committees and lawyers such as Langston turned the antislavery cause from a moral battle into a political battle. They said that slavery was not only evil, it was contrary to democracy. They demanded more than abolition. They also demanded that African Americans be equal citizens under the law.

Taking Another Look

1. What were some of the ways that African Americans fought slavery?

2. What political demands did African American abolitionists begin to make in the mid-1800s?

3. **Critical Thinking** It has been said that the pen is mightier than the sword. Do you think that abolitionists would have achieved more through armed rebellions than they did through antislavery writings? Explain.

LOOKING AHEAD

From the 1830s on, African American and white abolitionists bombarded the nation with meetings, demonstrations, speeches, and newspapers calling for an end to slavery. Meanwhile, the most direct attack on slavery came through committees set up to help African American slaves escape and guide them safely to the North. A Mississippi governor claimed that between 1810 and 1850 the South lost some 100,000 slaves, valued at more than $30 million.

CLOSE UP: Chapter 13

I have ploughed and planted and gathered into barns, and no man could head [do better than] me! And ain't I a woman? . . . I have borne thirteen children, and seen them most all sold off to slavery. . . . And ain't I a woman?

Sojourner Truth spoke these words at a women's rights convention in 1851. Like many other women abolitionists, former slave Sojourner Truth saw the connection between slavery and the lack of rights for women. She joined others—African Americans and whites, women and men—in demanding full citizenship and equality for all.

In 1863, a petition to enact what became the 13th Amendment ending slavery was started by the Women's Loyal National League and supported by other abolitionists. But after the Civil War, a split developed within the movement. Feminists felt strongly that women's rights should be included in the 14th and 15th amendments. Others feared that this issue might endanger the passage of these amendments.

About the 14th Amendment, Frederick Douglass counseled: "This hour belongs to the negro." To this, Elizabeth Cady Stanton hotly replied: "Do you believe the African race is composed entirely of males?" The debate over women's suffrage continued until 1920 and passage of the 19th Amendment.

The Who, What, Where of History

1. **Who** was Sarah Douglass?
2. **Who** was William Lloyd Garrison?
3. **What** was *Uncle Tom's Cabin*?
4. **What** was the Declaration of Sentiments?
5. **What** does the term *militant* mean?
6. **Who** was Frederick Douglass?
7. **Who** was Sojourner Truth?

Making the Connection

What was the link between the women's rights movement and the antislavery movement?

Time Check

1. In what year was the American Anti-Slavery Society formed?
2. When did the first women's national antislavery convention take place?

What Would You Have Done?

1. Suppose that you were a middle-class American living in a northern city between 1820 and 1860. Which reform movement would you have worked for? Explain.
2. Would you have supported William Lloyd Garrison in his call for nonviolent change or would you have agreed with his critics? Explain the reasons for your decisions.

Thinking and Writing About History

1. Write your own *Declaration of Sentiments*. Include at least three reasons to abolish slavery.

2. Imagine that you were in the audience of the New England Anti-Slavery Society when Frederick Douglass spoke in 1842. Write a letter to a good friend or to a relative describing Douglass, his speech, and the effect his words had on you.

3. Imagine that you are an abolitionist in 1835. An important merchant in your town objects to the idea of founding an antislavery organization. He uses the following argument:

[W]e are not such fools as not to know that slavery is a great evil, a great wrong. But it was consented to by the founders of our Republic. It was provided for in the Constitution of our Union. A great portion of the property of the Southerners is invested [in it]; and the business of the North, as well as the South has become adjusted to it. . . . We cannot afford to let you and your associates succeed in your endeavor to overthrow slavery. It is not a matter of principle with us. It is a matter of business necessity.

Write a response to his argument.

Building Skills: Recognizing a Generalization

People who study and write about history are in some ways our official memory. It is their job to help us experience and understand events of the past. However, we don't want them to present us with a book containing every newspaper, every lecture, every debate from a time period—we want a shortened version.

As historians (and other writers) make their decisions about what to put in a book and what to leave out, they *generalize* about the events or trends of the past. A generalization is a broad conclusion that is based on many facts that are related to one another.

Here is an example of a generalization that could be made after reading Unit 4's "The Big Picture": "The nation was alive with progress." The sentences below are examples of some of the facts that support this generalization.

The nation was rapidly expanding its boundaries across the continent. Immigrants were arriving in ever increasing numbers from Europe. New roads, railroads, and canals carried goods from new factories to market.

It is not always easy to recognize a generalization. You should look for *broad* (as opposed to specific) and *summarizing* sentences (as opposed to examples).

On a separate sheet of paper, write the numbers of the sentences below that are generalizations.

1. The homes of New York City African American abolitionists were burned in 1834.

2. William Lloyd Garrison was strong-minded and courageous.

3. Reformers were strong-minded and courageous people.

4. In the 1800s, women in the United States had few of the rights of men.

5. Sojourner Truth worked against slavery and for women's rights.

Harriet Tubman (left) with some of the people she helped

Escaping from Slavery
(1800–1860)

THINKING ABOUT THE CHAPTER

How did African American slaves flee the South?

In 1846, two African American slaves in Macon, Georgia, got permission from their owners to marry. The couple— Ellen and William Craft—were skilled workers. Ellen was hired out as a seamstress. William's owner hired him out as a cabinetmaker. Neither owner treated the two badly. Ellen, however, feared having a child who might be sold away from them, so she plotted a way for the couple to escape.

Ellen was the light-skinned daughter of a white planter and an enslaved African American mother. She proposed dressing up as William's *male* owner and leading them out of the South. William's owner allowed him to earn money as a waiter at a local hotel, so he had some savings. Ellen persuaded William to use some of the money to buy men's clothes for her to wear. They would still have enough money to pay for their trip to the North.

In December 1848, they were ready. Ellen, who could neither read nor write, put her right arm in a sling so that she would not be expected to sign her name. She bandaged her jaw so that she could not speak and give herself away. Looking at her, no one could doubt that she was an invalid planter headed north for medical treatment accompanied by a loyal servant.

Ellen acted every inch a planter, walking with a manly swagger. The couple booked first-class passage on boats and trains and stayed at the best hotels. In January 1849, they arrived in Philadelphia. Here, the Crafts met abolitionist William Wells Brown, who guided them to Boston and safety.

From the earliest days of slavery, thousands of African Americans escaped to freedom, by one means or another. Some traveled unaided like the Crafts, but from the 1830s to the 1860s, many more traveled by Underground Railroad.

1 PATH TO FREEDOM
▼ What were the risks for those who ran
▼ or used the Underground Railroad?

In 1848, an African American slave in Richmond, Virginia, named Henry Brown stepped into a specially made box and had a friend nail it shut. The friend then shipped the box to the office of an anti-slavery committee in Philadelphia.

Twenty-six hours later, the wooden box arrived at the committee's office. Four abolitionists pried off the lid. One of them, the African American William Still, long remembered Brown's words. Still later wrote: "Rising up in his box, he reached out his hand, saying, 'How do you do, gentlemen?'"

After his spectacular escape, Brown became famous as Henry "Box" Brown. He joined others who had escaped slavery, including Ellen and William Craft, on lecture tours. Their appearances helped abolitionists raise money to bring other African Americans to freedom.

Look for the "Drinking Gourd." Some African American slaves fled the South to avoid the auction block. Others wanted to find a loved one or to escape

What did Henry "Box" Brown's escape from slavery show about African Americans' desire for freedom?

1793 Congress passes a fugitive slave law.

1830s–1860s The Underground Railroad helps hundreds of African American slaves escape.

1848 Henry "Box" Brown escapes to the North.

1849 Ellen and William Craft escape to the North.

1850 Congress passes Fugitive Slave Law as part of the Compromise of 1850.

Harriet Tubman begins leading African American slaves out of the South.

the whip of a cruel overseer. Most, however, slipped away just to find freedom.

Planters tried to keep slaves ignorant of geography, but most slaves knew the magic word *North*. To head north, they searched the evening sky for the "Drinking Gourd," or Big Dipper. In this way, they found the North Star—their guide to the North. On starless nights, they felt for moss on the north side of trees.

Slave owners often used packs of dogs to hunt down runaways. If the runaways refused to halt, their pursuers might shoot them. Some slaves chose death over the brutal punishment that awaited them if they were caught.

Slaves knew the risks of running away. They had seen runaways crippled so that they could not flee again. Still, many African American slaves ran. "Many of dem had no idea where dey going," recalled former slave Edward Lycurgas. "But, one and all, dey had a good strong notion [desire] to see what it was like to own your own body."

The Underground Railroad. The obstacles faced by African Americans who wished to escape aroused sympathy among some whites. Northern Quakers were the first to shelter runaways. Others joined the Quakers when Southern slave owners convinced Congress to pass a federal fugitive slave law in 1793.

Early in the 1800s, African American and white abolitionists set up an informal network to protect runaways from capture. By the early 1830s, this network had grown into the **Underground Railroad**, a system aimed at helping slaves flee the South. The "tracks" of this railroad consisted of country roads, backwoods trails, and rivers. Its "stations" were homes where runaway slaves could receive food and shelter. Its "conductors" were abolitionists, both African American and white, who defied federal and state laws to guide slaves to freedom in the North and Canada.

Antislavery societies sent agents into the South to tell African American slaves about the Underground Railroad. The agents posed as peddlers, map makers, and census takers. Some agents were daring escaped slaves on "return runs" to the South to help others. From 1830 to 1860, perhaps 2,500 slaves a year took the Railroad to freedom.

A Dangerous Operation. From their first stop on the Underground Railroad to their last, slaves were in constant risk of capture. They traveled at night and slept during the day. They waded through streams to cover their tracks. Mothers muffled the cries of their children.

Agents and conductors faced danger, too. White abolitionists who were caught in the South helping slaves escape risked being sent to prison. Calvin Fairbanks of Kentucky served over 17 years in jail for

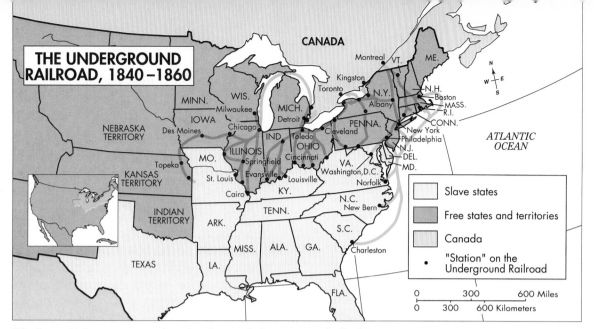

THE UNDERGROUND RAILROAD, 1840–1860

CANADA

Montreal · VT. · ME.

Kingston
Toronto · N.Y. · N.H.
· Albany · Boston
· MASS.
MINN. · WIS. · R.I.
· Milwaukee · MICH. · CONN.
IOWA · Detroit · PENNA. · New York
NEBRASKA · Chicago · Cleveland · Philadelphia
TERRITORY · Des Moines · IND. · Toledo · N.J.
· OHIO · DEL.
ILLINOIS · Cincinnati · MD.
· Springfield · VA.
MO. · Evansville · Washington,D.C.
Topeka · St. Louis · Louisville · Norfolk
KANSAS · Cairo · KY. · N.C.
TERRITORY · New Bern
INDIAN · TENN.
TERRITORY · ARK. · S.C.
· MISS. · ALA. · GA. · Charleston
TEXAS · LA.
· FLA.

ATLANTIC
OCEAN

Slave states

Free states and territories

Canada

• "Station" on the Underground Railroad

0   300   600 Miles
0   300   600 Kilometers

Why do you think many escapees chose Canada instead of remaining in the North?

delivering slaves to Levi Coffin, one of the Quaker founders of the Underground Railroad. Elijah Anderson died in a Kentucky prison for the same offense.

African American agents faced higher penalties. Slave owners placed a price on the heads of some. David Ruggles, head of the New York Vigilance Committee, which aided runaway slaves, regularly changed residence to avoid kidnappers. A judge ordered Samuel Burris, a free African American agent in Delaware, to be sold at auction. Luckily, the highest bid came from a white abolitionist.

Conductors in the North. From the start, free African Americans in the North took a leading role in sheltering runaways. Two business owners in Pennsylvania— Robert Purvis of Philadelphia and William Whipper of Columbia—kept stations on the Railroad. Purvis hid runaway slaves in a room of his house reached only by a trapdoor. Whipper shipped runaways

Steubenville, Ohio, on the opposite shore of the Ohio River, was a magnet for African Americans fleeing from slavery at this crossing on the river.

north in the false end of a railroad car he owned. Frederick Douglass and Henry Highland Garnet also kept busy stations.

One of the best-known African American conductors of the Underground Railroad was William Still. Some 2,000 slaves passed through his station.

William Still escaped slavery when his mother fled from Maryland to New Jersey with as many of her children as she could carry. Here, she joined Still's father, and they saved money to buy the rest of their children. At age 23, William Still moved to Philadelphia to find work. He took a leading role in the Philadelphia Society for the Abolition of Slavery. Still helped push the city's Underground Railroad routes farther north and deeper into the South. His activities led him to be described as the "president of the Underground Railroad." In 1872, he published a firsthand account of African American abolitionists in action in *The Underground Railroad.*

Still's book documents one of the most courageous figures of the Underground Railroad—Harriet Tubman. Southerners called her a criminal. African American slaves called her Moses.

Taking Another Look

1. What risks did African American slaves face in running away?

2. In what ways was the Underground Railroad like a real railroad?

3. **Critical Thinking** Would you have worked for the Underground Railroad? Explain. Consider the risks and the rewards.

2 A WOMAN CALLED "MOSES"

▼ How did Harriet Tubman earn the title "the Moses of her people"?

One night, around 1860, Thomas Cole set out from an Alabama plantation with bloodhounds on his heels. He shuddered with fear as he heard the howl of dogs behind him. Recalled Cole, "I was hopin' and prayin' all de time dat I could meet up wid dat Harriet Tubman woman. . . . I never did see dis woman, but I thinks she was a brave woman, anyway."

Liberty or Death. By the time Cole fled the South, Harriet Tubman had become a legend.

Born in 1820, **Harriet Tubman** was one of the 11 children of Harriet and Benjamin Ross —two field hands on a Maryland plantation. She tasted her owner's whip for the first time at age 7. From that time on, she recalled, "[I] prayed to God to make me strong and able to fight." Fight she did, for at 13, she tried to save another African American slave from being punished. Her enraged owner hit her on the head with a rock, fracturing her skull.

At 20, her owner married her to John Tubman, also a slave. One day in 1849, Harriet Tubman learned that she and several of her brothers were to be sold into the Deep South. That night she fled. Later, Harriet recalled her feelings: "I had reasoned this out in my mind; there was one of two things I had a *right* to, liberty or death; if I could not have one, I would have the other; for no man should take me alive."

Joining the Underground Railroad. Freedom felt good to Tubman. But she also felt sorrow, for her family remained enslaved. After settling in Philadelphia, she turned to William Still for help. He sent Tubman traveling on the Underground Railroad.

In 1850, Tubman rescued one of her sisters and her two children from being sold at auction. A few months later, she led one of her brothers and two other men out of Maryland. In 1851, she went back for her husband. But John Tubman had taken another wife and refused to see her. Heartbroken, Harriet decided "to drop him out of my heart." She told Still to put her to work full-time saving other African American slaves.

In all, Tubman made 19 trips south. Armed with a gun and a firm belief in God, she delivered more than 300 people to freedom in the North.

Tubman maintained that she never let "a train run off the track," meaning that she had never lost anyone in a rescue operation. But few in her charge dared falter. Those who lagged behind or had second thoughts stared into the barrel of her gun and heard her husky voice order, "Go north or die."

Any slave owners who matched wits with Tubman lost. They placed a $40,000 price on her head, but nobody was able to collect it. Not even the Civil War stopped her from rescuing African Americans from slavery. As a scout and spy for the Union army, she once helped free more than 750 slaves. Frederick Douglass later wrote a stirring tribute to the woman called Moses.

The midnight sky and silent stars have been the witness of your devotion to freedom and your heroism. . . . I know of no one who has willingly encountered more perils and hardships to serve our enslaved people than you have.

Taking Another Look

1. How did Harriet Tubman become involved in the Underground Railroad?

2. What risks did Tubman take?

3. **Critical Thinking** If Tubman rescued only a small portion of the total number of African American slaves who escaped, why do you think slave owners considered her to be so dangerous?

LOOKING AHEAD

The conductors of the Underground Railroad were able to rescue as many African American slaves as they did because of the moral, practical, and financial support of dedicated abolitionists. Included among those who supported the Underground Railroad were African American churches. They served as stations and raised money for conductors. They gave shelter to runaways—and fueled the hope that God would one day deliver all African Americans out of chains.

FOCUS ON

Leading the Way to Canada

Mary Ann Shadd was the first woman ever to speak before the Colored National Convention. In 1855, Shadd hoped to sway delegates to the 11th annual convention to support the relocation of African Americans to Canada. Of Shadd's speech, a reporter wrote: "The House was crowded and breathless in its attention to her masterly exposition [explanation] of our present condition."

Shadd had moved to Canada after the passage of the Fugitive Slave Law of 1850. In the next decade, more than 15,000 African Americans relocated there. In Canada, African American men could vote and own property, and African American children could go to school.

Shadd settled in Windsor, Canada, a final stop for western Underground Railroad routes. She opened a school in Windsor for fugitive slaves and also started a newspaper, *Provincial Freeman*. Many African Americans, including Frederick Douglass, believed abolitionists should stay in the United States to fight slavery. Shadd, however, saw more hope of freedom in Canada.

During the Civil War, the U.S. government asked Shadd to recruit African American soldiers in Canada. She convinced hundreds to join the Union army. After the war, Shadd moved to Washington, D.C., to earn a law degree from Howard University and enter a new fight—the struggle for women's rights.

CLOSE UP: Chapter 14

The Who, What, Where of History

1. **Who** were Ellen and William Craft?
2. **Who** was Henry "Box" Brown?
3. **What** was the "Drinking Gourd" to which escaping slaves often referred?
4. **What** was the Underground Railroad?
5. **Who** was Levi Coffin?
6. **Who** was William Still?
7. **Who** was Harriet Tubman?

Making the Connection

What was the connection between the Fugitive Slave Law and the Underground Railroad?

Time Check

Use the time line on pages 130–131 to answer the following questions.

1. During what years did the Underground Railroad operate?
2. Did the year in which Harriet Tubman began to lead African American slaves out of the South come closer to the beginning or to the end of the years the Underground Railroad was in operation?

What Would You Have Done?

1. Suppose you were a slave who wanted to escape to the North. List some qualities or skills that you possess that you think would have helped you reach freedom safely.
2. Imagine that you are a white farmer in Indiana. One night you hear noises and realize that several escaping Afri-

can American slaves are trying to hide in your barn. You know that if you try to help the slaves and you are caught, your family may go to prison and you will lose the farm. What course of action would you take?

Thinking and Writing About History

1. Write a short play about an episode in the escape of Ellen and William Craft. Choose a simple event, such as registering at a hotel or eating a meal in the dining car of a train.

2. Write a song or poster about the Underground Railroad using its code words of "tracks," "stations," and "conductors."

Building Skills: Recognizing a Generalization

In the last chapter you learned about generalizations, broad statements based on many related facts. Read this account of the Underground Railroad and answer the question that follows:

[T]he Underground Railroad . . . needed capital [money to operate]. The fugitives required food and clothing, and frequently there were unexpected expenses such as boarding a train in order to evade a pursuing owner, or displaying affluence [wealth] to convey the impression that one had been free long enough to accumulate wealth. Quakers and similar groups raised funds to carry on the work. The vigilance committees . . . solicited [asked for] money. Philanthropists [wealthy people who give to charity] contributed, as did the conductors and other "officials" of the Railroad.

1. Number the sentences in the quotation from 1 to 5. Which of the sentences contain generalizations?

Next, read the following selection and answer the questions.

As a historian attempting to research the Underground Railroad, I have found, with a mixture of admiration and chagrin [disappointment], that [an] atmosphere of secrecy endures. So much is uncertain. Even the origin of the term "Underground Railroad" is obscure. No one knows how many fled from bondage along its invisible tracks. . . . What we do know is a mere fragment of the whole, but it is enough. Ordeals may have gone unrecorded and names have been forgotten, but such records as have survived in the memories of men like my grandfather and the memoirs of those who risked all for freedom and brotherhood make it clear that the flight to freedom on the Underground Railroad was an epic of American heroism.

2. Number the sentences in the quotation from 1 to 6. Which of the sentences contain generalizations?

3. In the last sentence the author indicates that he has based his generalizations on certain kinds of information. What information do you think he used? Explain what kinds of facts would be necessary to tell the story of the Underground Railroad.

Philadelphia's Mother Bethel African Methodist Episcopal Church

African American Churches: Agents for Change

(1787–1860)

THINKING ABOUT THE CHAPTER

What part did African American churches play in the struggle for equality?

The day in 1833 when Thomas James was ordained a minister in the African Methodist Episcopal Zion Church was a milestone in the life of this former slave. As he stood in the pulpit preparing to give his first sermon, his mind went back to the events that had brought him there.

Born enslaved in upstate New York in 1796, James remembered being auctioned off at 17 "in exchange for a yoke [pair] of steers, a colt, and some additional property." Fleeing slavery, he supported himself by digging canals and chopping wood. Gradually, he made his way to Buffalo, New York, where he discovered a Sunday school that changed his life. The church, he decided, would be his life's work.

Once ordained, in 1833, James frequently used his pulpit to speak out against slavery. On several occasions, white mobs beat him for his strong words. That did not stop him. In 1835, he became an antislavery missionary and went on to found African Methodist Episcopal Zion churches in Syracuse, Ithaca, and Sag Harbor, New York.

In 1839, James left New York State for a post in New Bedford, Massachusetts. In the church where he became pastor, he met a young man who spoke so eloquently that he "licensed him to preach." One night, James was giving an antislavery speech when he spotted the young man in the audience. He called on him to speak. The man was Frederick Douglass. Years later Douglass said that he had found his purpose in life that night—to use his voice against slavery.

Both James and Douglass long credited their antislavery awakenings to the same source—the African American church.

1 THE SEARCH FOR RELIGIOUS ▼ EQUALITY
▼ Why did African Americans organize their own churches?

In November 1787, two months after the end of the Constitutional Convention, African American worshipers filed into the St. George Methodist Episcopal Church in Philadelphia. The church had always allowed them to be seated on the main floor. But church officials had grown uneasy at the large number of African Americans attending the church. On that November Sunday, they met African Americans at the door and forced them to climb to the upstairs gallery instead.

Two prominent African Americans, Richard Allen and Absalom Jones, founders of the Free African Society (see page 79), walked up the steps to the gallery with the others. They headed to the front of the gallery and knelt in prayer. Unknown to them, church officials had closed off this spot, too.

"We had not been long upon our knees," Allen later recalled, "before I heard considerable scuffling and low talking." Allen lifted his head from prayer and saw a white usher pulling Jones from his knees. "Wait until prayer is over," pleaded Jones, "and I will trouble you no more." The usher called for help to remove Jones by force.

After prayer had ended, the African American worshipers walked out of the church together. They were furious at the treatment they had received. "We were filled with fresh vigor," said Allen, "to get a house erected to worship God in." Thus began the independent African American church movement in the United States.

New Churches. Richard Allen and Absalom Jones agreed that African Americans had to have their own church. But they disagreed on the direction they should take in founding a new church. In 1794, Allen founded the Mother Bethel African Methodist Episcopal Church in Philadelphia and became its first minister. Still stinging from his treatment by the St. George Methodists, Jones joined the Episcopalians. In 1794, he opened the doors of the St. Thomas Free African Church, also in Philadelphia.

Locally, some **denominations**, or religious groups, especially the Episcopalians and Quakers, did not believe it was wise for African Americans to form separate churches. But Allen and Jones defended the move. They recalled the treat-

1787 African American church movement begins.

1794 Richard Allen founds Mother Bethel African Methodist Episcopal Church.
Absalom Jones opens St. Thomas Free African Church.

1809 Independent Baptist churches are organized by African Americans in New York City and Boston.

1816 First African American denomination in North America is organized.

1830s White Southerners move against African American churches.
African American churches in the North increase opposition to slavery.

ment they had received in racially mixed churches. Accordingly, they admitted only members of African descent to their churches. They did, however, organize a number of joint activities with white churches, including Bible readings, picnics, and lectures.

Over the next 20 years, Allen's followers demanded greater freedom from the white Methodist church authorities. In 1816, African American Methodists from various cities met in Philadelphia to set up a new denomination—the African Methodist Episcopal (AME) church. This was the first African American denomination in North America. Trustees of the church elected Allen their bishop.

As African American Methodists moved toward independence, African American Baptists did the same. On May 14, 1809, 13 African Americans organized Philadelphia's first Baptist church for African Americans. That same year, African Americans, under the leadership of Reverend Thomas Paul, organized independent Baptist churches in New York City and Boston. Already active among African Americans in the South, the Baptist church soon competed with the Methodists in importance to African Americans.

Churches in the Mid-1800s. Discrimination in mixed churches continued in the mid-1800s. Once Frederick Douglass stormed out of a church when the minister refused African Americans communion until all white worshipers were served. Douglass called on African Americans to push into white pews, go limp, and force ushers to haul them into the streets. In 1837, the New York *Colored American* called for "stand ins." Do not sit in separate pews, demanded the journal:

> Stand in the aisles, and rather worship God upon your feet, than become a part to your own degradation [humiliation]. You must shame your oppressors, and wear out prejudice by this holy practice.

Separate Sunday school classes, separate pews, separate communion services—these were only some of the practices in many Christian churches in the mid-1800s.

Most free African Americans protested these actions by forming their own **congregations**, or groups for worship. A handful of African American abolitionists, including Frederick Douglass, came to object to this practice. Douglass believed that separate churches made true racial equality hard to attain. Most African

The Reverend Lemuel Haynes, who had fought in the American Revolution, was one of the few African American ministers who preached to white congregations.

American abolitionists, however, felt that the independent churches gave them a freedom to organize protests that might otherwise have been denied them. Thomas James, Douglass's former ally, was among this group. Whether or not Douglass's view had merit, independent churches became vital forces for change. They gave African Americans a place not only to express themselves spiritually but to assemble freely.

Taking Another Look

1. Why did African Americans first form independent churches?

2. How did African American churches serve their people?

3. **Critical Thinking** Why do you think the independent African American church movement took shape in the North rather than in the South?

2 JOINING THE ANTISLAVERY BATTLE

How did African American churches contribute to the antislavery cause?

In 1855, police burst into a meeting of African American church officials in Washington, D.C. They seized one Bible, two books on morality, and an agreement drawn up for the purchase of a woman slave. Of the 24 church members arrested, a judge ordered one to be whipped, four jailed, and the rest fined.

Further Restrictions in the South. Farther south, white fears of African American assemblies grew. Fear of slave rebellions still gripped the minds of many white Southerners. The fact that both Denmark Vesey and Nat Turner had been preachers strengthened opposition to separate African American churches in the region.

Beginning in the 1830s, African American preachers in much of the South had to be approved by white ministers. In many Southern states, only white ministers could preach to African American congregations. A handful of independent African American churches operated. But most existed in cities—and under the close watch of whites.

Opposition in the North. African American ministers such as Henry Highland Garnet and Samuel Ringgold Ward blasted white church officials for not taking a strong stand against slavery. Even the Quakers, who supported abolition, were attacked for discriminatory practices. "They give us good advice," said Ward of the Quakers. "They will aid in giving us a partial education—but never in a Quaker school, beside their own children. Whatever they do for us savors of pity, and is done at arm's length."

Ward's militant words expressed the new spirit among African American abolitionists in the 1840s. He spoke so eloquently that some said he surpassed Frederick Douglass as a speaker.

African American clergymen were joined by many white ministers, like the owner of this house on the Ohio River, in providing safe havens for runaways from slavery.

Samuel Ringgold Ward was born in 1817 on a Maryland plantation. His enslaved parents escaped and carried him to freedom in New York. There, he received an education and became a minister in a white Presbyterian church in South Butler, New York. But Ward abandoned his ministry in 1839 to become a full-time antislavery agent. His stirring words shook audiences. "If I cannot go to heaven as black as God made me, let me go down to hell and dwell with the Devil forever," declared Ward in one speech. When Congress passed the 1850 Fugitive Slave Law, Ward fled to England and then to the Caribbean island of Jamaica, where he later died.

Places of Protest. African American churches received their funds from African American parishioners, or church members. This permitted them to support antislavery causes without fear of losing membership. In fact, the tradition of self-help went back to the mutual-aid societies of the 1700s (see page 79). It inspired African Americans to dig deeply into their pockets to help the churches in their fight to end slavery.

Time and again, the churches threw open their doors to abolitionists who were denied meeting places elsewhere. Generally, the churches charged no fees. In fact, they sometimes made donations to fund the meetings.

African American churches also provided safe places for runaways. More than one church acted as a station on the Underground Railroad. Richard Allen, for example, operated a station at Mother Bethel Church in Philadelphia until his death in 1831. The congregation continued the practice until the Civil War.

In another antislavery move, African American churches in Pennsylvania and New York led a drive to boycott products made by slaves. They called upon antislavery supporters to buy only goods produced by free labor. When white abolitionist Angelina Grimké married, she ordered a baker to use "free sugar" in her wedding cake. In 1834, William Whipper opened a free-labor grocery store next to the Mother Bethel Church in Philadelphia. He stocked shelves with free-labor sugar, cloth made from free cotton, and a full supply of abolitionist pamphlets.

Taking Another Look

1. How and why did white Southerners restrict African American churches after 1830?

2. What methods did African American churches use to protest slavery and racial inequality in the North?

3. **Critical Thinking** If you were a free African American, would you have agreed with Richard Allen's or Frederick Douglass's view on separate churches for African Americans? Explain.

LOOKING AHEAD

The growth of separate African American churches went hand in hand with the growth of the antislavery movement in the North. Both developments stemmed from the same root—the desire for equality. By the 1850s, the activities of abolitionists further increased the division between North and South. Rumblings of war could be heard as Southerners threatened to leave the Union rather than give up slavery. But abolitionists showed no signs of backing down.

In 1794, Richard Allen hitched his horses up to a blacksmith shop and hauled it to a lot at Sixth and Lombard streets in Philadelphia. He dedicated the building as a church and named it Bethel—"the house of God to the gathering of thousands of souls." Four church buildings called Bethel have stood on this site. The fourth and present church is called Mother Bethel—for its historical leadership of the African Methodist Episcopal (AME) churches.

Today, AME churches span the globe. They can be found throughout the United States, and in Central and West Africa, the Caribbean, Bermuda, South America, and Europe. But the heart of the AME network still lies in Philadelphia. The present Mother Bethel Church, which is over a 100 years old, has been named a national landmark.

The congregation of Mother Bethel Church currently numbers about 700 and includes a direct descendant of Richard Allen. Over its long history, members of Mother Bethel Church have supported Allen's twin concepts of self-help and freedom for African Americans. For example, the church served as a station on the Underground Railroad in the mid-1800s. In the 1960s, church members marched in the Civil Rights Movement. Today, the church runs a summer day-care program, and church members are active in city affairs.

CLOSE UP: Chapter 15

The Who, What, Where of History

1. **Who** was Thomas James?
2. **Who** was Richard Allen?
3. **Who** was Absalom Jones?
4. **Where** was the African Methodist Episcopal Church established?
5. **What** does the term *denomination* mean?
6. **Who** was Samuel Ringgold Ward?

Making the Connection

What was the connection between African American churches and the antislavery movement?

Time Check

Use the time line on pages 130–131 to answer the following questions.

1. In what year did the African American church movement begin?
2. How many years after the beginning of the African American church movement was the first African American denomination in North America formed?
3. Approximately how many years after the foundation of the first African American denomination did white Southerners begin to suppress African American churches?

What Would You Have Done?

1. Imagine that you are attending church at the St. George Methodist Episcopal Church in Philadelphia on the day that ushers forcibly removed Absalom Jones from the gallery. You are a friend of Jones. What would you have done? Explain your actions.

2. Imagine that you have just read an editorial in which Frederick Douglass objects to the practice of forming separate African American congregations. He disapproves on the grounds that separate churches make racial equality hard to obtain. How would you have responded to his editorial in a letter to the editor?

3. Imagine that you are Samuel Ringgold Ward. An acquaintance of yours who is a Quaker heard you say that the Society of Friends carries on discriminatory practices against African Americans. Your friend says you are wrong because Quakers support freedom for African Americans. Write a dialogue in which you and your friend discuss your differences. Use your most convincing evidence to prove your position, and then suggest ways in which the Quakers can remedy the situation.

Thinking and Writing About History

1. Write a paragraph that describes the many roles the church played in the lives of African Americans.

2. Write the words for a plaque to be erected on the site of an African American church. The church was founded in 1820 and served as a station on the Underground Railroad. Many important abolitionists spoke at the church.

Building Skills: Making a Generalization

We make generalizations all the time. Suppose that you eat a pizza with anchovies—and you don't like it at all, although you usually love pizza. Then at a restau-rant you try a dip that tastes terrible. When you ask what's in it, you find out it contains anchovies. You might generalize from those two experiences that you do not like anchovies and do not wish to eat any more of them.

Read each of the following groups of related facts. Use the facts to make a generalization, a broad conclusion, based on each group of facts.

1. a. Church officials of the St. George Methodist Episcopal Church in Philadelphia decided to forbid African Americans from sitting on the main floor of the church.

   b. Richard Allen and Absalom Jones were removed from the front of the gallery of St. George's because church officials did not wish African Americans to sit in that part of the church.

   c. In one church the minister refused to give communion to African Americans until all the white worshippers had received.

   d. Many churches maintained separate Sunday schools, separate pews, and separate communion services for African Americans.

2. a. Thomas James used his ministry in an African American church to speak out against slavery.

   b. Abolitionists were able to organize protests through African American churches.

   c. The African American churches provided training for African leaders of the abolitionist movement.

   d. African American churches gave money to antislavery causes.

UNIT 6

Dred Scott and Harriet Scott

HOPE FOR A NEW WAY OF LIFE
(1820–1880)

An African American cowboy

14th U.S. Colored Infantry
at Ship Island, Mississippi

Unit 6 traces the story of one of the most bitter periods in U.S. history. From 1819 on, the North and the South were on a collision course over slavery. The climax came in the 1860s with the **Civil War.** When the war ended in 1865, the government set about restoring the **Union** (the United States). This period, called **Reconstruction,** lasted until 1877. With the Civil War came the end of slavery, and with Reconstruction came the promise of a new life for freed African Americans—a promise that was not to be fully realized.

THE MISSOURI COMPROMISE, 1820

CANADA

MAINE admitted as a free state

Missouri R.

MISSOURI admitted as a slave state

MISSOURI COMPROMISE LINE

Louisiana Purchase, 1803

Free states

Free territories

Slave states and territories

MEXICO

Latitude 36°30'N

VT. ME. N.H. MASS. N.Y. R.I. CONN. N.J. PENNA. DEL. OHIO MD. IND. ILL. VA. MO. KY. N.C. TENN. S.C. MISS ALA. GA. LA.

ATLANTIC OCEAN

0   300   600 Miles
0 300 600 Kilometers

What was the purpose of the Missouri Compromise Line? Which new states did the Missouri Compromise create?

The Missouri Compromise.   As more Americans began moving to the new territories of the Louisiana Purchase, the debate over slavery went with them. Should slavery be allowed to expand into these new territories or should it be limited to the states where it was already established?

This issue was angrily debated in Congress when Missouri applied in 1819 for admission to the Union as a **slave state,** a state in which slavery would be allowed. Its resolution would have important political consequences. In 1819, there were 11 **free states** and 11 slave states. The North opposed admitting Missouri as a

slave state because the South would then have more votes in the U.S. Senate than the North. This would tip the balance of power in the Senate in favor of the South.

Northerners and Southerners in Congress finally reached a compromise in 1820. Known as the **Missouri Compromise,** it admitted Missouri as a slave state, and Maine was admitted as a free state. At the same time, a line was drawn at latitude 36° 30′ N across the territory of the Louisiana Purchase. North of the line, except for Missouri, slavery would be barred "forever." South of the line, slavery would be allowed.

The issue of slavery in new territories flared up again 30 years later. This time the controversy centered on the huge area that Mexico had given up to the United States after the Mexican War (1846–1847). The new lands included California, New Mexico, and most of present-day Arizona, Nevada, Colorado, and Utah. What was to be done about slavery in these new territories?

An African American Speaks

A war undertaken and brazenly [shamelessly] carried on for the perpetual [everlasting] enslavement of colored men calls logically and loudly for colored men to help suppress [stop] it.

—Frederick Douglass

161

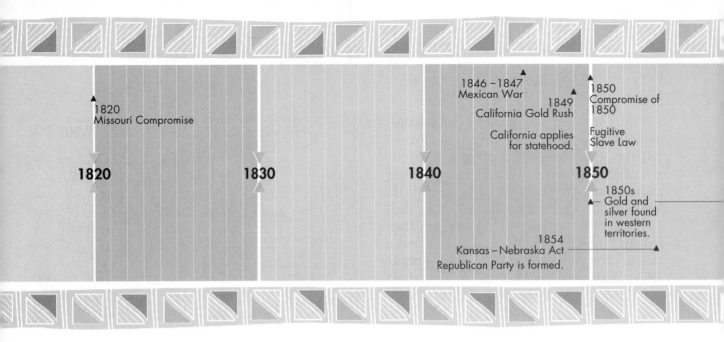

1820
Missouri Compromise

1846–1847
Mexican War

1849
California Gold Rush

California applies
for statehood.

1850
Compromise of
1850

Fugitive
Slave Law

1820　　　**1830**　　　**1840**　　　**1850**

1850s
Gold and
silver found
in western
territories.

1854
Kansas–Nebraska Act
Republican Party is formed.

The Compromise of 1850. When California applied for admission to the Union as a free state in 1849, Northerners and Southerners in Congress once again compromised. According to the **Compromise of 1850,** California was to enter the Union as a free state. In the other former Mexican lands, settlers would vote on whether or not to allow slavery. This voting plan was called **popular sovereignty.**

To gain Southern support, the compromise included a tough **Fugitive Slave Law** to help slave owners capture runaways. Not surprisingly, many Northerners, even those who were not abolitionists, bitterly objected. One Northern member of Congress declared that returning a fugitive to slavery would be the same as murder.

The Kansas-Nebraska Act. An even more bitter clash over slavery occurred four years later. A bill to organize a Kansas Territory and a Nebraska Territory came before Congress. The Mis-

souri Compromise had barred slavery in that area. The new proposal, however, would repeal the Missouri Compromise, and the question of slavery would be decided by popular sovereignty. Although Northerners flooded Congress with protests, the **Kansas-Nebraska Act** became law in 1854. As a result, armed bands fought one another in Kansas over the issue of slavery. So much violence occurred in 1856 that the territory became known as **Bleeding Kansas.**

Lincoln. One effect of the Kansas-Nebraska Act was the formation of a new political party in 1854 by opponents of the extension of slavery. They called themselves the Republican party.

In 1860, the Republicans chose Abraham Lincoln of Illinois as their candidate for President. Although Lincoln strongly opposed slavery, he did not plan to end it in the South. His aim was to prevent its spread into the western territories. However, many Southerners thought that Lin-

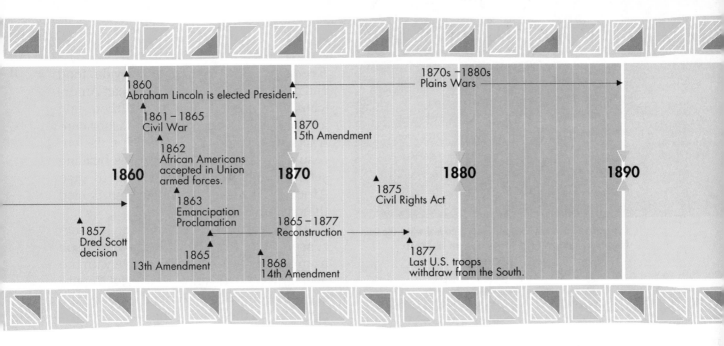

1860
Abraham Lincoln is elected President.

1861–1865
Civil War

1862
African Americans accepted in Union armed forces.

1863
Emancipation Proclamation

1857
Dred Scott decision

1865
13th Amendment

1868
14th Amendment

1860

1865–1877
Reconstruction

1870
15th Amendment

1870s–1880s
Plains Wars

1875
Civil Rights Act

1877
Last U.S. troops withdraw from the South.

1870

1880

1890

coln was an abolitionist. His main support came from the North and West, and he won the 1860 presidential election.

Secession. The news of Lincoln's victory outraged the South. Six weeks later, South Carolina **seceded,** or left the Union. It was soon joined by Mississippi, Florida, Alabama, Georgia, Louisiana, and Texas. In February 1861, delegates from these states met at Montgomery, Alabama, and formed the Confederate States of America.

On April 12, Confederate forces at Charleston, South Carolina, fired on Fort Sumter, in Charleston harbor. This fort was a **Union,** or Northern, stronghold. These shots were the first of the Civil War. Soon after, Virginia, North Carolina, Tennessee, and Arkansas joined the **Confederacy.** That left Lincoln the President of only the 23 states of the North, Midwest, and West.

The Civil War. The Civil War lasted from 1861 to 1865. It was the bloodiest war in U.S. history. About 620,000 people were wounded or killed, including 38,000 African Americans. In the beginning, the North appeared to have all the advantages over the South. The Union had over 22 million people. The South had 8 million, of whom 3.9 million were enslaved African Americans. The North had 92 percent of the nation's factories and almost all its iron, coal, and copper. Seventy percent of the country's railroads were in the North. Yet the South's armed forces were commanded by outstanding military leaders, and they fought with such determination that at times, especially in the early years of the war, the South appeared close to victory.

The Emancipation Proclamation. Early in the war, Lincoln was criticized by many for not freeing enslaved African Americans. In August 1862, he replied to his critics: "My paramount [main] object in this struggle is to save the Union, and is not either to save or destroy slavery."

Four years of a bloody Civil War were launched when the Confederates bombarded Fort Sumter on April 12, 1861.

However, as the war dragged on and Union forces suffered heavy losses, Lincoln reversed himself. On January 1, 1863, Lincoln signed the **Emancipation Proclamation,** which declared free all African Americans in those parts of the South that were still in rebellion. This move, he believed, would give the North a strong moral reason for continuing the terrible struggle. It would also encourage slaves to run away and thus further damage the economy, or system of producing goods and services, of the South.

The year 1863 was the turning point of the war. From then until April 1865, the Union armies scored one major victory after another. On April 9, 1865, General Robert E. Lee, the Confederate commander, surrendered to General Ulysses S. Grant, of the Union army, at Appomattox, Virginia. The Union had little time to celebrate, for less than a week later, President Lincoln was assassinated by a Southerner who blamed him for the South's defeat.

The Reconstruction Years. With the war at an end, the federal government had to decide what to do about the defeated South and how to rebuild, or reconstruct, the Union. Before the war had

even ended, Congress had set up the **Freedmen's Bureau** to provide food and clothing to newly freed African Americans. The bureau also helped them find jobs and homes and negotiated labor contracts with landowners. Perhaps the bureau's most important work was building schools and providing teachers to give African Americans the education denied them under slavery.

After Lincoln's assassination, his successor, Vice President Andrew Johnson from Tennessee, ran into trouble with the plan for Reconstruction. Powerful Republicans in Congress attacked the plan as too generous to the South. The plan did, however, force the Southern states to ratify the 13th Amendment, banning slavery in the United States. This was the first of three Reconstruction Amendments. As a reaction against the 13th Amendment and the Freedmen's Bureau, many white Southerners passed **Black Codes** in their states. These laws severely limited the rights of African Americans.

Beginning in 1867, Radical Republicans pushed through their own tough plan to reorganize the South. The Radicals were bitter against the South and wanted to set much harsher terms than did President Johnson. They believed that the South should be treated as a conquered nation and that African Americans should have the same rights as white Americans.

The Radicals were joined by moderate Republicans who shared some of the same goals as well as the desire the keep Republicans in power in the South. Their plan divided the South into five military districts, each governed by a U.S. Army general with troops to back up his orders. Before any Southern state could be readmitted to the Union, it had to accept the 14th Amendment and to write a new constitution giving African American men the right to vote.

▶▶ THE RECONSTRUCTION AMENDMENTS

13th Amendment (1865)

Forbids slavery in any state of the Union.

14th Amendment (1868)

States that all persons born in the United States are U.S. citizens and cannot be deprived of "life, liberty, (or) property, without due process of law" nor be denied "equal protection of the laws."

15th Amendment (1870)

Forbids states to deny the right to vote to male citizens "on account of race, color, or previous condition of servitude."

Which Reconstruction amendment ended slavery? Which gave citizenship to African Americans?

White Southern Reaction. Many white Southerners bitterly resented the new state governments set up during Reconstruction. Some joined secret societies like the Ku Klux Klan, whose purpose was to terrorize African Americans and prevent them from voting. Many African Americans who tried to vote were beaten. Some were **lynched**—or murdered by mobs for supposed crimes. As Southern white men regained their right to vote, they replaced Reconstruction governments with ones made up of former supporters of the Confederacy.

The End of Reconstruction. By the mid-1870s, some of the leading Radical Republicans had died, and the nation was worried about economic problems. Many Northerners wanted to "leave the South alone," which meant abandoning its African Americans. By 1877, the last U.S. troops had been withdrawn from the South, and Reconstruction, a stormy period in U.S. history, was over.

Going West. Beginning in the late 1840s, the lands west of the Mississippi began to attract more and more people, African Americans among them. The Gold Rush of 1849 brought thousands to California seeking to strike it rich quick. Thousands more followed when gold and silver were discovered in the 1850s in what are today the states of Colorado, Nevada, Idaho, Montana, and South Dakota; and in the 1870s in the present-day states of Arizona, Wyoming, Utah, and New Mexico.

After the Civil War, these same territories attracted ranchers and farmers looking to start new lives. Many were from Europe, as hundreds of thousands of immigrants flooded into the nation. African Americans joined the move westward to escape the growing oppression of the post–Civil War South.

These western lands, however, were not empty. Native Americans lived along the Pacific Coast, in the Rocky Mountains, and on the Great Plains—the land between the Mississippi River and the Rocky Mountains. In a series of plains wars, white and African American troops of the U.S. Army killed or sent to reservations thousands of Native Americans.

Taking Another Look

1. Describe the laws passed between 1820 and 1854 to try to settle the debate over slavery's expansion.

2. Explain the advantages the North had over the South in the Civil War.

3. How did the Emancipation Proclamation affect the war?

4. **Critical Thinking** If you had been a newly freed African American, would you have gone west? Explain.

165

A victim of the 1850 Fugitive Slave Law

The Road to the Civil War

(1820–1860)

THINKING ABOUT THE CHAPTER

What important events affecting African Americans occurred in the years immediately before the Civil War?

In 1854, cholera (KOL-uhr-uh), a dreaded disease, struck Pittsburgh. Dr. Martin Robison Delany, one of the few African American doctors in the city, drew praise from both African Americans and whites for the devotion and energy he showed in taking care of the sick.

When the scare was over, Delany returned to attacking another dread disease—slavery. For years, he had been a leader in rescuing African Americans from slavery through the Underground Railroad. Delany was also one of the African American abolitionists who never hesitated to emphasize his pride in his heritage. His friend Frederick Douglass once said of him, "I thank God for making me a man simply, but Delany always thanks him for making him a black man."

166

When the Fugitive Slave Law was passed in 1850, Delany's fury knew no bounds. Addressing a meeting in Pittsburgh, which included the city's mayor, he declared:

Sir, my house is my castle. . . . If any man approaches that house in search of a slave—I care not who he may be, whether constable or sheriff, magistrate or even judge of the Supreme Court—nay, let it be he who sanctioned [approved] this act to become a law [President Millard Fillmore], . . . and I do not lay him a lifeless corpse at my feet, I hope the grave may refuse my body a resting-place, and righteous Heaven my spirit a home.

Delany's strong words reflected the anger of many abolitionists at the new law. They were also typical of the debate over slavery that heated up in the 1850s.

1 CHALLENGES TO THE FUGITIVE SLAVE LAW

What was the effect of the Fugitive Slave Law on African Americans?

Late in 1850, fear was spreading among free African Americans in the North because of the Fugitive Slave Law, passed by Congress in September. This law put the power of the federal government behind the efforts of slave owners to capture African American slaves who had escaped to the North. It authorized federal marshals to hunt down runaways and return them to slavery. It provided stiff penalties for law officers and even ordinary people who did not assist slave catchers.

Law officers were paid a fee for capturing runaways. Professional slave catchers frequently kidnapped free African Americans and took them South. The Fugitive Slave Law denied African Americans who were arrested as runaways a trial by jury or the right to testify in their own defense. Many free African Americans in the North no longer felt secure, and hundreds sought safety in Canada.

Many Northerners—white and African American—defied the law and stepped up their efforts to help African American slaves to escape. Despite these efforts, over 330 fugitives were returned to slavery in the 1850s.

The Case of Anthony Burns. The recapture of one runaway African Ameri-

Angry Bostonians bought hundreds of copies of this pamphlet about the recapture of Anthony Burns.

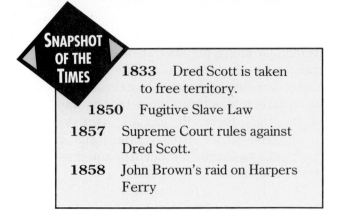

SNAPSHOT
OF THE
TIMES

1833   Dred Scott is taken
        to free territory.
1850   Fugitive Slave Law
1857   Supreme Court rules against
        Dred Scott.
1858   John Brown's raid on Harpers
        Ferry

can, Anthony Burns, attracted national attention in 1854. A Virginian, Burns had stowed away on a ship to Boston, where he found work as a tailor. But his owner discovered where he was and headed north to claim his "property."

Burns was arrested on May 24 and placed under guard in the federal courthouse. Soon after, a crowd of African American and white abolitionists held a protest meeting. Stirred by the speakers, they resolved that "resistance to tyrants [unfair rulers] is obedience to God."

Led by a white minister, Thomas Wentworth Higginson, the abolitionists stormed the courthouse with axes, revolvers, and a battering ram. Higginson and an African American broke through the door but were driven back by marshals swinging clubs. A shot was fired and a deputy fell dead.

Although the attack failed, local authorities sent an appeal to President Franklin Pierce for help. He ordered federal soldiers to Boston to strengthen the guard around the courthouse. He also sent a telegram to the local district attorney: "Incur [undertake] any expense to insure the execution of the law."

Lawyers tried to win Burns's freedom in court, but failed. Other Bostonians raised money to buy Burns's freedom, but the district attorney would not allow it. A

In May 1854, over the protests of the people of Boston, troops escorted Anthony Burns to the ship that returned him to slavery after his trial at the courthouse.

federal commissioner had ruled that under the Fugitive Slave Law, Burns had to be returned to Virginia. A U.S. gunboat waited in the harbor to take him.

On June 2, about 1,500 troops began marching Burns to the ship. Some 50,000 angry Bostonians lined the streets crying "Shame!" Buildings were draped in black. Flags were hung upside down. Church bells rang mournfully as Burns was hustled aboard the ship.

Enslaved Again. Back in Virginia, Burns was jailed, but eventually his owner agreed to sell him to a group of Northerners. Freed by them, Burns attended Oberlin College, became a minister, and moved to Canada. While Burns was in jail, he put his thoughts on his escape from slavery in a letter:

> Look at my case. I was stolen and made a slave as soon as I was born. . . . God made me a *man*—not a slave; and gave me the same right to myself that he gave the man who stole me to himself. The great wrong he has done me . . . in compelling [forcing] me to work for him many years without wages, and holding me as merchandise—these wrongs could never put me under obligation to stay with him, or return voluntarily, when once escaped.

Freedom Laws. To prevent abuses in the recapture of African American slaves, several Northern states, including Pennsylvania and Massachusetts, passed **personal liberty laws.** Some forbade state officials and anyone else from helping to enforce the Fugitive Slave Law. Some laws also tried to guarantee a fair trial for runaways who were caught.

Although these laws did not free a single captured African American, they were important. They showed a new willingness among Northerners to fight the Fugitive Slave Law. They also showed that people were ready to use state laws to try to overturn a federal law.

Taking Another Look

1. What effect did the Fugitive Slave Law have on runaway African American slaves?

2. In what ways did abolitionists try to get around the Fugitive Slave Law to help runaways?

3. **Critical Thinking** Abolitionists who helped runaway slaves were breaking the Fugitive Slave Law. Do you think they were justified? Explain.

2 THE DRED SCOTT CASE, A TEST OF SLAVERY

▼ Why was the Supreme Court decision in the Dred Scott case important in the fight to end slavery?

On March 6, 1857, anxious listeners on both sides of the slavery question packed the Supreme Court's chambers to hear the Court's decision in an important case. Only two days before, President James Buchanan had commented on the case in his inaugural address. He had also written to the Supreme Court justices, hoping that the Court would settle the slavery question once and for all by its decision in this case. Buchanan and many others believed that since legislation had failed to settle the slavery issue, a decision by the Supreme Court was needed. The case was about the future of an African American named Dred Scott.

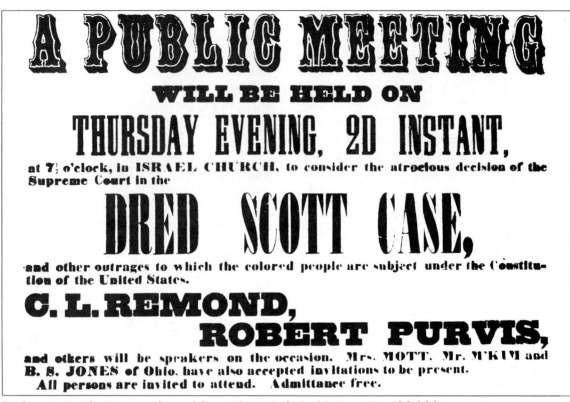

A PUBLIC MEETING

WILL BE HELD ON

THURSDAY EVENING, 2D INSTANT,

at 7½ o'clock, in ISRAEL CHURCH, to consider the atrocious decision of the Supreme Court in the

DRED SCOTT CASE,

and other outrages to which the colored people are subject under the Constitution of the United States.

C. L. REMOND,
ROBERT PURVIS,

and others will be speakers on the occasion. Mrs. MOTT. Mr. M'KIM and B. S. JONES of Ohio, have also accepted invitations to be present.
All persons are invited to attend. Admittance free.

Few Supreme Court decisions aroused as much furor as the one in the Dred Scott case. Here Philadelphians are invited to attend a meeting to protest the decision.

The Dred Scott Case. In 1833, Dred Scott's owner took him from Missouri, a slave state, to Illinois, a free state, and then to the Wisconsin Territory. The Missouri Compromise banned slavery there. Scott's owner later returned him to Missouri. In 1846, white friends of Scott advised him to sue for his freedom on the grounds he had lived in a free state and then a free territory, even though he had been taken back to a slave state. Eventually, Scott's case reached the U.S. Supreme Court.

On that fateful March day, Chief Justice Roger B. Taney led the other eight justices into the courtroom. Five of them, including Taney, were from slave states. A hush fell over the courtroom as Taney began to speak.

Issues of the Case. The justices had debated three issues in the case. Was Scott a citizen and therefore entitled to sue in a federal court? Did his residence on free soil entitle him to freedom in Missouri? Finally, was the Missouri Compromise, which had made the territories free, constitutional?

The Court ruled, Justice Taney said, that African Americans could not be citizens, because neither the Declaration of Independence nor the U.S. Constitution was ever meant to be applied to them. Therefore, Scott did not have the right to sue in court.

The fact that Scott had lived on free soil did not entitle him to freedom. Why? Scott was a slave and as a slave he was the property of his owner. Congress could not deprive a person of the right to take his or her property anywhere.

Finally, the Supreme Court ruled that the Missouri Compromise was **unconstitutional** (un-kon-stuh-TOO-shuhn-uhl), not permitted by the Constitution. The right to hold slaves was a property right, and Congress could not interfere with a person's property rights. Congress could no more take away a Southerner's right to his or her slaves than it could take away a Northerner's right to a horse or mule or any other property.

Only two of the nine justices, both from the North, opposed the majority decision.

Reactions to the Decision. The Court's ruling was greeted with jubilation in the South. One newspaper wrote, "Southern opinion on the subject of Southern slavery . . . is now the supreme law of the land."

Once the meaning of the decision was realized—that all federal territories would now be open to slavery—Northerners were enraged. They held mass meetings to protest the decision. In Philadelphia, a convention of African Americans denounced the ruling. For African Americans, of course, the decision was particularly bitter. Not only did it permit slavery in the territories, but also it supported the idea that African American slaves were no more than property.

Frederick Douglass, however, believed that the Supreme Court's decision would actually hasten the end of slavery. He said:

The Supreme Court is not the only power in this world. We, the abolitionists and colored people, should meet this decision, unlooked for and monstrous as it appears, in a cheerful spirit. This very attempt to blot out forever the hopes of an enslaved people may be one necessary link in the chain of events preparatory to the complete overthrow of the whole slave system.

The Supreme Court had not settled once and for all the question of slavery in the territories, as President Buchanan had hoped. Instead, it had, in the words of one historian, "exploded a bombshell."

Taking Another Look

1. On what grounds did Dred Scott claim that he should be a free person?

2. Why was the Supreme Court's decision such a disappointment to opponents of slavery?

3. **Critical Thinking** Which part of the Dred Scott decision do you think upset abolitionists the most? Explain.

3 JOHN BROWN'S RAID

Why did John Brown's raid stir up such strong feelings?

Although most abolitionists at the time believed in ending slavery by trying to show how evil it was, the Fugitive Slave Law convinced some that direct action might be necessary. Frederick Douglass, for one, had never advocated violence as a way of ending slavery. Now, however, he took the position that "who would be free must himself strike the first blow." Others agreed with Douglass and went even further.

John Brown, a fiery abolitionist, said in disgust, "Talk! Talk! Talk! That will never free the slaves. What is needed is action—action!" Brown believed that victory over slavery could only be won by a violent slave uprising. Brown himself was no

"Bleeding Kansas" was a battleground of proslavery and antislavery forces. In May 1856, proslavery men attacked the antislavery town of Lawrence, Kansas, provoking John Brown to strike back.

stranger to violence. In Bleeding Kansas he had led an attack against proslavery settlers at Pottawatomie Creek, five of whom were killed.

John Brown's Plan.   Brown had been planning a slave uprising for a long time. In May 1858, he had met secretly with 34 former African American slaves who now lived in Chatham, Canada. They drew up a constitution for a nation of liberated African Americans to be set up in the mountains of Virginia.

Brown also sought the help of Frederick Douglass. In August 1859, the two met in an old stone quarry near Chambersburg, Pennsylvania. "Come with me, Douglass," he said. "I want you for a special purpose. When I strike, the bees will swarm, and I shall want you to hive [orga-

nize] them." Douglass refused. He believed that Brown's mission was suicidal and "would array [set] the whole country against us." He warned Brown, "You will never get out alive."

The Raid on Harpers Ferry.   Brown was disappointed but went on with his plans. On the night of October 16, 1859, Brown and 18 men, including 5 African Americans, crossed a railroad bridge over the Potomac River from Maryland to Harpers Ferry, Virginia. There they seized the federal arsenal, capturing several million dollars worth of arms. Brown sent out patrols to rouse African American slaves in the surrounding area. But the hoped-for uprising never occurred.

Soon a church bell rang out, warning farmers and neighboring militia that there was trouble. Local residents and troops rallied, and the shooting began. Trapped inside the arsenal, one after another of Brown's supporters fell. In the morning, marines stormed the arsenal and captured the remaining defenders. One of Brown's African American supporters, Osborne Perry Anderson, escaped and later wrote a book about the raid.

Reaction to Brown's Raid. The first reaction to the raid in both the North and the South was shock. In Virginia, angry mobs clamored for Brown's blood, and authorities feared a lynching. In the North, even some abolitionists saw Brown's raid as misguided and rash, the work of a "madman."

Brown, who was slightly wounded, was tried for treason to Virginia. His quiet and dignified behavior at his trial won over much public opinion in the North. More and more Northerners began to see Brown as a martyr. A group of African American women in Brooklyn, New York, expressed this view in a letter to Brown shortly before he was hanged:

We, a portion of the American people, . . . recognize in you a Saviour commissioned [sent] to redeem us, the American people, from the Great National Sin of Slavery; and though you have apparently failed in the object of your desires, yet the influence that we believe it [the raid] will eventually exert [have] will accomplish all your intentions.

Such expressions of sympathy enraged many in the South even more. A Baltimore newspaper asked if the South could afford any longer "to live under a government, the majority of whose subjects or citizens regard Brown as a martyr and a Christian hero?"

Taking Another Look

1. What was the purpose of Brown's raid on Harpers Ferry?

2. **a.** In what ways did Brown's raid fail? **b.** What, if anything, did it achieve?

3. **Critical Thinking** Should John Brown be considered a hero or an enemy of the state? Explain.

LOOKING AHEAD

Hopes for a peaceful settlement of the slavery issue faded rapidly in the 1850s. The Fugitive Slave Law of 1850 angered abolitionists and other Northerners. The U.S. Supreme Court's decision in the Dred Scott case further provoked abolitionists. An attempt by the abolitionist John Brown to stir up a revolt among enslaved African Americans failed but produced more angry voices—this time in the South. By now, many people in both the North and the South believed an armed conflict over slavery had become unavoidable.

How can you tell that the painter of this picture of John Brown's last moments was sympathetic to Brown?

CLOSE UP: Chapter 16

On April 6, 1846, Dred Scott and his wife Harriet climbed the stairs of the St. Louis Courthouse in St. Louis, Missouri. Thus began the Scott family's long journey through the legal system—from state courts to the federal court of appeals to the Supreme Court of the United States. Their walk up the steps that day made the Scotts and the Old Courthouse famous.

Lawyers battled out the first two trials in the Old Courthouse in 1847 and in 1850. The Scotts did not return to the building until 1858, a year after their Supreme Court loss. Climbing the stairs in 1858 were Dred Scott, Harriet, and their daughters Eliza and Lizzie. They had come to the Old Courthouse to apply for licenses to remain in Missouri as "free negroes."

In the 1930s, President Franklin D. Roosevelt declared the Old Courthouse an historic site. In 1977, a group of African Americans placed a plaque at the site of the actual courtroom of the Scott trials. It read: "Dred Scott: American Pioneer, participant in the legal struggle for citizenship that rocked America."

Today, the State Bar Association of Missouri holds mock trials in that courtroom to commemorate the case. Once again, the Scotts, as actors, stand in the Old Courthouse awaiting their freedom.

The Who, What, Where of History

1. **What** was the Missouri Compromise?
2. **What** was the Compromise of 1850?
3. **What** was the Fugitive Slave Law?
4. **Who** was Anthony Burns?
5. **What** were personal liberty laws?
6. **What** was the Supreme Court's decision in the Dred Scott case?
7. **What** did John Brown do?

Making the Connection

1. What was the connection between the Fugitive Slave Law and personal liberty laws?
2. What was the connection between Dred Scott's claim to freedom and the Missouri Compromise?

Time Check

1. When was the Fugitive Slave Law passed?
2. Which of these events happened *first:* John Brown's raid, the Dred Scott decision, the capture of Anthony Burns in Boston?

What Would You Have Done?

1. If you had lived in Boston in 1854, would you have tried to help Anthony Burns? Explain.
2. If you had lived in the North when the Fugitive Slave Law was passed, would you have obeyed or disobeyed that law? Explain.

Thinking and Writing About History

1. Imagine that you are a former African American slave living in New York State in 1854. Write a letter to a friend explaining why you are moving to Canada.

2. Look at the picture of John Brown by Horace Pippin in "The Artist's View." Review the chapter for information about Brown, then write a brief newspaper article about the event in the painting.

Building Skills: Primary and Secondary Sources

If you ever watch mystery or detective shows on television, then you know something about how a detective solves a crime. First, the detective looks for clues.

When a historian tries to decide what really happened at a certain time in the past, he or she acts much like a detective. Some of the clues that historians use come from *primary sources.* A primary source is an original document that comes from the actual time period being studied. Letters, journals, legal records, autobiographies—all these are primary sources. A *secondary source* is an account written at a later time that describes or analyzes an event or person from the past. Usually, the writer of a secondary source, such as a textbook or a biography, has used primary sources to find the facts.

1. In this chapter, several primary sources are quoted. Scan the text to find three primary sources used in this chapter.

2. To be sure that you can tell the difference between primary and secondary sources, study the list of books and articles below. On a separate sheet of paper, write the letters of the primary sources and explain why each is a primary source.

a. "John Brown's Last Statement to the Court"

b. a book called *From Slavery to Freedom* by John Hope Franklin, first published in 1947

c. a book called *Narrative of the Life and Adventures of Henry Bibb, an American Slave, Written by Himself,* first published in 1850

d. a biography of Frederick Douglass called *Frederick Douglass,* by William McFeely, published in 1991

e. a book called *John Brown of Harpers Ferry,* by John Anthony Scott, published in 1988

f. *Army Life in a Black Regiment,* by Thomas Higginson, published in 1870

g. articles about the raid on Harpers Ferry from the October 18, 1859, New York *Herald*

h. *The Black Americans: A History in Their Own Words, 1619–1983* edited by Milton Meltzer, published in 1987 in paperback

i. "The Execution of John Brown," *The Anglo-African Magazine,* published in 1859

54th Massachusetts Infantry at the Battle of Fort Wagner

CHAPTER 17

The Civil War and the End of Slavery

(1861–1865)

THINKING ABOUT THE CHAPTER

What was the impact of the Civil War on African Americans?

It was not until 1862 that African Americans were officially allowed to enlist in the Union army. But once they joined, they fought with valor. Perhaps the most famous battle in which African Americans fought was the attack on Fort Wagner, which guarded the harbor of Charleston, South Carolina. The assault began at dusk on July 18, 1863, and was led by the 54th Massachusetts Infantry, an African American regiment. Its white commander, Colonel Robert Shaw, was eager to prove the ability, skill, and courage of his men.

At 7:45 P.M., 600 men of the 54th charged up an open beach toward the fort. Some 1,700 Confederate defenders raced to the walls of the fort and opened fire on them. Despite the heavy fire, African American soldiers reached the top wall of the fort and held it for an hour before being forced back. The 54th lost nearly half its men in the battle, including Colonel Shaw.

Although the attack failed, it proved the courage of African American soldiers. White Northerners who had believed African Americans would run in battle now saw them differently. The *Atlantic Monthly* declared, "Through the cannon fire of that dark night, the manhood of the colored race shines before many eyes that would not see."

The Civil War began as a war to save the Union, and African American troops made a significant contribution to reaching that goal. In 1863, a second and equally important goal of the war became the freeing of enslaved African Americans.

1 ON THE ROAD TO ENDING ▼ SLAVERY

▼ What did the Emancipation Proclamation do?

On a hot summer night in 1862, President Abraham Lincoln walked across the White House lawn to the nearby telegraph office. Borrowing some paper, he sat down at an old desk and began to write. Sometimes, he crossed out words, or chewed on his pencil as he thought. Finally, he put his notes in his pocket and walked back to the White House. What he had written was an early draft of the historic Emancipation Proclamation, a major step in ending the enslavement of African Americans in the United States.

Pressure to Free the Enslaved. Since the beginning of the Civil War, in 1861, Lincoln had been under increasing pressure from abolitionists to free African American slaves. Free African Americans were particularly outspoken in urging that

the war be fought to end slavery. Frederick Douglass argued:

> The negro is the key of the situation—the pivot [hinge] upon which the whole rebellion turns. . . . Tell the rebels and traitors that the price they are to pay for the attempt to abolish this Government must be the abolition of slavery.

Lincoln resisted. He said that his main goal was to save the Union, not to destroy slavery. Lincoln personally opposed slavery, but he feared that outlawing it would drive the four **border states**—Missouri, Kentucky, Maryland, and Delaware—into the Confederacy. These were slave states that had remained loyal to the Union. Lincoln was once told that freeing the slaves would put God on the Union side. He replied, "We would like to have God on our side, but we must have Kentucky."

Beginning in spring 1862, however, Lincoln took a series of steps that climaxed in the Emancipation Proclamation. In April 1862, he supported a bill that freed all African American slaves in Washington, D.C. Owners were paid up to $300 for each individual. The same bill outlined a plan to pay for the passage of those African Americans who wished to move to Haiti, in the Caribbean, or to Liberia, in Africa. This was consistent with Lincoln's belief that African Americans and whites could not live together peacefully in the United States.

In June 1862, Lincoln signed a bill abolishing slavery in the territories. It was followed by a law setting free all African American slaves who had escaped their Confederate slave owners and came into Union-held territory. Lincoln also tried, unsuccessfully, to persuade the border states to free their slaves gradually.

1861–1865 Civil War

1862 Congress passes law freeing African American slaves in District of Columbia.

Slavery is abolished in the territories.

Law passed freeing all African American slaves who cross into Union-held territory.

Union army recruits African Americans.

1863 Emancipation Proclamation

54th Massachusetts Infantry distinguishes itself at Battle of Fort Wagner.

1865 Confederacy recruits African Americans.

African American units lead Union army into Richmond.

The Emancipation Proclamation.
Meanwhile, the war was going badly for the Union and Lincoln had to do something. In July 1862, he presented a plan to his cabinet for the emancipation of African American slaves. To make emancipation an aim of the war would weaken the South by encouraging enslaved African Americans to desert their owners. As a result, there would be no one to raise food or perform heavy labor and other noncombat jobs for the Confederate army.

Lincoln also believed that making emancipation a goal of the war would inspire abolitionists and other Northerners with a moral reason to fight, rather than merely a political one. It would be an "act of Justice," he declared in the Emancipation Proclamation. He waited for a Union victory before announcing the Emancipation Proclamation. Otherwise, it might appear that the Proclamation was a sign of weakness. The victory, a costly one, came at Antietam, Maryland, on September 17, 1862.

Five days later, Lincoln announced that on January 1, 1863, he would issue an Emancipation Proclamation. It would free all African American slaves in areas that were in rebellion against the United States—in other words, those areas still held by the Confederate armies. It would not free the more than 800,000 enslaved African Americans in the border states or those in areas that were already in the hands of Union troops.

The Celebration of Emancipation.
Even though at the time it was issued, the Emancipation Proclamation did not free most of the 3.9 million enslaved African Americans in the South, African Americans greeted it with joy. Frederick Douglass spoke for most African Americans when he declared, "We shout for joy that we live to record this righteous decree."

When the Emancipation Proclamation went into effect, on January 1, 1863, celebrations were held in many Northern cities. African Americans were proud of the part they had played in bringing about this historic declaration and overjoyed at their victory—if still only a partial one. Henry M. Turner, an African American minister in Washington, D.C., described the scene in that city:

White and colored people shook hands, songs were sung, and by this time cannons began to fire at the navy-yard. . . . Great processions of colored and white men marched to

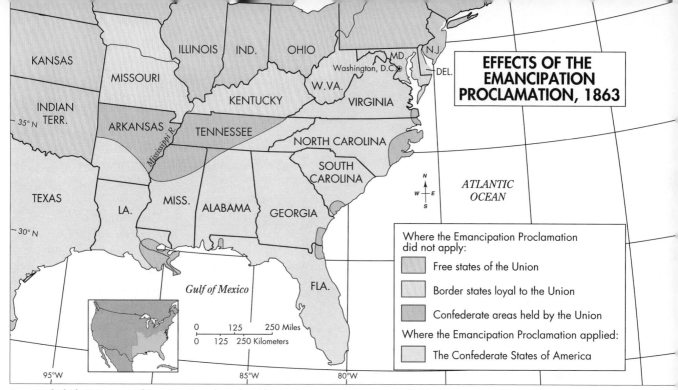

EFFECTS OF THE EMANCIPATION PROCLAMATION, 1863

Where the Emancipation Proclamation did not apply:
- Free states of the Union
- Border states loyal to the Union
- Confederate areas held by the Union

Where the Emancipation Proclamation applied:
- The Confederate States of America

In parts of which states were African American slaves freed by the Emancipation Proclamation? Where in the South were they not freed by the Proclamation?

and fro and passed in front of the White House and congratulated President Lincoln on his proclamation. The President came to the window and made responsive bows, and thousands told him, if he would come out of that palace, they would hug him to death. . . . It was indeed a time of times, and a halftime, nothing like it will ever be seen again in this life.

Taking Another Look

1. How did African Americans want the goal of the Civil War to change?

2. What did the Emancipation Proclamation provide?

3. **Critical Thinking** Why was the Emancipation Proclamation greeted so enthusiastically if it actually freed only a small portion of enslaved African Americans?

2 ON THE HOME FRONT

How did the Civil War affect African American slaves and former slaves?

Fear of uprisings by African American slaves, always strong in the South, intensified after the Emancipation Proclamation. One Southern leader wrote: "Our Negro population are going to give us great trouble. . . . The necessary pains to keep them on our side and in order have been unwisely and sadly neglected." Some slave owners were so terrified at the idea of bloody uprisings that they even appealed for protection to Union troops that had pushed into their area.

How African American Slaves Resisted. Actually, there was little violence by African American slaves against their owners. They resisted their owners in other ways. The most common method was running away. As Northern troops pushed deeper into Southern territory,

179

These African American slaves are fleeing to Union territory across Virginia's Rappahannock River. What were such slaves called after they reached Union lines?

thousands fled—often at great risk—to freedom behind Union lines.

One of those who escaped was Susie King Taylor, aged 14, of Savannah, Georgia. This was her recollection:

The whites would tell their colored people not to go to the Yankees, for they would harness them to carts . . . in place of horses. I asked grandmother one day if this was true. She replied, "Certainly not!", that the white people did not want slaves to go over to the Yankees, and told them things to frighten them. . . . I wanted to see those wonderful "Yankees" so much, as I heard my parents say the Yankee was going to set all the slaves free. Oh, how those people prayed for freedom!

Another form of resistance was refusing to work or to submit to punishment. One disgusted planter said, "*I wish every negro would leave the place* as they will do only what pleases them, go out in the morning when it suits them, come in when they please, etc." Some Louisiana slaves demanded wages for their work. Giving information to Union troops and seizing or destroying owners' property when Union troops arrived were other forms of resistance.

Forced Aid to the Confederates. By 1862, the Confederacy was faced with a severe labor shortage. At that time, it began forcing African American slaves into service to build fortifications and repair destroyed railroads. They were also forced to work in factories that made weapons for the Confederate army. Large numbers of African American slaves performed heavy labor for the army. They were also cooks, teamsters, mechanics, nurses in hospitals, and ambulance drivers.

Behind Union Lines. Over time, about half a million African American slaves fled to the Union side during the war. Some 200,000 of them went to work for the army not as soldiers but as laborers, cooks, teamsters, carpenters, and nurses. Some of these former African

180

American slaves, known as **contrabands,** also provided the army with important information about Confederate supplies and troop movements.

Life was hard for many former African American slaves who escaped to the Union lines. Often they were regarded as burdens by the army. Many were put back to work on the land they had recently tended as slaves. Sometimes they had to work for their old owners. Although free, they were often brutally treated and received only a fraction of the pay they were entitled to.

Taking Another Look

1. How did enslaved African Americans in the South resist their owners during the Civil War?

2. What services did escaped African Americans perform for the Union army?

3. **Critical Thinking** Why do you think Union officers often considered former African American slaves to be burdens?

3 ON THE WAR FRONT

What was the contribution of African American soldiers to Union victory?

Why does the government reject the negro? Is he not a man? Can he not wield [handle] a sword, fire a gun, march and countermarch and obey orders like any other? . . . This is no time to fight with one hand when both are needed; this is no time to fight with only your white hand and allow your black hand to remain tied.

With these words, Frederick Douglass urged the U.S. government to change its policy and allow African Americans into the armed forces in the Civil War. When the war began, many African Americans volunteered to serve in the Union army, but they were turned down. In Cincinnati, whites shouted at them, "Keep out of this; this is a white man's war!" A great many whites at this time considered African Americans "inferior" and did not want them in the army.

President Lincoln opposed African American enlistment for political reasons.

These soldiers of the 4th U.S. Colored Infantry were part of the defense of the nation's capital.

Robert Smalls—Pilot in Charleston harbor; took control of Confederate ship and turned it over to Union

William Bronson—Member of first African American company to see action in the war

Nicholas Biddle—One of the first African American Union soldiers to be wounded in the war

Charles L. Mitchell—Captain in a Massachusetts regiment; captured two Confederate cannons and turned them on the enemy in battle at James Island, South Carolina

William H. Carney—Sergeant with 54th Massachusetts Infantry, received Medal of Honor for bravery in planting the flag under fire at the Battle of Fort Wagner

William H. Carney

Peter Vogelsang—Lieutenant with the 54th Massachusetts Infantry; one of three African Americans to be made officers in the regiment

Powhatan Beaty—Received Medal of Honor for assuming command of his company when all officers had been killed or wounded in 1864 battle

Decatur Dorsey—Received Medal of Honor for heroism in battle at Petersburg, Virginia, in 1864

Aaron Anderson—Served in Union navy, received Medal of Honor for courage in an 1865 naval battle

Milton M. Holland—Awarded Medal of Honor for taking command of his company after the officers had been killed or wounded

Harriet Tubman—Conducted raids on Confederate territory; spied for the Union

---

It was essential, he believed, to keep the slave-owning border states from joining the Confederacy. "To arm the negroes," he said, "would turn 50,000 bayonets from the loyal Border States against us. . . . "

Change in Union Policy. Union defeats on the battlefield between 1861 and the first half of 1862 persuaded the government to change its policy about enlisting African Americans. In July 1862, Congress passed an act that permitted the President "to use as many persons of African descent" as he needed "for suppression of the Rebellion."

African Americans, free and slave, flocked to recruiting offices. Many runaways hoped that their joining the army would bring victory for the Union—and with it, freedom. Elijah Marrs, an African American who had escaped from slavery in Kentucky, recalled the moment when he joined the Union army: "I felt freedom in my bones," he said.

In time, some 186,000 African Americans saw combat in the Union army. About 29,000 African Americans served

In order to urge African Americans to volunteer in 1863, the Union army circulated advertisements showing this picture of African American troops in uniform.

in the Union navy. African Americans made up about 10 percent of the Union's armed forces, although they represented less than 1 percent of the population of the North. Between 75 and 100 became officers. Twenty African American soldiers were awarded the Medal of Honor, the Union's highest military honor.

About 38,000 African American troops died in the war, a much higher rate than for white soldiers. Often African American soldiers were inadequately trained and given inferior weapons. Many died because of poor medical care. The high death rate of African American troops was also a result of their frequent attacks on the strongest enemy positions.

African American women played a role in the war, too. Some served as nurses for the army. Harriet Tubman, the Underground Railroad conductor, led raids into Confederate territory and served as a

Union spy. In some Southern cities captured by Union troops, African American women organized relief committees.

African Americans as Union Soldiers. Even though African Americans were recruited, they were generally not treated as the equal of white soldiers. For the most part they were used as laborers, rather than fighters. They were paid $10 a month minus clothing expenses, while white soldiers got $13 a month plus clothing expenses. African American soldiers objected strongly to this discrimination. Finally, in 1864, the War Department began paying them the same amount as whites. Throughout the war, African Americans served in separate units, almost always commanded by whites.

Many African Americans who enlisted complained that they were no better off than slaves. African American units were employed mainly in the backbreaking work of building fortifications behind the lines. An African American soldier from Louisiana wrote a letter of protest to Lincoln. "Instead of the musket," he said, "it is the spade and the wheelbarrow and the axe."

Finally, an order was issued limiting the amount of heavy labor by African American troops to "their fair share . . . to prepare them for the higher duties of conflicts with the enemies." Eventually, African American soldiers saw action against Confederate forces in hundreds of engagements.

Southern White Reaction. The use of African American troops by the North enraged most Southerners. They regarded African American soldiers as rebellious slaves who should be treated as such. But when the tide of war had turned

against the South, some Confederate leaders, commanding general Robert E. Lee and president of the Confederacy Jefferson Davis among them, agreed that African Americans should serve as Confederate soldiers. President Davis's decision in 1865 to recruit African Americans came too late to help the Confederacy. The South was already defeated and would surrender within weeks.

Confederate Secretary of War James A. Seddon reacted to the news of African American Union troops by saying, "We ought never to be inconvenienced with such prisoners. . . . Summary [quick] execution must therefore be inflicted on those taken." Some Southern commanders carried out Seddon's directive. The worst example occurred at Fort Pillow, on the Mississippi River, on April 12, 1864. After its capture by Confederate forces under the command of General

What does this picture of an army cook show about how the Union army used many African Americans?

The aftermath of the battle of Fort Pillow was one of the worst examples of Southern revenge on African American troops. Why do you think Forrest ordered the massacre?

Nathan B. Forrest, all African Americans taken as prisoner were massacred.

Despite the fear of such acts, African Americans fought valiantly throughout the war. On the day Union troops finally marched into Richmond, Virginia, the Confederate capital, African American units were in the lead.

Taking Another Look

1. Why did President Lincoln at first oppose the enlistment of African Americans?

2. Why did the Union change its policy?

3. **Critical Thinking**   About 125 years after the Battle of Fort Wagner, a major motion picture about the 54th Massachusetts Infantry was made. What qualities about the men of this regiment would you expect to see in this movie?

LOOKING AHEAD

The release of the Emancipation Proclamation changed the Civil War from a war to save the Union to a war that also sought to free African American slaves. Hundreds of thousands of them escaped to Union lines, depriving the South of their invaluable labor. Others slowed down their work, reducing the production of food and other goods needed by the South.

Both free African Americans and contrabands entered the Union army in large numbers and played a substantial role in winning the war. The conduct of African American troops in battle won the admiration of many. Having played a major part in the war, African Americans now looked forward to living as free Americans.

CLOSE UP: Chapter 17

Union soldiers charge up the hill toward the fort. Confederate soldiers open fire. Many of the Yankees, including their commanding officer, fall, mortally wounded. "Cut!" yells the director.

This is not a real battle but the filming of a scene from the civil war movie *Glory*. The movie tells the story of the 54th Massachusetts Volunteer Infantry—an African American regiment in the Union army.

Glory won three Academy Awards in 1989. Denzel Washington won the award for best supporting actor for his portrayal of Trip, an African American slave who enlists in the Union army. The movie also won for sound and cinematography.

Historian Shelby Foote helped the filmmakers make the movie realistic. For example, the film shows that the soldiers were not given a left shoe and a right shoe. Instead, both shoes were the same, becoming "left" and "right" after soldiers wore them. The film also paid attention to battle details, such as soldiers marching shoulder to shoulder. Historian Peter Burchard wrote: "It took great heart . . . to tell the story of the 54th as it is told in *Glory*—from the point of view of the regiment's rank and file [ordinary soldiers]."

The Who, What, Where of History

1. **What** was the 54th Massachusetts Infantry?
2. **Who** was President of the Union during the Civil War?
3. **What** does the word *secede* mean?
4. **What** does the word *emancipation* mean?
5. **What** were the four border states?
6. **What** did the Emancipation Proclamation do?
7. **What** did African American slaves do to resist during the war?
8. **Who** were the contrabands?
9. **What** jobs were African Americans first given in the Union army?

Making the Connection

1. What was the connection between President Lincoln's refusal to free African American slaves and the border states?
2. What was the connection between the battles fought between 1861 and the first half of 1862 and the decision to enlist African Americans in the Union army?

Time Check

By the end of 1865, all African American slaves in the United States were free. Use the Snapshot on page 178 and the information in the chapter to answer this question: In which of the following places did slavery end *last:* Washington, D.C.; Kansas Territory; Richmond, Virginia?

What Would You Have Done?

1. If you had been a free African American man during the Civil War, would you have enlisted in the Union army? Explain.

2. If you had been an African American slave during the Civil War, would you have resisted slavery? Explain.

3. If you had been a free African American in the North on January 1, 1863, would you have celebrated the Emancipation Proclamation? Explain.

Thinking and Writing About History

1. Design a recruiting poster encouraging African Americans to enlist in the Union army. Give at least two reasons to join the army.

2. Choose one of the heroes listed in the Honor Roll of the Civil War. Write a letter to the state senators of the state where he or she lived explaining why you think that person should have a memorial in the state capitol. Write an inscription for the plaque that would be on the statue. See page 174 for a model.

Building Skills: Interpreting a Primary Source

Have you ever seen a mystery movie in which all the clues point to one suspect, but in the end you find out that someone else committed the crime? A good detective always interprets clues carefully. A good historian has to interpret carefully the sources he or she uses, as well.

Primary sources often express opinions. A historian must decide what value to place on the opinions he or she finds in a source. For example, sometimes the opinions are not based on facts; sometimes the opinions may be biased by a speaker's prejudices.

Imagine that you are a historian working on a book about the role of African American soldiers in the Civil War. You have found a letter dated 1864 about African American soldiers in the Union army. It says, in part:

At Milliken's Bend, at Port Hudson, Morris Island and other battlefields, they have proved themselves among the bravest of brave, performing deeds of daring and shedding their blood with a heroism unsurpassed by soldiers of any other race.

You are trying to interpret the letter and to decide how much value to place on it. Answer the following questions about the letter:

1. Does the letter express facts and/or the writer's opinion?

2. List the facts and/or opinion.

3. Is the opinion, if any, based on facts?

4. How could you find out?

5. Suppose the letter was written by one of two people: the editor of an abolitionist newspaper or Secretary of War Edwin Stanton writing to President Lincoln. Whose opinion would you value most in this case? Explain.

Sharecroppers during Reconstruction

The Promise and Failure of Reconstruction

(1865–1877)

THINKING ABOUT THE CHAPTER

What were the benefits and disappointments of Reconstruction for African Americans?

Slavery was over at last, but what would freedom be like? How would the 4 million African Americans who had been slaves live? How would they find work? The account of a woman who had been enslaved in Mississippi typified the feelings of many newly freed African Americans as they faced the unknown world of freedom:

> When freedom come, folks left home, out in the streets, crying, praying, singing, shouting, yelling, and knocking down everything. Some shot off guns. Then came the calm. It was sad then. So many folks dead, things tore up, and nowhere to go and nothing to eat, nothing to do.

In the 12 years of Reconstruction, from the end of the Civil War, in 1865, to 1877, enormous changes occurred in the lives of African Americans. As you will read in this chapter, Reconstruction was both a period of hope and achievement for African Americans and a time of great disappointment for them.

1 CHANGES IN FAMILY LIFE, RELIGION, AND EDUCATION

▼ What changes occurred in family life, religion, and education as a result of Reconstruction?

"Samuel Jefferson." "Charles Washington." These were the names two African Americans gave when they went to vote for the first time. Before emancipation, their white owners had called them by their first names only. But after the Civil War, many newly freed African Americans were able to use their **surnames,** or family names. Enslaved African Americans had chosen these names themselves, and they were often the names of early owners. These surnames helped to weave together a vast network of family— grandparents, great grandparents, aunts, uncles, and cousins—who lived on a particular farm or plantation. When a family was broken up through sale, its surname helped to preserve a sense of family among separated members.

At emancipation, those African Americans who did not already have surnames took them, but rarely chose the name of their recent owner. They often took the names of famous people like George Washington or Thomas Jefferson. Whatever their choices, newly freed African Americans were ready for a new life.

Reunited Families.   During slavery, thousands of African American families had been broken up when husbands, wives, children, and other family members were sold to distant plantation owners. With freedom came the chance for separated families to reunite. Many African Americans appealed to the Freedmen's Bureau for help in finding long-gone relatives. Other African Americans took off on their own in search of their families. In September 1865, one freed African American walked more than 600 miles, from Georgia to North Carolina, looking for his wife and children.

New Patterns of Family Life.   Now that they were free, African Americans wanted to establish a normal family life. Under slavery, many men and women lived together without having been formally married. Now, many insisted on being legally joined in marriage.

African American men now assumed the role of head of their family, a role often denied them under slavery. Many refused to allow their wives to work in the fields, as they had before the Civil War. Men also took over the disciplining of their children, a right their former owners had frequently exercised.

Churches of Their Own.   Before emancipation, most African American slaves did not have their own churches. They worshiped in separate sections of white churches. There were some African American churches in the South before the Civil War, but, after emancipation, the number of such churches grew very rapidly.

Across the South, church members pooled their resources to buy land and erect houses of worship. There were many Baptist churches, but there were also African Methodist Episcopal and African Methodist Episcopal Zion congrega-

1865 Southern white secret societies begin campaign of terror.

1865–1877 Reconstruction

20 African Americans serve in U.S. House of Representatives, 2 in the Senate, 600 in Southern state legislatures.

1867 Freedmen's Bureau has set up almost 4,500 schools.

1867–1868 Southern states draw up new constitutions.

1870 Hiram Revels is sworn in as U.S. Senator from Mississippi.

1870s Public schools replace Freedmen's Bureau schools.

1874 Blanche K. Bruce is elected to U.S. Senate.

1877 White Democrats are in power in all former Confederate states.

tions. More than places of worship, they also housed schools, social gatherings, and political meetings.

African American ministers were often the most respected people in their communities, and they were expected to be leaders. Many of the African American men elected to political office were ministers. In the African American community today, ministers still hold a central position of power and esteem.

The Thirst for Education.

It is surprising to me to see the amount of suffering which many of the people endure for the sake of sending their children to school. . . . They are anxious to have the children 'get on' in their books and do not seem to feel impatient if they lack comforts themselves.

This is how a Northern white woman described the eagerness of former African American slaves for the chance to educate their children and themselves. Before the war, some free African Americans in the South had gone to school. Some African American slaves had learned to read and write on their own or with the help of sympathetic owners. Their numbers, however, were small.

After the war, groups of African Americans throughout the South raised money to buy land, build schools, and pay teachers' salaries. Also, by 1867, the Freedmen's Bureau had set up almost 4,500 schools. These schools were not free, and paying tuition was a considerable burden for families. Tuition often represented 10 percent or more of their monthly income. Yet the schools were full. By 1870, bureau schools enrolled 250,000 pupils.

Many of the teachers were African American women. A resident of Selma, Alabama, wrote, "I trust the fact will never be ignored that Miss Lucy Lee, one of the emancipated, was the pioneer teacher of the colored children."

In the 1870s, the bureau schools were replaced by public schools. During the short period when racially **integrated** governments ruled Southern states, the same schools were open to both African American and white children.

Taking Another Look

1. List two important changes that occurred in African American family life during Reconstruction.

2. What part did churches play in Southern African Americans' lives?

3. How did the Freedmen's Bureau help to provide education for Southern African Americans?

4. **Critical Thinking** Why do you think education for former African American slaves has been described as the most revolutionary result of Reconstruction?

2 NEW WORKING CONDITIONS
▼ What changes occurred in how African Americans in the South earned their living?

Until Reconstruction, African American slaves had worked for their owners. Now, they had the chance to work for themselves. This was one of the most satisfying changes for African Americans that resulted from the Civil War. "I felt like the richest man in the world," a former African American slave in Arkansas declared after receiving one dollar for work he had done for a railroad.

Why do you think freed African Americans built their cabins away from the landlord's house?

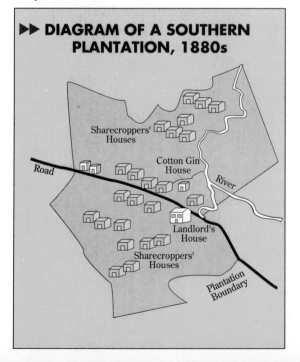

DIAGRAM OF A SOUTHERN PLANTATION, 1880s

Sharecroppers' Houses

Road

Cotton Gin House

River

Landlord's House

Sharecroppers' Houses

Plantation Boundary

What does this picture of a Freedmen's Bureau school tell you about the students' desire to learn?

New Freedoms. Not only could they work for wages, but African Americans in the South were free to work where they wanted. Although many worked for their former owners at their old jobs, others did not. One African American woman who, as a slave, had worked as a cook for a South Carolina family explained why she chose to leave: "I must go," she said. "If I stay here, I'll never know I'm free."

Those who did stay refused to live in the old slave quarters, which were generally near the owner's house. Instead, they insisted that their pay include money to build new cabins far from their old homes and far from the prying eyes of the plantation owner.

The Sharecropping System. Earning a living in the ruined South turned out to be very difficult. Few former slaves could afford to buy land, and even if they could, whites would not sell it to them. Many states had laws that prohibited African Americans from owning land. How then were newly freed African Americans to survive?

At the end of the Civil War, newly freed African Americans were given the im-

Despite its drawbacks, why did sharecropping seem to African Americans to be an improvement over slavery?

money was left that the family needed more credit to start again.

As a result, sharecropping became a cycle of poverty and debt. As John Solomon Lewis, an African American sharecropper, put it, "I was in debt and the man I rented land from said every year I must rent again to pay the other year, so I rents and rents and each year I gets deeper and deeper in debt."

Taking Another Look

1. List three changes in African Americans' working conditions after the Civil War.

2. How did the sharecropping system work?

3. **Critical Thinking**   Do you think an African American might have thought sharecropping was better than slavery? Explain.

pression that they would receive "40 acres and a mule" from the federal government. This would have enabled them to become independent farmers. Without land, they would be at the mercy of their former owners. Some African Americans did become landowners, but hopes of government help never materialized. Gradually, a system of farm labor known as **sharecropping** developed.

Under this system, a family farmed a small plot of land belonging to another, in return for a share of the crop. Having little means of support until the harvest, the family bought supplies and groceries on **credit,** the promise to pay in the future. After the harvest, the landowner or storekeeper who was sometimes the same person, subtracted these growing debts from the money the family would receive from the sale of the crop. So little

3 RECONSTRUCTION GOVERNMENTS

▼ What part did African Americans play in Southern governments during Reconstruction?

During Reconstruction, African Americans in the South became politically active. Once given the right to vote, they used it to elect many African Americans to local, state, and federal offices. The high point of their political participation may have come on February 25, 1870. On that day, Hiram Revels, a Republican from Mississippi, was sworn in as senator, becoming the first African American ever to serve in the U.S. Senate. What made the event even more noteworthy was that Revels had been elected to fill the seat once held by Jefferson Davis, the former president of the Confederacy.

African Americans in State Conventions.

The Reconstruction plan enacted by Congress in 1867 called for conventions to be held in the former Confederate states to draw up new constitutions. All of the conventions had African American delegates, but they made up a majority only in South Carolina.

The state constitutions drawn up in 1867 and 1868 abolished property qualifications for voting and holding office. They granted the right to vote to adult males, except for some former Confederates.

African Americans in State Offices.

Backed by the presence of U.S. troops, African American men flocked to the polls. They represented about 80 percent of Republican voters, and they helped elect Republican legislatures that included African American members. Yet African Americans did not dominate any state government. In South Carolina, they had a large majority in the lower house of the legislature. However, whites controlled the upper house, and there was always a white governor.

In all, more than 600 African Americans served in Southern state legislatures during Reconstruction. Eighteen held

How did Hiram Revels make history when he was sworn in as a U.S. Senator from Mississippi?

such major offices as lieutenant governor, treasurer, superintendent of education, and secretary of state. In Louisiana, Lieutenant-Governor P. B. S. Pinchback became governor for 43 days when the elected governor was impeached. Pinchback was the first African American governor in U.S. history.

Reconstruction governments, with considerable pressure from African Americans, greatly expanded services for both newly freed African Americans and poor whites. Public schools, hospitals, and institutions for the mentally ill were established for the first time in many areas. South Carolina pioneered medical care for needy citizens. Alabama was the first state to provide legal aid for poor defendants. State legislatures did away with earlier Black Codes, outlawed corporal punishment, and reduced both capital punishment and the penalties for theft.

African Americans in the Federal Government.

From 1869 to 1876, 20 African Americans were elected to the

A candidate for office campaigns. Why do you think the women were listening, even though they could not vote?

U.S. House of Representatives, and 2 served in the U.S. Senate. As you have read, one of the senators was Hiram Revels. The other was Blanche K. Bruce, also from Mississippi.

Born a slave in Virginia in 1841, **Blanche K. Bruce** (1841–1898) ran away to freedom when the Civil War began. He later attended Oberlin College in Ohio for two years, until his money ran out. In 1869, Bruce went to Mississippi, where he entered politics.

In 1871, he ran as a Republican candidate for sheriff of Bolivar County, Mississippi, against a white Democrat. In a debate, the Democrat accused Bruce of having been "a slave who did nothing but wait on his master." Bruce replied, "It is true that I was a house slave. But I freed myself, educated myself, and raised myself up in the world. If my opponent had started out where I did, he would still be there." Bruce won the election.

In 1874, Bruce was elected to the U.S. Senate. As a senator, he fought for the rights of African Americans. When he died, in March 1898, it was said that he was second in importance only to Frederick Douglass as a leader of his people.

A White Backlash. In taking back their state governments after 1877, many Southern whites accused Reconstruction governments of corruption. They ignored the fact that in the years after the Civil War, dishonesty in state and local governments was widespread—in North and South, among Democrats and Republicans, and whites and African Americans.

Another charge whites leveled against African Americans in government was that they were uneducated. In fact, almost all African American officeholders on the state and federal levels could read and write. Many were professionals with advanced degrees, or owned businesses and had at least high school educations.

Taking Another Look

1. In what ways did the new state constitutions benefit African Americans?

2. What did Reconstruction state governments accomplish?

3. **Critical Thinking** What qualities did Blanche K. Bruce have that would make all Americans proud of him?

4 A CAMPAIGN OF TERROR
▼ Why did Southern whites try to intimidate African Americans?

Many white Southerners were unable to accept the idea of African Americans' being free, attending school, being able to vote, and holding public office. Almost as soon as the Civil War was over, secret societies grew up in the South to terrorize African Americans. Groups such as the Ku Klux Klan and the White Camelia used violence, arson, and murder to keep African Americans "in their place." In time, the major aim became to destroy the Reconstruction governments.

Between 1865 and 1866, about 5,000 African Americans were murdered in the South in racial incidents. In a typical incident in 1866, a white mob in Memphis,

Tennessee, burned African American homes, churches, and schools, and killed 46 African Americans. Years later, an African American, a former slave, recalled Klan activity in North Carolina:

> The government built schoolhouses, and the Ku Klux Klan went to work and burned 'em down. . . . The Ku Kluxes . . . wore long sheets and covered the horses with sheets so you couldn't recognize 'em. Men you thought was your friends was Ku Kluxes, and you'd deal with them in stores in the daytime, and at night they'd come out to your house and kill you.

For the most part, such activities went unpunished. Sometimes local white officials even participated. State and federal law enforcement officials did nothing to stop the murders and bring the murderers to justice.

Inevitably, the reign of terror against African Americans and their white allies had its effect. Although some African Americans voted in spite of threats, more and more African Americans stayed away from the polls in fear. The result was that Republican candidates were defeated and were replaced by white Democrats. One by one, the Reconstruction governments fell. By 1877, when the last U.S. troops were withdrawn from the South, white Democrats were in power everywhere in the former Confederacy. The hopes of African Americans for their equal rights and economic independence were dead in the South.

Taking Another Look

1. Why did white Southerners conduct a campaign of terror against African Americans?

2. How successful were the Ku Klux Klan and similar organizations in their campaign against African Americans?

3. **Critical Thinking** Why do you think white state and local officials allowed the terror to continue without punishing the participants?

LOOKING AHEAD

Reconstruction has been called "America's unfinished revolution." African Americans took advantage of freedoms denied them under slavery. They formed their own churches, worked through political action to achieve full citizenship for males, and eagerly took advantage of the education available to men and women and children.

But generally African Americans remained poor and dependent on white landowners, after Congress failed to give them land of their own. Before long, whites were using terror and violence to destroy the Reconstruction governments. African Americans would have to fight long and hard for the promise of Reconstruction to become a reality.

Ku Klux Klan members disguised themselves before their raids. What was the purpose of the group?

CLOSE UP: Chapter 18

> *The slave went free; stood for a brief moment in the sun; then moved back again toward slavery.*

So said W.E.B. Du Bois of Reconstruction. The laws passed during Reconstruction held out great hope for African Americans. Yet, for nearly a century after the end of Reconstruction, the federal government failed to enforce them.

The laws were passed to strike at terrorism by the Ku Klux Klan in 1870–1871. Local officials had refused to act against the Klan, so federal agents stepped in—as the new laws allowed. The laws enabled the government to enter into brutality cases in which a public official, such as a police officer, violated a person's civil rights.

The laws were not enforced again until the Civil Rights Movement of the 1960s. In a 1964 case, sheriff's deputies were charged with murdering three civil rights workers near Philadelphia, Mississippi. The federal government cited Reconstruction laws to justify its intervention into the local matter.

The laws passed during Reconstruction are still used and carry stiff penalties. If convicted, a person can receive up to ten years in prison for each civil rights violation, and a maximum life sentence for those violations that end in death.

The Who, What, Where of History

1. **What** was Reconstruction?
2. **What** is sharecropping?
3. **What** was the Freedmen's Bureau?
4. **Who** was Hiram Revels?
5. **When** were Freedmen's Bureau schools replaced by public schools?
6. **What** does the word *integrated* mean?
7. **What** were Black Codes?
8. **Who** was Blanche K. Bruce?

Making the Connection

1. What was the connection between the end of slavery and African Americans' going to school?
2. What was the connection between the end of slavery and sharecropping system?

Time Check

1. When was Reconstruction?
2. **a.** Use the timeline on pages 162–163 to find out what amendments to the Constitution were passed during Reconstruction. **b.** Explain each one.

What Would You Have Done?

1. Imagine that you are a newly freed African American in the South during Reconstruction. Will you exercise your newly acquired right to vote? Explain.
2. Imagine that you are a newly freed African American. The plantation where you spent all your life was burned during the war. You have very little to eat. Your former owner has

asked you to stay and work on the land. You have no money and no idea of where else to get a job. Will you stay on your old plantation? Explain.

Thinking and Writing About History

1. Imagine that you are a former enslaved African American woman, a wife and mother. Write a short autobiography. Describe at least two ways your life has changed with the end of slavery.

2. Imagine that you are a candidate for the Florida legislature in the first election after the Civil War. Write a campaign speech explaining what laws you will work to pass.

Building Skills: Classifying Information

Imagine trying to shop in a music store that didn't *classify* tapes and CDs by type of artist, music, and so on. You might have to dig through every item in the store to find what you wanted.

Classifying means grouping or arranging items into classes, or categories, based on similarities. We classify pieces of information for the same reasons we classify CDs and tapes—to keep them organized and to find what we want easily.

In this chapter, you have studied the many effects of Reconstruction. One way to keep these effects straight is to classify them into groups. Three categories into which you might classify the effects are *political, economic,* and *social.*

Review the chapter, looking for effects of Reconstruction that fall into these categories. On a separate piece of paper, organize them into a chart like the one below. Note that sample entries have been made in each category. Be sure to include at least three other effects in each category on your chart.

After you have completed the chart, review it. In which category do you think the effects of Reconstruction were most important? On a separate sheet of paper write a paragraph explaining your choice.

Effects of Reconstruction

Political Effects	Economic Effects	Social Effects
Passage of the 15th Amendment	Development of sharecropping	Reuniting of many African American families

African American settlers on the Great Plains

CHAPTER **19**

Miners, Farmers, and Cowhands

(1849–1880)

THINKING ABOUT THE CHAPTER

Why did African Americans leave the South and move west?

> I one day said to the man I rented land from, "It's no use. I works hard and raises big crops and you sells it and keeps the money, and brings me more and more in debt. So I will go somewhere else and try to make headway like white workingmen."

These words were written in 1879 by an African American sharecropper who saw no hope for a decent life in the South. Out west, beyond the Mississippi, was a new chance. There African Americans might escape from the limited opportunities, violence, and racism of the South. In the years after the Civil War, thousands of African Americans went west, where they worked as miners, merchants, servants, farmers, and cowhands. Their lives were not easy, but they were better than they had been in the South.

1 THE GOLD RUSH AND AFTER

▼ What roles did African Americans play in the gold fields of California and Colorado?

In 1849, "gold fever" was sweeping the country. Tens of thousands of people were rushing to seek their fortunes in California, where gold had been discovered the year before. The human stampede resulted in an enormous increase in California's population, from 10,000 in 1848 to 100,000 by the end of 1849. Some

The California gold fields attracted many people in 1849. Did most African Americans earn their living mining?

came through Beckwourth Pass (see page 89) in the Sierra Nevada.

The California Gold Fields. Two thousand free African Americans were among those who arrived in California hoping to strike it rich. A number of African American slaves also came with their owners, who expected them to work in the gold fields. Some African American slaves saw California as an opportunity to win their freedom.

Among them were people like Alvin Coffey, his wife, and their three children. With Coffey working on his own at night, he and his family saved more than $5,000 to buy their freedom. Their owner took the money and then sold the Coffeys to another white man. The Coffeys again went to work and soon earned enough money to purchase freedom from their new owner. In time, the Coffeys became the wealthy owners of a laundry in northern California.

Like the Coffeys, few African American settlers in California spent their time searching for gold. Most of them made their living as merchants, barbers, and craftworkers. A few owned newspapers or restaurants.

▶ **William Alexander Leidesdorff,** who arrived in California in 1841 as a ship captain, is an example of a successful African American settler. Born in the Virgin Islands, Leidesdorff soon established himself as a merchant in Yerba Buena, renamed San Francisco in 1847. He built a considerable business with the ships that came to the harbor and with nearby merchants and ranchers. In time, he owned a 35,000-acre (14,165-hectare) ranch and became an important civic and educational leader of the city.

SNAPSHOT OF THE TIMES

1849　African Americans join California Gold Rush.

1857　African Americans join Colorado Gold Rush.

1876　Deadwood Dick gets his nickname.

1870s　African Americans move west.

1879–1880　Exodusters migrate to Kansas.

Taking Another Look

1. Why did African Americans—free and slave—go to California?

2. How did most African Americans in California earn their living?

3. **Critical Thinking** What qualities do you think the Coffeys, William Leidesdorff, and Clara Brown had in common?

The Colorado Gold Fields. In 1857, gold was discovered in Colorado, and once again, African Americans were among those who "rushed" there to make their fortunes.

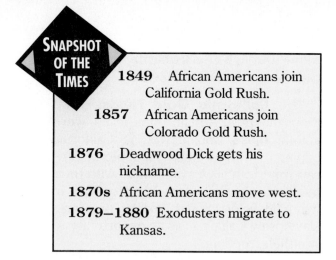

One of them was **Clara Brown,** born into slavery in Virginia in 1803. At the first news of the gold strike, she bought her freedom with her savings and headed for Central City, Colorado. There, cooking and washing clothes for the miners, she saved enough money to bring many of her relatives to Colorado after the Civil War. She also invested in the mines and in time became one of Colorado's richest citizens. Clara Brown was equally well known for her contributions to charities that benefited both African Americans and whites.

2 THE EXODUSTERS AND THE SODBUSTERS

▼ What was life like for African Americans on the Great Plains?

John Solomon Lewis, an African American sharecropper, lived in Tensas Parish, Louisiana. This was a heavily African American, Republican county that had been terrorized in the 1878 election by whites seeking to keep African Americans from voting. Lewis was angered not only by the violence but also by his family's poverty. He decided to move. Despite the landowner's threats to prevent them from leaving, Lewis, his wife, and their four children gathered up their belongings and headed west.

The Lewises were among the thousands of African Americans who fled the South in 1879 and 1880 and joined the exodus, or flight, westward. They called themselves **Exodusters** after the Book of Exodus in the Bible that described the Israelites' exodus from Egypt to the Promised Land. The Exodusters saw no other way to escape the poverty of sharecropping and the terror of the Ku Klux Klan than to leave the South.

Leaders of the Exodus. The exodus was organized by two African Americans, Henry Adams and Benjamin

"Pap" Singleton. Adams, a former slave who had served in the U.S. army, organized a Committee of 500 to live among the newly freed African Americans and report on their condition. Adams recalled:

> We looked around. . . . We said that the whole South had got into the hands of the very men that had held us slaves. . . . Then we said there was no hope for us and we had better go.

Adams and Singleton believed that the way out of poverty and oppression for African Americans was to set up separate African American communities. These communities, they believed, would provide the same economic opportunity for African Americans as the settlements established by white pioneers did for white Americans.

Singleton, a former slave from Tennessee, believed that he had a God-given mission to lead African Americans out of the South. To him, Kansas was the Promised Land where African Americans would find their salvation.

As early as February 1879, groups of Exodusters, ranging in number from 50 to 600, began arriving in St. Louis for the trip west on the Missouri River to Kansas. Others traveled over land. In all, as many as 50,000 Exodusters went to Kansas and other western areas between 1879 and 1881. No one knows how many others tried to go but were turned back by armed bands of whites.

Settling the Great Plains. The Exodusters were not the only African Americans who left the South for territories beyond the Mississippi in the late 1870s and the 1880s. Hundreds of others also headed west and for many of the same reasons. They settled in Kansas,

Why did thousands of African Americans head west?

Oklahoma, and other areas farther west and north.

Some African American settlers set up their own towns. Most of them, however, moved to farm areas on the Great Plains. Life on the Great Plains was hard. With few trees for lumber, settlers built their houses of sod, the top layer of soil that is thick with grass. For this reason, the settlers were called **sodbusters.** Every season brought its hardships: in spring, swollen streams swept away homes; in summer, intense heat and frequent droughts withered crops and killed livestock; in fall, there were prairie fires; in winter, howling blizzards.

A New Life. Despite these hardships, African American sodbusters were better off than they had been as sharecroppers. Some even managed to buy large farms. Within a few years, African Americans had bought thousands of acres. The example of Henry Carter from Tennessee explains how some African Americans were able to start new lives.

Henry Carter and his wife were penniless in 1879 when they arrived in Topeka, Kansas. They trudged on foot to distant Dunbar with their only possessions—

some bedding and a few hand tools. By 1880, they had cleared 40 acres of land, built a small cottage, and owned a horse and two cows. Carter had earned the money by working on nearby ranches.

In the western states and territories, African Americans also found they were much freer than they had been in the white-controlled South. They could go where they pleased, when they pleased, and for as long as they pleased. There were no curfews. Racial prejudice existed, but it was not as severe as in the South. Although city schools separated whites and African Americans, rural schools, where most African Americans lived, did not.

Sympathetic whites in Kansas even helped some African American newcomers get settled. In May 1880, a newspaper in Topeka reported that about one third of the new settlers had received teams of horses and farm tools and should be self-supporting within a year. In general, the African Americans who fared best were those who had skills and some resources of their own. Only a few African Americans gave up and returned to the South.

Taking Another Look

1. Why did Henry Adams and Pap Singleton want to set up separate African American communities?

2. What was life like for African American settlers in the Plains?

3. Why did few settlers return to the South?

4. **Critical Thinking** Why do you think African American settlers faced less prejudice west of the Mississippi than they did in the South?

3 ▼ CATTLE DRIVES AND COWHANDS

▼ What part did African Americans play in the cattle country?

After the Civil War, Texas ranchers found a way to make money from the millions of longhorn cattle that roamed wild on the plains. By 1865, railroads were pushing westward across Missouri and into Kansas. Enterprising Texans began driving herds of cattle 1,000 miles (1,600 kilometers) northward to Abilene and Dodge City, Kansas. There, the cattle were loaded onto railroad freight cars and shipped to market in the East, to be sold at $40 a head.

Countless movies and television programs have portrayed these cattle drives, but rarely, if ever, have African American cowhands been shown. Yet over 5,000 cowhands were African American. A typical trail crew of eight usually included two African Americans.

Some were brought west as slaves and were herding cattle before they were freed. Others came west after emancipation. They were seeking a new life where skill counted for more than the color of a person's skin.

Life on a Cattle Drive. As a rule, African American cowhands suffered less discrimination than African Americans in other occupations. Working and living conditions on the trail were always difficult, sometimes dangerous. All hands had to be prepared for stampedes, cyclones and tornadoes, rainstorms and snowstorms, and attacks by wild animals. Ranch owners, trail bosses, cowhands—all had to share the same rough living conditions. Even life back home on the ranch wasn't easy. But whereas African Americans were welcomed as cowhands and were paid the same wages as other cowhands—usually a dollar a day—they were rarely promoted to trail boss.

A Living Legend. The most famous African American cowhand was probably Nat Love, better known by his nickname, Deadwood Dick.

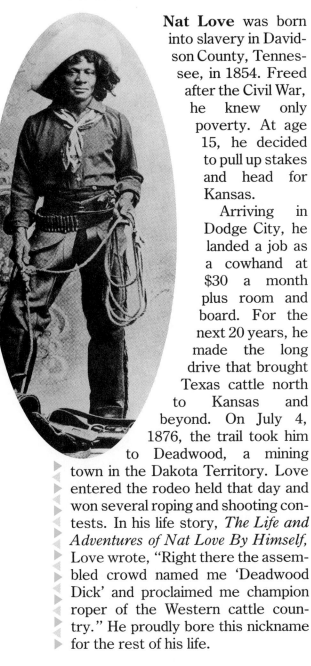

Nat Love was born into slavery in Davidson County, Tennessee, in 1854. Freed after the Civil War, he knew only poverty. At age 15, he decided to pull up stakes and head for Kansas.

Arriving in Dodge City, he landed a job as a cowhand at $30 a month plus room and board. For the next 20 years, he made the long drive that brought Texas cattle north to Kansas and beyond. On July 4, 1876, the trail took him to Deadwood, a mining town in the Dakota Territory. Love entered the rodeo held that day and won several roping and shooting contests. In his life story, *The Life and Adventures of Nat Love By Himself,* Love wrote, "Right there the assembled crowd named me 'Deadwood Dick' and proclaimed me champion roper of the Western cattle country." He proudly bore this nickname for the rest of his life.

Cowhands who wrote about themselves were usually boastful, and Love was no exception. But if much of what Love wrote seems unbelievable, his book does give a glimpse of the "Wild West" era and its code for cowhands.

In time, the railroads went south into Texas, making the long cattle drives unnecessary. But the legendary deeds of cowhands on the trail live on in countless stories, films, and TV shows. Contrary to history, however, these **folk heroes** are rarely shown as African Americans.

Taking Another Look

1. How do cattle drives shown in movies and TV programs differ from the way they really were?

2. **Critical Thinking** What did African American cowhands have in common with Exodusters and other settlers in the western states and territories?

LOOKING AHEAD

For thousands of African Americans, as for white Americans, the western states and territories seemed a promised land where it was possible to start life over. Some African Americans—free and slave—went as far as Colorado and California in the mining days. The largest single migration of African Americans took place in 1879 and 1880, when thousands fled the South and settled in Kansas and other parts of the Great Plains. The great majority of African Americans, however, remained in the South. There, in the last quarter of the 1800s, conditions worsened as white legislatures enacted laws to enforce separation from whites and to deprive African Americans of the right to vote.

They were the Buffalo Soldiers—African American soldiers sent west by the federal government during the Plains Wars. Native Americans gave the soldiers their nickname. Knowing the respect Native Americans had for the buffalo, the troops took the name as a compliment, and used it proudly for more than 80 years.

The Buffalo Soldiers came into being on July 28, 1866, when Congress created six African American regiments. Congress wanted some way to end fighting between Native Americans and new settlers on the Great Plains. The job fell to the 24th and 25th Infantries and the 9th and 10th Cavalries.

Some doubted that the newly formed African American units could fight. But 14 Buffalo Soldiers won the Congressional Medal of Honor for service on the Plains.

Buffalo Soldiers fought until 1952, when the federal government ended segregated army units. Today, three paintings of the soldiers hang in the Pentagon office of General Colin L. Powell, head of the Joint Chiefs of Staff. Sculptor Eddie Dixon has created a monument honoring the Buffalo Soldiers. It stands in Fort Leavenworth, Kansas, the original home of the 9th and 10th Cavalries.

CLOSE UP: Chapter 19

The Who, What, Where of History

1. **Where** was gold discovered in 1849?
2. **What** did most African Americans do in the gold fields?
3. **Who** was Clara Brown?
4. **Who** were the Exodusters?
5. **Who** were the sodbusters?
6. **Where** are the Great Plains?
7. **Who** were Henry Adams and Benjamin "Pap" Singleton?
8. **What** are folk heroes?
9. **Who** was Nat Love?
10. **When** did the largest western migration of African Americans from the South take place?

Making the Connection

1. What was the connection between the end of Reconstruction and the exodus of African Americans to the Great Plains?
2. What was the connection between slavery and the number of African American cowhands?

Time Check

1. Did the gold rushes in California and Colorado happen before or after the Civil War?
2. Did the Exoduster movement happen before or after the end of Reconstruction?

What Would You Have Done?

1. If you had been an African American determined to leave the South in 1879, where would you have gone? Would you have chosen to be an

Exoduster, a sodbuster, or a cowhand? Explain.

2. If you had been an Exoduster, would you have settled in one of Adams and Singleton's separate communities or in a racially mixed community? Explain.

Thinking and Writing About History

1. Imagine that you are an Exoduster. Write a letter to a friend urging him or her to join you on the trip to Kansas.

2. In the library, find stories and legends of cowhands. Then write your own story about an African American cowhand in which the hero defeats a dangerous opponent, either human or a force of nature.

Building Skills: Drawing Conclusions

A conclusion is a statement that is supported by facts. Every conclusion must have facts that support it. For example, the following sentence is a conclusion: "Despite hardships, African American sodbusters were better off than they had been as sharecroppers." What facts support this conclusion? Here is one supporting fact: "Some African Americans managed to buy large farms." Here is another: "Within a few years, African Americans had bought thousands of acres of land."

Each conclusion below has a set of facts that follow it. Some facts support the conclusion; others do not. For each conclusion, write the letters of the facts that support it.

1. Out west, beyond the Mississippi, African Americans had a new chance.
   a. African Americans might escape from the limited opportunities, violence, and racism of the South.
   b. In the years after the Civil War, thousands of African Americans went west, where they worked as miners, merchants, servants, farmers, and cowhands.
   c. Their lives were easier than in the South.

2. Life on the Great Plains was hard.
   a. In spring, swollen streams swept away homes.
   b. Some African American settlers set up their own towns.
   c. In summer, intense heat and frequent droughts withered crops and killed livestock.

3. In the western states and territories, African Americans found they were much freer than they had been in the South.
   a. City schools separated whites and African Americans.
   b. African Americans could go where they pleased, and for as long as they pleased.
   c. Racial prejudice existed, but it was not as severe as in the South.

4. African American cowhands were not usually victims of discrimination on their jobs.
   a. African Americans were welcomed as cowhands both on ranches and on trail drives.
   b. African American cowhands were paid the same wages as white cowhands, about a dollar a day.
   c. All cowhands, including African Americans, as well as ranch bosses shared the same living conditions on the job.

UNIT 7

MAPLE LEAF RAG.

the King of Ragtime writers Scott Joplin.

From the cover of the sheet music

FREEDOM WITHOUT EQUALITY
(1877–1910)

Students at Tougaloo College, Tougaloo, Mississippi

THE BIG PICTURE

Unit 7 traces the changes that took place in the lives of African Americans in the period from the end of Reconstruction, in 1877, to the early years of the 1900s. Growth is the key for this period.

During this time, the United States grew from a nation that was still basically agricultural into one of the world's great industrial powers. It was a time when "big business" expanded and took control of the nation's industry. Immigrants from Europe poured into the factories, mines, and farmlands of the nation. The population almost doubled, and cities mushroomed in the North and Midwest. Such rapid growth and change brought problems as well as benefits, and African Americans experienced more than their share of the problems.

The Growth of Industry. In the 1850s, an Englishman named Henry Bessemer and an American named William Kelly invented a way of making steel quickly and cheaply. When U.S. steel mills began using what was called the Bessemer process in 1867, the country was producing only small amounts of steel. Within 30 years, the United States was turning out 7 million tons (6.4 metric tons) a year, and by 1910, four times that amount. This strong, inexpensive metal was used to manufacture everything from farm equipment and girders for buildings to safety pins.

The greatest immediate use of steel was to enlarge the nation's railroad system. From 52,000 miles (83,700 kilometers) in 1870, it grew to over 166,700 miles (268,000 kilometers) by 1890. With the railroad, products—and people—crisscrossed the nation both quickly and inexpensively.

Two other developments played major roles in the **industrialization** of the United States. In 1879, Thomas Alva Edison, with coworkers such as Lewis H. Latimer, an African American, invented the incandescent light bulb. Later, they developed other applications of electricity. Industries replaced their steam-driven machinery with electrically run machinery. Electric trolleys replaced horse-drawn streetcars in the cities. The telephone, invented in 1876 by Alexander Graham Bell, became a necessity in every office and factory.

Industrial production soared. In the 33 years between 1879 and 1912, the **gross national product**, which is the total value of all goods and services produced in a country, soared from $11.2 billion to $39.4 billion. No other country in the world matched the United States in such growth or such wealth.

The Rise of Big Business. As industrial wealth grew, competitors used various ways to gain larger and larger shares

---

An African American Speaks

The first and dearest rights the Negro of the South wants are the right to pay for his labor, his right of trial by jury, his right to his home, his right to know that the man who lynches him . . . shall be convicted.

—Thomas E. Miller,
Member of Congress, 1891

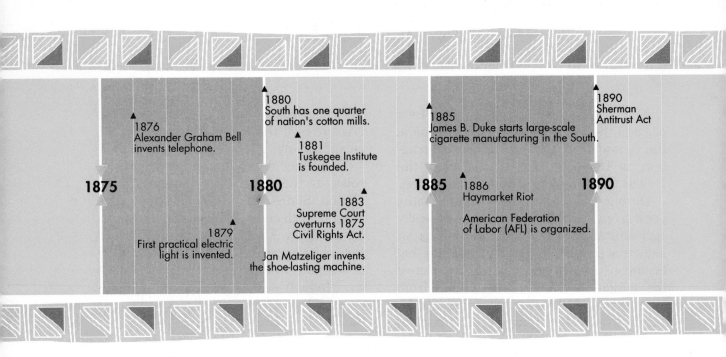

1876
Alexander Graham Bell
invents telephone.

1880
South has one quarter
of nation's cotton mills.

1881
Tuskegee Institute
is founded.

1890
Sherman
Antitrust Act

1885
James B. Duke starts large-scale
cigarette manufacturing in the South.

1875

1880

1885

1890

1879
First practical electric
light is invented.

1883
Supreme Court
overturns 1875
Civil Rights Act.

Jan Matzeliger invents
the shoe-lasting machine.

1886
Haymarket Riot

American Federation
of Labor (AFL) is organized.

of business for greater and greater profits. Oilman John D. Rockefeller forced competing oil companies to sell out to him or be driven into bankruptcy.

Steel giant Andrew Carnegie chose another path to growth. He bought the mining companies that supplied him with iron ore, the shipping companies and rail lines that brought the ore to his factories, and the warehouses that stored his finished steel. By owning all steps of the steel business, Carnegie was able to outsell his competitors and force most of them out of business.

Through these and other means, more and more large companies secured **monopolies** in their industries. A monopoly is the complete, or nearly complete, control of an industry. As the next step, many large corporations joined together to form even larger corporations, called trusts. Their goal was to control entire industries. By 1888, trusts existed in a wide range of industries—sugar, whiskey, steel, paper bags, plows, and glass.

Many Americans were worried about the power of these giant corporations. Demands for government regulation grew. In 1890, Congress passed the Sherman Antitrust Act in an attempt, largely unsuccessful, to ban the formation of trusts and monopolies.

Labor and Unions. While the owners of big business grew wealthy, the men and women who worked in their mills, mines, and factories received only a small share of this wealth. In 1900, the average income of a male factory worker was between $400 and $500 a year. The one fifth of U.S. women who worked in industry received even lower wages. The workweek was long—six days a week, ten hours a day. Children as young as ten worked alongside adults for the same long hours and low pay. Working conditions

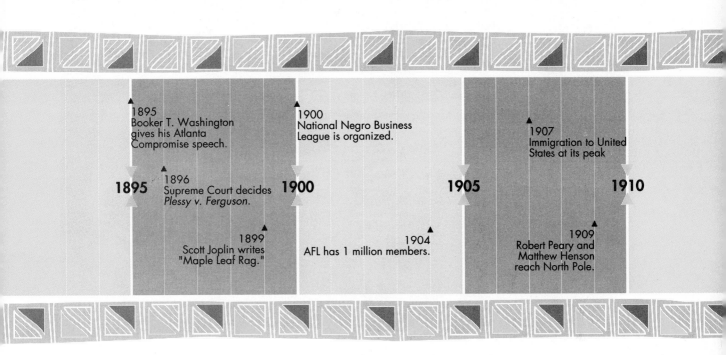

1895
Booker T. Washington gives his Atlanta Compromise speech.

1896
Supreme Court decides *Plessy v. Ferguson.*

1899
Scott Joplin writes "Maple Leaf Rag."

1900
National Negro Business League is organized.

1904
AFL has 1 million members.

1907
Immigration to United States at its peak

1909
Robert Peary and Matthew Henson reach North Pole.

1895   **1900**   **1905**   **1910**

were often unsafe. Injuries and even death from industrial accidents were common. In one year, 195 workers died in Pittsburgh steel plants alone.

Workers sought to improve their lives by forming **labor unions**. In 1869, workers organized the Knights of Labor. It was one of the few unions that accepted African American workers. Its goal was equal pay for men and women, an end to child labor, and a shorter workday.

In 1886, strikers against the McCormick Harvester Company held a meeting in Haymarket Square, Chicago, to protest the shooting of striking workers by the police. Someone threw a bomb into a group of policemen patrolling the meeting. Although the Knights of Labor condemned the attack, the union was accused of favoring violence. Its membership declined sharply.

The American Federation of Labor (AFL) organized the same year as the Haymarket attack and was more successful than the Knights of Labor. It won higher wages, shorter hours, and improved working conditions for its members. By 1904, the AFL was the most powerful union in the United States, with 1 million members. It did not, however, accept African Americans as members.

Immigration. The many new workers who were needed by the growing industries in the North and Midwest came from two sources. Some were U.S.-born farm workers, including African Americans, who left the land to work in the mines and factories. Others were immigrants, who came to the United States in great numbers in the late 1800s and early 1900s from eastern and southern Europe. In 1907, the peak year of immigration, 1,285,000 people entered the United States. Of these almost 70 percent were from Poland, Russia, Hungary, Bohemia,

These immigrants from southern Europe joined the millions of others who have fled persecution and poverty and found refuge in the United States.

Italy, and Greece. Most of them were unskilled and willing to take jobs at lower wages than native-born white workers and earlier immigrants. Not surprisingly, hard feelings developed against the newcomers, and they experienced prejudice for many years.

Growth of Cities. Almost all the new industries were located in cities in the Northeast and Midwest. As people streamed into the cities looking for jobs, the cities mushroomed in number and size. In 1870, there were only 14 cities in the United States with populations over 100,000. By 1910, that number had grown to 50. In 1870, fewer than 27 out of every 100 U.S. residents lived in cities. By 1910, that figure had almost doubled. In the same period, Chicago's population doubled, and New York's increased by more than 50 percent.

These large cities had separate Italian, Polish, Russian, Hungarian, and African American neighborhoods. Living conditions in these areas were harsh. Families often lived in one room. Sanitary conditions were lacking, and diseases such as typhoid flourished.

Yet, for many of the newcomers, the cities also served as steppingstones into American culture. Their children were educated in the public schools and, in the course of a generation or two, moved into the growing middle class. At the same time, the cities and the nation were enriched by the cultural traditions of each new ethnic group.

The New South. Beginning with Reconstruction, Southern merchants, bankers, and other businesspeople realized that the South could not continue with an economy based on agriculture if it was to prosper. Leading the call for change was Henry Grady, the white editor of the *Atlanta Constitution.* Grady proclaimed the opportunity for a "New South." He saw a South with a variety of farm crops, decent relations between African Americans and whites, and growing industry. Of these goals, only industrialization was to become a reality.

Attracted by the region's water power and rich coal, iron, and oil resources, Northerners invested in the South. They were also attracted by cheap, nonunion labor. Southern factory workers, almost all of them white, were paid about half the Northern wage scale. African Americans were given only the lowest factory jobs.

Across the South, new mills and factories went up. By 1880, the South had one quarter of the nation's cotton mills. Birmingham, Alabama, became a center of the iron and steel industry. Mining, smelting, and lumber industries developed. Between 1880 and 1890, railroads in the South doubled their track mileage in order to transport the new products.

Tobacco manufacturing, which had always been an important Southern industry, flourished after 1885. An aggressive Southern businessman, James B. Duke, bought the rights to a cigarette-making machine and gained almost a complete monopoly of the tobacco market.

Westward Expansion. While the cities of the Northeast and Midwest were expanding, so were the western borders of the United States. Thousands of farmers, cattle ranchers, and miners settled the lands west of the Mississippi. In the process of settlement, however, they destroyed the livelihood and culture of the many Native American peoples who had lived on the land for thousands of years.

Taking Another Look

1. In what ways did U.S. industry grow between 1877 and 1910?

2. How did cities change in this period?

3. **Critical Thinking** What groups did U.S. growth benefit at this time?

This steel mill in Birmingham, Alabama, employed hundreds of workers after the Civil War. As in most Southern industries, African Americans were allowed to work at only the lowest-paying jobs.

Sharecroppers' cabins

African Americans in the New South

(1877–1910)

THINKING ABOUT THE CHAPTER

Why were the closing decades of the 1800s and the first years of the 1900s a difficult time for African Americans in the South?

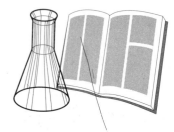

One day in 1832, a popular white entertainer named Thomas Rice stood in the alley outside a theater in Baltimore, Maryland. He was watching an African American street performer sing and dance. The song went:

> Wheel about, turn about,
> Do it jus' so,
> An' every time I wheel about
> I jump Jim Crow.

Rice was so impressed by the man's performance that he added it to his own act. Dressed in an exaggerated version of the street performer's clothes, he per-

Rice as Jim Crow

formed "Jim Crow" before laughing white audiences everywhere. Soon, the term *Jim Crow* began to be used by whites to apply to all African American people.

This is one of many versions of the origin of the term *Jim Crow*. Whatever its origin, however, *Jim Crow* at first was used to make fun of African Americans.

In the years after Reconstruction, the meaning of the term changed. Rather than being applied to African Americans, **Jim Crow** was used to refer to the laws being passed in the South to segregate African Americans in housing, transportation, and many other aspects of daily life. These laws were enacted at a time when African Americans were finding it difficult just to earn a living.

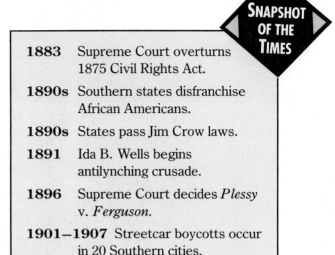

SNAPSHOT OF THE TIMES

1883 Supreme Court overturns 1875 Civil Rights Act.

1890s Southern states disfranchise African Americans.

1890s States pass Jim Crow laws.

1891 Ida B. Wells begins antilynching crusade.

1896 Supreme Court decides *Plessy* v. *Ferguson*.

1901–1907 Streetcar boycotts occur in 20 Southern cities.

1 HARD WORK AND MORE POVERTY

▼ What was the economic condition of African Americans in the South in the late 1800s?

In 1884, T. Thomas Fortune, a leading African American journalist, wrote that African Americans in the South were "more absolutely under the control of the Southern whites; they are more poorly housed, clothed and fed, than under the slave regime [system]." He added, "The African American is an alien [stranger] in his native land."

Families in the Fields. No African Americans would have agreed more with Fortune than those who worked as sharecroppers on the farms and plantations of the South. When sharecropping began during Reconstruction (see page 190), African Americans saw it as a way to earn a living. But as the post-Reconstruction years rolled on, life under the sharecropping system turned more and more bitter. Not only was the work terribly hard, but

sharecroppers were also constantly in debt to their landowners, who often cheated them.

Jobs in Industry. African Americans also provided needed labor in the industries of the New South. They filled low-level jobs in lumbering, mining, shipping, manufacturing, and some trades. African Americans also built the New South's roads, dug its sewers, and cleaned its streets. Although the pay was low, it was higher than what African Americans could earn from sharecropping, and they saw these jobs as a step up the economic ladder. The jobs were backbreaking, and some were dangerous as well. In the lumber industry, for example, forest workers could be killed by falling trees. African Americans were able to get these jobs because few white men wanted them.

Most African American women worked in laundries and in white people's homes, as cleaning women, cooks, or washerwomen. They earned the lowest pay of anyone in the United States, as little as $5.00 a month.

White and African American workers who did the same jobs did not always get

An African American officer of the Knights of Labor introduces union head Terence V. Powderly at a meeting.

the same pay. An African American fireman on the Southern Railway explained:

> If I take a train from here to Greenville, South Carolina, I get for that trip $2.60, the white engineer gets $6.00. But if that same train had the same engineer and a *white* fireman, the engineer would get his $6.00 just the same but the fireman would get $3.25. He gets 65 cents more for doing the same work I do.

A skilled African American woman working in Columbia, Georgia, earned between $5.00 and $6.00 a month. An unskilled white woman worker in the Columbia cotton mill, where African Americans were not allowed to work, earned from $35.00 to $45.00 a month.

Labor Unions. Although labor unions were not strong in the post-Reconstruction South, when they did exist, they too discriminated against African Americans. White workers rarely allowed African Americans to join their unions. An exception was the Knights of Labor, which had 90,000 African American members in 1886.

When union members went on **strike,** or stopped work in an attempt to gain better pay and working conditions, employers sometimes offered their jobs to African Americans. In the 1870s, for example, mine owners brought African American workers to Ohio and Illinois to break strikes by white mine workers. Such incidents increased the ill will of the white workers toward African Americans. In other places, because African Americans would work for less, employers threatened to hire them and fire white workers.

On rare occasions, African Americans joined forces and went on strike also. This happened in the Southern sugar fields in 1880. African American workers struck to gain an increase in their pay from 75 cents a day to $1 a day. The strikers were arrested, and the strike was broken.

The Convict-Lease System. Imprisoned African Americans were organized, and literally chained together, in work gangs that were leased out to individuals or companies. Working under the most brutal conditions, these chain gangs built roads, and labored in lumber mills, quarries, factories, mines, and brickyards. The **convict-lease system** had the effect of decreasing the number of paying jobs available for others.

Taking Another Look

1. Describe some of the injustices suffered by African American workers in the South.

2. In what way did labor unions and the convict-lease system affect the job opportunities of African Americans in the South?

3. **Critical Thinking** What do you think T. Thomas Fortune meant when he said, "The African American is an alien in his native land"?

2 THE LAND OF JIM CROW

▼ What rights were denied African
▼ Americans by law?

Although white Southern political leaders returned to office in the years right after Reconstruction, many African Americans continued to vote. They sent African Americans both to state legislatures and to Congress. Between 1876 and 1895, for example, there were 57 African Americans in the North Carolina House of Representatives and 47 in the South Carolina General Assembly. There were three African Americans in Congress in 1890. That situation was soon to change.

Losing the Vote. In the 1890s, the Democrats, who by then controlled politics in the South, made an important decision. It was now clear that the federal government had lost interest in making sure that African Americans were not prevented from voting in Southern states. This left Southern states free to pass laws **disfranchising** African American men. Such laws denied them the rights of citizenship, especially the right to vote. The states developed a number of ways by which African American men could be

▶▶ STATE BARRIERS TO VOTING BY AFRICAN AMERICANS

Poll Tax	A fee a voter must pay in order to vote; in effect, a voting tax that many African Americans were too poor to pay
Property Test	Requirement that a man must own a certain amount of property in order to vote; a test that few African Americans and poor whites could meet
Literacy Test	Requirement that to vote, a man must be able to read; white election registrars decided who passed the test
Grand-father Clause	Waived literacy and property tests for those men whose grandfathers had been eligible to vote before the Civil War, a test that few African Americans could meet
White Primary Elections	Primary, or nominating election, from which Southern Democrats could ban African American men because such elections were not covered by the 15th Amendment, which had given African Americans the vote

By 1910, seven Southern states had adopted some of these measures to disfranchise African Americans. Why did whites want to keep them from voting?

denied their voting rights. The table on this page lists the most widely used of these devices.

The measures described in the table above worked. In one Southern state after another, the number of African Americans who were able to vote dropped sharply. In Louisiana, for instance, 130,000 African Americans had voted in 1896. Two years later, after the grandfather clause had gone into effect there, the number dwindled to 5,000. By the end of the 1800s, African Americans had lost their power to elect officials.

The Rise of Jim Crow. Keeping African American men from voting was only one way the South attacked the rights of African Americans. The Southern states also saw to it that laws were passed establishing strict separation between African Americans and whites. Separation, or **segregation,** became the law. African Americans and whites could not ride in the same streetcars or railway cars or even sit in the same passenger stations. African Americans could not drink from the same public water fountains as whites. They had to sit in separate sections of theaters. African Americans and whites could not be treated in the same hospitals or buried in the same cemeteries. This was the system that became known as Jim Crow.

Plessy v. Ferguson. African Americans believed that Jim Crow laws violated the 14th Amendment, which guaranteed American citizens "the equal protection of the law" (see page 165). One African American who decided to test the legality of Jim Crow laws was Homer Plessy. While on a train trip in Louisiana, Plessy sat in a whites-only railroad car. When he refused to move to a car for African Americans, he was arrested.

Louisiana law required separate accommodations for African Americans and whites in public facilities. By riding in the whites-only car, Plessy had broken this law. He was found guilty by a Louisiana court, but he appealed his case to the U.S. Supreme Court.

In 1896, in the case known as *Plessy* v. *Ferguson,* the Supreme Court ruled against Plessy. As long as facilities for African Americans and whites were equal, keeping the races separate was constitutional. The Court reasoned that the 14th Amendment "could not have been intended to abolish distinctions based on color." This ruling established

Why do you think whites set up Jim Crow?

▶▶ SOME JIM CROW LAWS, 1870 – 1965

Date/Place		Intent of Law	Date/Place		Intent of Law
1870	Georgia	separate schools	1915	Oklahoma	separate phone booths
1891	Georgia	separate seating in railroad cars	1915	S. Carolina	unequal spending for education
1900	S. Carolina	separate railroad cars	1922	Mississippi	separate taxicabs
1905	Georgia	separate parks	1932	Atlanta	separate baseball fields
1906	Alabama	separate streetcars	1935	Oklahoma	no boating or fishing together
1910	Baltimore	separate residential blocks	1937	Arkansas	segregation at race tracks
1914	Louisiana	separate entrances and seating at circuses	1944	Virginia	separate airport waiting rooms
1915	S. Carolina	separate entrances and work areas in factories	1965	Louisiana	no state money for schools not segregated

These African American children are attending a segregated school in the nation's capital, which followed Southern segregationist policies.

what became known as the separate-but-equal principle.

The Spread of Jim Crow. Two years after the *Plessy* decision, a bill to make it illegal for African Americans and whites to ride in the same railroad cars was before the South Carolina legislature. The editor of a white newspaper wrote an editorial making fun of the proposal. "Why stop there?" he asked jokingly.

> If there must be Jim Crow cars on the railroads, there should be Jim Crow cars on the street railways. Also on all passenger boats. . . . There should be Jim Crow waiting saloons at all stations, and Jim Crow eating houses. . . . Jim Crow sections of the jury box, and a separate Jim Crow dock and witness stand in every court—and a Jim Crow Bible for colored witnesses to kiss. . . . Perhaps, the best plan would be, after all, to take the short cut . . . by establishing two or three Jim Crow counties at once, and turning them over to our colored citizens for their [use].

Except for the Jim Crow witness stand and the separate counties, everything the editor poked fun at eventually came true—even the Jim Crow Bible. The separate-but-equal doctrine of *Plessy* v. *Ferguson* became the South's justification for segregating all kinds of facilities, from schools, parks, and water fountains to cemeteries. It didn't matter that facilities for African Americans were rarely equal to those for whites. The separate-but-equal doctrine was to keep Jim Crow alive for more than 50 years.

Lynch Law. Added to the loss of African Americans' voting rights and the spread of Jim Crow was a campaign of terror against African Americans. For example, one day in March 1892, 12 armed white men attacked a grocery store owned by three African Americans in Memphis, Tennessee. The partners were armed and fought back. They were arrested and jailed on conspiracy charges. Some whites, outraged at the African Americans' actions, stormed the jail, dragged the partners out to the street, and shot them to death.

This was just one example of the wave of lynchings that swept the South at this time. Between 1882 and 1900, over 3,000 people—most in the South and mostly all African Americans—were lynched. This reign of terror continued well into the 1900s, as you will read in Chapter 23.

Taking Another Look

1. Describe three measures taken by Southern states to prevent African Americans from voting.

2. How did the *Plessy* v. *Ferguson* decision help the South justify its policy of segregation?

3. **Critical Thinking** As you will read later in this book, the separate-but-equal doctrine was eventually overturned by the Supreme Court. What wording in the *Plessy* decision might point to the outcome?

3 THE AFRICAN AMERICAN RESPONSE

▼ What did African Americans do to protect themselves?

"It is time to face the enemy and fight inch by inch for every right he denies us." This was the advice of journalist T. Thomas Fortune to his fellow African Americans, living in the world of Jim Crow, lynchings, and absence of **civil rights**. Civil rights are those rights given to all citizens of the United States by the Constitution and its amendments.

Facing the Enemy. Many African American organizations took Fortune's advice and petitioned Congress for a new civil rights bill. In 1875, Congress had passed a civil rights law that outlawed racial discrimination in public places. The Supreme Court declared the law unconstitutional in 1883. African Americans then petitioned individual states. As a result, 15 Northern states passed or strengthened their civil rights laws.

Some African Americans took more direct action. In over 20 cities across the South from 1901 to 1907, African Americans boycotted streetcar companies that segregated their cars. In doing so, they were obeying the words of African American newspapers like the Savannah *Tribune*, which wrote, "Do not trample on our pride by being 'jim crowed.' Walk!" In some cities, the boycotts forced streetcar companies into bankruptcy. In some cases, African Americans then formed transit companies of their own.

Attack on Lynching. In the 1890s, one African American was lynched about every two days. One person who did more than anyone else to fight lynching was Ida B. Wells.

Ida B. Wells  was born a slave in 1862 in Holly Springs, Mississippi. When she was 14, she became a teacher. She later continued her own education by attending Fisk University in Nashville.

One day, when she was 22, Wells sat in the "white ladies only" car of a Memphis train. The conductor told her to move, and she refused. He grabbed her arm to pull her off, and she bit his hand. It took three men to force the embattled Wells from the coach. She sued the railroad for damages and won $500, although she later lost her case on appeal by the railroad.

In 1891, Wells became the editor and part owner of a Memphis weekly newspaper, *Free Speech,* in which she attacked lynching. A grocery-store owner who had been lynched in Memphis had been a close friend of Wells. After his murder, she wrote an editorial demanding the lynchers' arrest, but nothing was done. Wells advised her fellow African Americans to leave Memphis. "We are out-numbered and without arms," she wrote. "There is only one thing left we can do—leave a town which will neither protect our lives and property nor give us a fair trial, but takes us out and murders us in cold blood."

Some whites, angry at what Wells had written, destroyed her printing presses and threatened to hang her in front of the Memphis Courthouse. Wells had to flee the city for her own safety. She settled in Chicago, where she later married Ferdinand L. Barnett. After her marriage she was known as Ida B. Wells-Barnett.

Wells dedicated herself to the anti-lynching crusade. She investigated lynchings and wrote about them for the African American press. In 1895, she compiled *The Red Record,* a study of lynchings that had occurred during the past three years. Within three years after she began her campaign, the number of lynchings dropped from 235 a year to 180. Until her death in 1939, Wells continued to fight lynch law. She also fought in other ways for the freedom and equality of African Americans, especially women, and was one of the founders of the NAACP.

Taking Another Look

1. Describe three ways African Americans fought racism in the South.

2. How did Ida B. Wells-Barnett fight against lynching?

3. **Critical Thinking** As you read in the story of Ida B. Wells-Barnett, fighting racial hatred could be dangerous. Why do you think many African Americans fought back despite the danger to them?

LOOKING AHEAD

Disfranchisement, Jim Crow laws, and lynching made life in the South unbearable for many African Americans. Unwilling to accept such conditions, African Americans fought back, none more actively than Ida B. Wells-Barnett. One man, however, Booker T. Washington, became the spokesman for a different path for the betterment of African Americans.

CLOSE UP: Chapter 20

In 1892, African American and white farmers gathered in Texas to support the newly formed Populist party. "I am an emancipated slave of this state," declared one African American delegate, "[yet] my interest is yours and yours mine." To unseat the Republicans and Democrats, the Populists openly courted and won the backing of African American voters in the South.

In 1892, the Populists seated more than 90 African American delegates at their national convention. African Americans voted in large numbers and helped the Populists win many state and national offices throughout the South.

When the Populists declined in the late 1890s, many white Southerners vowed that never again would they allow African American votes to decide elections. In 1901, the last African American representative from the South, George H. White of North Carolina, left Congress. "This . . . is perhaps the Negro's temporary farewell to the American Congress," said White, "but . . . he will rise up some day and come again." That day came in 1972 when Georgia elected Andrew Young to the House of Representatives.

The Who, What, Where of History

1. **What** does the term *Jim Crow* mean?
2. **What** was the New South?
3. **What** are labor unions?
4. **What** was the convict-lease system?
5. **What** does the word *disfranchising* mean?
6. **Who** was Homer Plessy?
7. **What** was *Plessy* v. *Ferguson*?
8. **What** is a lynching?
9. **Who** was Ida B. Wells?

Making The Connection

1. What was the connection between strikes by labor unions in the South and increased anger of whites toward African Americans?
2. What was the connection between low employment rates in the South and the convict-lease system?

Time Check

1. When did the Supreme Court overturn the 1875 Civil Rights Act?
2. When did the Supreme Court decide *Plessy* v. *Ferguson*?

What Would You Have Done?

1. Imagine that you are an African American offered a job in a Southern textile mill during a strike. You are not allowed to join the union that is on strike. Would you become a strikebreaker? Explain.

2. Would you have taken Ida B. Wells's 1891 advice to leave Memphis? Explain in a letter to a friend.

Thinking and Writing About History

1. Write a paragraph that explains why sharecroppers could not get out of debt regardless of how hard they worked.

2. Write a journal entry describing a day in the life of an African American child living in a small Southern city in 1900. Include a description of the "separate but equal" facilities that the child must use.

Building Skills: Comparing Charts

Comparing charts that show differences over time can be a bit tricky. You need to be sure that you know what you are looking at before you start to make comparisons.

The two charts below, for example, show the requirements for voters in Southern states in 1860 and 1930. The chart for 1930, however, does not have the same categories as the chart for 1860. Look at the two charts and answer the following questions.

1. What category(ies) does the 1860 chart include that the 1930 chart does not have?

2. What category(ies) is a part of the 1930 chart but not of the 1860 one?

3. Which states had poll taxes in 1930?

4. Which states had an education requirement in 1930?

5. Using the information in the two charts, write a sentence explaining whether an African American had a better chance of voting in 1860 or 1930 and why.

▷ ▷ Voter Qualifications in 1860

State	Race	Residence	Citizenship
Alabama	White	1/2 year	U.S.
Arkansas	White	1/2 year	U.S.
Florida	White	1/2 year	U.S.
Georgia	White	1/2 year	U.S.
Kentucky	White	2 years	State
Louisiana	White	1 year	U.S.
Maryland	White	1 year	U.S.
Mississippi	White	1 year	U.S.
Missouri	White	1 year	U.S.
North Carolina	White	1 year	U.S.
South Carolina	White	2 years	U.S.
Tennessee	White	1/2 year	U.S.
Texas	White	1 year	U.S. or state
Virginia	White	2 years	State

▷ ▷ Voter Qualifications in 1930

State	Residence	Education	Property
Alabama	2 years	Read, write English	Poll tax, 40 acres
Arkansas	1 year	—	—
Florida	1 year	—	Poll tax
Georgia	1 year	Read, write English	Poll tax, 40 acres or $500
Kentucky	1 year	—	—
Louisiana	2 years	Read, write English	Poll tax, $300
Maryland	1 year	—	—
Mississippi	2 years	Read Constitution	Poll tax
Missouri	1 year	—	—
North Carolina	1 year	Read, write English	—
South Carolina	2 years	—	Poll tax
Tennessee	1 year	—	Poll tax
Texas	1 year	—	Poll tax
Virginia	2 years	Read Constitution	Poll tax, $300

George Washington Carver at Tuskegee Institute

Living in the Jim Crow World

(1877–1910)

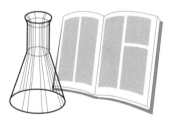

THINKING ABOUT THE CHAPTER

What strategies were advanced in the late 1800s and early 1900s to improve the lives of African Americans?

Atlanta, Georgia, on September 18, 1895, was as hot as it usually is at that time of year. For the whites and African Americans crammed into the building where the Cotton States and International Exposition was to open, the heat was almost unbearable. Yet, when an African American whom the New York *World* described as "tall, bony," with a "high forehead . . . and strong, determined mouth" began to speak, the heat was forgotten. "Within ten minutes," continued the *World*, "the multitude [audience] was in an uproar of enthusiasm. . . . The fairest women of Georgia stood up and cheered."

The speaker who aroused such spirited response was Booker T. Washington. From that day on, he was thought

by many to have succeeded Frederick Douglass as the leader of African Americans. At a time when African Americans such as Ida B. Wells-Barnett were vigorously protesting the wave of lynchings and the Jim Crow world in which African Americans lived, Washington had another answer. African Americans would succeed, he believed, not by protests but through industrial education, self-help, and business ownership. Washington devoted his life to making these goals a reality for African Americans.

1 A STRONG LEADER

▼ What were Booker T. Washington's accomplishments as educator and leader of African Americans?

Somehow 16-year-old Booker T. Washington heard of Hampton Institute in Hampton, Virginia, and was determined to attend the school. But it was 500 miles (800 kilometers) from his home in West Virginia, and he had no money to get there or to pay for classes. That did not stop Washington. If it meant walking the 500 miles, he would walk. If it meant getting up at four in the morning to work as a janitor to pay his expenses, that's what he would do. Booker T. Washington never regretted either decision. His education at Hampton became his steppingstone to leadership of Tuskegee Institute. Building Tuskegee into a first-class educational institution for African Americans was the proudest accomplishment of Washington's life.

Washington's Early Years. In many ways, Booker T. Washington's early years were typical of those of a Southern African American boy after Reconstruction.

Booker T. Washington was born into slavery on a small plantation in Virginia in 1856. He never met his father, who was said to be a white man living on a nearby plantation. After the Civil War, when he was nine years old, his family moved to West Virginia, where he worked first in a coal mine and then in a salt mine. He squeezed in a few hours at the local school whenever he could.

Washington was a bright student and learned enough to think seriously of attending Hampton Institute. Hampton had been founded in 1868 by General Samuel Chapman Armstrong as a college for African Americans. Armstrong believed that along with their basic academic studies, African Americans should learn practical skills that would help them get jobs and earn a living. Washington was especially attracted to this part of the Hampton program, and it influenced his later leadership at Tuskegee Institute.

Washington did well at Hampton, and in 1879, Armstrong offered him a job teaching there. After teaching for two years, he was given a chance to head Tuskegee, a new school in Alabama.

When Washington arrived at Tuskegee, he discovered that the school had no buildings and no land suitable for building. Undismayed, Washington and his small staff of teachers taught classes in a shanty lent him by the local African American church and had his students help clear the land.

1881 Tuskegee Institute is founded.

1888 First African American insurance company is founded.

First African American bank is founded.

1895 Booker T. Washington delivers Atlanta Compromise speech.

1900 National Negro Business League is organized.

Washington's Goals for Tuskegee. Washington's goals for what students should learn at Tuskegee were clear. As he wrote in his famous autobiography, *Up From Slavery:*

> We wanted to give them such a practical knowledge of some one industry, together with the spirit of industry, thrift, and economy, that they would be sure of knowing how to make a living after they had left us. We wanted to teach them to study actual things instead of mere books alone.

For the next 15 years, Washington worked to offer as fine an industrial education at Tuskegee as his students would have received at Hampton Institute. In addition to academic subjects, male students were taught farming, brick making,

Teaching African Americans to be skilled craftworkers was one of Booker T. Washington's goals for Tuskegee. Here students are assembling horse-drawn carriages.

Why did Booker T. Washington think an industrial education was important for African Americans?

carpentry, and other skills. Female students also learned cooking and sewing.

Under Washington's guidance, Tuskegee grew and prospered. By 1906, it had 1,500 students and a staff of 155. Among the staff was scientist George Washington Carver (see page 240), who came to Tuskegee at Washington's invitation in 1896. Many of Tuskegee's graduates became teachers, who carried the school's message into all the Southern states and to African nations.

Washington as Leader. As you read at the beginning of this chapter, Washington was invited to deliver an address at the Cotton States and International Exposition in Atlanta, Georgia, in 1895. That speech brought him national fame and guided his work as a national leader until his death in 1915.

In his Atlanta speech, which came to be called the **Atlanta Compromise**, Washington made public his belief that African Americans should advance not through political protest, but through education and job skills. According to Washington,

being able to earn a living and buy property was more important than being able to vote. Washington urged African Americans to take advantage of opportunities around them. This was his message:

Cast down your bucket [seize the opportunity] where you are. . . . Cast it down in agriculture, in mechanics, in commerce, in domestic service, and in the professions. . . . No race can prosper till it learns that there is as much dignity in tilling a field as in writing a poem. It is at the bottom of life we must begin and not at the top.

Washington also urged whites to hire African Americans instead of looking to European immigrants as workers. As a reward, he promised, "you and your families will be surrounded by the most patient, faithful, law-abiding, and unresentful people that the world has seen."

Washington then addressed the question of whether African Americans and whites should mix together socially. He assured the white members of his audi-

African Americans debated the merits of Washington's programs. Which of the people quoted above would have approved of them?

ence that economic integration did not mean social integration. In what became the most remembered part of his speech, he said, "In all things that are purely social we can be as separate as the fingers, yet one as the hand in all things essential to mutual progress."

African Americans' Views of Washington. Washington seemed to be advising African Americans to ignore the evils of Jim Crow and discrimination. However, most ordinary African Americans supported him and viewed him as their leader.

However, the response of other African American leaders to Booker T. Washington was mixed. Some agreed that he was a great leader. Others were not so sure. They criticized his apparent acceptance of segregation and disfranchisement. They thought his system of industrial education kept African Americans in lower-paying jobs at a time when modern industry needed workers with more advanced skills. The table is a sampling of opinions about Washington by some of his African American contemporaries.

Washington's Influence Among Whites. Many prominent white leaders were pleased with Booker T. Washington's philosophy. It did not call for any basic change in the country's treatment of African Americans. Some whites called Washington the Moses of the Negro race. Influential business people also praised him. The wealthy industrialist Andrew Carnegie said that Washington was "certainly one of the most wonderful men living or who has ever lived."

Political leaders also admired Washington's philosophy. President Theodore Roosevelt invited him to dine at the White House in 1901, and he often consulted with him on racial policy. The President thought Washington was "a genius such as does not arise in a generation" and said he did not know "a white man of the South who is as good a man as Booker Washington today."

Even conservative Southern politicians liked Washington. His influence with them was so great that no African American could be appointed to an important politi-

Washington was very influential among politicians and businessmen. Here he is shown with President William Howard Taft (left) and Andrew Carnegie (right).

cal or educational position without Washington's approval.

While Washington publicly advised African Americans to accommodate themselves to segregation and Jim Crow, in private, he opposed these policies. He secretly financed court cases that challenged voting laws, segregation, and discrimination. He also tried to get more African Americans to register and vote. He was careful to keep this work hidden, however, believing that public knowledge would hurt his ability to help African Americans.

Taking Another Look

1. What kind of education did Tuskegee Institute offer under Washington?

2. What was Booker T. Washington's stated policy on segregation?

3. **Critical Thinking** Why do you think Washington's speech in Atlanta came to be known as the Atlanta Compromise?

2 ▼ AFRICAN AMERICAN BUSINESSES

▼ What did African Americans accomplish in the business world in the late 1800s and early 1900s?

Booker T. Washington did not believe that industrial education alone was the way for all African Americans to better themselves. According to him, business ownership was also a way for African Americans to succeed.

In 1900, five years after his Atlanta speech, Washington launched the National Negro Business League. Meeting for the first time, in Boston, 115 delegates from 20 states, mostly from the South, heard Washington declare that the purpose of the organization was to promote business.

By 1905, more than 300 local business leagues had been organized, and the number of businesses owned by African Americans had grown substantially. However, the total number of such businesses was still small and involved only a fraction of the African American population. Nevertheless, these businesses were the vehicle by which a significant number of African Americans were able to launch themselves into the middle class.

African American Businesses. Between the end of Reconstruction and 1910, African Americans set up a wide variety of small businesses in the South. They included food stores, restaurants, drugstores, cigar stores, dry-cleaning establishments, and shoe-repair shops. Other businesses provided personal services that whites refused to offer African Americans. Among these were beauty parlors, barbershops, and undertaking establishments. Almost all of these small businesses were located in the segregated African American neighborhoods of cities and towns.

More substantial than the retail businesses were the banks and insurance companies owned by African Americans. Since white insurance companies often refused to insure African Americans or charged them very high rates, many African American self-help societies set up their own insurance companies. The first of these was founded in Virginia by the Grand United Order of True Reformers in 1881. The North Carolina Mutual Life Insurance Company was founded in Durham. Under the leadership of C. C. Spaulding, it became the largest U.S. business owned and operated by African Americans.

Banks provided two services to the community. African American churches preached the virtues of thrift, and African Americans who took this advice needed a place to deposit their savings. At the same time, in order to grow, African American businesses needed credit, which white banks often denied them. Again, it was the Grand United Order of True Reformers that pioneered in the establishment of banks. It set up the True Reformers Bank in Richmond, Virginia, in 1888. By 1910, about 50 African American banks were operating throughout the South.

Problems of African American Businesses. African American businesses did not have an easy time, and many failed. One reason was that African Americans did not have experience in business and often made poor business decisions. Some banks, for example, made loans that were out of proportion to the amount of money they had on deposit.

Since small businesses had little money, they frequently could afford to locate only in the least desirable, and therefore cheapest, areas of African American communities, where few customers were likely to come. Often, African American small businesses also had to compete with white-owned businesses located in African American neighborhoods. The white owners usually had more capital and could offer lower prices.

A Success Story. One of the great African American success stories was that of businesswoman Madame C. J. Walker. Her company was also unusual in that it was one of the few successful African American businesses that was not established in the South.

Madame C. J. Walker built a successful business and amassed a fortune from her beauty products. Born in Louisiana as Sarah Breedlove in 1867, she was raised in St. Louis, Missouri. While working as a laundress over a washtub she asked herself what she was going to do when she got old and her back got stiff. Her answer came, she said, in a dream in which an old man gave her a formula for a hair conditioner. She began to make the conditioner and sell it door to door. Encouraged by her success, she introduced a line of cosmetics and opened a chain of beauty parlors. By 1910, her company had sales of $1,000 a day and employed 5,000 saleswomen around the world. She died in New York City in 1919.

Importance of African American Businesses. Despite their problems, these early businesses were an important chapter in the story of African American economic progress. The people who owned these businesses and the many who worked in them demonstrated that they were capable of being more than the farm workers, laborers, and servants who made up most of the African American population of the period. People in business often had an economic stability that most African Americans had never experienced. The middle class of African American businesspeople of the time was small. However, it provided a base for the growing number of educated African Americans who would appear in the years ahead.

Taking Another Look

1. What kinds of businesses did African Americans establish in the late 1800s and early 1900s?

2. What difficulties did African American businesses face?

3. **Critical Thinking** Why do you think most African American businesses were established in the South rather than in the North?

LOOKING AHEAD

Although Booker T. Washington had his critics among prominent African Americans, most ordinary African Americans saw him as their spokesman. In fact, the years of his leadership are sometimes called the Age of Booker T. Washington. This was also the period when African Americans began to establish businesses in record numbers and enter the nation's growing middle class.

The African American middle class was increasing in numbers in the late 19th century. Here, a Washington, D.C., family poses for a family portrait.

At the same time, educators were establishing colleges for the growing number of African Americans who wanted to become professionals like doctors, teachers, and lawyers. African American artists, writers, and inventors were also breaking new ground.

CLOSE UP: Chapter 21

The first funds for what is now Tuskegee University came at the urging of an unlikely pair—Lewis Adams, a former slave, and George W. Campbell, a former slave owner. At their request, the Alabama legislature approved $2,000 for African Americans in Tuskegee to start a school of higher learning. Adams and Campbell then chose Booker T. Washington to work a miracle with the small amount of money.

On July 4, 1881, Washington met his first 30 students. Their campus consisted of a rundown church and a small building. In 1882, Washington borrowed $200 and bought 100 acres of abandoned farmland. He then asked his students to create a school—bricks for the walls, furniture for the classrooms, food for the dining hall—and they did.

Today, those early buildings are a National Historic Site and form the northern end of a 200-acre campus nicknamed Skegee. The school has grown from a technical-training center to an accredited university with more than 4,000 students. Nearly 90 percent of the students receive some financial aid, in keeping with Washington's aim: "quality education for those who are economically, educationally, or culturally disadvantaged."

The Who, What, Where of History

1. **Who** was Booker T. Washington?
2. **Where** is Tuskegee Institute?
3. **What** was the Atlanta Compromise?
4. **What** was the National Negro Business League?
5. **Who** was Madame C. J. Walker?

Making the Connection

What was the connection between the African American self-help groups and the African American insurance companies and banks?

Time Check

When did Booker T. Washington deliver his Atlanta Compromise speech?

What Would You Have Done?

1. Would you have agreed with Booker T. Washington that earning a living and buying property were more important for African Americans than voting? Explain your reasons.
2. Imagine that you are an African American who wants more education in 1900. However, you do not agree with Booker T. Washington about the importance of practical education. You wish to study Latin, Greek, and literature. Your church has offered you a scholarship to Tuskegee. Do you go to Tuskegee? Explain.

Thinking and Writing About History

1. Imagine that you are a student at Tuskegee in 1902. Write a letter to a friend describing your studies and your plans for the future.

2. Write an off-the-record interview with Booker T. Washington in which you question him on his views on voting and the use of the courts to win civil rights for African Americans.

Building Skills: Drawing Conclusions

Sometimes the information that you *don't* have is more important than the information you *do* have. Suppose that you are buying a car. You know the total cost of the car, but before you can decide for sure if you can afford it, you need to know how much you will have to pay each month. Without that information, you cannot make an informed decision.

When you look at information and sources as you study history, you may find that you do not always have all the information you need in order to draw reasoned conclusions.

In this chapter you read about the first African American insurance companies. Insurance is still an important business for African Americans. The chart below gives you some information about the largest insurance companies owned by African Americans in the late 1980s.

Use the chart to answer the following questions. For the questions that you cannot answer from the chart, write a description of the information you need.

1. How many of the largest African American–owned insurance companies are *not* located in the South?

2. How many of these companies were founded after 1925?

3. Is the North Carolina Mutual Life Insurance Company the largest African American–owned business in the United States?

▶ ▶ Largest African American-Owned Insurance Companies

Rank	Company	Location	Year Founded	Assets*
1	North Carolina Mutual Life Insurance Company	Durham, North Carolina	1898	$216,357
2	Atlanta Life Insurance Company	Atlanta, Georgia	1905	126,421
3	Golden State Mutual	Los Angeles, California	1925	119,229
4	Universal Life Insurance Company	Memphis, Tennessee	1923	66,327
5	Supreme Life Insurance Company of America	Chicago, Illinois	1921	58,954
6	Chicago Metropolitan Mutual Assurance Company	Chicago, Illinois	1927	54,474
7	Booker T. Washington Insurance Company	Birmingham, Alabama	1932	34,033
8	Mammoth Life and Accident Insurance Company	Louisville, Kentucky	1915	29,101
9	The Pilgrim Health & Life Insurance Company	Augusta, Georgia	1898	16,457
10	Protective Industrial Insurance Co. of Alabama, Inc.	Birmingham, Alabama	1923	12,973
11	United Mutual Life Insurance Company	New York, New York	1933	12,550
12	Golden Circle Life Insurance Company	Brownsville, Texas	1958	7,365
13	American Woodmen's Life Insurance Company	Denver, Colorado	1966	6,168
14	Winnfield Life Insurance Company	Natchitoches, Louisiana	1936	5,958
15	Central Life Insurance Company of Florida	Tampa, Florida	1922	5,800
16	Williams-Progressive Life & Accident Insurance Company	Opelousas, Louisiana	1947	4,627

*millions of dollars

The Fisk Jubilee Singers

Advances in Education, the Arts, and Science

(1877–1910)

THINKING ABOUT THE CHAPTER

What were the educational, artistic, and scientific achievements of African Americans in the years after Reconstruction?

CHAPTER **22**

George White, the treasurer of newly founded Fisk University, was desperate. The school had run out of money, and bills were beginning to pile up. Fisk might have to shut its doors. Then, White had an idea. He loved listening to students sing the old spirituals from slavery days. Maybe other people would, too.

Soon afterwards, on a cold autumn day in 1871, nine young men and women set out on a series of concert tours to raise money for Fisk. For seven years, the Fisk Jubilee Singers toured the United States and Europe to wildly enthusiastic audiences.

The singers raised enough money to erect the buildings that form the core of Fisk today. The dedication of the

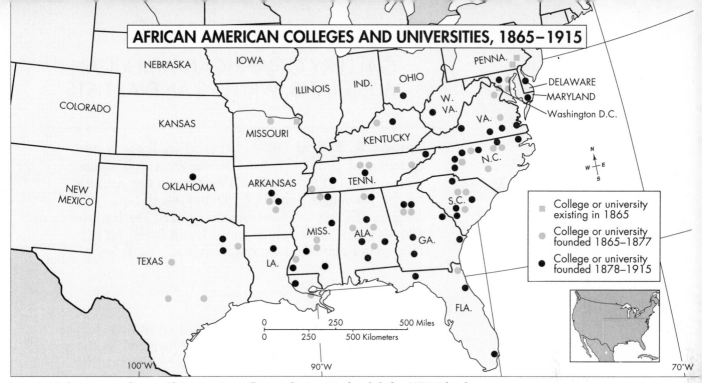

AFRICAN AMERICAN COLLEGES AND UNIVERSITIES, 1865–1915

Legend:
- College or university existing in 1865
- College or university founded 1865–1877
- College or university founded 1878–1915

In which states were the most African American colleges and universities founded after 1877? What does this tell you about where most African Americans lived?

young singers was only one of the many ways that African Americans showed how important education was to them.

1 EDUCATION
▼ What educational institutions were founded for African Americans?

As you read in Unit 6, the Freedmen's Bureau established thousands of schools for African Americans in the South after Reconstruction. It also founded colleges and universities, as did missionary societies and wealthy Northerners.

Public Education. After Reconstruction, public elementary and high schools in the South were segregated by race. Public schools for African Americans received much less financial support than schools for whites. Elsewhere in the United States, many African American children also had to attend segregated, underfinanced, poorly equipped schools.

Nevertheless, by 1910, over 70 percent of the African American population nationwide was literate. This was more than twice the number who could read in 1863. Over 1,700,000 African Americans were attending public schools, and 35,000 African Americans were teachers.

Higher Education. During and after Reconstruction, colleges for African Americans were built across the South. By 1900, more than 2,000 students had graduated from these institutions of higher learning.

The most prestigious was Howard University in Washington, D.C., which opened in 1867. Its goal was to train future African American leaders. Over the years, it graduated about half of the country's African American doctors and dentists, a fourth of its lawyers, and many of its engineers.

In their early years, schools like Hampton Institute and Tuskegee gave their stu-

GALLERY OF AFRICAN AMERICAN MUSICIANS, WRITERS AND ARTISTS

James A. Bland (1854–1911) Bland was a performer and composer, who wrote over 600 songs. These included the popular favorites "In the Evening by the Moonlight" and "Oh, Dem Golden Slippers." Virginia officially adopted Bland's "Carry Me Back to Old Virginny" as its state song. Bland lived and performed in England for almost 20 years.

Charles W. Chesnutt (1858–1932) A novelist and short-story writer, Chesnutt was recognized as the first important African American writer of fiction. His works, such as the novels *The House Behind the Cedars* and *The Marrow of Tradition*, dealt with the racial problems of his characters, especially those of mixed African American and white background.

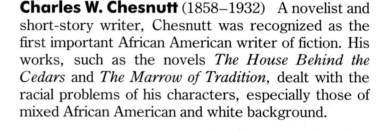

Paul Laurence Dunbar (1872–1906) Dunbar was one of the first African American writers of poetry and fiction to be nationally known. He wrote many widely admired dialect poems, which he composed at the urging of white editors. Some of his best poems deal with the anger and hurt of the African American experience.

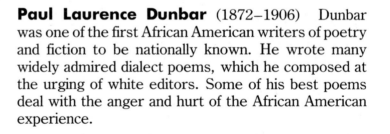

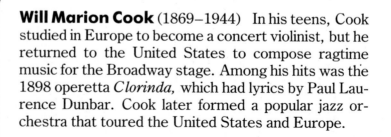

Will Marion Cook (1869–1944) In his teens, Cook studied in Europe to become a concert violinist, but he returned to the United States to compose ragtime music for the Broadway stage. Among his hits was the 1898 operetta *Clorinda,* which had lyrics by Paul Laurence Dunbar. Cook later formed a popular jazz orchestra that toured the United States and Europe.

W. C. (William Christopher) Handy (1873–1958) Although Handy did not invent the blues, he became known as the Father of the Blues because he wrote two of the earliest blues songs to be published. These were "Memphis Blues," which appeared in 1912, and "St. Louis Blues," which he wrote in 1914. These songs introduced blues to the general public.

Scott Joplin (1868–1919) Composer and pianist, Joplin fought for the recognition of ragtime as a legitimate musical form. "Maple Leaf Rag," written in 1899, was the first of his many popular ragtime compositions. It was the first piece of sheet music to sell a million copies. Joplin also wrote ballet music and the folk opera *Treemonisha,* which was not produced in his lifetime.

Edmonia Lewis (1845–1890) Lewis was one of the few women sculptors of her time. She received her art training in Boston and in Rome. She specialized in portraits, producing highly admired busts of the abolitionists John Brown, Wendell Phillips, and Charles Sumner. Another famous work is *Forever Free,* which shows a newly freed African American mother and her child (see **The Artist's View**).

Henry Ossawa Tanner (1859–1937) Tanner began his career as a painter of scenes of plantation life. In 1891, discouraged by the racial prejudice in the United States, he moved to Paris, where he spent the rest of his life. In Paris, he painted many large scenes of Biblical subjects. These won him wide acclaim in Europe, but little recognition in the United States in his lifetime (see **The Artist's View**).

GALLERY OF AFRICAN AMERICAN SCIENTISTS AND INVENTORS

▽▲▽

George Washington Carver (1864–1943) Carver helped to revolutionize the agriculture of the South. He persuaded Southern farmers to raise less cotton, which wore out the soil, and raise other crops such as peanuts, sweet potatoes, and soybeans, which enriched the soil. To make these crops profitable, he invented over 300 uses of the peanut, over 100 for the sweet potato, and many for the soybean.

Matthew A. Henson (1866–1955) Henson was a member of Robert E. Peary's expedition to the North Pole in 1909. Henson claimed that he and the expedition's Eskimo guides reached the North Pole on April 4, 1909, an hour before Peary. They were the first people to stand on top of the world. Henson wrote about his feat in the book *A Negro Explorer at the North Pole.*

Lewis H. Latimer (1848–1928) Latimer was a draftsman and inventor whose father was an escaped slave. Latimer worked with inventor Thomas Edison, making improvements in the incandescent electric lamp. He supervised the installation of the electric lighting systems of New York City, Philadelphia, Montreal, and London.

Jan Matzeliger (1852–1889) In 1883, Matzeliger invented a machine that attached the upper part of a shoe to the lower part. This shoe-lasting machine cut the cost of making shoes in half and revolutionized the shoe industry. Matzeliger's invention was used to make almost all the shoes in the United States and was adopted by countries all over the world.

Elijah McCoy (1844?–1929) McCoy, the son of slaves who escaped to Canada, was the inventor of the lubricating cup. This allowed machines to be oiled while still in operation. It is thought that the expression "the real McCoy," meaning the genuine article, came about because people insisted that the machinery they buy be equipped with McCoy's invention.

Norbert Rillieux (1806–1894) In 1881, Rillieux invented a revolutionary method of refining sugar, which is still used today. Born in New Orleans, Rillieux was educated in Paris, where he taught at a school for engineers. His sugar-refining process was also used in the manufacture of soap, glue, and condensed milk.

Daniel Hale Williams (1856–1931) In 1893, Dr. Williams performed the first successful heart operation in history. The operation was performed at Chicago's interracial Provident Hospital, which Williams founded in 1891 as a place where African American doctors and nurses could be trained and African American patients could be treated.

Granville T. Woods (1856–1910) Called the Black Edison, Woods is best known for his invention of the automatic air brake for railroad trains. He also developed a telegraph system for sending messages between moving trains, an invention that helped avoid train collisions.

The cakewalk, a high-stepping dance that developed among African American slaves to poke fun at plantation owners, became a national dance craze in the 1890s.

dents industrial-arts training. However, most African American colleges offered the same education as the leading white colleges of the time. Other important colleges were Spelman College in Atlanta; Wilberforce University in Wilberforce, Ohio; and Shaw University in Raleigh, North Carolina. Spelman admitted only women, and the emphasis at Wilberforce was training men for the ministry. Shaw had one of the first medical schools for African Americans. Most of the college-educated African Americans of the period were graduates of African American colleges and universities.

Taking Another Look

1. How did the literacy rate of African Americans change between 1863 and 1910?

2. List two African American institutions of higher learning and explain their importance.

3. **Critical Thinking**   How did the establishment of African American colleges help African Americans?

2 THE ARTS
What were some of the contributions of African Americans to the arts?

In 1890, many African Americans were making music their profession. Many military bands had only African American musicians. African American composers wrote classical music and Broadway shows, and African American stage performers sang and danced in shows that reached the general public.

By the turn of the century, two new kinds of music had been born—ragtime and blues. **Ragtime**, based on offbeat rhythms, became a national craze. By the 1870s, African American musicians—banjo players and piano players, on riverboats and in urban social clubs—were "ragging" their music.

No one knows when or how the **blues** began. The best guess is that the style grew out of the work songs sung by African Americans as they worked in the fields as slaves.

The blues used the call-and-response pattern of African music (see page 28). Blues songs became widely popular in the early 1900s with W. C. Handy's compositions such as "St. Louis Blues."

African American writers produced a variety of works in the last quarter of the 1800s and the early 1900s. Older writers such as abolitionist William Still Grout and William Wells Brown wrote about the years of slavery. Younger writers such as Charles W. Chesnutt and Paul Laurence Dunbar told about the experiences of African Americans in the freer, but still restricted, world of their own time.

In the late 1800s, prominent African American painters and sculptors faced bitter struggles for recognition in the United States. To escape racial prejudice at home, some artists moved to Europe to work.

Taking Another Look

1. What is ragtime?

2. Why did some African American artists leave the United States to work in Europe?

3. **Critical Thinking** The types of music described in this section were popular with both African Americans and whites. Why do you think this was so?

3 ACHIEVEMENTS IN SCIENCE AND INVENTION

▼ What inventions were African Americans responsible for in this period?

In 1900, Henry E. Baker, of the U.S. Patent Office, published four thick volumes that described inventions made by African Americans. Many people were amazed that there were any African American inventors, let alone enough to fill four volumes with their work.

Inventions were the fuel that fired the industrialization of the United States in the late 1800s. African American Jan Matzeliger was among the inventors who worked on their own, while Lewis H. Latimer was one of those who worked in Thomas Edison's vast "invention factory." Along with white inventors, African Americans created new labor-saving devices, new uses for electricity, and new ways to increase the efficiency of machines.

In the years after Reconstruction, African American colleges and universities were just beginning to turn out graduates with substantial training in the sciences. It is not surprising, then, that few African Americans made significant scientific contributions in this period. Therefore, the work of George Washington Carver and Dr. Daniel Hale Williams is especially noteworthy.

1867	Howard University is founded.
1871	Fisk Jubilee Singers begin tours.
1872	Elijah McCoy invents device for oiling machines.
1883	Jan Matzeliger invents the shoe-lasting machine.
1893	Dr. Daniel Hale Williams performs first successful heart surgery.
1899	Scott Joplin composes "Maple Leaf Rag."
1909	Matthew Henson reaches North Pole.
1912	W. C. Handy writes "Memphis Blues."

Taking Another Look

1. What did Jan Matzeliger and Lewis H. Latimer have in common?

2. Why were there only a few African American scientists in the late 1800s and early 1900s?

3. **Critical Thinking** Explain the importance of African Americans' inventions.

LOOKING AHEAD

The achievements of African Americans in education, the arts, and science in the years between 1877 and 1910 are impressive. This is all the more so since these were years when African Americans suffered from legal, political, and economic discrimination. But the times were changing, and new leaders would emerge to challenge Booker T. Washington's Atlanta Compromise.

"I cannot offer you money, position, or fame. I offer you in their place work—hard, hard work—the task of bringing a people from degradation, poverty and waste to full manhood!" With these inspiring words, Booker T. Washington convinced George Washington Carver to teach agricultural science at Tuskegee Institute.

In the fall of 1896, Carver stepped into his laboratory—an empty room. He gave students their first assignment: search for jars, bottles, pots, bits of rubber—anything that might be turned into lab equipment. Carver called his makeshift laboratory "God's little workshop."

Carver was born into slavery in 1864, the last year of the Civil War. He earned a masters degree in science when high school diplomas were rare. Carver's experiments earned him national fame and the nickname the Wizard of Tuskegee.

Carver's inventions touch our lives today. He developed over 300 uses for peanuts, including peanut butter. He proved the nutritional value of soybeans. Carver even made plastic out of soybeans! About himself, Carver remarked: "All I do is prepare what God has made, for uses to which man can put it. It is God's work—not mine."

CLOSE UP: Chapter 22

The Who, What, Where of History

1. **What** is Howard University?
2. **What** is ragtime?
3. **Who** was W.C. Handy?
4. **Who** was Charles W. Chesnutt?
5. **Who** was Paul Laurence Dunbar?
6. **Who** was Scott Joplin?
7. **Who** was Edmonia Lewis?
8. **What** did George Washington Carver do?

Making the Connection

1. What was the connection between colleges and universities such as Howard and Spelman and the growth of an African American middle class?
2. What was the connection between the patterns used in African music and the blues?

Time Check

1. When did Elijah McCoy invent a device for oiling machines?
2. When did Matthew Henson reach the North Pole?

What Would You Have Done?

Imagine that you are an African American opera singer in the early 1900s. Your career is at a standstill because discrimination will not allow you to sing on stage of the great opera houses of the country. You can see two choices: move to Paris or Rome and try to continue a career in opera, or switch to singing blues or show tunes. What would you choose? Give reasons for your answer.

Thinking and Writing About History

1. Imagine that you are about to graduate from one of the African American colleges in 1912. Write a short speech that you will deliver at graduation. The topic of your speech is "The Value of College Education for African Americans."

2. Imagine that you are a newspaper reporter about to interview Granville T. Woods, Daniel Hale Williams, or Matthew A. Henson. Prepare at least three questions for the interview about your subject's inventions or discovery.

Building Skills: Identifying Point of View in Poetry

The poetry and fiction of a time period can tell you a great deal about the ideas, feelings, and life styles of the authors and their audiences. Reading fiction and poetry requires different skills than reading other kinds of writing.

Reading poetry is sometimes similar to reading a secret message. The poet leaves clues for you to unravel. You may unravel only a few clues and still get much meaning from the poem. Of course, if you unravel many clues, you will understand and enjoy the poem on a deeper number of levels.

A poem always has a *voice*, an attitude toward the reader. It may be friendly, cold, sarcastic, or joyous. We can figure out a poem's voice from the choice of words, from the use of details, and from the rhythm of the poem.

When you read the poem below by Paul Laurence Dunbar for the first time, read it through, experiencing it with no particular ideas in your mind. Then read it a second time, making sure you know the meanings of all the words Dunbar uses. Then read the poem a third time to answer the questions about the voice in the poem.

We Wear the Mask

We wear the mask that grins and lies,
It hides our cheeks and shades our
    eyes—
This debt we pay to human guile;
With torn and bleeding hearts we
    smile,
And mouth with myriad subtleties.

What should the world be otherwise,
In counting our tears and sighs?
Nay, let them only see us while
We wear the mask.

We smile, but O great Christ, our
    cries
To thee from tortured souls arise.
We sing, but oh the clay is vile
Beneath our feet, and long the mile,
But let the world dream otherwise,
We wear the mask.

1. What is "human guile"?

2. Give an example of how you might "mouth with myriad subtleties."

3. Who is the "we" of this poem? Who is "them"?

4. Why does the speaker say that "we" choose to wear a mask?

5. What does the poem tell you about how African Americans lived and acted in the early 20th century?

▼U N I▼T

8

Flappers in Harlem

PROTEST AND HOPE IN A NEW CENTURY

(1900–1941)

Steel workers during World War I

**Emergency unemployment
relief line**

THE BIG PICTURE

Unit 8 tells of the experiences of African Americans in the first 40 years of this century. This period opened with economic growth and a spirit of optimism. It ended with the nation trying to overcome the worst economic crisis in its history. As it did, growing conflicts in Europe and Asia threatened to pull the United States into global war for the second time in a little over 20 years. These events had a powerful impact on the lives of African Americans, leading to changes in where they lived, in the kinds of work they did, and in the political loyalties they held.

The Progressive Era. In 1900, the United States was in the midst of a period of remarkable economic growth. During the 35 years after the Civil War, the country had become a great industrial power.

Since its beginnings, the United States had been a rural nation, with most of its citizens living in small towns or on farms. With the growth of industry had come the growth of industrial cities, located mainly in the Northeast and the Midwest. This expansion would soon turn the United States into an urban nation.

Many of the new city dwellers had left farms and country towns seeking increased opportunities. They were joined by throngs of immigrants from Europe who also found jobs in the booming mills and factories.

A variety of problems accompanied the growth of this new, urban United States. Workers—male and female—toiled 10- and 12-hour days for low pay, often in unsafe factories. Child labor was common, as families scraped for every penny to make ends meet.

Off the job, conditions were not much better. Workers often lived in poor, overcrowded areas, or **slums**. Poor water supplies and sanitation facilities encouraged the spread of disease there. City governments were often more concerned with collecting bribes than with correcting problems.

Conditions like these encouraged the growth of reform movements. Individuals and organizations crusaded to improve unsafe working conditions and fight corruption in city, state, and federal governments. Some tried to limit the influence of big business. Others aimed at bettering the lives of working people. Together, these movements were known as **Progressivism**.

Progressive Achievements. The Progressives had success in a number of areas. Jane Addams of Chicago founded Hull House in a poor immigrant neighborhood to help the people improve their lives. The National Consumers League pushed for new laws protecting custom-

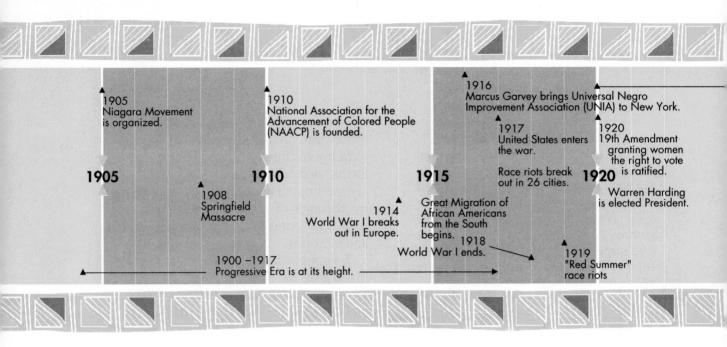

1905
Niagara Movement is organized.

1910
National Association for the Advancement of Colored People (NAACP) is founded.

1916
Marcus Garvey brings Universal Negro Improvement Association (UNIA) to New York.

1917
United States enters the war.

1920
19th Amendment granting women the right to vote is ratified.

1905   **1910**   **1915**   **1920**

1908
Springfield Massacre

1914
World War I breaks out in Europe.

Great Migration of African Americans from the South begins.

Race riots break out in 26 cities.

Warren Harding is elected President.

1918
World War I ends.

1919
"Red Summer" race riots

1900 –1917
Progressive Era is at its height.

ers from worthless or dangerous products. "Good government" organizations introduced new plans of government in many cities to improve efficiency and reduce corruption.

Progressives also brought change to the federal government. Their ideas led to constitutional amendments that permitted an income tax, gave women the right to vote, and banned the manufacture and sale of alcoholic drinks.

Most Progressives were white and middle class, and their efforts tended to focus on Northern and Midwestern cities. As a result, the Progressive movement had limited impact on the lives of African Americans, most of whom still lived in the rural South. One important exception, however, was the **NAACP** (National Association for the Advancement of Colored People). This organization, founded by African American and white Progressives in 1910, became a major force in attempts to win equal rights for African Americans.

World War I. The Progressives were chiefly concerned with conditions within the United States. In the summer of 1914, their concerns and those of many other citizens shifted abroad as war broke out in Europe. On one side, called the Central Powers, were Germany and Austria-Hungary. Great Britain, France, and Russia were the main countries on the other side, known as the Allies. Because the war eventually involved countries in all parts of the world, it became known as the World War.

When the war began, the United States declared its neutrality—that is, that it would not aid either side in the war. Gradually, however, it was drawn toward the Allied side, mainly because of actions of the German government. For example, German submarines sank ships in an effort to keep supplies from reaching Great Britain. Some of these ships were from the United States or carried U.S. passengers. In 1917, this nation entered the war on the Allied side.

U.S. troops, including many African Americans, reached Europe in large numbers the following year. The German army, on one side, and the British and

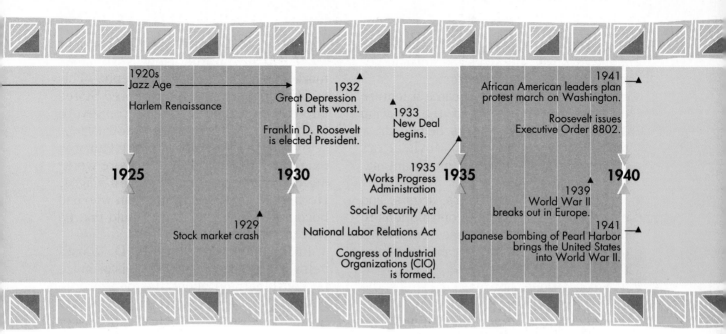

1920s Jazz Age
Harlem Renaissance

1925

1929
Stock market crash

1932
Great Depression is at its worst.

Franklin D. Roosevelt is elected President.

1930

1933
New Deal begins.

1935
Works Progress Administration

Social Security Act

National Labor Relations Act

Congress of Industrial Organizations (CIO) is formed.

1935

1941
African American leaders plan protest march on Washington.

Roosevelt issues Executive Order 8802.

1939
World War II breaks out in Europe.

1941
Japanese bombing of Pearl Harbor brings the United States into World War II.

1940

French armies, on the other, had fought to a standstill. The arrival of the U.S. soldiers finally turned the war in the Allies' favor, and in November 1918, Germany asked for peace.

The Home Front. The war brought changes into the lives of people at home. Factories had to increase their output to equip U.S. forces. But a military draft had taken many young men into the army, creating a shortage of workers. One result was the hiring of women to do what had been thought of as men's jobs.

Another result was the recruiting of African American agricultural workers from the South to do factory jobs in the North. By the end of the war, this **Great Migration** had brought more than 500,000 African Americans to industrial cities of the Northeast and Midwest.

The Aftermath of War. After the war, many people seemed more suspicious of immigrants and minorities. A revolution in Russia in 1917 had ended in a takeover of that country's government by Communists. As a wave of strikes swept the United States after the war, some people feared that Communists were trying to start a revolution here.

The "Red Scare" that followed resulted in the arrest and deportation of many immigrants. Reacting to such fears, Congress soon passed laws limiting immigration to the United States. Suspicion of minorities also led to a rebirth of the Ku Klux Klan and new tensions between whites and African Americans. Many African Americans lost their lives in riots and lynchings in the years after the war.

The Roaring Twenties. In 1920, Warren Harding, the Republican candidate—promising a "return to normalcy"—won election as President. "Normalcy" for many Americans seemed to mean making money and having a good time. They had little interest in working for Progressive reform.

For a large number of people, the decade of the 1920s was a time of prosperity. Industry was growing, and wages

245

were going up. Many people had enough money to play the stock market and get richer with no apparent effort.

Mass entertainment became a feature of what has been called the Roaring Twenties. Radio networks helped draw the nation closer together. Movie actors and sports stars became important national figures.

African American writers, artists, and entertainers made major contributions to popular culture during these years. This outpouring of creativity became known as the **Harlem Renaissance**.

Not everyone, however, did well in the 1920s. Farmers suffered from low prices, and so did agricultural workers, including most African Americans.

Pittsburgh steel workers greet Secretary of Labor Frances Perkins, first woman to serve in the Presidential Cabinet.

The Great Depression. In October 1929, prices on the New York stock market fell suddenly and deeply. This stock market crash led the United States into the greatest **depression**, or severe economic slump, it had ever known.

By 1932, one person in every four was out of work, and many others were working only part time or at reduced wages. Herbert Hoover, the Republican who had become President in 1929, could find no way to get a recovery started.

In 1932, Democrat Franklin D. Roosevelt was elected President on his promise to do something about the depression. His cheerful and optimistic personality helped restore the people's confidence. "The only thing we have to fear, is fear itself," he announced, and he seemed to believe it.

The New Deal. In his election campaign, Roosevelt had promised "a new deal for the American people." Roosevelt quickly began to deliver on his promise. In his first 100 days in office alone, the President asked for, and Congress passed, 15 major bills.

This **New Deal** created dozens of new government bodies to deal with different aspects of the nation's economic problems. The federal government provided money for food and clothing for the needy. It created jobs for the unemployed. Some policies aimed to raise farmers' incomes; others tried to regulate industrial production.

One important bill, the National Labor Relations Act, guaranteed workers the right to **collective bargaining** through unions. A later law for the first time set a national minimum wage and a national maximum workweek.

In 1935, Congress also passed the Social Security Act. Now, millions of citi-

During the Great Depression, thousands of homeless people built shacks like these in New York City. Why were such shanty towns called "Hoovervilles?"

zens were guaranteed old-age and unemployment insurance.

Not all New Deal laws proved successful, nor did all citizens benefit equally from them. Sharecroppers in the South, for example, many of whom were African Americans, were harmed by the New Deal's agricultural policies. But the New Deal gave people the feeling that something was being done.

As Roosevelt neared the end of his second term in 1940, unemployment was still high, but the worst of the Great Depression was over. More people were working, and farmers were better off.

In Europe, however, a new war had broken out, into which the United States would soon be drawn. That war and its aftermath would bring profound changes in the lives of all African Americans.

Taking Another Look

1. What were some successes of the Progressive movement?

2. How did the New Deal attempt to solve problems caused by the depression?

3. **Critical Thinking** If you had been an African American voter in the election of 1920, would you have voted for a candidate who promised a "return to normalcy"? Explain.

The NAACP-sponsored Silent March to protest lynching, 1917

The Civil Rights Struggle
(1900–1941)

THINKING ABOUT THE CHAPTER

What gains in civil rights did African Americans make in the first half of the 1900s?

On the evening of July 30, 1903, Boston's African Methodist Episcopal Zion Church was packed with some 2,000 spectators and journalists. They had come to hear Booker T. Washington speak before the National Negro Business League. He would present his long-held view that African Americans should concentrate on trying to achieve economic success and temporarily accommodate themselves to segregation.

In the audience sat William Monroe Trotter, publisher of the African American newspaper the *Guardian*. Unlike Washington, Trotter wanted immediate equality for African Americans. Tonight he was going to raise a series of questions designed to embarrass Washington.

248

As Trotter started to ask his questions, Washington's supporters began to protest. Trotter had to shout his questions above the noise. Someone shouted, "Throw Trotter out the window!" Fistfights broke out around the room. Finally, the Boston police stepped in and arrested Trotter. He was later fined $50 and sentenced to 30 days in jail.

Newspapers across the country seized upon the incident, labeling it the "Boston Riot." The real news, though, was that some African Americans were openly questioning the views of Washington. This was the man who had long been regarded as the spokesman for African Americans (see page 223). In this chapter, you will read about how their rising voices led to new strategies in the fight for civil rights.

1 W.E.B. DU BOIS

▼ What were the basic differences between W.E.B. Du Bois's views and those of Booker T. Washington?

The events in Boston revealed divisions among African Americans. Certainly, by the early 1900s, many were beginning to turn away from Booker T. Washington and his ideas. But who would take Washington's place? What ideas would the new leader have?

A New Thinker. In 1903, a 35-year-old professor of history and economics at Atlanta University published a book called *The Souls of Black Folk*. It included a bitter attack on Booker T. Washington's strategy for African American advancement and proposed a new course of action. Its author, W.E.B. Du Bois (doo-BOYZ), was to become the most important leader of African American protest in the first half of the 1900s.

William Edward Burghardt Du Bois was born in 1868 in Great Barrington, Massachusetts, and was raised in a single-parent family. From an early age, Du Bois viewed education as the way to a better life. Supported by hard-earned scholarships, he graduated from Fisk University in Nashville, Tennessee. He later went on to become the first African American to receive a doctoral degree from Harvard University. For ten years, Du Bois was a professor at Atlanta University, doing research on slavery and the African American community.

Du Bois gradually came to realize that his work as a scholar would not end such evils as Jim Crow, lynching, unfair housing practices, and unequal treatment of African Americans in the courts. Not long after his 1903 book was published, he gave up his teaching career to apply himself full-time to the fight for civil rights. He devoted the rest of his life to this cause. In 1961, dissatisfied with the progress of African Americans, the 93-year-old Du Bois became a Communist and moved to Ghana. He died there two years later.

Du Bois, unlike Booker T. Washington, was not a great public speaker. Even his friends said he sometimes put them to sleep with his cold, intellectual speeches. His influence came through his writings, which were read by well-educated African Americans and by sharecroppers and factory workers.

Du Bois's Leadership. "The American Negro demands equality, and he is never going to rest satisfied with anything less." This was the core of Du Bois's ideas. It was founded on the belief that peaceful resistance would gain civil rights and economic progress for African Americans. Du Bois opposed Washington's belief that going along with segregation would win these goals.

Du Bois believed that "the Negro race, like all other races, is going to be saved by its exceptional men." By "exceptional men," Du Bois meant those men—and women—who made up the well-educated upper 10 percent of the African American population. He called this group the **Talented Tenth**. According to Du Bois, the most intelligent African Americans had a duty to become teachers, lawyers, doctors, politicians, artists, and other professionals and African American colleges had an obligation to educate them. Du Bois declared:

> The Talented Tenth of the Negro race, must be made leaders of thought and missionaries of culture among their people. No others can do this work, and Negro colleges must train men [and women] for it.

Du Bois also believed that African Americans should take pride in both their rich cultural heritage and their own abilities. He urged African Americans to look to Africa for their heritage and develop literature and art of their own. They had to see the beauty in their blackness.

Du Bois realized that more than words was going to be needed to make his program a reality. African Americans had to find ways or make ways to make their voices heard. "We must organize," Du Bois declared.

POINTS OF

As you have read, the freedom that African Americans gained as a result of the Civil War left them with many problems. What could African Americans do to fight discrimination? No two African American leaders differed more sharply as to the best course for African Americans than Booker T. Washington and W.E.B. Du Bois.

Booker T. Washington's View

No race can prosper until it learns that there is as much dignity in tilling [plowing] a field as in writing a poem. It is at the bottom of life we must begin, and not at the top. . . .

The wisest among my race understand that the agitation [stirring up] of questions of social equality is the extremest folly [greatest mistake], and that progress in the enjoyment of all the privileges that will come to us must be the result of severe and constant struggle rather than of artificial forcing. No race that has anything to contribute to the markets of the world is long in any degree ostracized [shut out]. It is important and right that all privileges of the law be ours, but it is vastly more important that we be prepared for the exercises of these privileges. The opportunity to earn a dollar in a factory just now is worth infinitely more than the opportunity to spend a dollar in an opera house.

—*from the* Atlanta Compromise Speech, *1895*

VIEW

W.E.B. Du Bois's View

[African Americans] do not expect that the free right to vote, to enjoy civic rights and to be educated, will come in a moment . . . but they are absolutely certain that the way for a people to gain their reasonable rights is not by voluntarily throwing them away and insisting that they do not want them; . . . on the contrary, Negroes must insist continually, in season and out of season, that voting is necessary to proper manhood, that color discrimination is barbarism, and that black boys need education as well as white boys. . . .

So far as Mr. Washington preaches Thrift, Patience, and Industrial Training for the masses, . . . we must strive with him. . . . But so far as Mr. Washington apologizes for injustice, North or South, does not rightly value the privilege and duty of voting, . . . and opposes the higher training and ambition of our brighter minds—

. . . we must unceasingly and firmly oppose [him].

—*from* The Souls of Black Folk, 1903

Taking Another Look

1. How does Washington think African Americans will gain full rights?

2. What is Du Bois's solution to African Americans' problems?

3. **Critical Thinking** Do you think that it is possible to agree with both Washington and Du Bois? Explain.

Taking Another Look

1. What was the basic difference between Du Bois's ideas and those of Booker T. Washington?

2. What part did education play in Du Bois's program for African Americans?

3. **Critical Thinking** Why might some African Americans object to the idea of a Talented Tenth? What do you think about Du Bois's idea?

2 ORGANIZING FOR JUSTICE
▼ What was the purpose in establishing the NAACP?

On a warm August day in 1906, W.E.B. Du Bois, William Monroe Trotter, and other members of the year-old **Niagara Movement** traveled to Harpers Ferry, West Virginia, for their annual meeting. There, 47 years before, the white abolitionist John Brown had tried to start a private war against slavery (see page 171). Now these African Americans were pledging to renew the struggle for their full civil rights.

We claim for ourselves every single right that belongs to a free born American. How shall we get them? By voting where we may, by persistent [determined], unceasing agitation, by hammering the truth, by sacrifice and work.

Earlier Pioneers. The Niagara Movement was not the first group to start a national civil rights organization. Sixteen years earlier, T. Thomas Fortune, a newspaper editor, had organized the Afro-American League of the United States in Chicago, Illinois. Its members worked in Northern cities to promote citi-

251

SNAPSHOT OF THE TIMES

1903 Du Bois writes *The Souls of Black Folk.*

1905 Niagara Movement is organized.

1908 Springfield Massacre

1909 First National Negro Conference

1910 NAACP is founded.

Why did African American leaders found the Niagara Movement? How successful was it?

zenship rights and economic opportunity for African Americans. In 1896, the National Association of Colored Women elected Mary Church Terrell as its first president. Her goal was to organize women's clubs nationwide to work for voting rights and health and educational programs for African American women.

The Niagara Movement. What made the Niagara Movement different from these earlier groups was its sense of urgency. Its members demanded immediate action. They insisted on an immediate end to all racial discrimination, on equal justice and fair housing for all African Americans, and on full voting rights for African American men.

To symbolize its views, the group first met near Niagara Falls, Canada. This area had once been an important station on the Underground Railroad (see page 146). Also, the members wanted to use the mighty falls to symbolize the power of their beliefs.

Despite its ambitious goals, the Niagara Movement never attracted many followers. This was partly because many African Americans, including Booker T. Washington, opposed its program as too extreme. Failing to attract wide support, the Niagara Movement disbanded in 1908. However, it had laid the groundwork for a more successful organization—the NAACP.

Gathering Momentum. In August 1908 in Springfield, Illinois, the home of Abraham Lincoln, white prejudice against African Americans erupted into two days of race rioting. Three African Americans and four whites died. Over 70 people were injured, and the entire African American community was terrorized.

The Springfield Massacre, as the riot came to be called, shocked the entire nation. A white journalist named William English Walling wrote a bitter newspaper article called "Race War in the North," in which he condemned the Springfield Massacre. He also pleaded for a "large and powerful body of citizens" to help African

252

Americans in their fight for political and social equality.

The response to his appeal was a meeting of nearly 300 African Americans and whites in New York City in May 1909 to discuss African American rights. Among the African Americans who attended this first National Negro Conference were W.E.B. Du Bois; Ida Wells-Barnett, the antilynching activist (see page 219); and the Reverend Francis Grimké, husband of the Reconstruction teacher Charlotte Forten. Booker T. Washington was not invited. Among the whites were Protestant and Jewish clergy; social workers such as Jane Addams; and Oswald Garrison Villard, grandson of abolitionist William Lloyd Garrison (see page 131). Grimké and Garrison were reminders that the struggle for African American freedom and equality went back many years and many battles.

Not all African Americans who attended the meeting were pleased that whites were involved. Du Bois later reported that at one point an African American woman cried out, "They are betraying us again—these white friends of ours." Nevertheless, the conference made progress. It condemned U.S. attitudes toward its African American citizens "as the greatest menace that threatens the country." It also set up a Committee of Forty to form a permanent organization.

Setting Up the NAACP. The Committee of Forty met in 1910 and founded a new organization called the National Association for the Advancement of Colored People (NAACP). Its objective was to secure "equal rights and opportunities for all." The NAACP was an interracial organization that brought together African Americans who had been involved in the Niagara Movement and white reformers. The NAACP soon became the most active and effective fighter for the rights of African Americans.

Taking Another Look

1. What were the goals of the Niagara Movement?

2. What led to the founding of the NAACP?

3. **Critical Thinking** Why do you think Booker T. Washington was not invited to the first National Negro Conference?

3 THE NAACP'S FIGHT FOR CIVIL RIGHTS

What tactics did the NAACP use to achieve its goals?

A blond, blue-eyed young man was being sworn in as a sheriff's deputy in a county in Oklahoma. After the ceremony, another deputy turned to him and told him he could now go out and kill any black he saw, "and the law'll be behind you."

The new deputy's name was Walter White. Despite the fact that he was usually taken to be white, he was an African American. He was also an undercover agent for the NAACP. For ten years, starting in 1920, he risked his life to gather evidence about race riots and lynchings. In 1930, White became executive secretary of the NAACP.

Organizing Nationwide. The NAACP had quickly built a strong national organization. The first local branch was established in Chicago, Illinois, in 1911. By the end of its first decade, the NAACP had over 400 local branches, with more

1912	Desegregates New York City theaters
1913	Leads campaign against segregation in U.S. Post Office and Treasury departments
1915	Supreme Court rules grandfather clause (see page 215) in Southern states unconstitutional
1917	Organizes New York City parade protesting lynching. Supreme Court bans legal African American ghettoes in Southern cities
1923	Supreme Court rules African Americans must be permitted to serve on juries
1925	In Detroit, Michigan, wins right of African Americans to use force in self defense
1930	Active in strong protests leading to U.S.Senate's rejection of appointment of John H. Parker, opponent of African Americans' voting rights, to Supreme Court
1933	Helps organize committee to fight discrimination against African Americans in New Deal programs
1935	Forces University of Maryland through court action, to admit its first African American student
1936	Files first suit in campaign to end differences in salaries between African American and white teachers
1940	Begins drive against segregation in the armed forces

What kinds of activities did the NAACP engage in to end discrimination?

than 91,000 members. The NAACP was committed to achieving its goals through legal, peaceful means.

Spreading the Word. The NAACP believed that public opinion was "the main force upon which [to rely] for victory of justice." The NAACP took out ads in newspapers to spread the word about lynchings and other acts of racial violence. Its own publications printed research studies about the living conditions of African Americans.

Soon after the NAACP was set up, W.E.B. Du Bois became director of publicity and research. His major role, however, was as editor of the NAACP's magazine, the *Crisis*. The *Crisis* reported on the organization's activities and the challenges that it faced. It published not only political articles, but also poetry and stories by African American writers. The

magazine was so successful that by 1912 it had a circulation of 16,000 copies an issue, when the NAACP had only 1,000 members. By 1919 the circulation had reached 100,000 copies.

Fighting Against Lynching. The articles and editorials in the *Crisis* urged the federal government to take action against lynching. From 1900 to the outbreak of World War I, more than 1,100 African Americans were lynched. To stop the killing, the NAACP in 1921 persuaded a member of Congress to introduce legislation making lynching a federal crime. Although the bill passed the House of Representatives, senators from the South prevented the law from being enacted. Later NAACP-sponsored bills met the same fate. Nevertheless, the NAACP's efforts kept the national spotlight on the problem of lynching.

Fighting in the Courts From the start, the NAACP fought some of its most important battles in the courts, as you can see from the table on page 254. Its long-term strategy was to attack laws that discriminated against African Americans. The NAACP, from the mid-1920s through the 1930s, won important court victories in the fields of housing, education, and voting rights. It also gave legal aid to African American victims of race riots. By 1935, the NAACP began to challenge segregation in the nation's schools, as you will read in Unit 9.

Taking Another Look

1. How did the NAACP attempt to use public opinion?

2. What action did the NAACP take in regard to the lynchings of African Americans?

3. **Critical Thinking** Do you think the *Crisis* was a good title for the NAACP magazine? Explain.

LOOKING AHEAD

In 1929, W.E.B. Du Bois summed up the accomplishments of the NAACP in these words:

> Twenty years ago . . . it was said . . . that the real effective organization for the attainment of the rights of black men in America was impossible. . . . But we went in for agitation. We pushed our way into the courts. We demanded the right to vote. . . . We stand today at the threshold [edge] of a new generation.

Despite its record of achievements, the NAACP appealed largely to the middle and upper classes of African Americans. By focusing on political and social discrimination, it often ignored the bread-and-butter economic concerns of most African Americans. To them, the NAACP seemed an organization of well-off African Americans and whites who had little understanding of the day-to-day difficulties they faced.

W.E.B. DuBois (standing, right), was the editor of *Crisis,* the NAACP magazine, for many years.

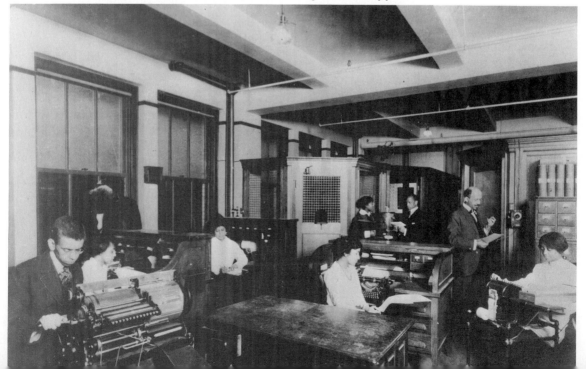

The NAACP began in 1910 in a small room of a New York City apartment. Its members included a handful of African Americans and whites. Among them were W.E.B. Du Bois, Mary Church Terrell, Mary White Ovington, Henry Moskowitz, and William English.

Today, the national headquarters of the NAACP occupies a five-story building in Baltimore, Maryland. The 80-person staff coordinates the activities of nearly 2,200 local chapters and over 500,000 members.

In the beginning, the organization fought most of its battles in the courts. It focused on winning equality for African Americans and scored important victories during the Civil Rights Movement of the 1950s and 1960s.

Today, the NAACP still fights discrimination, but it has also branched out. Says NAACP director Dr. Benjamin Hooks: "We have programs to inspire students to stay in school . . . and get them back in when they drop out. We have drug programs and a prison project." The NAACP has youth-oriented projects such as ACT-SO—Academic, Cultural, Technological, and Scientific Olympics. However, the NAACP will never abandon the fight against racism. "If we do," asks Hooks, "who's left?"

The Who, What, Where of History

1. **What** was Progressivism?
2. **Who** was William Monroe Trotter?
3. **What** was the *Guardian*?
4. **Who** was W.E.B. Du Bois?
5. **What** was the Talented Tenth?
6. **Who** was T. Thomas Fortune?
7. **Who** was Mary Church Terrell?
8. **What** was the Niagara Movement?
9. **What** was the NAACP?
10. **What** was the *Crisis*?

Making the Connection

1. What was the connection between the Niagara Movement and the NAACP?
2. What was the connection between the Springfield Massacre and the organization of the first National Negro Conference?

Time Check

Use the timeline on pages 244–245 and the Snapshot on page 252 to answer these questions.

1. How many years separated the writing of *The Souls of Black Folk* and the formation of the NAACP?
2. How many years separated the formation of the Niagara Movement and the formation of the NAACP?

What Would You Have Done?

1. If you had been an African American living in the early 1900s, would you have joined the Niagara Movement? the NAACP? Explain the reasons for your decisions in a letter to a friend.

2. Imagine that you have attended a lecture at which Du Bois explains his idea that the Talented Tenth will "save" African Americans. After the lecture, you have the chance to talk with Du Bois. Explain why you either agree or disagree with his idea.

Thinking and Writing About History

1. Write a short newspaper article about the "Boston Riot" of 1903. Make sure you answer the questions *who, what, when, where,* and *why.*

2. Review what you read in Chapter 21 about Booker T. Washington. Then write two paragraphs comparing the ideas of Washington and of Du Bois on the subject of how African Americans should achieve civil rights and economic progress.

Building Skills: Interpreting a Primary Source

W.E.B. Du Bois criticized Booker T. Washington's strategy for African American advancement. Read the following selection from Du Bois's *The Souls of Black Folk.* Then answer the questions that follow.

Mr. Washington distinctly asks that black people . . . concentrate all their energies on industrial education, and accumulation of wealth, and the conciliation of the South. This policy . . . has been triumphant for perhaps ten years. . . . In these years there have occurred:

1. The disfranchisement of the Negro.

2. The legal creation of a distinct status of civil inferiority for the Negro.

3. The steady withdrawal of aid from institutions for the higher training of the Negro . . .

Mr. Washington . . . faces the triple paradox [contradiction] of his career:

1. He is striving to make the Negro artisans business people and property-owners; but it is utterly impossible . . . for workingmen and property-owners to defend their rights and exist without the right of suffrage.

2. He insists on thrift and self-respect, but at the same time counsels a . . . submission to civic inferiority such as is bound to sap . . . any race in the long run.

3. He . . . depreciates institutions of higher learning; but neither the Negro common-schools, nor Tuskegee itself, could remain open a day were it not for teachers trained in Negro colleges, or trained by their graduates.

1. On what has Washington asked African Americans to focus?

2. What have been the results of Washington's policies, according to Du Bois?

3. What do you think Du Bois means when he says that it is impossible "for workingmen and property-owners to defend their rights and exist without the right of suffrage"?

4. Do you agree or disagree with Du Bois's criticisms of Washington? Explain the reasons for your position.

Cotton on the way to market in 1910

The Great Migration

(1915–1930)

THINKING ABOUT THE CHAPTER

How did the thousands of African Americans who left the South for the cities of the North and Midwest adjust to their new lives?

Bearing postmarks from distant worlds—Chicago, Milwaukee, New York, Philadelphia—letters and postcards poured into the South from 1910 through the 1920s. They were read aloud in rural African American churches and city markets and passed from hand to hand until they were too tattered to read.

Yet their message remained clear: There really were places in the United States where African Americans could live with dignity and a chance for financial security. A man from Hattiesburg, Mississippi, newly arrived in Philadelphia in 1917, proclaimed these wonders in a letter home:

Well, Dr . . . I am making very good. I make $75 per month. I can ride in the electric street and steam car anywhere I get a seat . . . and if you are first in a place here shopping you dont have to wait until the white folks get thro trading. . . . I am praying that God may give every well wisher a chance to be a man regardless of his color.

What began as a trickle of people swiftly became a river. Between 1915 and 1930, over a million African Americans abandoned the South. In this chapter, you will read why so many joined this Great Migration to the industrial cities of the North and Midwest and what their lives were like once they got there.

1 LEAVING HOME

▼ What conditions led many African Americans to leave the South?

On a cotton plantation in southern Georgia in 1910, 15 African American families—the Harrisons, the Battles, and 13 others—tried to scratch out a living as sharecroppers. By the end of 1917, not a single family remained. Like thousands of other African American families in the South, they had been the victims of a series of crushing blows.

Sharecroppers' Woes. First had come the boll weevil. Starting east from Texas in the 1890s, these insects came in giant, hungry swarms, stripping fields bare of cotton. By 1922, they had ruined more than 85 percent of the South's cotton fields. Meanwhile, a series of fierce, driving rains brought deadly floods. Sharecroppers, many of whom were African Americans, were broke, tired, and close to starving.

Nature was not the only cause of their troubles. Sharecropping had not changed since Reconstruction. The plows that sharecroppers turned the soil with, the cotton seeds they planted, and the shacks they lived in belonged to the landowner.

Once the harvest was sold and their debts to the landowner were paid, the farm family had to make do on whatever was left until the next planting season. But by the fall of 1916, there was hardly any cotton left to harvest. Throughout Georgia, Alabama, Mississippi, Florida, and Louisiana, the boll weevil and the rains had done their work.

Trapped in the South. There was not much hope of finding other jobs. Georgia state law, for example, forbade sharecroppers from leaving their fields until they had paid off their debts. If they tried to move to nearby towns or cities, local sheriffs had the legal right to hunt them down and bring them back. Southern law condemned the Harrisons, the Battles, and thousands of other families to a form of economic slavery.

SNAPSHOT OF THE TIMES

1890s	Boll weevils attack cotton fields.
1910	National Urban League founded.
1914–1918	World War I
1915	Great Migration of African Americans from the South begins.
1916	Cotton declines as important crop in the South.
1917	United States enters World War I.
	W.E.B. Du Bois urges African Americans to support the war.
	U.S. troops land in Europe.
	Race riots occur in 26 U.S. cities.
1919	U.S. troops are welcomed home.

In addition, white prejudice and the threat of brutality hung over African Americans. Many had seen friends and neighbors dragged off to jail for such "crimes" as being outside their homes past 10 P.M. The fear of lynching was very real. Few African Americans felt safe from local police, even inside their homes. For many, life seemed to lead to a dead end. "I am in the darkness of the South," a lonely voice cried, "and I am trying my best to get out."

Pulled to the North. Three thousand miles away, World War I was raging across Europe. Even before the United States entered the war in 1917, the nation was feeling the economic effects.

The war choked off the steady supply of cheap immigrant labor that Northern and Midwestern industries depended on. Then, in 1917, 4 million white workers were called into the U.S. armed forces. Factory owners had little choice but to recruit African Americans to work their steel furnaces, meat-packing plants, railroads, loading docks, and brickyards.

Company agents combed the South, armed with free railroad passes and promises of jobs that paid five dollars a day. Field hands who survived on less than a dollar a day and workers who sweated in Southern factories for 14 cents an hour leapt at the offer. They could make in a day what they earned in a week.

"Northern fever" was also intensified by headlines in African American newspapers. "Get out of the South," one paper shouted. Another, the *Chicago Defender,* urged, "For the hard-working . . . there is plenty of work."

The call was irresistible. One night in 1917, the 12 members of the Battle family slipped quietly away from their Georgia cotton plantation and boarded a train for Chicago. This scene was repeated thousands of times across the South.

Taking Another Look

1. What prompted many African Americans to leave the South between 1915 and 1930?

2. What attracted African Americans to Northern and Midwestern cities?

3. **Critical Thinking** Imagine yourself as a Southern sharecropper in 1917. Explain why you would or would not join the Great Migration.

2 AFRICAN AMERICAN URBAN CULTURE

How did African Americans respond to life in the cities?

The El rumbled to a halt above Chicago's South State Street. As the doors of the elevated train opened, a tide of weary women and men spilled onto the platform. They were mothers and wives, bone-tired from scrubbing fashionable homes on the shore of Lake Michigan. They were husbands and fathers back from the

What were some of the advantages that Southern arrivals found in Northern cities?

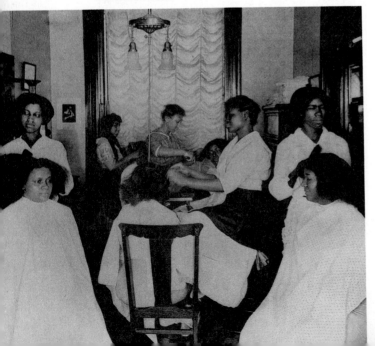

The Artist's View

Statue; Ife, Nigeria
By A.D. 1000, the city-state of Ife, founded by the Yoruba, was the center of a powerful kingdom. Its craftworkers were famous for their wood, clay, and bronze figures.

Kente cloth; Ghana
The National Museum of
African Art and the National
Museum of Natural History,
Smithsonian Institution,
Washington, D.C.
Kente cloth, like this piece
made at the turn of this
century, is created by stitching
narrow, handwoven strips
together. In the past, only
nobles wore robes made from
this fabric. Today, Asante
weavers create this fabric
for collectors.

A2

Bronze head; Ife, Nigeria
British Museum, London
The metalworkers of Ife used the lost-wax process
for making bronze figures like this head of a king, or
oni. First, they made a wax model and covered
it with clay. They then poured hot metal into the
mold. The wax melted and was replaced by the
metal. The ancient Egyptians may have developed
this process.

Ceremonial mask; the Congo
Africans used masks made of wood, ivory, and other materials in their religious ceremonies. Masks like this one inspired European artists such as Picasso and Derain to use elements of African art in their work.

A3

Bronze plaque;
Benin, Nigeria
Museum of African Art,
Smithsonian Institution,
Washington, D.C.
Benin plaques like this
one from the 1600s were
made to glorify the
deeds of rulers. The size
of the individuals in the
plaques showed their
importance in
the society.

A4

Harriet Powers, pictorial quilt
Museum of Fine Arts, Boston
Harriet Powers of Athens, Georgia, worked from 1895 to 1898 on this quilt depicting
scenes from the Bible and from local history. To create the pictures, Powers
sewed, or appliqued, pieces of fabric onto a backing.

A5

Joshua Johnston, Portrait of a Cleric
Bowdoin College Museum of Art, Brunswick, Maine
Painted in 1805, this is Joshua Johnston's only
known portrait of an African American subject.
Working from 1789 to 1825, Johnston, the most
celebrated African American artist of his time,
had to paint portraits of wealthy whites to
make a living.

Thomas Day,
detail from a mantle
Thomas Day's fine
cabinetwork often had
African-inspired designs.
He worked as a cabinet-
maker creating mahogany
furniture and architectural
pieces from 1818 to 1858.

A6

Henry O. Tanner,
The Banjo Lesson
Hampton Institute, Virginia
Painted in 1893, this is one of
Henry O. Tanner's few works
with an African American
subject. After Reconstruction,
the U.S. art world rejected
African American art so
Tanner fled to Paris and
turned to religious themes.

N. Elizabeth Prophet, Congolais
*The Whitney Museum of American Art,
New York*
Nancy Elizabeth Prophet, one of the
many African American artists who
lived and worked abroad, sculpted
this figure reminiscent of a Masai
warrior in 1931.

Face vessel, South Carolina
This porcelain face vessel was made in the 1800s.
Called "monkey pots" by the African American slaves
who crafted them, the style of these water jugs have
their roots in West Africa where wooden sculptures
have similar features.

A7

Palmer Hayden, The Janitor Who Paints
National Museum of American Art, Smithsonian Institution, Washington, D.C.
Painted about 1937, this painting suggests the period when Hayden, like other African American artists, was forced to take odd jobs to support himself. The masklike faces of the woman and child show Hayden's tie to African art.

A8

Edmonia Lewis, Forever Free
Howard University Art Gallery, Washington, D.C.
Sculpted of marble in 1867, Edmonia Lewis's
Forever Free celebrates the ratification of the
13th Amendment outlawing slavery. Her
sculptures often reflected her Chippewa
and African American heritage.

Aaron Douglas, "Song of the Tower,"
Aspects of Negro Life
*Schomburg Center for Research in
Black Culture, New York*
This work, from a four-panel series, illustrates
the reasons African Americans migrated to the
industrialized North. In this 1930 series, Aaron
Douglas painted African American history
and experiences.

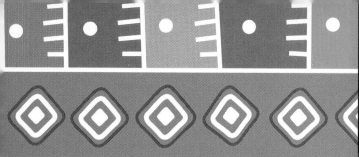

Lois Mailou Jones, Les Fetiches
National Museum of American Art,
Washington, D.C.
The African mask in this work painted in 1938
reflects Lois Mailou Jones's commitment to
her African American heritage. She often
employed African images in her work.

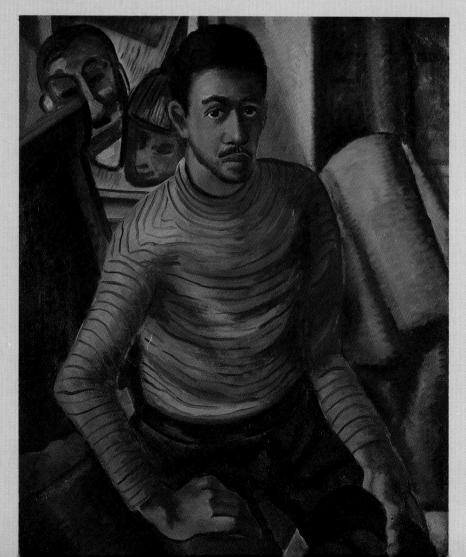

Malvin Gray Johnson,
Self-Portrait
National Museum of
American Art, Smithsonian
Institution, Washington, D.C.
This self-portrait was
painted in 1934, the year
Johnson died. Although he
lived only 38 years, he left
a legacy of paintings of
African American life,
especially of the South.

Jacob Lawrence, from The Migration of the Negro
Museum of Modern Art, NewYork
Jacob Lawrence painted his 60-panel series *The Migration of the Negro* between 1940 and 1941. The series details the conditions that pushed and pulled many African Americans to move to the North.

A11

Horace Pippin, John Brown Going to His Hanging
Pennsylvania Academy of Fine Arts, Philadelphia
Horace Pippin creates a powerful effect using mainly gray, black, and white in this
last in a series of paintings illustrating John Brown's life. As a young girl, Pippin's
mother, an African American slave, had seen Brown's execution.

A12

Sargent Johnson, Mask
San Francisco Museum of Modern Art
This copper mask, made in 1933, reveals Sargent Johnson's effort to suggest but not copy forms from Africa. He interpreted the artistic traditions of Africa in contemporary African American art.

Xenobia Bailey, Royal Crown #5
Schomburg Center for Research in Black Culture, New York
Xenobia Bailey created this hat in 1985 from acrylic, yarn, and other materials. She was inspired by the Yoruba idea that the head is the center of thought and moral strength.

A13

John Biggers, Jubilee—Ghana Harvest Festival
The Museum of Fine Arts, Houston
A painter, sculptor, and printmaker, John Biggers painted murals in the middle
of this century. His work shows aspects of African and African American life.

Augusta Savage, Gamin
*The Schomburg Center for Research
in Black Culture, New York*
Augusta Savage sculpted this piece
in 1930, using plaster as her medium.
She was the first African American
in the National Association of
Women Painters and Sculptors.

Faith Ringgold, Bitternest Part II: ▶
Harlem Renaissance Party
Bernice Steinbaum Gallery, New York
This 1988 mixed media piece made of cloth and
acrylic represents Faith Ringgold's campaign
for equality in every aspect of life for women
and African Americans.

A14

Romare Bearden, Trio
The Estate of Romare Bearden
Working in 1964 on this collage, Romare Bearden combined forms from African art with photographs, cloth, and painted paper to represent various experiences of African Americans.

Sultan Rogers, Walking Stick
University Museums, University of Mississippi Cultural Center, University of Mississippi
This wooden walking stick carved in 1985 is reminiscent of a chief's symbol in Africa. It has snake designs and patterns from West African textiles.

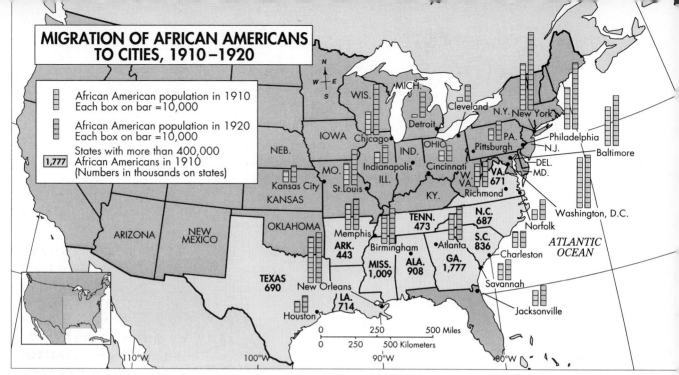

MIGRATION OF AFRICAN AMERICANS TO CITIES, 1910–1920

African American population in 1910
Each box on bar = 10,000

African American population in 1920
Each box on bar = 10,000

States with more than 400,000
African Americans in 1910
(Numbers in thousands on states)

What three cities gained the most African American population between 1910 and 1920?

grimy glass factories, stockyards, and blast furnaces that ringed the city. They were African Americans glad to be home from the white world.

It was payday for some, and they rushed to deposit their paychecks in African American banks. Some stopped to buy African American newspapers. Sports fans scanned the papers for the latest baseball scores from the professional Negro League.

As they fanned out to their homes, some passed a crowded record store where Jelly Roll Morton could be heard playing his "Smokehouse Blues" on the piano. From another store a record of Bessie Smith's "Nobody Knows You When You're Down and Out" was playing. This was a typical day in any city where African Americans had come to live.

City Living.   In Chicago, it was called the South Side. In New York, Harlem. In Philadelphia, the Seventh Ward. In Washington, D.C., Northeast. These and similar neighborhoods in Northern and Mid-

western cities were where African Americans lived—usually not by choice. In time, the African American sections of cities became known as **ghettoes.** A ghetto is a section of a city in which many members of one **ethnic group,** people who share a common culture, are forced to live, because of discrimination. Jews, Mexicans, and Asians were among other groups who lived in ghettoes.

Often because of lack of government interest, these neighborhoods were, or would soon become, the most rundown and neglected parts of cities. Nevertheless, rents were so high that several families of **migrants,** people who had moved looking for better economic opportunity, often had to share one apartment. In most cities, African American children attended neighborhood schools. Since their neighborhoods were almost all African American, so too were their schools.

City Churches.   As in the South, African Americans looked to their churches for spiritual comfort, community support,

How would these children's lives be different if they were raised in the South?

and help in many parts of their lives. Older, established African American churches welcomed newcomers to the city. Sometimes a whole congregation moved North and rented a storefront for their church. New religious organizations such as the Church of God in Christ and the **Nation of Islam** (see page 337) also began to attract followers.

At a typical Sunday service, community concerns often took as much time as strictly religious matters. A sermon on the need for African Americans to vote might be followed by a report on the annual clothing drive to help the needy.

National Urban League. The goal of the **National Urban League,** founded in 1910, was also to help migrants. The League focused on helping them gain their economic and political rights. It aided new city dwellers in finding housing and work and made sure they were treated fairly on the job.

On crowded docks and in bustling train stations, Urban League workers searched out migrant families and directed them to apartments they had personally inspected. They demanded that union bosses and factory owners teach African American workers the skills that brought higher wages. If money was needed to build a playground or a health care center, for example, the Urban League helped raise the funds and often supervised the construction.

African American Newspapers. Newspapers helped strengthen ties in the African American communities. The *Washington Bee,* the *New York Age,* the *Cleveland Gazette,* the *Pittsburgh Courier,* and many others not only reported community news but also spoke out for the rights of African Americans. The most influential paper was the *Chicago Defender.* As you read earlier in this chapter, the *Defender* encouraged African Americans to leave the South. It also attacked discrimination, segregation, and lynching. The founder of the *Defender* was Robert S. Abbott.

Raised in Savannah, Georgia, **Robert S. Abbott** graduated from Kent Law School in Chicago. After being told that he was "too dark" to practice law in the United States, he decided to enter the newspaper business. In 1905, he brought out the first issue of the weekly *Defender,* which sold 300 copies. Abbott began to attract readers by using bold headlines and dramatic articles to announce both the ambitions and the accomplishments of African Americans. At its peak, Abbott's newspaper was distributed in cities from Chicago to New Orleans and had a circulation of over 300,000.

Taking Another Look

1. What living conditions did African American migrants face in the cities?

2. How did the African American community help migrants?

3. **Critical Thinking** Did the benefits of city life outweigh the social and economic hardships migrants found there? Explain.

3 WORLD WAR I: OPPORTUNITIES AND SETBACKS

How were African Americans involved in World War I?

According to President Woodrow Wilson, the goal of the United States in World War I was to make the world "safe for democracy." However, few African Americans saw democracy at work in the nation's armed forces. The Marine Corps barred them from service. The navy took them only as cooks, kitchen helpers, and boiler-room workers. Only the army reluctantly used them as fighting men.

Serving in the Armed Forces. When the nation began drafting men for the armed forces in July 1917, it also drafted Jim Crow. African American recruits were stationed throughout the country in segregated training camps. Many of these camps were in the South, where it seemed that whites disliked African American soldiers more than they did the German enemy.

A bitter racial incident took place in Houston, Texas, in August 1917. For several weeks, tensions had been building between soldiers and townspeople. One afternoon, several uniformed African American soldiers flagged down a public streetcar to board it. In an instant, they were surrounded by a gang of whites, who pulled them off, hurling racial insults at them. News of the incident quickly reached the training camp. Seizing their weapons, a band of angry African American soldiers raced to town. During the street fight that followed, 12 white civilians were killed.

After a brief trial, an army court-martial found 13 soldiers guilty of murder and ordered them hanged. Fourteen others were jailed for life. No whites were punished. The incident led to nationwide protests by African American organizations and white supporters. To prevent further violent flare-ups, the army began to ship some of its African American troops to Europe even before they had finished their training.

Serving Overseas. The U.S. Army trained over 370,000 African American

Known as the Harlem Hellfighters, the 369th Infantry returned in triumph to New York City in 1919. The unit also served in the Persian Gulf War in 1991.

soldiers for combat. Yet three out of four spent their time in the army in labor battalions. They hauled supplies, broke roads, or built fortifications. Although U.S. generals questioned the fighting fitness of African Americans, about 100,000 did see combat and most performed with distinction. They served in all-African American regiments, commanded for the most part by white officers. Only 1,400 African Americans became officers, none above the rank of colonel.

Despite the attitude of the American high command, their war-weary French allies gladly accepted African American units. Strapping on French backpacks and shouldering French rifles, African American soldiers fought under French officers in one vicious trench battle after another.

For their heroic efforts, African Americans were welcomed in French restaurants, hotels, and clubs. The French chose to ignore a secret memorandum from the U.S. high command warning against treating African American soldiers too well.

Serving at Home. Most African Americans backed the war. W.E.B. Du Bois spoke for many when he declared, "If this is our country, then this is our war." He hoped that by supporting the war, African Americans would win the respect of the public and gain better treatment from whites.

African Americans stepped in to help fill the gap left by workers who had gone to war. They mined the coal that fueled the factories, and they labored to build badly needed tanks, trucks, and battleships. They bought Liberty Bonds to help finance the war and supported the Red Cross. African American women worked in army canteens.

However, events at home did not seem to reward their support. Race riots broke out in 26 major U.S. cities in 1917, including East St. Louis, Illinois, where 39 African Americans were killed. In protest, the NAACP organized a silent protest parade in New York City (see page 248). In the nation's capital, President Wilson, who had once promised "absolute fair dealing" for African Americans, ordered federal offices to be segregated.

Taking Another Look

1. What obstacles did African Americans face during World War I?

2. How did African Americans contribute to the war effort at home?

3. **Critical Thinking** Compare the reasons African Americans fought for the Union in the Civil War with their reasons for fighting in World War I.

LOOKING AHEAD

Huge parades in the nation's towns and cities greeted returning veterans of World War I. In New York City, nearly a million people lined Fifth Avenue to salute their heroes, among them Harlem's battle-hardened 369th Regiment. A grateful Chicago closed its schools and businesses to honor its triumphant warriors. For African Americans would this holiday from racism last?

From the NAACP magazine the *Crisis,* W.E.B. Du Bois issued a call to arms for African Americans. He proclaimed, "Make way for democracy! We saved it in France, and by the Great Jehovah, we will save it in the United States of America, or know the reason why."

World War I veteran

World War I Honor Roll

Henry Johnson and Needham Roberts—First African Americans to receive the highest French award, the Croix de Guerre; awarded for fighting off attacking German soldiers while wounded

Sergeant Matthew Jenkins—Received the Distinguished Service Cross and the Croix de Guerre for holding a position against the enemy by himself for 36 hours

Corporal Isaac Valley—Awarded Distinguished Service Cross for covering a grenade with his foot to protect fellow soldiers

First Battalion of the 367th Infantry Regiment of the 92nd Division—Awarded the Croix de Guerre for bravery

369th Infantry Regiment of the 93rd Division—Cited 11 times for bravery; awarded the Croix de Guerre

FOCUS ON: JAZZ IN THE 1920s

In 1919, the 369th U.S. Infantry marched triumphantly through New York, back from duty in Europe. When the African American regiment reached Harlem, its 60-piece band, led by Lieutenant James Europe, switched to **jazz**—the same music it had played to wildly enthusiastic crowds in France, Belgium, Britain, and Germany. European love of jazz began with James Europe's band.

Jazz is a unique musical form that developed in the United States at the turn of the century and then spread throughout the world. Blending a number of musical traditions, jazz combines West African rhythms, European harmonies, and African American spirituals and blues.

The popularity of jazz grew in Europe and the United States in the 1920s. However, many jazz musicians preferred playing in Europe, partly because Europeans were more appreciative of jazz than Americans were. African American musicians also found less racial discrimination in Europe, where talent was more important than skin color. But at home and abroad, African American musicians, including Billie Holiday and Jelly Roll Morton, drew large audiences. Their music later inspired present-day musicians like Wynton Marsalis, Hiram Bullock, and Grover Washington.

The Who, What, Where of History

1. **What** was the Great Migration?
2. **What** was the boll weevil?
3. **What** are migrants?
4. **What** are ghettoes?
5. **What** was the National Urban League?
6. **Who** was Robert S. Abbott?
7. **Where** was a silent protest parade held in 1917?

Making the Connection

1. What was the connection between the boll weevil and an increase in the African American population of cities of the North and Midwest?
2. What was the connection between state laws and the inability of African Americans to move from farms to cities in the South?
3. What was the connection between World War I and the increased employment of African Americans in manufacturing jobs?

Time Check

1. When did World War I begin?
2. When did the Great Migration of African Americans begin?
3. When did U.S. troops join the fighting in World War I?

What Would You Have Done?

1. Suppose you were starting a new weekly newspaper designed for African Americans. How would you attract readers?

2. If you had been an African American man in 1918, would you have chosen to try to get a factory job or to enlist in the army? Explain your choice.

Thinking and Writing About History

1. Imagine that you are an African American migrant who has come to Chicago in 1918. Write a letter to a friend in Mississippi explaining why you think the friend should or should not join you in the city.

2. Imagine that you are a member of the National Urban League in 1916. Write a letter to a friend explaining what sort of work you do for the league and why you enjoy it.

3. Write an editorial for the *Defender* about the court-martial of the soldiers following the racial incident in Houston in August 1917.

Building Skills: Making Generalizations Based on Statistics

Suppose your friend tells you that in 1988 Darryl Strawberry hit more home runs than José Canseco. You don't think he's right, and you consult an almanac, a record book, or your baseball cards. You've just used some *statistics*—or as they call them in sports, *stats*. Statistics are numerical facts about a subject.

Historians often look at statistics to form ideas about trends and developments. They make generalizations from the information they find.

Following is a table that gives information about tenant farmers during the Great Depression. A tenant farmer is one who works land owned by another person. The tenant pays rent to the landowner. Study the table, then answer the questions that follow.

▷ ▷ Tenant Farmers in 1930			
State	Percentage of farmers who were tenants	State	Percentage of farmers who were tenants
AL	64.7	NE	47.1
AZ	16.4	NV	12.9
AK	63.0	NH	5.3
CA	18.0	NJ	15.6
CO	34.5	NM	20.2
CT	6.2	NY	13.2
DE	33.8	NC	49.2
FL	28.4	ND	35.1
GA	68.1	OH	26.3
ID	25.3	OK	61.5
IL	43.1	OR	17.8
IN	30.1	PA	15.9
IA	47.3	RI	12.5
KS	42.3	SC	65.1
KY	35.9	SD	44.6
LA	66.6	TN	46.2
ME	4.5	TX	60.9
MD	26.5	UT	12.2
MA	5.6	VT	9.7
MI	15.5	VA	28.1
MN	31.1	WA	17.0
MS	72.2	WV	18.6
MO	34.8	WI	18.2
MT	24.5	WY	22.0

1. What do the numbers in the table represent?

2. a. Which are the five states with the highest percentage of tenants? **b.** Which five have the lowest?

3. Write a generalization based on your answers to question 2.

4. Look at the percentages for Washington, Oregon, Utah, Arizona, California, Idaho, Nevada, Montana, Wyoming, Colorado, and New Mexico. Write a generalization about farm tenancy in the western states.

Marcus Garvey at right

Black Nationalism
(1916–1929)

THINKING ABOUT THE CHAPTER

Why did African Americans become interested in black nationalism in this period?

On a steamy August day in 1920, some 50,000 African Americans set out on a march through the streets of Harlem, New York City's African American community. The march marked the opening of the first International Convention of the Negro Peoples of the World.

Thousands more African Americans lined the sidewalks, cheering the marchers. A sense of pride swept through the crowd. Many waved flags of black, red, and green—the black standing for their race, the red for their blood, and the green for their hopes.

The loudest cheers went up when a stocky Jamaican-born man in a gold-trimmed uniform rolled into view in an open car. This was Marcus Mosiah Garvey, the president-general of the convention.

That night, Garvey addressed 25,000 African Americans gathered at Madison Square Garden. "We are descendants of a people determined to suffer no longer," he proclaimed. "We shall now organize the 400 million Negroes of the world into a vast organization to plant the banner of freedom on the great continent of Africa." A participant in the meeting later recalled, "It was the greatest demonstration of colored solidarity [unity] in American history, before or since."

Garvey served as the inspiring leader of many African Americans for only a brief time. However, his ideas still move African Americans. He believed that they should take pride in their blackness and study and identify, or connect, with the history and culture of Africa. He also felt that, to get ahead, African Americans should rely on themselves rather than on white people. These ideas make up what has been called **black nationalism.**

1 THE APPEAL OF BLACK ▼ NATIONALISM

▼ Why were African Americans attracted to black nationalism?

A little over a year before Garvey addressed the convention in New York,

W.E.B. Du Bois had announced to African Americans that, "We are cowards . . . if now that the war is over we do not marshal every ounce of our brain and brawn [muscle] to fight a sterner, longer, more unbending battle against the forces of hell [discrimination] in our own land." Events in the coming months would demonstrate just how bitter that battle was to be.

Losing Ground. For many whites, the 1920s were good years. Spirits and fortunes soared as new jobs were created. The stock market and the nation's economy boomed.

Most African Americans, however, still faced discrimination, and many were jobless. African Americans who had found wartime jobs in the factories of the North and Midwest often lost them to returning white veterans. Barred from joining the powerful labor unions, African Americans could not protect themselves against such layoffs.

A revived Ku Klux Klan was again threatening African Americans and also Catholic, Jewish, and immigrant whites. By day, its members staged parades in Northern as well as Southern cities and put pressure on white politicians to support Klan policies. Under the cover of

This photo of Garvey's African Motor Corps was taken by Harlem photographer James Van Der Zee.

1916	Marcus Garvey brings Universal Negro Improvement Association to New York.
1919	"Red Summer" race riots
1920	First International Convention of the Negro Peoples of the World
1922	Garvey is charged with mail fraud.
1927	Garvey is deported.

darkness, its night riders assaulted African Americans in their homes. The number of lynchings, which had fallen during the war, began to rise again.

Race Riots. The Great Migration had steadily increased the African American populations of cities in the North and Midwest. Whites often resented these new neighbors, and tensions between the groups mounted steadily. Then, less than eight months after the end of World War I, tensions erupted in a series of race riots across the nation.

During the "Red Summer" of 1919, as this violent season was called, casualties mounted. Six died and 150 were injured in two days of fighting in Washington, D.C. The toll in Chicago stood at 38 dead and 537 injured. By year's end, race riots had ripped through 25 cities and towns, including Knoxville, Tennessee; Longview, Texas; and Tulsa, Oklahoma.

Fighting Back. This violence provoked a new spirit of defiance among African Americans. Tired of being the victims of discrimination and violence, many African Americans chose to fight back. "The time for cringing [shrinking away in fear] is over," announced the Kansas City *Call*, an African American newspaper. From New York City, the Jamaican-born poet Claude McKay agreed, writing in the poem "If We Must Die,"

> If we must die, let it not be like hogs
> Hunted and penned in an inglorious [undignified] spot.
> . . . .
> Like men we'll face the murderous, cowardly pack,
> Pressed to the wall, dying but fighting back!

Nevertheless, few believed that violence could permanently solve the problems that African Americans faced in the nation. Members of the NAACP and the National Urban League, who were mostly middle-class African Americans, still looked to legal and political strategies to bring about change.

Pan-Africanism. Some African Americans began to identify more closely with their African roots. Led by W.E.B. Du Bois, they championed the idea of **Pan-Africanism.** Pan-Africanists be-

Two million members of the revived Ku Klux Klan conducted a new reign of terror in the 1920s.

lieved that people of African descent had common interests and should join in a common struggle for freedom, at home and abroad (see page 274).

The roots of Pan-Africanism in the United States went back to the early 1800s. One of its earliest promoters was Paul Cuffe. He encouraged African Americans to leave the United States and make Africa their home (see page 124).

In the 1920s, there was renewed interest in Pan-Africanism. The ideas of black nationalism that Marcus Garvey developed, for example, stressed the importance of their African heritage to African Americans.

Taking Another Look

1. What does the term *black nationalism* mean?

2. List three responses of African Americans to conditions after World War I.

3. **Critical Thinking** Which of the responses you listed promised the strongest hope of success? Explain.

2 MARCUS GARVEY
▼ What message did Marcus Garvey bring to African Americans?

The violence of the Red Summer strengthened the resolve of many African Americans to make a new life for themselves. "Lynchings and race riots," said one leader, "all work to our advantage by teaching the Negro that he must build a civilization of his own or remain forever the white man's victim."

The speaker was Marcus Garvey, organizer of the International Convention of the Negro Peoples described at the beginning of the chapter. Garvey had a vision of new strength for African peoples around the world. That vision and his plans for making it happen won him the title "Black Moses."

Marcus Mosiah Garvey was born in 1887 in Jamaica, in the British West Indies. He left school at the age of 14 to help support his family. In his early 20s, Garvey worked his way through Central and South America. As he traveled, Garvey was struck by the hardships black people everywhere faced.

At age 25, Garvey went to London to learn more about conditions for Africans in the British Empire. There he met African scholars, students, and workers. It was in London that supporters of Pan-Africanism opened his eyes to his rich African heritage.

Garvey believed that African peoples could win equality with whites only through economic, political, and cultural independence. He returned to his native Jamaica in 1914 and founded the Universal Negro Improvement Association (UNIA) to work toward this goal.

Beginnings of a Movement. Marcus Garvey stood at the center of a whirlwind of activity that swept out of Harlem from 1916 through the early 1920s. Garvey had brought the UNIA to New York from Jamaica in 1916. "Up you mighty race!" he preached to African Americans. "You can accomplish what you will." Garvey thus started the first extensive black nationalist movement in

U.S. history that appealed to the great mass of the African American people.

Garvey set in motion a variety of UNIA programs aimed at fostering political, economic, and cultural independence. The UNIA's newspaper *Negro World* carried stories about African American leaders and heroes usually left out of white publications. Its meeting halls became the scene of rallies and of exhibitions highlighting the African American experience.

Garvey's Plans.   Garvey warned African Americans that "a race that is solely dependent upon others for its economic existence sooner or later dies." He felt that businesses owned and managed by African Americans offered a path to independence for them. With the UNIA as a base, Garvey began to develop such businesses.

In 1919, he founded the Black Star Line. He hoped this steamship company would develop commercial ties between African peoples the world over. Garvey also started the Negro Factories Corporation in 1919. Within a short time, the corporation operated grocery stores, a restaurant, a laundry, a publishing house, and several other businesses.

Yet, even if African Americans succeeded in owning businesses, Garvey believed that the "monster evil of prejudice" would deny them justice and equality in the United States. He therefore called upon black workers to join him in Africa and create a powerful nation there. "Let Africa be a bright star among the constellation of nations," he proclaimed. As part of a plan to develop the continent, the UNIA sent teams of surveyors and engineers to map potential settlement sites in Liberia (see page 131).

Garvey's Appeal. Programs like these won Garvey a huge following. His approach differed from that of earlier African American leaders. Du Bois had focused on the Talented Tenth at the top of African American society. The NAACP's programs likewise attracted the upper and middle classes and professionals.

Garvey, however, tailored his appeal to ordinary African Americans. He offered pride, pageants, and uplifting messages. He was, according to one observer, "the first Negro to capture the imagination of the masses." The masses responded by flocking to join the UNIA. By 1920, Garvey claimed 4 million members for the organization. His critics protested that this figure was wildly exaggerated.

The masses also gave money—for contributions, membership fees, and pur-

Garveyite families valued their African heritage and belief in black nationalism.

chases of stock in Garvey's companies. Between 1919 and 1921, an estimated $10 million in nickels, dimes, and dollars poured in.

A Movement Collapses. As Garvey's popularity reached its peak, rumors began to spread that his Black Star Line was in danger of sinking. Garvey was a poor business manager, more comfortable in a crowded lecture hall than running a company. As a result, he left many key decisions in the hands of associates who lacked practical business experience. They spent huge sums on leaky ships and ill-trained crews to run them.

The federal government began an investigation of the Black Star Line. In 1922, Garvey was arrested for mail fraud. The government charged that he had known the company was on the verge of ruin but had continued to urge people to invest in it.

Garvey was found guilty and sentenced to five years in prison. President Calvin Coolidge freed Garvey in 1927, after he had served two years. Upon his release from prison, Garvey was deported from the United States. Without its leader, Garvey's movement soon collapsed. His later efforts to restart the UNIA failed. Garvey died in London in 1940.

Garvey's Legacy. At the time of his death, Garvey was almost a forgotten figure. After his movement had collapsed in the 1920s, many African Americans had dismissed his programs as foolish schemes. Some leaders protested that the UNIA had taken attention away from better-planned efforts to gain equality.

However, as black nationalism resurfaced during the 1960s, people rediscovered Garvey. Publishers rushed his collected speeches and essays into print. In the 1970s, New York City named a housing project the Marcus Garvey Park Village. In 1987, an African American member of Congress presented a bill to reverse Garvey's 1925 conviction and clear his name.

African Americans had finally taken note of Garvey's major accomplishment. He had begun a movement to make African Americans a united people. He had also left them a lasting gift. "In a world where black is despised," said New York's *Amsterdam News,* "he taught them that black is beautiful."

Taking Another Look

1. How did Garvey attempt to build economic independence among African Americans?

2. How did Garvey's programs differ from those of earlier African American leaders?

3. **Critical Thinking** What benefits would the powerful African nation that Garvey wanted to build offer for African Americans?

LOOKING AHEAD

When Marcus Garvey announced membership figures for the UNIA, critics attacked him. The real numbers were only a tenth of Garvey's figures, they said. But critics' charges did not bother him. "No one will ever know accurately the membership of the Universal Negro Improvement Association," he said, "because every second Negro you meet, if not an actual member, is one in spirit." Already, this spirit was flowering in a creative explosion of African American art and culture that would come to be known as the Harlem Renaissance.

CLOSE UP: Chapter 25

You have opened my eyes to liberty. I shall never rest until I have carried your message to Africa.

So wrote Kwame Nkrumah (KWAH-mee uhn-KROO-muh) as he left the United States at the end of World War II. The message that he carried back to his native Ghana and to all of Africa could be summed up in just two words—independence and unity.

Nkrumah and other young African thinkers at the time were caught up in the excitement of a movement known as Pan-Africanism. Inspired by W.E.B. Du Bois and Marcus Garvey, this movement stressed the shared interests and common struggle of all peoples of African descent.

The movement also emphasized Africa's historical importance. Du Bois promoted these ideas at a series of five international conferences that Nkrumah and other future African leaders, including Kenya's Jomo Kenyatta, attended. The objective was to help Africans shake off their colonial rulers.

In the 1950s and 1960s, the nations of Africa did win their freedom. Nkrumah, first president of Ghana, tried to forge a united Africa, but political turmoil prevented it. In spite of that, a desire still burns among Africans to chart their own independent course in world affairs.

The Who, What, Where of History

1. **Who** was Marcus Garvey?
2. **What** is black nationalism?
3. **What** is Pan-Africanism?
4. **What** was the Red Summer?
5. **What** was the UNIA?
6. **What** was the Black Star Line?

Making the Connection

What was the connection between the end of World War I and the increase in the unemployment rates among African Americans?

Time Check

1. When was the First International Convention of the Negro People of the World held?
2. How many years were there between Garvey's bringing the UNIA to the United States and his deportation?

What Would You Have Done?

1. Imagine that you are the editor of an African American newspaper in Chicago. It is September 1919. Write an editorial for your paper about the events of the Red Summer.
2. If Marcus Garvey had asked you which of his ideas you thought was most useful to African Americans, what would you have answered?

Thinking and Writing About History

1. Imagine that you are one of the founding members of the UNIA. Write a short paragraph explaining the goals and purposes of the organization.

2. Design a poster that advertises some UNIA-sponsored business or event.

3. Write an obituary for Marcus Garvey that might have appeared in a Harlem newspaper.

4. Shortly after Garvey's death, one scholar said:

> *That is the difference between success and failure. Had Garvey succeeded in his undertakings, he would have been uncontestably the greatest figure of the twentieth century. Having failed, he is considered a fool.*

Do you think this summary is still valid? Explain.

Building Skills: Recognizing Propaganda

When people hear the word *propaganda*, they often think of something sneaky or evil. However, propaganda is merely a method of using ideas and information to influence people's views. Some widely used propaganda techniques are listed below:

1. *Glittering generalities:* broad, sweeping statements that sound good but, in fact, mean little.

2. *Name calling:* trying to devalue something by attaching a bad label to it.

3. *Bandwagon:* trying to win support for something by conveying the idea that "everybody's doing it."

4. *Testimonial:* having a well-known person endorse an idea or product.

5. *Plain folks:* showing that something comes from ordinary, down-to-earth people, and is, therefore, good.

6. *Card stacking:* distorting facts and evidence to present only one side of an issue favorably.

7. *Transfer:* trying to shift the positive associations from a person or thing to something not directly related.

After studying the propaganda techniques above, see if you can recognize them at work. Read the list below. Write the type of propaganda each illustrates on a separate sheet of paper.

1. "Almost everyone on the block has joined the UNIA already. Why don't you sign up now?"

2. "To join an organization like the UNIA is un-American."

3. "The Black Star Line presents to every African American man, woman, and child the opportunity to climb the great ladder of industrial and commercial progress."

4. "Marcus Garvey has already bought a thousand shares of stock in this company. Why don't you buy some?"

5. "I'm a workingman just like you, so you know that if I'm willing to put my hard-earned money in this company, it must be a safe investment."

6. "Don't you want to invest in the Black Star Line? After all, its flagship is the S.S. *Frederick Douglass*."

7. "Look, the stock is selling for $5.00 a share right now. That's a great buy! You don't need to know what it was selling for last month."

125th Street in New York City's Harlem

CHAPTER 26

The Harlem Renaissance

(1920–1930)

THINKING ABOUT THE CHAPTER

How did conditions in New York City during the 1920s influence the work of African American writers, artists, and musicians?

New York City's African American community of Harlem lay to the north of fashionable white residential and business areas. Yet on Saturday nights in the 1920s, it seemed the world was traveling uptown to catch Harlem's fastest-rising stars. Along Lenox Avenue, caravans of taxicabs and limousines shuttled the well-to-do to New York City's hottest clubs and dance palaces.

The crowds might be bound for the Cotton Club, which billed itself as the "Aristocrat of Harlem" and limited its audience to whites only. There, high-stepping African American dancers in feathers and sequins pranced to the beat of an orchestra led by Duke Ellington.

The more daring downtown whites might head for the clubs that accepted mixed audiences—places like Mexico's and the Catagonia Club—to hear jazz. Or they might join the crowds of African Americans that packed the glittering Savoy Ballroom. There they learned the Charleston or the Savoy Stomp on the Savoy's nearly block-long dance floor.

Uptown Saturday night entertainment was only the most visible part of the outpouring of African American artistic achievement in the 1920s. This burst of creativity by writers, musicians, and artists is known as the Harlem Renaissance.

The "New Negro." The Harlem Renaissance was another of the developments that affected the African American community after World War I. African American writers and thinkers proclaimed the appearance of a "New Negro." One African American newspaper announced, "The NEW NEGRO, unlike the old time negro, does not fear the face of the day."

For writers and artists this meant a new willingness to explore African American themes and topics. One poet stated,

We younger Negro artists now intend to express our individual dark-skinned selves without fear or shame. If white people are pleased, we are glad. If they are not, it doesn't matter.

Harlem. It seemed only natural that the New Negro Movement, as it is sometimes called, was centered in Harlem. The Great Migration had turned an almost all-white neighborhood into the nation's largest African American community. Here lived the most prominent African American leaders, such as W.E.B. Du

Bois and Marcus Garvey. The NAACP and the National Urban League had their headquarters in New York. The nation's largest collection of material on African American history and culture, which belonged to Arthur Schomburg, a Puerto Rican of African descent, could be found in Harlem as well. As African Americans poured into Harlem, once-spacious apartments were divided into smaller flats, and rents soared.

As buildings became overcrowded, landlords neglected them and decay set in. Yet the elegant houses of "Strivers' Row," the homes of doctors, dentists, and professionals, stood in the center of the community. They were symbols of the financial success that African Americans could achieve in New York. "Better to be a dishwasher in New York," commented one writer, "than to be head of a high school in Kansas City."

Near which streets did Langston Hughes live? Where was the Apollo Theater? the Savoy Ballroom?

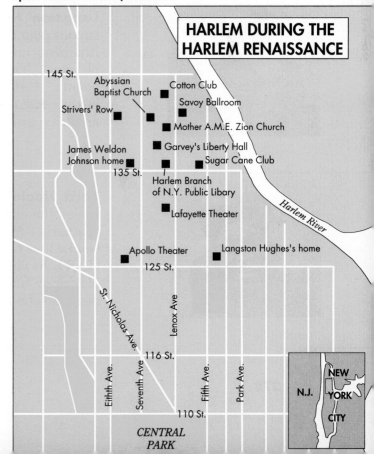

HARLEM DURING THE HARLEM RENAISSANCE

GALLERY OF AFRICAN AMERICAN WRITERS

Countee Cullen (1903–1946)   Cullen explored the African American experience in delicate poetry. One of his finest poems, "Heritage," deals with the importance of his African roots. Other poems describe emotional scars that prejudice caused. A popular Harlem high school teacher, Cullen also wrote a literary column that introduced new African American writers to a wide audience.

Jessie R. Fauset (1885–1961)   Fauset was a novelist, editor, teacher, and poet. As literary editor of *Crisis*, the NAACP magazine, she tirelessly promoted the work of promising young African American writers. Both in her poetry and in her four successful novels, she gave readers the first real and compassionate picture of middle-class African American life.

Langston Hughes (1902–1967)   Harlem's most famous poet captured the rhythms and spirit of African American music—especially jazz and the blues—in his work. Originally from Missouri, Hughes wrote poems, stories, plays, essays, autobiographies, and histories that helped define the African American urban experience.

Zora Neale Hurston (1901–1960)   Hurston revealed the emotional intensity and genuine speech of southern African Americans in novels like *Jonah's Gourd Vine* (1934) and *Their Eyes Were Watching God* (1937). As an anthropologist, she pioneered the study of African American folktales and spirituals in her 1935 nonfiction book *Mules and Men*.

James Weldon Johnson (1871–1938) Johnson began to write poetry late in his life, after a brilliant career as a lawyer, diplomat, and civil rights activist. During the Harlem Renaissance, he wrote and edited several major volumes of poetry and championed new writers. He wrote the lyrics to "Lift Ev'ry Voice and Sing," the unofficial African American national anthem.

Claude McKay (1890–1948) This Jamaican writer's poetry helped define the spirit of the Harlem Renaissance. McKay first won critical acclaim in the United States for his widely published protest poem "If We Must Die." He set many of his short stories (*Gingertown,* 1932) and novels (*Home to Harlem,* 1928) in African American communities.

Wallace Thurman (1902–1934) A successful, sharp-tongued writer, Thurman was the first African American senior editor in a major publishing company. He cofounded the experimental magazine *Fire!!* and wrote the controversial novel *The Blacker the Berry,* which explores color prejudice within the African American community.

Jean Toomer (1894–1967) Though he published only one novel, Toomer is considered one of the most original American writers of his time. In *Cane* (1923), he combined elements of poetry, drama, and fiction to depict African American life both in the rural South and in Northern cities.

GALLERY OF AFRICAN AMERICAN MUSICIANS AND PERFORMING ARTISTS

Louis "Satchmo" Armstrong (1900–1971)   Some people mark the beginning of the Jazz Age as 1922, when Louis Armstrong brought his golden cornet from New Orleans to Chicago. Armstrong's brilliant playing and remarkable musical invention forever changed the sound of U.S. music. Starting in 1932 with his first international tour, he served as the United States' global ambassador of music.

Duke Ellington (1899–1974)   Beginning with a 1927 Cotton Club engagement, Ellington made his swinging orchestra a vital part of U.S. popular music. Radio broadcasts, annual concerts at Carnegie Hall, and sold-out tours made him a household name. Ellington wrote over 2,000 compositions, including the hits "Sophisticated Lady" and "Mood Indigo."

Rose McClendon (1884–1936)   Recognized for her great dramatic range, McClendon became one of the finest American actresses of her day. First winning acclaim in the 1926 play *Deep River,* she later toured the United States and Europe in *Porgy,* a play about African American life in coastal South Carolina. McClendon was an original founder of the Negro People's Theater in Harlem.

Florence Mills (1895–1927)   Mills was a celebrated singer and comedienne. A favorite of Harlem's cabarets and nightclubs, she won national attention in the 1921 Broadway show *Shuffle Along.* Later performances in *Dixie to Broadway* and *Blackbirds* added to her fame. When she died at 32, some 100,000 people lined the streets of Harlem to bid her goodbye.

Paul Robeson (1898–1976)   An athlete, scholar, lawyer, and actor, Robeson was also one of the most popular singers of his day. His career included performances in such plays as *The Emperor Jones* and *All God's Chillun Got Wings,* as well as recitals of African American spirituals in concert halls. Robeson was also a forceful activist for African American civil rights.

Bessie Smith (1894–1937)   Hailed by fans and fellow musicians as the Empress of the Blues, Bessie Smith sold more than 2 million copies of her 1923 recording of "Down Hearted Blues". In the 1920s and 1930s, her traveling blues show thrilled African American audiences across the nation. Through her records, Smith's musical style continues to influence popular vocalists to this day.

William Grant Still (1895–1978)   The "Dean of African American Composers" combined European classical music with American jazz and blues. His *Afro-American Symphony* was the first work by an African American to be performed by a major symphony orchestra. Still wrote operas and ballets, as well as sound tracks for television and movies.

Ethel Waters (1896–1977)   Known as Sweet Mama Stringbean, Waters was one of Harlem's leading entertainers. During the 1920s, her clear, seemingly effortless blues sound won her millions of fans. In 1927, she began a career on the Broadway stage. She achieved her greatest successes in the 1940 musical drama *Cabin in the Sky* and the 1950 drama *Member of the Wedding.*

GALLERY OF AFRICAN AMERICAN ARTISTS

▽▲▽▲▽▲▽▲▽▲▽▲▽▲▽▲▽▲▽▲▽▲▽▲▽▲▽▲▽▲▽▲▽▲▽▲▽▲▽

Aaron Douglas (1899–1979) Douglas was an artist who rejected stereotyped portraits of African Americans. During the Harlem Renaissance, his illustrations graced the books of such writers as Langston Hughes and Countee Cullen. Aaron used ideas drawn from African sculpture, most notably in his murals depicting African American history and life (see **The Artist's View**).

Richmond Barthé (1901–1989) Though he began his artistic career as a portrait painter, Barthé made his reputation as a great sculptor. His small, realistic works reveal the inner grace, strength, and pride of African Americans. Among his best known sculptures are *The Singing Slave, The Blackberry Woman,* and *African Boy Dancing.*

Romare Bearden (1913–1988) After experimenting with different art styles, Bearden achieved his greatest success with collage. In works using combinations of textured papers, vibrant colors, and delicate brush strokes, he explored the rituals and social customs of African American city dwellers (see **The Artist's View**).

Meta Vaux Warrick Fuller (1877–1967) Fuller was one of the first African American artists to make black people the chief subject of her work. Her sculptures, such as the bronze *Water Boy,* are prized for their intimate appeal and human warmth. Her life-size sculpture *Awakening Ethiopia* symbolized the rebirth of African American culture for many Harlem artists.

Sargent Johnson (1888–1967)   Like many African American visual artists of his time, Johnson looked to Africa for artistic inspiration. He once explained that the purpose of his art was to demonstrate "the natural beauty and dignity of the . . . American Negro." He sculpted in metal, wood, and ceramic. His finest works include *Sammy* and *Esther* (see **The Artist's View**).

Horace Pippin (1888–1946)   A self-taught artist, Pippin overcame a severe World War I injury to his painting arm to emerge as one of the nation's leading artists. Using an original technique, he first burned the outlines of figures into wooden boards, then filled them in with brilliant colors. His paintings deal with the drama of African American history (see **The Artist's View**).

Augusta Savage (1900–1962)   Working in marble, wood, and plaster, this sculptor and teacher used art to express her outrage at racial injustice. She won acclaim for her busts of W.E.B. Du Bois and Marcus Garvey and her antiwar sculpture *Glory*. Savage directed the Harlem Community Art Center, which provided many younger sculptors with steady work during the Depression (see **The Artist's View**).

Hale Woodruff (1900–1979)   Woodruff was one of the nation's great mural painters. While at Atlanta University, he began to use painting as a tool for social change. His *Shantytown* and *Mudhill Row* shocked Atlanta citizens into building better urban housing. In 1948, he began a series of murals depicting the contributions of African Americans to California history.

Paul Robeson, shown here as Shakespeare's Othello, was a noted actor and singer of African American spirituals. He spent many years abroad because of discrimination.

The Arts. Visions of success lured promising African American artists to Harlem from other parts of the nation. In the 1920s the *Crisis* and *Opportunity,* the magazines of the NAACP and the Urban League, offered cash prizes for outstanding writing. The Harmon Foundation, a white charitable organization, likewise offered cash prizes for African American writers and artists. It also arranged important exhibitions of work by African American painters and sculptors.

In addition, Harlem lay just north of midtown Manhattan, center of the nation's commerce. The major book and magazine publishers were there. The Broadway theaters offered national recognition to performers and playwrights. Just around the corner, Tin Pan Alley, the hub of the music publishing business, attracted songwriters and musicians.

Perhaps most important, in Harlem aspiring artists could meet and exchange ideas. In this atmosphere of excitement and hope, many new talents blossomed. They included writers like Jean Toomer, Countee Cullen, Claude McKay, Zora Neale Hurston, and Langston Hughes. Such figures recognized that their history as African Americans had given them a unique perspective as writers. They probed many different aspects of the African American experience, dealing with the effects of racism and prejudice. They proudly used regional accents and dialects and sometimes worked the rhythms of the blues into their stories and poems. The works of such writers found an audience not only among African Americans, but among white readers as well.

Painters and sculptors, such as Aaron Douglas and Hale Woodruff, were an important part of the Harlem Renaissance. Many of them drew inspiration from African art or dealt with different aspects of African American history in their work. Traveling exhibitions sponsored by the Harmon Foundation brought the work of such artists to national attention.

African American musicians had an enormous impact on the nation and on the world, producing what has been called "an explosion of genius." The music played in the clubs, ballrooms, and theaters of Harlem by figures such as Fletcher Henderson, Fats Waller, and Duke Ellington was jazz. This musical form had grown out of the mixing of blues and ragtime (see page 266) in New Orleans early in the 1900s. Jazz had moved north in the Great Migration, and was further developed by artists like King Oliver, Louis Armstrong, and Jelly Roll Morton.

Soon the appeal of jazz extended to white audiences. Jazz reached the Broadway stage in shows such as *Shuffle Along* and *Hot Chocolates*. Dances such as the Charleston, the Black Bottom, and the Lindy Hop became wildly popular. The rhythms of jazz captured the spirit of the times so well that the decade of the 1920s is often called the Jazz Age.

Taking Another Look

1. How did some organizations encourage the Harlem Renaissance?

2. What were the roots of jazz?

3. **Critical Thinking** Do you think the "Jazz Age" was an appropriate name for the 1920s from the point of view of African Americans? Explain your answer. Suggest an alternative name for the period.

LOOKING AHEAD

African American artists continued creating new poems, books, plays, songs, musicals, and paintings after the 1920s. But the Harlem Renaissance did not survive the decade.

The nation had experienced an economic boom during much of the 1920s. Then in 1929 the stock market crashed. Banks failed, factories closed, and millions of people lost their jobs. African Americans for the most part had not shared in the boom. Now, they suffered greatly in the depression that followed.

A band leader, pianist, and composer, Duke Ellington, shown here at the piano, was one of the great jazz artists of all time. His career spanned almost 50 years.

In the 1950s, African American artists such as Fats Domino, Little Richard, and Chuck Berry brought a new vitality to popular music. They wrote lyrics and music that excited teenagers, added a driving beat, and called the new sound rock 'n' roll. Its popularity spread so quickly that one music critic called it "the sound heard 'round the world."

Although rock burst on the scene in the 1950s, its roots lay in the distant musical past. Rock developed from many sources, including jazz, blues, and gospel—sources inspired by African rhythms. Rock grew most directly out of another African American music style, the rhythm and blues, or R & B, of the 1940s.

African American influence on rock did not end in the 1950s. Jimi Hendrix used distortion and feedback to produce hard rock in the 1960s. The Motown sound, written and performed by African Americans and produced by Motown Records, an African American company, appealed to teenagers of all ethnic groups. Today, rap stars such as L.L. Cool J and M.C. Hammer, musicians such as Luther Vandross, and groups such as Living Colour continue the tradition of African Americans and rock 'n' roll.

The Who, What, Where of History

1. **Where** is Harlem?
2. **What** was the Harlem Renaissance?
3. **Who** was Aaron Douglas?
4. **Who** was Langston Hughes?
5. **Who** was Louis Armstrong?
6. **Who** was Zora Neale Hurston?
7. **Who** was Hale Woodruff?
8. **What** was the Harmon Foundation?

Making the Connection

1. What was the connection between New York City and the work of African American artists in the 1920s?
2. What was the connection between jazz music and the cities of New Orleans and New York?

Time Check

When did the Harlem Renaissance occur?

What Would You Have Done?

1. Imagine it is 1922, and you are a young African American who aspires to be a great writer or artist. Would you move to Harlem from Kansas? Assume that you have little money and no friends in Harlem.
2. Imagine that you work for an advertising agency in New York City in the 1920s. A group of Harlem business owners has hired your company to plan a campaign to attract more tourists to Harlem. Design a poster to use in the campaign.

Thinking and Writing About History

1. Write a travel article about Harlem for the Chicago *Defender*, an African American newspaper. The time is 1922.

2. Write one paragraph explaining why the Harlem Renaissance was important to U.S. cultural development.

3. Aaron Douglas was one of the leading artists of the Harlem Renaissance. Study the painting by Douglas in "The Artist's View." Write a paragraph explaining what you think Douglas's picture represents.

Building Skills: Understanding Points of View

Suppose that you are a teenager writing an essay about the Harlem Renaissance in the present day. How likely is it that what you have to say will be similar to an essay about the development in Harlem by a French scholar living there in the early 1920s? If you said "Not very likely," you are probably correct. You have one point of view, and the French professor had his.

Any author, whether a writer of fiction, history, poetry, or biography, has a *point of view*—a particular way of looking at things. A person's point of view is shaped by his or her experiences, family, education, reading, and friends. A person's point of view is also shaped, at least to some extent, by the times in which he or she lives.

Read the following poem by Langston Hughes and see what you can learn about his point of view.

The Negro Speaks of Rivers

I've known rivers:
I've known rivers ancient as the world
*   and older than the flow of human blood*
*   in human veins.*

My soul has grown deep like the rivers.

I bathed in the Euphrates when dawns
*   were young.*
I built my hut near the Congo and
*   it lulled me to sleep.*
I looked upon the Nile and raised the
*   pyramids above it.*
I heard the singing of the Mississippi
*   when Abe Lincoln went down to New*
*   Orleans, and I've seen its muddy*
*   bosom turn all golden in the sunset.*

I've known rivers:
Ancient, dusky rivers.

My soul has grown deep like the rivers.

1. What rivers does Hughes use? Where are they located?

2. Based on this poem, do you think that Langston Hughes was sympathetic to the ideas of Pan-Africanism? Explain your answer.

3. Who do you think is "the Negro" who is speaking in the poem?

4. Why do you think the poem emphasizes the great age of the rivers?

5. Explain what you think Hughes means by the line "My soul is deep like the rivers."

6. Do you think Hughes was proud of his African American background? Explain your answer.

New Deal work project

The Great Depression and the New Deal

(1929–1941)

THINKING ABOUT THE CHAPTER

How did the Great Depression affect the lives of African Americans?

On the sidewalk in front of a Chicago apartment building one day in the early 1930s, an African American family stood surrounded by their furniture and belongings. Unable to pay their rent, they had been evicted from their home. A crowd of neighbors gathered, determined to help them regain their apartment.

Police cars screeched up. Officers sprang out and ordered the people to move on. The angry crowd refused, and one man stepped forward to say, "All we want is to see that these people, our people, get back into their home. We have no money, no jobs, and sometimes no food. We've got to live someplace. We are just acting the way you or anyone else would act."

Scenes like this were common in the 1930s all across the United States. The stock market crash of 1929 had set off a depression that almost paralyzed the nation's economy. The Great Depression affected all parts of U.S. society, but African Americans bore some of the greatest hardships. As writer Langston Hughes put it, "[T]he Depression had brought everyone down a peg or two. And the Negroes had but a few pegs to fall."

1 FIGHTING THE GREAT DEPRESSION

▼ How did the Great Depression affect the lives of African Americans?

The effects of the stock market crash quickly spread out through the economy. Banks failed, factories closed down, and stores shut their doors. Often, people lost their savings as well as their jobs.

Hard Times. Even during good times, African Americans received lower wages and had higher unemployment rates than whites. As the economy slumped, these conditions grew worse. One member of the Urban League stated, "At no time in the history of the Negro since slavery has his economic and social outlook seemed so discouraging."

At the beginning of the 1930s, most African Americans still lived in the rural South. As cotton prices plunged from 18 cents a pound to 6 cents, sharecroppers, who had always had a difficult time, could no longer make a living on the land. Thousands gave up and moved out of the South seeking jobs in the cities.

They found little hope there. African Americans had usually held the lowest paying, least desirable jobs. Jobs such as janitor, porter, and street sweeper were "Negro work."

But as jobs became scarce for everyone, whites increasingly took on "Negro work." Unemployment among African Americans soared. In Chicago, the unemployment rate for African American men reached 40 percent, in Pittsburgh it was 48 percent, and in Detroit it rose to 60 percent. The rates of unemployment among African American women were even higher.

Seeking Relief. Without regular paychecks coming in, people could not afford to pay their rents or mortgages or even to buy food and clothing. Many families quickly spent what little savings they had. Often they had to pawn clothes or furniture to buy food or keep a roof over their heads.

Private organizations and charities tried to help the needy. Such groups, however, often practiced discrimination. Soup kitchens sometimes turned away African Americans seeking food. Clothing meant for the poor often was not distributed to African Americans.

Needy people looked to government to help them. President Herbert Hoover, however, did not believe relief for the needy was the federal government's concern. Instead he tried to help big businesses and farms with loans, hoping this aid would "trickle down" to the rest of U.S. society.

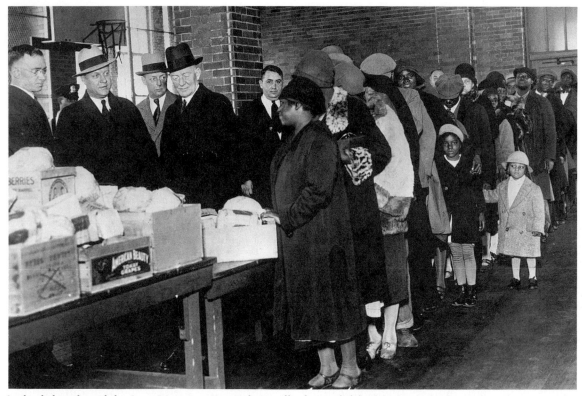

In the darkest days of the Great Depression, New York City officials provided food for hundreds of Harlem's unemployed African Americans.

States and cities had programs that provided food or small sums of money to the needy. But so many people now needed help that state and local governments could not help them all. In addition, relief programs often discriminated against African Americans. At times, they received smaller payments than whites, or they had to meet stricter standards to qualify for relief.

Self Help.   The economic outlook continued to worsen through 1931 and 1932. As it did, African Americans began to work together to do what the federal government refused to: defeat unemployment and hunger.

For the first time, many African American churches became involved in welfare work, starting soup kitchens and distrib-

uting clothing to the needy. The National Urban League organized emergency relief committees. Their members set up survival shelters where the needy could get food, clothing, medical care, and help in finding the few jobs available.

The Fight for Jobs.   The fight for jobs during the depression led to scenes like one in a Northwest Washington, D.C., neighborhood. There, a line of African American picketers marched in a circle in front of the Hamburger Grill, a popular restaurant. Many carried signs reading "Buy Where You Work—Buy Where You Clerk."

After weeks of being picketed, the white restaurant manager admitted his defeat. He agreed to rehire those African American workers he had replaced with whites. Inspired by this success, community leaders expanded their campaign to other stores. Soon what was called the New Negro Alliance was winning jobs for African Americans in white-owned department and grocery stores.

"Don't Buy Where You Can't Work" campaigns spread to Chicago, New York, and 23 other cities. Although they had some success in gaining jobs for African Americans, such campaigns could not hope to solve all the problems that the Great Depression created for African Americans.

The Election of 1932.   By 1932, many Americans had become convinced that strong federal action offered the only hope of curing the nation's economic ills. In the presidential election of that year, Republican Herbert Hoover stood by his belief that the federal government should play only a limited part in solving the crisis. Democrat Franklin D. Roosevelt, whose cheerful manner inspired confidence, promised a "new deal for the American people."

For African American voters, the election presented a difficult choice. The Republican party had been Lincoln's party—the party that had passed the civil rights laws of Reconstruction. The Democratic party was the party of white Southern governments—the party that helped pass Jim Crow laws.

Could African Americans now "turn Lincoln's picture to the wall" and vote for a Democrat as President, as African American newspaper publisher Robert Vann urged? In 1932, the answer was no. Over two thirds of African American voters backed Hoover that year, but Hoover was soundly defeated by Roosevelt nevertheless. In the years that followed, Roosevelt's policies won the backing of African American voters. In huge numbers, they shifted their loyalty to the Democratic party beginning with the election of 1936.

Taking Another Look

1. What limited the amount of government aid that reached African Americans at the beginning of the Great Depression?

2. How did African Americans organize to help themselves during the depression?

3. **Critical Thinking**   If you had been an African American voter during the election of 1932, would you have voted for Roosevelt or Hoover?

2   A NEW DEAL FOR AFRICAN AMERICANS?

How did President Franklin D. Roosevelt's recovery programs affect African Americans?

In the late 1960s, a man who had lived through the Great Depression was asked to comment on African Americans' feelings about Roosevelt in those years. He answered:

Oh yeah, that was something. He broke the tradition. My father told me: "The Republicans are the ship. All else is the sea." Frederick Douglass said that. They didn't go for Roosevelt much in '32. But the WPA came along and Roosevelt came to be a god.

The WPA, or Works Progress Administration, established in 1935, was one of the dozens of Roosevelt's New Deal programs. The hope these programs held out to African Americans had a great impact on their lives. By the 1936 election, 75 percent of African Americans supported Roosevelt. But in its beginnings, the New Deal seemed to offer little to African Americans.

New Deal Programs. "Our greatest primary task is to put people to work," Roosevelt announced on taking office in 1933. In the next 100 days, Congress passed a variety of New Deal measures aimed at restoring the nation's economy.

However, these programs did not aid African Americans and whites equally. "They don't give us any work and don't give relief to colored people," one African American woman complained to the NAACP about a work-relief program. "Kindly get in tutch with Washington. See why they don't."

The reason "why" was politics. To get his New Deal programs through Congress, Roosevelt needed the support of white Southern politicians. "First things come first," Roosevelt said, "and I can't alienate [lose] certain votes I need . . . by pushing any measures that would entail [involve] a fight."

This meant that Roosevelt at first did little to see that the benefits of New Deal programs were designed to reach African Americans on an equal basis with whites. Some New Deal measures called for lower pay for African American workers than for whites doing the same job. In other government work projects, African Americans had to live in segregated housing. Often, they were kept from skilled jobs on federally sponsored dam and electric-power projects. One NAACP member soon concluded, "The New Deal [is] the same raw deal."

Even the Social Security Act of 1935, widely hailed as the New Deal's greatest accomplishment, proved indirectly unfair

The Daughters of the American Revolution banned Marian Anderson from singing in Constitution Hall in 1939 because she was African American. Eleanor Roosevelt won permission for her to sing at the Lincoln Memorial in Washington, D.C.

to African Americans. The act provided millions of citizens with unemployment and old-age insurance. Yet, because it excluded farmers and domestic workers like house cleaners and cooks, the act kept nearly two thirds of African American workers from receiving benefits.

A Changing Deal. From the beginning, African Americans pressed for changes in these practices. They found that they had, as one African American newspaper reported, "a staunch [loyal] ally in the First Lady of the Land"— Eleanor Roosevelt.

Eleanor Roosevelt became a prominent worker for African American rights. She invited African American leaders to the White House. She defied Jim Crow laws by refusing to sit in a "whites only" section while attending a meeting in the South. She wrote newspaper columns that called for "fair play and equal opportunity for Negro citizens."

Most important, she pushed Franklin Roosevelt and other government officials to take action. Roosevelt began to name African Americans as advisers in different departments of the federal government. The leading figures made up what was called the **Black Cabinet,** an informal group of advisers to Roosevelt.

This group pushed for economic and political equality for African Americans. One of its members was Robert C. Weaver, who held several different posts in government and went on to become the first African American in President Lyndon Johnson's Cabinet in 1966. Another was William H. Hastie, dean of the Howard University Law School, who worked in the Department of the Interior. Perhaps the best-known was Mary McLeod Bethune.

Many considered that **Mary McLeod Bethune** was the glue that held the Black Cabinet together. A well-known educator, Bethune had founded and supervised Bethune-Cookman College, in Daytona Beach, Florida. Her work for the National Council of Negro Women focused new attention on the long-ignored subject of the rights of African American women.

As the director of the Division of Negro Affairs of the National Youth Administration (NYA), she traveled thousands of miles each month. Bethune's goal was to ensure that the funds that were targeted for African American high school and college students actually reached them. "I cannot rest," she told her friends, "while there is a single Negro boy or girl lacking a chance to prove his worth."

Some New Government Policies. Bethune's NYA was one of the New Deal agencies that actively sought to improve conditions for African Americans. It gave direct aid to over 300,000 African American young people seeking education.

The Public Works Administration (PWA) pressed contractors working on its projects to use African Americans for both skilled and unskilled labor. About a third of the space in PWA housing projects went to African Americans.

The Farm Security Administration (FSA) offered loans to poor farmers and sharecroppers. It saw that this money was distributed fairly among whites and African Americans.

Many unemployed young African Americans volunteered for the Civilian Conservation Corps (CCC). They served in segregated units to improve roads, plant forests, and create parks.

The Works Progress Administration (WPA) became one of the largest employers of African Americans. They made up 15 to 20 percent of the workers on its construction projects.

More and more bills passed by Congress to authorize New Deal programs included this statement: "There shall be no discrimination on account of race, creed, or color."

This order was not always obeyed, but the New Deal aided African Americans far more than any earlier administration had, and in many different ways. African American employees in the federal government jumped from 50,000 in 1933 to over 150,000 in 1941. A million African Americans took part in federally funded literacy programs. Relief funds and im-proved health care meant that the life expectancy of African Americans increased during the 1930s.

The New Deal did not end discrimination toward African Americans. Nor did it eliminate the huge economic inequalities that separated whites and African Americans. But it did begin to move toward these goals. As actor Paul Robeson remarked in 1939, "Conditions were far from ideal. . . . But change was in the air, and this was the best sign of all."

Taking Another Look

1. What was the Black Cabinet?

2. How did the New Deal improve job opportunities for African Americans?

3. **Critical Thinking** Reread Roosevelt's statement on page 292 about why he would not push for equal aid to African Americans. Then write your reaction to it.

3 GAINS FOR AFRICAN AMERICAN WORKERS

How did African Americans force a change in government policies on discrimination?

"A way must be found of gradually raising the living standards of the colored laborers. . . . " So said Secretary of Labor Frances Perkins in 1934. But African American workers were already taking steps to help themselves.

New Union Policies. One way African American workers helped themselves was by joining unions. In the past, many major U.S. unions had excluded African Americans. Some unions admitted African Americans but had rules that kept them out of skilled jobs, like pipe fitter or machinist, and in lower-paying jobs, like janitor or messenger, with little chance of advancement. The nation's largest labor organization, the American Federation of Labor (AFL) refused even to meet with African American leaders to discuss problems of discrimination. By 1930, African Americans made up only 1 percent of union membership. Half of those, some 50,000 workers, belonged to one segregated union.

The depression helped unions realize they needed to enlist African Americans to increase their membership rolls, in order to apply more pressure on employers. As one African American union organizer said, "We colored folks can't organize without you and you white folks can't organize without us."

New Deal laws like the National Labor Relations Act had guaranteed the right of workers to form unions. Labor leaders now aimed to organize workers in large industries—steel, textiles, and car manufacturing—that employed unskilled African American workers.

This history of African Americans was one of many valuable literary works created by WPA writers. (See the "Focus On . . .", page 298.)

A new labor group, the Congress of Industrial Organizations (CIO), formed in 1935. It opened its membership to African American workers. Thurgood Marshall, a noted NAACP lawyer, declared the CIO's charter of job equality for all workers, "a Bill of Rights for Negro labor." By 1940, the CIO had some 210,000 African American members.

A March on Washington. One African American labor leader hoped to translate this new union participation into increased political power. In the late 1930s, A. Philip Randolph, the founder and president of the Brotherhood of Sleeping Car Porters, had noted the outbreaks of fighting in Asia and Europe. He felt that the United States was heading into another world war.

U.S. factories were beginning to get rich on government defense contracts to manufacture guns, ammunition, airplanes and other war goods. Yet, many still refused to hire African American workers. When Randolph's pleas to end this discrimination went unanswered by President Roosevelt, Randolph launched a civil rights crusade.

In 1941, Randolph called on African Americans to join him in a "nonviolent demonstration of Negro mass power" in Washington, D.C., on July 1. Leading African American newspapers backed Randolph's call. March committees were organized, and press releases announced that 100,000 marchers were expected.

President Roosevelt feared that such a march might hurt him politically. He tried to get Randolph and the organizers to call it off. They refused unless the government took steps to end discrimination.

Finally, four days before the march was scheduled, Roosevelt gave in. He issued

African Americans joined white members of CIO unions to show their strength in a New York City protest march. Thousands of African American workers benefited from union membership.

Labor leader A. Philip Randolph, shown seated at the microphone, led the fight to pressure the New Deal administration to end job discrimination in defense industries.

Executive Order 8802, which barred discrimination in defense industries, government agencies, and work-training programs. To enforce the order, he set up the Committee on Fair Employment Practices (FEPC). For the first time since the Civil War, a U.S. President had issued an order guaranteeing the rights of African Americans.

Taking Another Look

1. Why did many African American workers join the CIO?

2. What was the purpose of Executive Order 8802?

3. **Critical Thinking** Why do you think President Roosevelt was so eager to stop Randolph's march on Washington?

LOOKING AHEAD

Organizers of the march on Washington in 1941 had also demanded an end to segregation in the nation's armed forces. Roosevelt, however, refused to take any action on that issue. Thus, when the Japanese bombing of Pearl Harbor brought the United States into World War II, African Americans were still serving for the most part in segregated units. Meanwhile on the home front, discrimination in the workplace still affected African Americans in spite of union gains, Executive Order 8802, and the FEPC.

Discrimination toward African Americans continued after World War II. Twenty-two years after A. Philip Randolph announced plans for a march on Washington, civil rights leaders again called on African Americans to come to the nation's capital and march for their rights. This time the march took place.

297

FOCUS ON: WPA WRITERS AND ARTISTS

During the Great Depression, the federal government hired writers and artists to create "American stuff." American stuff included anything from folktales and dramas to histories.

With government grants, African American scholars were able to research the history of their people. In one project, African Americans ranging in age from 70 to over 100 vividly described their experiences as slaves. The researchers published these interviews.

The Theater Project created 16 "Negro Units" to tour the country. These troupes staged impressive productions of Shakespeare with an African twist. These theatrical units added African drummers and other touches of African culture. The plays were hits.

These and other projects grew out of the Works Progress Administration—a program that paid artists, writers, musicians, and actors to create works of art for the nation. Such projects nurtured the careers of talented African Americans such as Ralph Ellison, Richard Wright, and Jacob Lawrence. As African American artist Ernest Critchlow observed, "Without that [WPA] aid, many of today's important artists might never have made their contributions to the nation's art."

CLOSE UP: Chapter 27

The Who, What, Where of History

1. **What** is an economic depression?
2. **Who** was Herbert Hoover?
3. **Who** was Franklin Roosevelt?
4. **Who** was Eleanor Roosevelt?
5. **What** was the Black Cabinet?
6. **Who** was Mary McLeod Bethune?
7. **What** was the PWA?
8. **What** was the WPA?
9. **Who** was A. Philip Randolph?
10. **Where** did Randolph plan to hold a great protest march of African Americans?

Making the Connection

1. What was the connection between the Great Depression and fewer jobs for African Americans?
2. Explain the connection that many African Americans saw between Lincoln and Hoover.
3. What was the connection between the Great Depression and increased African American membership in labor unions?

Time Check

1. When did the Depression begin?
2. When was Franklin Roosevelt first elected President?

What Would You Have Done?

1. Would you have participated in a "Don't Buy Where You Can't Work" picket line? Explain.
2. Would you have voted for Franklin Roosevelt in 1936? Explain.

Thinking and Writing About History

1. Write a paragraph comparing Hoover's beliefs about the role of the federal government during the Great Depression and Roosevelt's beliefs about what the government should do to end the depression.

2. Imagine that you are a reporter listening to President Roosevelt and A. Philip Randolph discuss the march on Washington. Write a newspaper article that includes "quotations" from their conversation.

Building Skills: Generalizing From a Primary Source

The following chart comes from the *Statistical Abstract of the United States, 1932*. The Department of Commerce puts together the *Statistical Abstract* every year, collecting information from many federal departments and agencies. Look at the chart and then answer the questions.

1. Look at the percentages of illiterate persons for the United States in 1920 and then for the United States in 1930. Now make a generalization based on the chart about whether illiteracy was increasing or decreasing in the United States as a whole in 1930.

2. Using the regional divisions, make a generalization about where schools were the poorest for African Americans and for all residents.

3. Make a generalization based on the information in the chart about illiteracy in rural areas.

Percentage of Illiterate Persons 10 Years of Age and Over: Continental United States, 1920 and 1930, and by Geographic Divisions, 1930.

Division and Age	Native White, Native White Parentage	Native White, Foreign or Mixed Parentage	Foreign-born, White White	Negro
United States 1920	2.5	.8	13.1	22.9
10–20 years	1.3	.6	5.7	13.0
21 years and over	3.0	.9	13.7	27.4
Urban, total	.8	.5	13.0	13.4
Rural, total	3.8	1.4	13.3	28.5
United States 1930	1.8	.6	9.9	16.3
10–20 years	.8	.3	1.3	7.5
21 years and over	2.2	.7	10.3	20.0
Urban, total	.6	.4	10.0	9.2
Rural, total	3.0	1.0	9.4	22.4
New England	.6	.7	11.6	5.5
Middle Atlantic	.6	.5	12.2	3.7
East North Central	.7	.6	8.8	4.7
West North Central	.8	.5	4.9	4.7
South Atlantic	3.9	.8	10.4	19.7
East South Central	5.1	1.2	7.4	22.0
West South Central	2.7	2.0	9.4	17.0
Mountain	1.5	.4	5.6	4.1
Pacific	.3	.3	4.9	3.1

UNIT 9

Civil rights march, Selma, Alabama, 1965

THE CIVIL RIGHTS REVOLUTION

(1941–1973)

Linda Brown in front of her school

World War II troops heading home

In 1941, the United States entered World War II. Four years of warfare led to a victory that left the nation one of the strongest in the world—a superpower. Spared the destruction of war at home, the United States was now the world's mightiest economic power.

Over the next 25 years, the United States reached a new height of prosperity. The nation also played a larger part in world affairs than it ever had before. The United States presented itself as a model of democracy that nations around the world could follow.

At the same time, African Americans complained that the democracy the nation's leaders were praising still did not apply to them. They renewed their efforts to secure their civil rights. In doing so, they brought about the greatest changes in U.S. society since the days of the Civil War and Reconstruction.

World War II. In 1939, war broke out in Europe, with Germany and Italy opposing Great Britain, France, and, after 1941, the Soviet Union. By 1941, Germany, under its Nazi dictator, Adolf Hitler, had conquered much of Europe. In Asia, war had been going on since 1937, when Japan invaded China.

The United States managed to keep out of the fighting until December 7, 1941. On that date, the Japanese attacked Pearl Harbor, a U.S. naval base in Hawaii, destroying many ships and killing more than 2,000. Four days later, Germany and Italy, who had an alliance with Japan, also declared war on the United States.

As in World War I, the United States quickly prepared to fight the war. The Great Depression came to a swift end as industrial production soared to meet the demands of war. African Americans benefited not only because there were more jobs, but also because A. Philip Randolph's efforts had made the jobs more available to them (see page 296). As in the earlier war, many African Americans moved from the rural South to the industrial cities of the Northeast and Midwest, seeking jobs.

The armed forces grew until, by 1945, there were more than 12 million men and women in uniform. Of these, about 1 million were African Americans. Most of them served in segregated army units.

The Truman Years, 1945–1953. In 1945, shortly before the end of World War II, President Roosevelt died. His successor was Vice-President Harry S Truman. During Truman's first years in office, the United States found itself caught up in the **Cold War**. The Cold War was a conflict with the Soviet Union that stopped short of actual warfare between the two nations. For almost half a century, it would shape U.S. attitudes and policies toward the rest of the world.

In 1950, the Cold War turned hot when Soviet-backed North Korea invaded

---

An African American Speaks

I have a dream that one day this nation will rise up and live out the meaning of its creed: "We hold these truths to be self-evident—that all men are created equal."

—Martin Luther King, Jr.
Civil Rights Movement leader

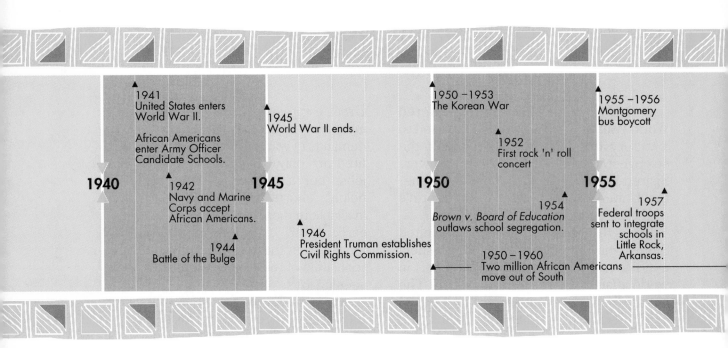

1941
United States enters World War II.

African Americans enter Army Officer Candidate Schools.

1945
World War II ends.

1950 –1953
The Korean War

1955 –1956
Montgomery bus boycott

1952
First rock 'n' roll concert

1940

1942
Navy and Marine Corps accept African Americans.

1945

1950

1955

1954
Brown v. Board of Education outlaws school segregation.

1957
Federal troops sent to integrate schools in Little Rock, Arkansas.

1944
Battle of the Bulge

1946
President Truman establishes Civil Rights Commission.

1950 –1960
Two million African Americans move out of South

U.S.-backed South Korea. The United States joined the war on South Korea's side. China, which, like the Soviet Union, had a Communist government, entered the war on North Korea's side. The Korean War ended in a stalemate in 1953.

At home, Truman proposed many New Deal-style programs. In addition, he pressed hard for civil rights legislation. In 1946, he established a Civil Rights Commission. Its report, which Truman supported, called for a complete end to segregation in U.S. life.

In 1947, Truman issued an order integrating African Americans into all army units. Later orders by Truman and his successor, Dwight Eisenhower, completed the integration of the military. Truman's actions meant that during the Korean War, African American and white soldiers were fighting side by side in the same units for the first time since the early days of the Republic.

In 1948, Truman's loyalty to civil rights threatened his reelection. At the Democratic convention that year, Northern Democrats managed to have a strong pro-civil rights statement written into the party's platform. Many Southerners, called Dixiecrats, left the Democratic party to support a Southern candidate, but Truman won anyway.

In his second term Truman proposed laws to make lynching a federal crime, to protect African American voters, to abolish poll taxes, and to set up a federal commission to prevent discrimination in hiring. Because of Southern opposition, none of these laws was passed.

The Eisenhower Years, 1953–1961.
In 1953, Truman was succeeded by Dwight D. Eisenhower, a Republican. Eisenhower, or "Ike," a hero of World War II, was a popular President throughout his two terms in office.

In foreign affairs, Eisenhower continued the Cold War. At home, the country enjoyed growth and prosperity. For many white citizens, times were good. They couldn't see anything much that needed reform, and neither could Ike.

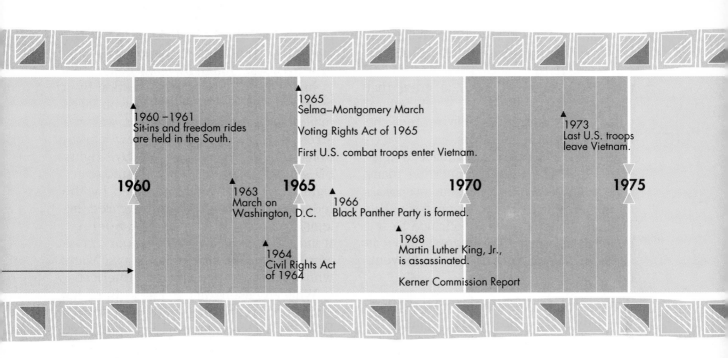

1960–1961
Sit-ins and freedom rides are held in the South.

1965
Selma–Montgomery March

Voting Rights Act of 1965

First U.S. combat troops enter Vietnam.

1973
Last U.S. troops leave Vietnam.

1960

1963
March on Washington, D.C.

1965

1966
Black Panther Party is formed.

1970

1975

1964
Civil Rights Act of 1964

1968
Martin Luther King, Jr., is assassinated.

Kerner Commission Report

For African Americans, this meant that the President took little interest in civil rights legislation. Eisenhower did, however, complete the integration of the military that Truman had begun, and he took steps to desegregate other branches of the federal government. In 1957, Congress passed the first civil rights law since Reconstruction. The law offered some protection to African Americans who had been denied the vote. It was weak, but it showed the federal government was willing to take some action on civil rights.

Challenging Segregation. By the time the civil rights bill passed, there had been important developments in other areas. In 1954, the Supreme Court overturned *Plessy* v. *Ferguson,* the 1896 case establishing the principle of "separate but equal." Now, in *Brown* v. *Board of Education,* the court unanimously ruled that segregation of public schools was illegal.

Actual desegregation was slow in coming. White Southern officials often tried to prevent African American chil-

dren from entering all-white schools. In many cases, integration came only after it was ordered by a federal court and overseen by federal marshals or troops.

The successful challenge to segregated education led to similar challenges in other areas. A young Baptist preacher, the Reverend Martin Luther King, Jr., soon emerged as the best-known leader of the growing **Civil Rights Movement** with his calls for nonviolent protest.

The Kennedy Years, 1961–1963. In 1960, King was arrested and jailed after a civil rights demonstration. John F. Kennedy, the Democratic candidate for President that year, helped King win release from jail. Kennedy's action gained him the support of African American voters, and he won a narrow victory.

Kennedy was sympathetic to African Americans. However, he hesitated to propose new civil rights laws because, like earlier Presidents, he wanted the support of white Southern politicians for other programs.

Meanwhile, King and other civil rights leaders organized protests that often met with violent resistance from whites. At times, the violence grew so great that Kennedy was forced to send federal troops and officials to help protect the rights of African Americans.

In June 1963, Kennedy made a televised speech strongly supporting many civil rights goals, and he sent proposals for several new laws to Congress. But Kennedy did not have the chance to see his proposals through Congress. He was assassinated in Dallas, Texas, in November 1963.

The Johnson Years, 1963–1969. Kennedy's Vice-President, Lyndon B. Johnson, a Texan who had spent many years in Congress, became the new President. As the nation mourned Kennedy, Johnson promised that he would work to have the civil rights bill passed as a memorial to the fallen leader. By applying enormous pressure in the Senate, he succeeded, and the Civil Rights Act of 1964

President Lyndon B. Johnson gives Dr. Martin Luther King, Jr., a ceremonial pen after signing the 1964 Civil Rights Act.

became law. The main provisions of the law dealt with outlawing segregation in public places. "Jim Crow" was dead.

In 1964, Johnson won reelection by a landslide, and the Democrats won large majorities in Congress. Johnson was in a strong position for enacting new legislation. In 1965, he proposed a civil rights bill guaranteeing that African Americans' right to vote would be enforced by the federal government. Johnson called his legislative program the **Great Society.** It included many laws to help poor or disadvantaged people in various ways. Many who benefited were African Americans.

While Johnson was trying to build his Great Society, he also continued the Cold War against communism. He sent large numbers of U.S. troops to Vietnam in Southeast Asia. In 1954, Vietnam was split by an international agreement. North Vietnam had a Communist government, while the U.S.-backed South Vietnam claimed to have a democratic one.

Soon after the division, North Vietnamese–backed guerrillas, seeking to reunite the country, began fighting against the government in the south. The South Vietnamese government kept telling U.S. Presidents that with a little more help, it could defeat the guerrillas. But the guerrillas apparently could not be defeated. By 1968, some 540,000 U.S. combat troops were in South Vietnam.

As the war dragged on, it became very unpopular in the United States. Antiwar demonstrations were held in many cities and on college campuses. Antiwar candidates challenged Johnson in the 1968 election. In early 1968, Johnson announced that he would not seek reelection.

During these same years, the Civil Rights Movement changed direction. The Civil Rights Act of 1964 and the Voting Rights Act of 1965 had ended legal segregation of African Americans. Yet many

▶▶ GREAT SOCIETY LEGISLATION, 1965

Elementary and Secondary School Act
  programs to improve schools and libraries

Medicare
  provides medical care for those over 65

Voting Rights Act of 1965
  ensures the right to register to vote

Omnibus Housing Act
  rent supplements and other housing funds
  for low-income persons

Economic Opportunity Act of 1964
  programs to help the poor, leading to Job
  Corps training and Head Start preschools

Department of Housing and Urban Development (HUD)
  aid to cities through urban planning and
  housing

Higher Education Act
  federal scholarships to college students

How might each of these pieces of legislation helped African Americans?

problems remained, often related to poor conditions in the cities where most African Americans now lived. Rioting broke out in many of these cities during the mid-1960s as African American rage exploded.

Violence seemed to overwhelm American society in the late 1960s. War raged abroad. Antiwar demonstrations often turned violent. Riots ripped major cities. Assassins killed Martin Luther King and Robert Kennedy, the brother of the slain President. Kennedy had been running for President as an antiwar and civil rights candidate at the time of his death.

People were dismayed and disheartened by these events. Not surprisingly, in the November 1968 election, many of them wanted a change in leadership. Voters elected the Republican candidate, Richard M. Nixon.

The First Nixon Term, 1969–1973.
Nixon had aimed his campaign at what he called the Silent Majority, people upset and angered by the turmoil of the 1960s. Although he did not try to change the civil rights laws of Johnson's administration, he was less enthusiastic about enforcing them. He also tried to cut back on some Great Society programs.

Nixon continued the Vietnam War, under a new policy of gradually replacing American troops with South Vietnamese. Antiwar protests continued. At Kent State University in Ohio, National Guard troops fired into a group of college students, killing four and wounding several others. Two African American students were killed by police at Jackson State University in Mississippi during another antiwar protest.

Early in 1973, representatives of the two Vietnams and the United States signed a cease-fire agreement, and the last U.S. forces pulled out. Two years later, the South Vietnamese government collapsed, and the North Vietnamese government took over. More than 58,000 U.S. citizens had died there, a high percentage of them African Americans.

Peace had come. But the changes that shook the United States in the 1960s would affect the nation and the lives of its African American citizens for years.

Taking Another Look

1. Where did the United States become involved in armed conflicts in its efforts to halt communism?

2. How did Nixon's approach to civil rights issues differ from Johnson's?

3. **Critical Thinking** How might the denial of civil rights to its African American citizens have affected the U.S. role as a world leader?

305

Dorie Miller receiving the Navy Cross

World War II and African Americans

(1941–1945)

THINKING ABOUT THE CHAPTER

How was this war different from World War I for African Americans?

When December 7, 1941, dawned over the U.S. naval base in Hawaii's Pearl Harbor, Dorie Miller was below decks of the battleship *West Virginia*. He was sorting laundry, part of his job as a mess attendant, a worker in the ship's kitchen. Suddenly, he heard bombs exploding above his head. He rushed up on deck, where he saw Japanese aircraft attacking the ship. Amid the noise and confusion of the attack, he spotted his captain lying wounded on the deck. Quickly, Miller dragged him to safety.

Then, although he'd never handled a machine gun before, Miller seized a gun and began firing at the planes zooming in for attack. He shot down four. Although the ship began to sink, he continued firing until an officer ordered him to leave the ship.

Five months later, Dorie Miller, the first hero of World War II, was awarded the Navy Cross for his bravery. However, Miller's job in the navy did not change. He was still only a mess attendant—just like most other African Americans in the navy at that time.

A million African Americans—men and women—took part in World War II. About 6,000 were officers. But African Americans fought a "Double-V" campaign—for victory over discrimination in the military and at home, and for victory over the enemy overseas.

1 IN THE ARMED FORCES
▼ What progress was made in desegregating the armed services?

In 1991, playwright Leslie Lee was talking about his new play, *Black Eagles*. "I want to rectify [make right] a wrong, and the wrong is that nobody knows about the Tuskegee airmen." In 1941, Tuskegee Institute had become a training base for African American fliers. The 99th Pursuit Squadron, which was attached to the 332nd Fighter Group, earned the name "Black Eagles" because of the success it had in escorting all-white bomber crews over Europe during the war.

By the end of the war, the Eagles had destroyed or damaged about 400 enemy aircraft yet never lost a bomber. In 1945, the 332nd Fighter Group was awarded a Distinguished Unit Citation. Together, the 99th Pursuit Squadron and the 332nd Fighter Group won 800 air medals and clusters. However, throughout their military service, like almost all other African Americans in the war, they were victims of segregation.

Protest by Black Leaders. At the beginning of World War II, fewer than 5,000 African Americans were in the armed forces. Not more than a dozen were officers. African Americans served in segregated units in the army and were barred from serving in the Army Air Corps and the marines. Of the 4,000 African Americans in the navy in 1940, most were mess attendants. This was the situation in a country that claimed to be opposed to the racism of the Nazis. Such discrimination was unacceptable to African Americans and many whites.

In September 1940, when the United States began to increase the size of its armed forces, three African American leaders visited President Roosevelt. Walter White of the NAACP, union leader A. Philip Randolph, and T. Arnold Hill of the National Urban League urged Roosevelt to end the segregationist policies of the military.

Many in the military opposed ending segregation, but eventually the services were forced to change their policies. In 1942, the navy and the Marine Corps began accepting African Americans to serve in many positions. The army's women's division, the Women's Army Corps (WAC), and the women's branch of the Navy, the WAVES, welcomed over 4,000 African American women during

Part of the 99th Fighter Squadron, these pilots were trained at Tuskegee. How did the armed forces policy in World War II about African Americans differ from World War I?

1941 U.S. enters World War II. Dorie Miller is hero of Pearl Harbor.

African Americans admitted to army Officer Candidate School.

1942 The Navy and the Marine Corps accept African Americans.

Army Air Corps trains African American pilots at Tuskegee.

African American women join WAC and WAVES.

1943 Detroit race riot

1945 World War II ends.

the war. As you have read, the Army Air Corps opened a post at Tuskegee to train African American pilots.

Continuing Segregation and Discrimination. Segregation was still the rule, however. African Americans and whites did not serve in the same units, nor did African American officers command white troops.

In addition, African American troops frequently faced discrimination and hostility in the small towns and cities around the military bases where they were stationed. One soldier recalled the time he and some other GIs entered a lunchroom in segregated Salina, Kansas:

> The owner said, "You boys know we don't serve colored here." . . . We . . . just stood there inside the door, staring at what we had come to see—the German prisoners of war who were having lunch at the counter. . . . The people of Salina would serve these enemy soldiers and turn away black American G.I.'s.

African American Officers. African Americans also wanted to be able to become officers. The military agreed because it needed officers to command the growing number of African Americans entering the armed forces. In summer 1941, African Americans began to enter army Officer Candidate School on an equal basis with whites. Two years later, the navy opened its officer ranks to African Americans.

During the war, one of the highest ranking African American officers was Colonel Benjamin O. Davis, Jr.

Benjamin O. Davis, Jr., was the son of the man who became the first African American general, in 1940. The younger Davis graduated from West Point in 1936, the first African American to do so in almost 50 years. He commanded the 99th Fighter Squadron, which fought in North Africa and Italy, and later he became commander of the 332nd Fighter Group. After the war, the younger Davis was made a major general, the first African American to hold such a high rank. In 1952, he was appointed commander of the 51st Fighter Interceptor Wing in Korea. He retired in 1970 with the rank of lieutenant general. In 1991, Davis wrote about the exploits of the Black Eagles in his autobiography.

African Americans Overseas. Of the 1 million African American men and women who were in the armed forces during World War II, half served overseas. They carried out essential, often dangerous, assignments on many fronts.

Twenty-two African American combat units—field artillery, antiaircraft artillery, tank battalions, and air combat units—took part in the invasion of Sicily, off the coast of Italy, in 1943, and the invasion of Normandy, in France, in 1944. In France, 1,500 African American truck drivers barreled down what was called the Red Ball Highway to supply General George S. Patton's Third Army. On Pacific islands, African Americans slashed through rain forests to build airplane landing strips as Allied forces pressed on to Japan.

African Americans in the navy were radiomen, gunner's mates, and supply officers on ships that escorted destroyers and tracked enemy submarines. They built naval bases in the Pacific. African American marines defended captured enemy outposts in the Pacific. On the supply ships of the merchant marine, African Americans and whites worked together as seamen, radio operators, and engineers.

The Battle of the Bulge. The officers commanding the army were slower to see how well integrated forces could work. Not until the closing days of the war did they move toward integrating combat troops. In late 1944, in the Ardennes Forest of Belgium and Luxembourg, the Germans launched a surprise counterattack. Short of soldiers to repel the attack, the army asked for volunteers. About 2,500 African Americans came forward. Fighting side by side, white and African American soldiers turned back a fierce Nazi attack, in what became known as the Battle of the Bulge. But once the Germans surrendered, the troops returned to their separate white and African American units.

Despite discrimination and segregation, African Americans in World War II had had more opportunity to serve their country than in any previous war. They had served well.

Taking Another Look

1. Why did the armed forces accept African Americans into Officer Candidate School?

2. What was the significance of the Battle of the Bulge for African Americans in the armed forces?

3. **Critical Thinking** How do you think African Americans who served in the war felt when they returned to a still-segregated nation?

2 ON THE HOME FRONT

▼ How did the war affect African Americans at home?

Sybil Lewis, a young African American, was trained to work in a defense plant and got a job riveting airplane parts. Lewis later told what happened on the job:

The women worked in pairs. I was the riveter, and this big strong white girl from a cotton farm in Arkansas worked as the bucker. . . . Bucking was harder than shooting rivets; it required more muscle. Riveting required more skill . . . . The boss came around one day and . . . assigned [the white woman] to do the riveting and me to do the bucking. . . . I was never given the riveting job back. That was the first encounter I had with discrimination in California, and it didn't sit too well with me.

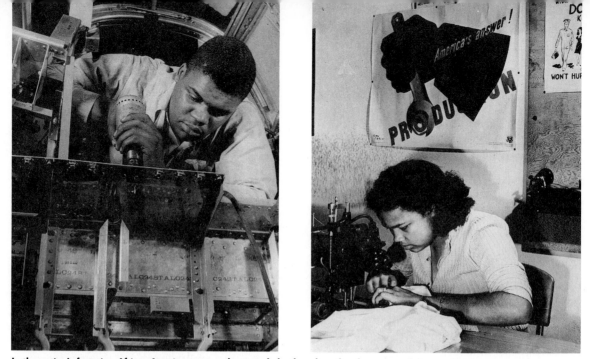

In the nation's factories, African American men and women helped produce the planes, parachutes, and other war equipment used by its armed forces.

World War II opened many jobs for African Americans in the nation's defense factories, but discrimination and segregation were still the rule.

Employment. Defense industries—aircraft, shipbuilding, iron and steel, and others—needed workers. As you read in Chapter 27, to make sure that African Americans would get their fair share of the new jobs, union leader A. Philip Randolph threatened to organize a massive march on Washington in May 1941. Only then did the government act. The following month, President Roosevelt set up the Fair Employment Practices Committee (FEPC) to end discrimination in defense industries.

With the FEPC to back them up, large numbers of African Americans got high-paying, skilled jobs in defense plants. They joined labor unions, too, even in the South.

Like Sybil Lewis, thousands of African American women worked alongside white women in the war plants. Women war workers, who were given the title "Rosie the Riveter," were praised for their patriotism. Most of the African American women workers earned higher wages than they ever had before.

Migration North. Defense work lured many African Americans to abandon Southern farms for the cities of the North, Midwest, and West. Once again, as in the early years of the 20th century, the cities swelled with thousands of newcomers (see page 259). They were not always received warmly. In a number of cities, friction between African Americans and whites erupted into riots.

The most serious riot took place in Detroit. Fifty thousand African Americans had come to work in the many defense plants of the city. One day in spring 1943, a fistfight between an African American man and a white man stirred up smoldering tensions. Within a few hours, a race riot blazed across the city. Whites roamed the streets beating African Americans and burning their cars. It took 30 hours and 34 deaths before 6,000 soldiers, called in by President Roosevelt, ended the riot.

Taking Another Look

1. How did World War II improve employment opportunities for African Americans?

2. Why did many African Americans leave the South during the war?

3. **Critical Thinking** What do you think were the causes behind race riots like the one in Detroit?

LOOKING AHEAD

World War II ended on September 2, 1945. Whether in the armed forces or at home, the lives of African Americans had been changed by the war. Many African Americans had worked at new jobs, gone to new places, and seen new things. For the first time, many had earned a decent living. After the war, some took advantage of the GI Bill, which gave them a chance for a college education. African Americans faced the future with more hope and greater expectations than ever.

WORLD WAR II HONOR ROLL

24th Infantry—Routed Japanese from New Georgia Islands

92nd Division—As part of the Fifth Army, pushed northward in Italy to the Arno River; lost over 3,000 men; won 65 Silver Stars, 65 Bronze Medals, 1,300 Purple Hearts

93rd Division—Fought in the Pacific: Treasury Islands, the Philippines, Dutch East Indies, and Bougainville

99th Pursuit Squadron—Downed eight Nazi planes in one of the fiercest fights of the Italian campaign

450th Anti-Aircraft Artillery Battalion—First African American unit in invasions of Africa and in Europe; cited by General Mark Clark for "outstanding performance of duty."

614th Tank Destroyer Battalion—Fought several important actions; one of its officers, Captain Charles L. Thomas, received Distinguished Service Cross for heroism in action

761st Tank Battalion—Won 391 awards for 183 days of combat; knocked out 331 machine-gun nests and captured a German radio station

969th Field Artillery—Won a Distinguished Unit Citation for "outstanding courage and resourcefulness and undaunted determination"

World War II soldiers

It was during World War II that the United States discovered a new type of soldier—women—and formed women's military branches. In World War I, women had been limited to working in the Red Cross as ambulance drivers and nurses. During World War II, women joined the military, where they served as clerks, typists, drivers, and nurses—but not fighters. Although this was a step forward for women, their units were not on an equal footing with the regular military.

In the service, African American women faced double discrimination—against skin color as well as gender. African American women were housed, fed, and trained in separate facilities from white women. At first, there were no African American women officers. Mary McLeod Bethune changed that. Bethune ensured that African American women were a part of the first women's Officers Training School. By 1946, there were 115 African American officers in the WACs. Among the outstanding African American officers were Major Charity B. Adams and Captain Abbie N. Campbell.

Today, women are integrated into all branches of the military. In 1991, Congress authorized women to fly combat missions.

The Who, What, Where of History

1. **Who** was Dorie Miller?
2. **Where** is Pearl Harbor?
3. **Who** is Leslie Lee?
4. **Who** were the Black Eagles?
5. **Who** is Benjamin O. Davis, Jr.?
6. **What** was the WAC?
7. **What** was the FEPC?

Making the Connection

1. What was the connection between World War II and the migration of African Americans to cities of the North and Midwest?
2. What was the connection between the Fair Employment Practices Committee and increased employment of African Americans in high-paying, skilled jobs?

Time Check

1. When did the bombing of Pearl Harbor occur?
2. In what year did the U.S. armed services' policies regarding segregation begin to change?
3. In what year did World War II end?

What Would You Have Done?

1. Reread the incident about the segregated lunchroom in Salina, Kansas, on page 308. If you had been one of the African American soldiers who was refused service, how would you have responded to the lunchroom owner's statement?

2. If you had been an African American woman during World War II, would you have chosen to join the military, or would you have taken a job in the defense industry? Explain.

Thinking and Writing About History

Imagine that you are one of the African American truck drivers who helped supply the Third Army during the Battle of the Bulge. Write a letter home explaining what you think about the work you are doing and how you think it might affect your life after the war.

Building Skills: Comparing Points of View

Friday night, Frank missed a party because he had to go to a family birthday celebration. The next morning, Frank asked his friend Sam about the party, and Sam said it was the worst party he had ever been to. Later Frank's friend Alexis told him that he'd missed a fantastic party.

Who was telling the truth? Both Sam and Alexis were, but they were giving their opinions, or points of view.

People writing about the same historical event can also have different points of view. A point of view represents someone's opinion or judgment. For the opinion to be valid, it should be supported by facts. It is important to figure out writers' points of view as you read, so that you can decide whether the evidence supports their views. Then you can logically agree or disagree with their judgments.

The two quotations below were both written by well-known, well-respected writers. Read the quotations and answer the questions that follow.

No one had expected it, . . . but the war had been the watershed of the postemancipation struggle for equality. These were the years when American Negroes began for the first time to fight for their rights effectively and independently. Their relationship to white America had undergone a fundamental change. Here was where the modern civil rights movement began; here was where it scored its first important victories.

—Geoffrey Perrett, *Days of Sadness, Years of Triumph*

The treatment accorded the Negro during the Second World War marks, for me, a turning point in the Negro's relation to America. To put it briefly, and somewhat too simply, a certain hope died, a certain respect for white Americans faded.

—James Baldwin, quoted in J. Milton Yinger, *A Minority Group in American Society*

1. Both writers believe that World War II marked a major change in the history of African Americans. Write the key words from each quotation that describe the change.

2. a. Would you say that Baldwin's view of the results of the war years is positive or negative?
 b. Do you think Perrett is positive or negative in his description?

3. Summarize in your own words the views of both writers.

4. With which point of view do you agree? Explain why.

5. Explain how both Perrett and Baldwin could be correct.

Mechanical cotton pickers

Gains and Losses in the Postwar Years

(1945–1960s)

THINKING ABOUT THE CHAPTER

What important changes took place in African Americans' lives in the decades after World War II?

On October 2, 1944, a crowd of people gathered at a cotton plantation in Mississippi. At the edge of a 42-acre (17-hectare) cotton field stood eight new bright red machines. At a signal, the operators of the machines began to drive along the rows of cotton, stripping the plants of their fuzzy white bolls. By the end of the day, not a single open boll of cotton was left in the field.

That day, the mechanical cotton picker foreshadowed the end of the centuries-old practice of picking cotton by hand. The bale of cotton that each machine picked cost the plantation owner a little over five dollars to harvest. If it had been picked by sharecroppers, it would have cost almost eight times more.

By 1960, mechanical cotton pickers had replaced almost all the sharecroppers who labored in the cotton fields. Just as the cotton gin had led to a massive increase in slavery in the 1800s, the mechanical cotton picker led to a massive migration of African Americans out of the South from the 1940s to the 1960s. This migration to the cities of the Northeast and the Midwest transformed the African American way of life.

1 A NEW WAVE OF MIGRATION

▼ Why did millions of African Americans leave the South in the years after World War II?

On a gray day in November 1951, a long-distance bus from Memphis, Tennessee, pulled into the Chicago bus terminal. Down the bus steps trudged 35 tired African Americans—men, women, and children—with battered suitcases, parcels of pots and pans, and children's toys. Relatives rushed up to greet some of the newcomers and take them home to their apartments. The others, bewildered by the noise and bustle, found their own way out of the bus terminal and to the African American neighborhoods.

To the Cities. In the ten years between 1950 and 1960, almost two million African Americans moved from the South to the nation's 12 largest non-Southern cities. With work on the cotton plantations shrinking every year and the discrimination and segregation of the South becoming more unbearable, migration North seemed the only answer.

Because the years after the war were times of general prosperity for the nation, jobs were not hard to find. However, most of the migrants had few skills that could be used in the industrial economy of the North. In addition, discrimination by whites often confined African Americans to low-paying "Negro work"—unskilled jobs, such as janitor or maid. Compared with those who remained in the South, though, their incomes were high.

Housing. Housing was expensive and in short supply. In segregated neighborhoods, African Americans had to live in older buildings. Low incomes for African Americans often meant more tenants had to share an apartment to meet the rent. Overcrowded buildings became run-down more quickly, and white owners often neglected repairs on buildings in

Many African American migrants from the south moved into housing projects like Chicago's Robert Taylor Homes. Built in the late 1950s and early 1960s, it is the largest housing project in the world.

1944	Development of mechanical cotton picker
1950–1960	2 million African Americans move to cities in Northeast and Midwest.
1950s	Bebop, cool jazz, free-form jazz, rock 'n' roll develop.
1953	Race riot in Chicago public housing
1954	Three African Americans elected to House of Representatives.
1952	Ralph Ellison publishes *Invisible Man*.
1959	*A Raisin in the Sun* opens on Broadway.

African American neighborhoods. When public housing projects began to be built in the 1950s, they seemed to offer a way out for African Americans.

However, bitter disputes broke out when African Americans tried to move into the new buildings. In 1953, violence erupted when several African American families moved into a Chicago housing project occupied by whites. For four years, police were assigned to maintain order there.

Eventually, whites moved away from many of the public housing projects in the cities, and African Americans became the large majority of tenants. Although this eased the housing shortage for them, before long the cities neglected the buildings. They became rundown and crime-ridden. African Americans in the cities thus became segregated in fact, rather than by laws as in the South. This **de facto segregation** applied not only to housing, but to schools as well.

Education. Schools in the African American neighborhoods had difficulty accommodating the rapid increase in students. After the 1954 *Brown* decision ending legally segregated schools (see page 323), more African American students shared classrooms with white students. However, city school budgets did not increase enough to solve the new problems of large classes, overcrowded school buildings, and low teachers' salaries. As neighborhoods became segregated, so did schools.

Political Power. The concentration of large numbers of African Americans in the big cities gave them greater political power. In 1954, for example, for the first time in this century, three African Americans—William Dawson of Chicago, the Rev. Adam Clayton Powell of New York City, and Charles C. Diggs of Detroit—were elected to seats in the House of Representatives.

In local politics, too, African Americans began to have political power. White politicians sought African Americans' votes in return for promises—not always kept—to improve African American neighborhoods. At the same time, the growing numbers of African Americans who were elected to city posts tried to make the local governments more responsive to the needs of the African American community, such as better schools.

Taking Another Look

1. What was the main reason for the migration of millions of African Americans from the South to the North in the 1940s through the 1960s?

2. How did the growing political power of African Americans in the cities show itself?

3. **Critical Thinking** Refer to Chapter 24 and compare the African American migration from 1915 to 1930 with that from the 1940s through the 1960s.

2 THE ARTS

▼ How did African Americans contribute to the nation's cultural life in the years after World War II?

Charlie Parker, a Kansas City high school student, knew that Count Basie, whose band was playing at a local nightclub, allowed amateurs to play with the band after hours. One evening, the intense, self-confident Parker, who was just 15, walked into the club with his saxophone, stepped up to the bandstand, and began playing. Before long, the players were jeering at Parker's poor performance, and one of them sounded the gong to get him off the stage. But Parker continued to play. Nothing stopped him until a cymbal crashed next to his ears. Reluctantly, Parker left the bandstand, more determined than ever to become the greatest saxophone player in the world.

For the next few years, Parker spent 11 hours a day practicing saxophone exercises from music books and playing along with jazz records. Eventually, Charlie "Bird" Parker became ranked with Louis Armstrong as one of the jazz greats.

When Parker came to fame in the mid-1940s, white Americans were gradually coming to appreciate African Americans in all the arts, not only music. However, segregation of African Americans and discrimination against them continued and as a result, social contacts between African Americans and whites were limited.

Writers. In 1940, the African American author Richard Wright wrote a novel called *Native Son,* about a 19-year-old African American in Chicago who kills a white woman. In it, Wright condemns the pressures of white society that lead the young man to commit the crime. The book quickly became a bestseller, the first by an African American writer. *Native Son* was important because it departed from earlier books by African Americans, which tended to avoid dealing with tensions between African Americans and whites. It was also important because it was so outspoken in its attack on the world in which African Americans were forced to live.

Wright led the way for books of protest by other writers. In 1952, Ralph Ellison wrote a novel, *Invisible Man,* that shows how African Americans are "invisible" to whites, who do not accept them as part of U.S. society. In his essays, poetry, and novels, James Baldwin also expressed the anger felt by African Americans. Imamu Amiri Baraka (LeRoi Jones) wrote works, including his play *Dutchman,* that deal with confrontations between African Americans and whites.

Saxophonist Charlie "Bird" Parker, with Dizzy Gillespie, introduced bebop.

Lorraine Hansberry won the Drama Critics Circle Award for Best American Play for the 1958–1959 Broadway season for *A Raisin in the Sun*. Sidney Poitier, right, starred in the movie version.

Women writers also explored the conditions African Americans faced in their daily lives. The poet Gwendolyn Brooks celebrated the life of African Americans in the ghetto. When Lorraine Hansberry's play *A Raisin in the Sun* opened on Broadway in 1959, audiences, mostly white, were astonished and delighted at the humor and warmth of the urban family in the play.

The works of the writers mentioned were huge successes with white readers and theatergoers as well as with African Americans. Rather than resenting the attacks of even the bitterest of the works, thoughtful whites welcomed them as unique contributions that enriched U.S. literature.

Music. "I'm playing the same notes, but it comes out different. You can't teach the soul. You got to bring out your *soul* on those valves." This was how African American trumpeter Dizzy Gillespie spoke about the new kind of jazz music he was playing. In the 1940s, Gillespie, Charlie Parker, and pianist Thelonious Monk developed what came to be called bebop, a form of jazz that soon rivaled the more rhythmic and more hard-driving traditional jazz.

In other developments, trumpeter Miles Davis later popularized a variation of bebop called cool jazz. Saxophonist Ornette Coleman moved modern jazz closer to contemporary classical music in what was called free-form jazz.

Gospel music made its way from the African American church to the popular stage. In her rich contralto voice, Mahalia Jackson sang gospel music throughout the United States and the world to enthusiastic African American and white audiences.

The 1950s saw the birth of rock 'n' roll. Small African American record companies first produced the strong, rhythmic music of African American performers such as Chuck Berry, Ruth Brown, Little Richard, and Fats Domino. Soon rock 'n' roll swept the country. In 1952, some 18,000 people attended the first rock 'n' roll concert, held in an auditorium in Cleveland, Ohio, that seated 10,000. All the performers were African American, but half the audience was white. Within a short time, rock became the most popular musical form among teenagers and spread to all corners of the world.

In its many forms, the music of African Americans in the 1940s, 1950s, and 1960s had an enormous impact. In earlier times, this music had been set apart as "race music" and sold mostly to African Americans. Now all Americans were beginning to appreciate and buy the music of African American musicians.

Artists. Although there were many African American visual artists in the 1950s and 1960s, few made the impact on U.S. culture that writers and musicians did. The best-known of the group was Jacob Lawrence. He represented the first generation of artists who were born in the African American community, had African American teachers, and devoted themselves to portraying the African American experience. Lawrence painted scenes of African American history and city life. Most noted are his 40 panels on the life of Frederick Douglass, a similar work on Harriet Tubman, and a longer series on the migrations of the African American people (see "The Artist's View").

Actors. For many years, African Americans were seen in movies mostly as servants or as objects of ridicule. That

Mahalia Jackson helped bring African American gospel music to the general public.

began to change in the 1950s and 1960s. Sidney Poitier won an Oscar as best actor of 1963 in a dramatic role. Harry Belafonte also had serious roles in pictures. In general, more films with African Americans as central characters were shown on the nation's screens.

Television programs also began to include African Americans as major figures. Bill Cosby became a nationwide favorite in his "I Spy" series, for which he won an Emmy in 1966.

Taking Another Look

1. Why was Richard Wright's *Native Son* an important book?

2. What new forms of jazz were introduced in the postwar years?

3. **Critical Thinking** Why do you think white audiences appreciated the work of African American writers, musicians, and artists?

LOOKING AHEAD

Despite rundown, overcrowded housing and segregated neighborhoods, the migration to the Northeast and Midwest benefited many African Americans. From the 1940s through the 1960s, jobs were plentiful. Although discrimination imposed limits on both wages and the types of job available to African Americans, even unskilled workers had more opportunities than they had had in the South. In the arts, especially in writing and music, the period was as rich in achievement as the Harlem Renaissance (see page 276).

While these economic and artistic developments were taking place, the fires of a new protest movement were being fanned as African Americans, joined by whites, sought to secure full civil rights for all Americans.

In a world of despair, we wanted to give hope. In a world of negative Black images, we wanted to provide positive Black images. In a world that said Blacks could do few things, we wanted to say they could do everything.

This is how African American publisher John H. Johnson described his reasons for founding *Ebony* in 1945. When *Ebony* first hit the newsstands on November 1, 1945, segregation and discrimination were facts of life for African Americans. Johnson struck back by publishing a glossy national magazine celebrating African American triumphs.

When it first came off the presses, *Ebony*'s total circulation was 25,000 copies. Since then, its readership has grown to more than 9.5 million. It is the world's best-selling African American publication.

Johnson's success did not stop with *Ebony*. In 1950, he published *Tan Confessions* which eventually became *Black Stars*, and he introduced *Jet*, a news weekly, in 1951. By 1962, Johnson Publishing Company was producing books. To acknowledge Johnson's achievements, the Chicago Junior Chamber of Commerce named him one of its men of the year—the first African American so honored.

The Who, What, Where of History

1. **What** was responsible for the end of the Southern sharecropping system?
2. **Who** was Adam Clayton Powell?
3. **Who** was Charlie Parker?
4. **Who** was Richard Wright?
5. **What** is *Invisible Man*?
6. **Who** was Lorraine Hansberry?
7. **What** is bebop?
8. **Where** was the first rock 'n' roll concert held?
9. **Who** was Jacob Lawrence?

Making the Connection

1. What was the connection between the mechanical cotton picker and the migration of African Americans to the North from the 1940s through the 1960s?
2. What was the connection between the migration of African Americans to the North and the election of increased numbers of African Americans to Congress?
3. What was the connection between *Native Son* and the writing of *Invisible Man* and of *Dutchman*?

Time Check

1. In what year was the mechanical cotton picker first used?
2. During which decade did 2 million African Americans move to cities in the North and Midwest?

What Would You Have Done?

If you had been an African American living in the South, would you have chosen to move to the North during the 1950s? Explain.

Thinking and Writing About History

Imagine that you are an 85-year-old African American living in a Northern city in 1968. Write a letter to a young relative explaining the differences you see between the lives and work of African Americans in 1968 and in the days when you were young.

Building Skills: Analyzing Fiction

A well-written fictional description of a time period can give the details and the feeling of being there that most historical works do not. Of course, when you are reading a work of fiction, you must remember that it *is* fiction. You may come away with the flavor and atmosphere of a time period, but you must remember that a writer of fiction doesn't have to list his or her sources as a historian does. Don't take everything in a piece of historical fiction as fact. Also, be very alert to the author's point of view.

Following is a brief excerpt from "Flying Home" by Ralph Ellison. Todd, an African American pilot in training during World War II, has been injured in a crash on a Southern farm. Read it, and on a separate sheet of paper, answer the questions that follow the reading.

"We kin ride him into town on old Ned," the boy said.

Ned? He turned, seeing the boy point toward an ox team browsing where the buried blade of a plow marked the end of a furrow. Thoughts of himself riding an ox through the town, past streets full of white faces, down the concrete runways of the airfield made swift images of humiliation in his mind. With a pang he remembered his girl's last letter. "Todd," she had written, ". . . And I have always known you to be as brave as anyone else. The papers annoy me. Don't you be contented to prove over and over again that you're brave or skillful just because you're black, Todd. . . . [T]hey don't want to say why you boys are not yet fighting. . . . Anyone with brains can learn to fly, but then what? What about using it, and who will you use it for? . . . I sometimes think they're playing a trick on us. It's very humiliating. . . ." He wiped cold sweat from his face, thinking, What does she know of humiliation? She's never been down South. Now the humiliation would come. When you must have them judge you, knowing that they never accept your mistakes as your own, but hold it against your whole race—that was humiliation.

1. What do you learn about African American pilots at the beginning of World War II?

2. What is the pilot's greatest fear?

3. What does the pilot indicate about the different attitudes toward African Americans in the North and South during World War II?

Jackie Robinson scoring a run

The Battle for Civil Rights

(1954–1963)

THINKING ABOUT THE CHAPTER

What tactics did civil rights workers use to win equality for African Americans?

On April 18, 1946, people packed the stands of the Jersey City, New Jersey, ballpark. They had come to see the first game played by the New York Giants since the end of World War II. In the exhibition game, the Giants faced the Montreal Royals—the top farm team for the Brooklyn Dodgers.

The excited crowd was waiting for Jackie Robinson to take his first turn at bat. Just six months before, Dodgers president Branch Rickey had made headlines by signing Robinson with the Royals. Now an African American was about to shatter the color barrier in baseball. Never before had an African American played outside the Negro National League.

His first time up, Robinson grounded out. The second time, he sent the baseball over the left-field fence.

Thus started a career that brought Robinson into major league baseball with the Dodgers in 1947 and into baseball's Hall of Fame in 1962. Robinson opened the way for other African American baseball greats—Roy Campanella, Willie Mays, and Hank Aaron, to name a few. Still, Robinson knew that winning equality for African Americans took more than hitting home runs. Like other African Americans, he soon became caught up in the Civil Rights Movement—the movement to extend the Constitution's promise of equality to all citizens.

1 ▼ EXPELLING JIM CROW FROM SCHOOL

▼ Why was the decision in *Brown* v. *Board of Education* a turning point in U.S. history?

About the same time that Jackie Robinson played his first game for the Dodgers, the University of Oklahoma admitted George McLaurin to its all-white law school. In 1938, the Supreme Court had ruled that states had to provide separate-but-equal graduate facilities for African Americans. Because Oklahoma did not have a separate law school for African Americans, the all-white law school had to admit McLaurin.

In 1948, the university accepted McLaurin on "a segregated basis." McLaurin studied at a segregated desk in the library. He sat in a roped-off area of classrooms or attended class alone. He ate in a separate part of the school cafeteria. Was he being offered an equal education with white students? Lawyers for the NAACP thought not.

Challenging Segregation Policies. The NAACP had set up the Legal Defense and Education Fund to tackle cases

1946 Jackie Robinson breaks the color barrier in baseball.

1954 *Brown* v. *Board of Education*

1955–1956 Montgomery bus boycott

1957 Federal troops sent to integrate schools in Little Rock, Arkansas.

Southern Christian Leadership Conference (SCLC) is founded.

1960 Students lead sit-ins in Greensboro, North Carolina.

Student Nonviolent Coordinating Committee (SNCC) is founded.

1961 Freedom rides

1962 James Meredith forces integration at University of Mississippi.

1963 Martin Luther King leads protests in Birmingham, Alabama.

March on Washington, D.C.

just like this. Thurgood Marshall, director of the fund, decided to take *McLaurin* v. *Oklahoma State Regents* all the way to the Supreme Court.

No one doubted that **Thurgood Marshall** had courage. He had a reputation as the African American "lawyer who stood up in white men's courts." Born in 1908 in Baltimore, Maryland, Marshall earned his law degree from Howard University. He then practiced under Charles

323

Hamilton Houston, a brilliant Harvard law graduate and legal director for the NAACP who inspired Marshall to use the courts to fight segregation. From the 1930s on, Marshall used the law to battle segregation and racism. In 1967, he became the first African American appointed to the Supreme Court. He served there until his retirement in 1991.

On June 5, 1950, Marshall faced the Court. He argued that the university had pinned "a badge of inferiority" on McLaurin by setting him apart from his fellow students. The Court agreed with Marshall and ordered an end to segregation at the law school. But the McLaurin decision affected only those schools that admitted African Americans in the first place. Many all-white schools denied African Ameri-

cans entry because supposed "separate but equal" facilities existed.

That same year, Marshall won another important victory in the case of *Sweatt* v. *Painter*. In it, he argued successfully that a separate law school established by the state of Texas for African Americans was anything but equal to the whites-only University of Texas Law School.

A Landmark Victory. The cases that the NAACP had won so far all involved colleges and universities. The Supreme Court's 1896 decision in *Plessy* v. *Ferguson* remained firmly in place in regard to public elementary and high schools. With the victory in *Sweatt* v. *Painter,* Marshall now felt he had the grounds on which to overturn *Plessy*.

Many African American lawyers, out of fear of the consequences, held back their

Which Supreme Court ruling do you think has had the greatest effect on African Americans?

▶▶ SELECTED SUPREME COURT DECISIONS AND AFRICAN AMERICANS

Case (year)	Decision Summary	Case (year)	Decision Summary
Dred Scott v. *Sandford* (1857)	African Americans are not U.S. citizens; Congress has no power to forbid slavery in U.S. territories.	*Swan* v. *Charlotte-Mecklenburg* (1971)	Busing can be used to integrate urban schools.
Plessy v. *Ferguson* (1896)	Segregation can be legal as long as the separate facilities are equal.	*Bakke* v. *University of California* (1978)	Race may be used as one factor—but not the only factor—in making affirmative action decisions.
Nixon v. *Herndon* (1927)	States cannot prohibit African Americans' voting in primary elections.	*Batson* v. *Kentucky* (1986)	Prosecutors in criminal cases cannot exclude jurors on the basis of race.
Brown v. *Board of Education* (1954)	Racial segregation in public schools is unconstitutional.	*Edmonson* v. *Leesville Concrete Co.* (1991)	Prosecutors and defendants in civil cases cannot exclude jurors on the basis of race.
Heart of Atlanta Motel v. *U.S.* (1964)	A motel may not refuse to rent rooms to African Americans.		

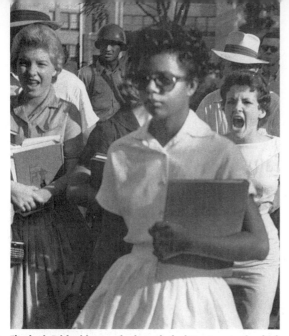

Elizabeth Eckford braves the hatred of whites to enter her high school in Little Rock, Arkansas, in 1957.

support. The risks were high. What if they lost? Segregation might then be more solidly in place than ever.

In the end, Marshall won enough support to continue the campaign against segregated schools. He convinced the NAACP to back parents suing to integrate school systems in four states and the District of Columbia. The Supreme Court lumped the cases together under *Brown* v. *Board of Education of Topeka, Kansas*. The decision in *Brown* would apply to all cases and to the nation as a whole.

Marshall's argument rested upon the psychological effects of segregation. He produced expert testimony demonstrating that segregation lowered the self-esteem of African American children. Thus, segregation violated the equal protection clause of the 14th Amendment.

In a unanimous 1954 decision, the Court declared segregation unconstitutional. Chief Justice Earl Warren read the majority opinion, which said in part:

To separate [those children] from others of similar age and qualifica-

tions solely because of their race generates a feeling of inferiority as to their status in the community that may affect their hearts and minds in a way unlikely ever to be undone. . . . Separate educational facilities are inherently unequal. . . . Any language in *Plessy* v. *Ferguson* contrary to these findings is rejected.

Resisting Desegregation. The Court ordered school districts to desegregate "with all deliberate speed." Many did. But resistance developed in the Deep South. A key test came in Little Rock, Arkansas, in 1957. There, Governor Orval Faubus called in the state's National Guard to prevent nine African American students from entering the city's public high school. When 15-year-old Elizabeth Eckford tried to walk into the school, soldiers with bayonets on their rifles turned her back. An angry mob of whites jeered "Lynch her!" She managed to escape with the help of a white bystander.

The crisis at Little Rock forced President Eisenhower to act. He took command of the Arkansas National Guard and sent the 101st Airborne Division to enforce the *Brown* decision.

The following year Faubus shut down Little Rock's high schools. The state set up "private" academies and blocked African Americans from entering them.

Desegregation did come—slowly. In 1957, Congress passed a new Civil Rights Act, increasing the power of the Attorney General to protect African Americans' rights. The Supreme Court also heard a new round of desegregation cases in the 1950s and 1960s. But it became clear that more than court decisions would end segregation. A new plan of action soon emerged in Montgomery, Alabama, the first capital of the Confederacy.

How did Rosa Parks make U.S. history in Montgomery, Alabama, in 1955?

Taking Another Look

1. What court decisions paved the way for the decision in *Brown*?

2. What arguments did Thurgood Marshall use to win the *Brown* case?

3. **Critical Thinking** Why do you think the NAACP made ending segregation in education a top priority?

2 RESISTING WITHOUT ▼ BITTERNESS

▼ What tactics did Martin Luther King, Jr., use to oppose segregation?

On December 1, 1955, Rosa Parks boarded a bus in Montgomery, Alabama. The 42-year-old African American seamstress took a seat in the first row of the "colored" section of the bus. An active church member and secretary of the local chapter of the NAACP, the soft-spoken Parks had no intention of violating the law that day. But by the time she left the bus, she had started a movement that would shake the nation.

As the white section of the bus filled up, the bus driver ordered Parks and three other people to stand. Parks stayed put. "Well, if you don't stand up," said the bus driver, "I'm going to call the police and have you arrested." "You may do that," answered Parks. The police arrested Parks and booked her for violating Montgomery's Jim Crow laws. News of Parks's arrest quickly spread through the African American community.

Taking to the Streets. E. D. Nixon, who had been a leader in the local chapter of the NAACP for years, posted bail for Parks. Nixon and Jo Ann Robinson, president of an African American organization, the Women's Political Council, came up with a plan to boycott segregated buses in Montgomery. Nixon marshaled the support of African American churches in the community, including the Dexter Avenue Baptist Church. Its pastor was 26-year-old Dr. Martin Luther King, Jr. King was elected head of the Montgomery Improvement Association, the organizing force behind the boycott.

African American volunteers mimeographed thousands of leaflets urging people to join the boycott. "Don't ride the bus to work, to town, to school, or any place on Monday," declared the leaflets.

African Americans made up nearly 75 percent of the city's bus riders. Most could not afford cars, but that Monday they stayed off the Montgomery buses.

The day of protest proved so successful that the boycott was extended to the next day and the next and the next. African Americans willingly endured the hardship of walking nearly every place they went. One older African American woman turned down the offer of a ride saying, "I'm not walking for myself, I'm walking for my children and my grandchildren."

The boycott lasted 381 days, nearly crippling Montgomery bus companies. In late 1956, the Supreme Court found that segregation on Alabama buses was unconstitutional. On December 21, King and other African Americans climbed aboard integrated Montgomery buses for the first time.

King's Beliefs. The success of the Montgomery bus boycott strengthened Martin Luther King, Jr.'s belief that nonviolent protest was the most effective tool for gaining civil rights. King had studied the ideas of India's Mohandas Gandhi, who earlier in the century had waged a struggle to free India from British rule. Gandhi had preached **nonviolence,** the peaceful refusal to obey unjust laws. King's study of history had convinced him that it would be suicidal to protest segregation with violence. He decided to draw upon the tactics that had helped Gandhi in India. He also drew upon a tradition of protest within his own family.

Martin Luther King, Jr., was born in Atlanta, Georgia, in 1929. He grew up in a devout Baptist family. Both his grandfather and father were ministers. King's grandfather led a protest to force Atlanta to build its first high school for African Americans. King's father continued speaking out for African American rights as pastor of Ebenezer Baptist Church. By age five, King could recite Bible passages from memory. By age 15, he had entered Morehouse College. By age 26, he had earned a Ph.D. in theology from Boston College. He soon moved to Alabama with his wife, concert singer Coretta Scott.

King quickly became the most visible and eloquent spokesperson of the Civil Rights Movement. In 1957, he joined with nearly 100 other church leaders in founding the Southern Christian Leadership Conference (SCLC). The SCLC reflected King's philosophy for change: "To resist without bitterness; to be cursed and not reply; to be beaten and not hit back."

In 1960, King moved the SCLC headquarters to Atlanta. There he served as SCLC president and as a part-time pastor in his father's church.

That same year, another civil rights group, the Student Nonviolent Coordinating Committee (SNCC), was formed. It was based in part on King's ideas of nonviolence. The young people who made up this organization had been teenagers when the Supreme Court handed down the *Brown* decision. Now, as college students, they stood ready to reshape the Civil Rights Movement.

Taking Another Look

1. What were the events leading up to the Montgomery bus boycott?

2. What was King's philosophy of protest and social change?

3. **Critical Thinking** How do you think King would have defined *courage?*

327

These civil rights demonstrators are determined to desegregate a lunch counter in Jackson, Mississippi.

3 A NEW GENERATION

▼ How did African American youth step up resistance to segregation?

On January 31, 1960, Ezell Blair, Jr., went to see his parents. Ezell, a freshman at North Carolina's Agricultural and Technical College in Greensboro, asked his parents a strange question. Would they be upset if he stirred up trouble in town. "Why?" they replied. "Because," explained Ezell, "tomorrow we're going to do something that will shake up this town."

Sit-Ins. On February 1, four students from the college walked into Woolworth's variety store in Greensboro. They bought a few items, then sat down at a "whites only" lunch counter. When a waitress asked what they were doing, one of them replied, "We believe since we buy books and papers in the other part of the store we should get served in this part."

The store manager refused them service. The four, including Blair, continued to sit. They were not served that day. But 20 students returned to sit at the counter the next day. More arrived the next day as news spread of the **sit-in,** as this form of protest came to be called.

Television cameras and radio and newspaper reporters poured into Greensboro. Within months, thousands of students—African Americans and a few whites—were staging sit-ins across the state. Whites beat them, jeered at them, and dumped food on them. The protesters refused to strike back.

Martin Luther King, Ralph Abernathy, and other leaders of the SCLC gave students their support. King called being arrested for taking part in sit-ins "a badge of honor." Over the next year, an estimated 70,000 students took part in sit-ins. Some 3,600 received their "badge of honor" by serving time in jail.

Freedom Rides. While sit-ins shook the South, the Congress of Racial Equality (CORE) organized another form of protest. James Farmer had struggled to keep CORE alive since its founding in Chicago in 1942. He worked without pay and recruited other dedicated volunteers to do the same.

The new burst of civil rights activity helped Farmer revitalize CORE into a national organization. Like the SCLC and SNCC, CORE followed a program of nonviolence. But the course of action chosen by CORE met with brutal backlash.

In May 1961, a group of 13 African American and white volunteers set out from Washington, D.C., for a **freedom ride** through the South. Six boarded a Greyhound bus; seven got on a Trailways bus. The freedom riders were testing the effectiveness of court orders barring segregation on interstate buses and in bus terminals. At first, the riders had few problems. But when they hit the Deep South, angry mobs of whites gathered. Both African American and white protesters received savage beatings. One bus was firebombed.

Farmer considered calling the freedom ride off. But now student leaders of SNCC wanted to carry them on. Diane Nash begged Farmer to let them continue the rides. "You know that may be suicide," warned Farmer. Responded Nash:

> We know that, but if we let them stop us with violence, the movement is dead! . . . Your troops have been badly battered. Let us pick up the baton and run with it.

Farmer agreed. The SNCC freedom riders rolled into Birmingham, Alabama. Sheriff Eugene "Bull" Connor's police beat the riders, took them into custody, and drove them into Tennessee. But the students came back and boarded a bus for Montgomery. Again they met with violence. Mobs cracked open heads and left students bleeding or unconscious.

The violence forced the Kennedy administration to act. Attorney General Robert Kennedy ordered federal marshals to protect the freedom riders as they headed farther south, chanting, "Freedom! Freedom!" In Mississippi, entire groups of freedom riders were arrested. Carried off to jail, they sang,

> I'm taking a ride on the Greyhound bus line
> I'm riding the front seat to Jackson this time.

As the freedom rides continued, the federal government issued tougher regulations barring segregation in interstate travel. It also put more pressure on local communities to obey the regulations.

Despite these measures, the turmoil over desegregation increased throughout the South. In 1961 and 1962, the Ku Klux Klan claimed credit for bombing four African American churches. In 1962, riots broke out in Oxford, Mississippi, when James Meredith tried to integrate the University of Mississippi. Federal troops had to escort him to and from classes.

Pressure mounted on the federal government to take stronger action for civil rights. On television, President Kennedy promised to send a new civil rights bill to Congress. It was 1963, the centennial of the Emancipation Proclamation.

Freedom riders in Anniston, Alabama, in May 1961 watch their burning bus, bombed by angry whites.

Taking Another Look

1. What was the purpose of the sit-ins and freedom rides?

2. What dangers did civil rights workers face in the Deep South?

3. **Critical Thinking** Why might it have seemed in 1963 as though the Civil War had never ended in the South?

4 MARCHING FOR FREEDOM

▼ How did the freedom marches of 1963 mark a turning point in the civil rights struggle?

On April 3, 1963, Martin Luther King, Jr., stepped off an airplane in Birmingham, Alabama. He had come at the invitation of Fred Shuttlesworth and other African American community leaders to start a new round of civil rights protests. King planned to celebrate the 100th anniversary of the Emancipation Proclamation by marching through one of the most stubbornly segregated cities in the South. King faced Bull Connor—the sheriff committed to crushing civil rights protests.

When reporters asked King how long he planned to stay in Birmingham, he replied, "[Until] Pharaoh lets God's people go." Bull Connor responded, "I got plenty of room in the jail." He also had club-wielding troopers, K-9 dogs, and fire hoses that could blast bark off a tree.

Freedom Now! Bull Connor had obtained a court order banning demonstrations until a full court hearing could be held. King and the other march leaders decided to go on with the protests anyway. Connor then set about arresting the demonstrators. At first, the protests were peaceful, and relatively few African Americans were jailed.

Then, on Good Friday, April 12, King stepped into the streets. Connor threw him into jail. Some whites believed King was openly courting crisis. King answered them in his "Letter from a Birmingham Jail."

For years now I have heard the word "Wait!" . . . when you have seen hate-filled policemen curse, kick and even kill your black brothers and sisters; when you see the vast majority of your twenty million Negro brothers in an airtight cage of poverty . . .; when you have to concoct an answer for a five-year-old son who is asking: "Daddy, why do white people treat colored people so mean?" . . . —then you will understand why we find it difficult to wait.

On April 20, King posted bail, but he did not leave Birmingham. Day after day, he and other civil rights workers marched. Then, on May 2, King decided to allow children in the marches.

Thousands of school-age students poured out of the public schools and into the street. Over 900 children went to jail that day. Helmeted police swept marchers off their feet with high-pressure hoses. Police dogs tore at marchers' arms and legs. As protesters lay helpless on the ground, police beat them with clubs and dragged them into waiting wagons.

Television cameras brought these scenes to a national audience. More rage and violence against the protesters followed. Bombs tore apart King's motel room and his brother's home.

Amid this crisis, Kennedy posted federal troops around Birmingham. An uneasy calm settled over the city as protesters agreed to halt demonstrations in exchange for an agreement that businesses would desegregate and also hire African Americans.

Events in Birmingham convinced President Kennedy to face the issue of civil rights. On June 10, the President addressed the nation: "Now the time has come for this nation to fulfill its promises." He demanded that Congress pass a new civil rights bill.

Within 24 hours of Kennedy's speech, an assassin crept up behind Medgar Evers, a leading Mississippi civil rights worker, and fired a bullet into his head. Evers fell dead.

The death brought African Americans together. They shot their fists into the air and shouted "Freedom Now!" Soon, a quarter of a million people would carry that cry to the nation's capital.

March on Washington. A. Philip Randolph and Bayard Rustin were among the African American leaders who organized a protest march on the nation's capital. On August 28, 1963, more than 250,000 people poured into Washington, D.C., from around the country. They had come to pressure Congress into passing the civil rights bill.

Amid memories of the recent violence, Martin Luther King spoke to the marchers about unity and racial harmony. "I have a dream," said King repeatedly. Each time he spoke these words, the crowd erupted in cheers. He then described his vision for the nation:

> When we let freedom ring, when we let it ring from every village and hamlet, . . . we will be able to speed up that day when all of God's children . . . will be able to join hands and sing in the words of that old Negro spiritual: "Free at last! Free at last! Thank God Almighty, we are free at last!"

"I have a dream," Dr. Martin Luther King, Jr., told the thousands at the March on Washington, D.C., in August 1963.

Taking Another Look

1. Why did King go to Birmingham?

2. What was King's dream for the United States?

3. **Critical Thinking** What role did television have in advancing the Civil Rights Movement?

LOOKING AHEAD

A few days after King's Washington speech, a bomb tore through an African American Bible school in Birmingham, killing four young girls. Two other African Americans were killed in the unrest that followed. On November 22, 1963, an assassin killed President Kennedy. His successor, Lyndon Johnson, pushed through Kennedy's civil rights bill in July 1964. But racial violence still ripped the nation. People prayed for the nightmare to end and King's dream to begin.

CLOSE UP: Chapter 30

On May 17, 1954, a crowd filed into the Supreme Court Building, passing beneath these words, carved over the entrance: "Equal Justice Under Law." Later that day, the Court lived up to the motto and ended more than 50 years of legal segregation. The Court ruled that racial segregation in public schools was unconstitutional.

The case before the Court that day, *Brown* v. *Board of Education*, involved an African American elementary student named Linda Brown. Brown's father had sued so his daughter could attend an all-white school in her neighborhood, rather than go across town to school.

In the 35 years after the *Brown* decision, most people agreed, Topeka had taken great strides toward ending school segregation. However, others, such as Linda Brown Smith, felt that integration was not going fast enough. In 1989, Smith tried to reopen the case to ensure that her grandson could attend a fully integrated school.

This time, however, the board of education worked with Smith to resolve their differences. All participants agreed with the goals of the *Brown* decision. Explained an African American board member: "It allowed my education experience to be part of the American mainstream."

The Who, What, Where of History

1. **Who** was Jackie Robinson?
2. **Who** was George McLaurin?
3. **What** arguments did Thurgood Marshall use to show that segregation was harmful to African Americans?
4. **What** was *Brown* v. *Board of Education*?
5. **Where** were federal troops sent in 1957 to enforce school integration?
6. **What** did Rosa Parks do to help end segregation?
7. **What** is the SCLC?
8. **Who** was Martin Luther King, Jr.?
9. **What** was SNCC?
10. **What** was a freedom ride?

Making the Connection

1. What was the connection between the decisions in *Sweatt* v. *Painter* and *Brown* v. *Board of Education*?
2. What was the connection between Rosa Parks's arrest and the Montgomery bus boycott?
3. What was the connection between Bull Connor's actions and the growth of public support for the Civil Rights Movement?
4. What was the connection between Martin Luther King and Mohandas Gandhi?

Time Check

1. When was the *Brown* decision handed down?
2. When did the Montgomery bus boycott take place?

What Would You Have Done?

1. If you had been a student in Greensboro, North Carolina, during the time of the sit-ins, would you have participated in them? Explain.

2. Imagine that it is 1963 and you are a student in Birmingham. How would you explain to your parents your decision to join the demonstrations?

Thinking and Writing About History

1. Write a letter to the editor of a Little Rock, Arkansas, paper giving your reaction to the governor's use of National Guard troops to prevent school desegregation.

2. Write a brief paragraph explaining why you agree or disagree with King's idea of nonviolent resistance.

Building Skills: Sequencing

It would make studying history easier if no two events happened at the same time. Then, you could read about how one event or movement began and ended, and how another event or movement began. It doesn't work like that, of course. Just as you often are involved in more than one thing at a time, events, and movements overlap in all sorts of ways.

The time lines at the beginning of each unit and chapter of your textbook give you a very clear, visual picture of the dates of the main events you are studying. A writer gives you such a picture, too, with words such as *before, after, during, while, meanwhile, at the same time, then, the next year, first, soon, next,* and *later.* These can help you to keep straight the flow of events. These and other transition words and phrases help place events in chronological, or time, order.

Read the following sentences from your textbook. Then answer the questions that follow.

On June 5, 1950, Marshall faced the Court. . . . That same year, Marshall won another important victory in the case of Sweatt v. Painter. *. . . A key test came in Little Rock, Arkansas, in 1957. There, Governor Orval Faubus called in the state's national guard to prevent nine African American students from entering the city's public high school. . . . The following year, Faubus shut down Little Rock's high schools. . . . Congress passed the 1957 Civil Rights Act. . . . The Supreme Court also heard a new round of desegregation cases in the 1950s and 1960s. . . . On December 1, 1955, Rosa Parks boarded a bus in Montgomery, Alabama. . . . In late 1956, the Supreme Court found that segregation on Alabama buses was illegal. . . . In 1957, [Martin Luther King, Jr.] joined with nearly 100 other church leaders in founding the Southern Christian Leadership Conference. . . . In 1960, King moved the SCLC headquarters to Atlanta.*

1. List two transition words and phrases used in the reading above.

2. List three events mentioned in the extract that happened in 1957.

3. List in order three things that happened between 1949 and 1957.

4. Did the Supreme Court rule against segregation on Alabama buses before or after Faubus shut down Little Rock High School?

Florida students being bused to school

New Directions in the Civil Rights Movement

(1964–1972)

THINKING ABOUT THE CHAPTER

What changes took place in the Civil Rights Movement after 1963?

On December 10, 1964, Dr. Martin Luther King, Jr., stepped forward to receive the Nobel Peace Prize in Oslo, Norway. Only two other blacks had ever claimed the award. In 1950, Ralph Bunche, the U.S. representative to the United Nations, had accepted the prize for negotiating an Arab–Israeli armistice after the creation of Israel in 1948. In 1960, Albert Luthuli won the award for his nonviolent drive for racial equality in South Africa. The 35-year-old King was the 14th American and the youngest person ever to receive the prize.

King won the award for his use of nonviolent resistance in the struggle for racial equality. Yet, equality still eluded African Americans. King stressed this fact in his acceptance speech:

I accept the Nobel Prize for peace at a moment when 22 million Negroes of the United States are engaged in a creative battle to end the long night of racial injustice. I accept this award in behalf of a civil rights movement which is moving with determination and a majestic scorn for risk and danger to establish a reign of freedom and a rule of justice.

This chapter tells the story of the Civil Rights Movement and the risks and dangers it faced during the late 1960s and early 1970s.

1 A LONG, HOT SUMMER

▼ Why did members of SNCC develop more militant attitudes during the mid-1960s?

A new resolve among African Americans filled the air as the election of 1964 neared. Republican candidate Barry Goldwater had voted against the Civil Rights Act of 1964. In response, civil rights workers vowed to campaign for the election of Democrat Lyndon Johnson.

Members of the NAACP, CORE, SNCC, and the SCLC formed the Council of Federated Organizations (COFO) to lead a voter registration drive in the South. They called the campaign Freedom Summer.

COFO sent some 1,000 African American and white volunteers into Mississippi alone. The state beefed up its police force to greet the "invaders." The Ku Klux Klan held white-sheeted rallies to intimidate activists who dared to cross state lines. But the young people came anyway.

On August 4, 1964, FBI agents found the bodies of three volunteers, an African American and two white students, in a Mississippi swamp. Missing since June,

the three had been brutally murdered. The FBI charged 20 men with conspiracy, including 7 Klan members who were charged with the killings. After three years of trials and appeals, convictions were upheld and the accused went to jail.

A New Mood. The murders were only part of a summer of violence. COFO officials in Mississippi reported 65 firebombings, 3 shootings, and 80 mob attacks. To make the nation aware of the violence, SNCC sent members of the Mississippi Freedom Democratic party (MFDP) to attend the Democratic National Convention. They came prepared to argue that the MFDP, rather than white politicians who supported segregation, truly represented the Democratic party in Mississippi. Fannie Lou Hamer spoke for the MFDP in a televised speech before the convention.

▶▶ **AFRICAN AMERICAN VOTER REGISTRATION BEFORE AND AFTER THE VOTING RIGHTS ACT OF 1965**

State	Years 1960	1966	Percent Increase
Alabama	66,000	250,000	278.8
Arkansas	73,000	115,000	57.5
Florida	183,000	303,000	65.6
Georgia	180,000	300,000	66.7
Louisiana	159,000	243,000	52.8
Mississippi	22,000	175,000	695.4
N. Carolina	210,000	282,000	34.3
S. Carolina	58,000	191,000	229.3
Tennessee	185,000	225,000	21.6
Texas	227,000	400,000	76.2
Virginia	100,000	205,000	105.0

Source: U.S. Department of Commerce, Bureau of the Census, *Statistical Abstract of the United States: 1982-83,* 103rd Edition

What did the Voting Rights Act provide? Which two states showed the greatest increase in voter registration?

Fannie Lou Hamer was the youngest of 20 children in a Mississippi sharecropping family. Hamer lost her job as a timekeeper on a Mississippi cotton plantation for registering to vote in 1962. The plantation owner had warned her: "Fannie Lou, . . . we are not ready for this in Mississippi." Replied Hamer: "I didn't register for you, I tried to register for myself." Mrs. Hamer left the plantation to join SNCC. She soon became involved in the voter registration drives of Freedom Summer.

In that June 1964 speech, Hamer told the nation what it was like to register African Americans in Mississippi. "I was beaten until I was exhausted," said Hamer of her treatment on one voter drive.

I began to scream, and one white man got up and began to beat me on the head and tell me to "hush." . . . All of this on account we wanted to register, to become first class citizens. [If] the Freedom Democratic Party is not seated now, I question America.

Support poured into the Democratic Convention for the MFDP. But Lyndon Johnson refused to allow the seating of MFDP delegates. He feared such a move would anger white Southern voters.

The MFDP and their young supporters in SNCC felt betrayed. In fall 1964, the leaders of SNCC, including Hamer, met in New York City to rethink their tactics. Here they met Malcolm X.

The Revival of Black Nationalism. The followers of Martin Luther King and the SCLC wanted an integrated society. The followers of Malcolm X preached black nationalism. They revived the spirit of African nationalism inspired by earlier leaders like Marcus Garvey (see Chapter 25). They sought unity among people of African descent throughout the world. They also looked to Africa for cultural models, including the practice of Islam.

In the 1950s and early 1960s, Malcolm X was a follower of Elijah Muhammad, head of a religious group known as the **Nation of Islam.** Muhammad had led the Black Muslims, as members were known, since the 1930s. He preached African American solidarity and said that advancement would come through self-help. Whites were "blue-eyed devils" to be avoided. Malcolm X became the most forceful spokesman of the Black Muslims. He saw in Muhammad's teaching a way to help African Americans gain control of their own destinies.

Born Malcolm Little in Omaha, Nebraska, about 1925, **Malcolm X** was one of 11 children. His father, an outspoken Baptist minister and a follower of Pan-Africanist Marcus Garvey, was harassed by the Ku Klux Klan. The family moved to Lansing, Michigan, where Malcolm's father died shortly after in an accident in which Malcolm believed whites had played a part. The troubled youth moved to Boston and later to Harlem, where an attempted burglary led to a seven-year prison term. In jail, Malcolm converted to Islam.

After his release in 1952, Malcolm devoted all his energies to the Nation of Islam. In 1964, after a trip to Africa and Mecca, he split with Elijah Muhammad to build his own movement. Malcolm changed his name to Al Hajj Malik al-Shabazz. His experiences abroad also convinced him to drop his hatred of whites and focus instead on building Pan-African American pride.

Malcolm X urged young people to think of themselves as part of an African majority, not an African American minority. "There can be no black–white unity unless there is first black unity," explained Malcolm. "We cannot think of unity with others until after we have first united among ourselves." He left the door open to cooperation with whites. But he stressed self-determination and self-defense by African Americans. "We won't get our problems solved depending on the white man," he declared.

Malcolm X attracted a large following, including many members of SNCC. A good number of these followers, however, focused on Malcolm's earlier message of anger toward whites.

Explosion in the Cities. In the sweltering heat of July 1964, the anger that many African Americans felt about living conditions in the decaying inner cities erupted. The first major riot in the central section of a U.S. city began in Harlem on July 18. There, an incident between white police and African American teenagers left a 15-year-old student dead. Before the rioting ended, casualties had risen into

What were the goals of the Nation of Islam under Elijah Muhammad?

the hundreds. Riots soon followed in Brooklyn and Rochester, New York; in Chicago; in Philadelphia; and in several New Jersey cities.

President Johnson tried to stop future rioting by announcing a "War on Poverty" with increased federal spending on programs to aid the nation's neediest citizens. But his efforts seemed too little, too late. More trouble lay ahead in 1965.

Taking Another Look

1. What events led SNCC to seek representation for the MFDP at the Democratic Convention?

2. What was the Nation of Islam?

3. **Critical Thinking** How did the programs of Marcus Garvey influence Malcolm X?

2 YEAR OF RAGE: 1965
▼ What troubles faced the Civil Rights
▼ Movement in 1965?

Malcolm X began 1965 with a new slogan: "Ballots or bullets." He focused on winning political power for African Americans, and he warned whites of a revolution if African Americans did not win such power. Malcolm X also let it be known that he would cooperate with other civil rights groups—and even whites—to achieve his goal. But he stuck fast to the need for a revolution in U.S. society. Peaceful or violent—the method of change was up to whites, said Malcolm X.

In following this broader course of action, Malcolm X turned his back on the separatism of the Nation of Islam. Because of this, he believed loyal followers of Elijah Muhammad might soon kill him for what they saw as his treason.

On February 21, Malcolm X addressed a crowd of about 400 followers in the Audubon Ballroom in Harlem. Three men in the audience, who may have been Black Muslims, suddenly pulled out guns and opened fire. At 39, Malcolm X, with his new vision of African nationalism, died. His death dramatized the conflict that increasingly tore at both the Civil Rights Movement and U.S. society.

Selma. In one of his last speeches, Malcolm X had said, "If white people realize what the alternative is, perhaps they would be more willing to listen to Dr. King." But in the South, white officials were trying everything possible to crush the Civil Rights Movement. SNCC decided to focus its voter registration drives on one stronghold of white power— Selma, Alabama.

At the beginning of 1965, some 15,000 African Americans lived in Selma. Only 65 dared register to vote. After SNCC volunteers—African American and white— poured into town, there were soon more African Americans in Selma jails than on its voting rolls.

King and the SCLC decided to join the SNCC campaign in Selma. They believed violent white resistance to voter registration would win them nationwide sympathy. Such sympathy could translate into support for a federal voting rights bill.

King announced a 50-mile march from Selma to Montgomery to ask the Alabama governor to protect African American voters. The march began on Sunday, March 7. News reports that night interrupted television programs to show what looked like a war. Claiming the marchers were breaking the law, the police tore into the demonstrators. Tear gas swirled around marchers. Police mounted on horseback charged into the crowd swing-

Civil rights marchers assemble in front of the state capitol in Montgomery, Alabama. What was the purpose of the five-day march from Selma to Montgomery in 1965?

ing billy clubs. The sight moved thousands to fly to Selma and join the march.

On March 15, President Johnson appeared on nationwide television to announce his support of a voting rights bill. The bill would allow federal examiners to register African American voters wherever discrimination was practiced.

Two days later, a federal judge gave the SCLC and SNCC a permit to complete their march. Johnson ordered federal troops to protect them. On March 25, some 25,000 marchers strode into Montgomery in triumph, with Nobel Prize winners Martin Luther King and Ralph Bunche in the lead.

Watts. The Selma march had helped win a civil rights victory for African Americans. Yet just four days after the federal Voting Rights Act of 1965 took effect came a reminder of the economic ills that African Americans faced. The reminder came from the nation's cities, where poverty-stricken families in ghettoes struggled not so much to win civil rights but simply to survive.

On August 11, 1965, police in a Los Angeles ghetto known as Watts pulled over 21-year-old Marquette Frye for drunken driving. When African Ameri-

cans saw one of the police pull a gun, tempers boiled over. Charges of police brutality flew. By evening, thousands of people had filled the streets.

For six days, violence ripped through Watts. Cars and stores were burned. Snipers shot at police and firefighters. Roving bands of looters stripped pawnshops and gunshops of weapons and ammunition. Nearly $45 million in property was destroyed.

The nation had seen riots before, but the violence in Watts was shocking. The rioters' rage about their treatment in U.S. society had fueled the destruction in Watts. It also fueled a new movement that had begun in the voter registration drives in the South: Black Power.

Taking Another Look

1. How did Malcolm X's approach to achieving his goals change in 1965?

2. What was the purpose of the SNCC and SCLC campaign in Selma?

3. **Critical Thinking** One commentator called the Watts riot "a purposeful symbolic protest." Explain why you agree or disagree.

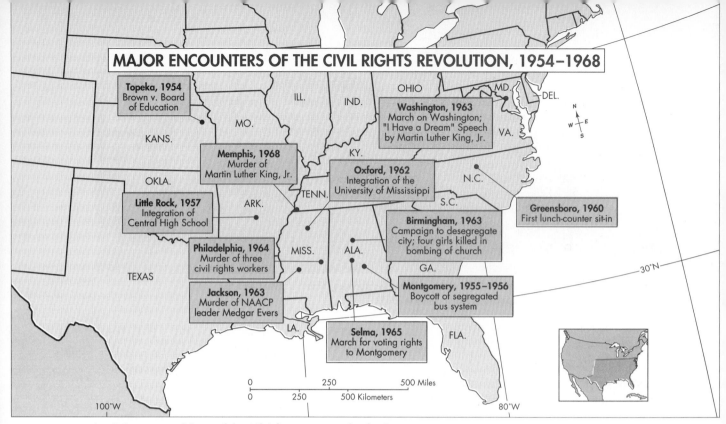

MAJOR ENCOUNTERS OF THE CIVIL RIGHTS REVOLUTION, 1954–1968

Topeka, 1954
Brown v. Board of Education

Washington, 1963
March on Washington; "I Have a Dream" Speech by Martin Luther King, Jr.

Memphis, 1968
Murder of Martin Luther King, Jr.

Oxford, 1962
Integration of the University of Mississippi

Greensboro, 1960
First lunch-counter sit-in

Little Rock, 1957
Integration of Central High School

Birmingham, 1963
Campaign to desegregate city; four girls killed in bombing of church

Philadelphia, 1964
Murder of three civil rights workers

Montgomery, 1955–1956
Boycott of segregated bus system

Jackson, 1963
Murder of NAACP leader Medgar Evers

Selma, 1965
March for voting rights to Montgomery

0   250   500 Miles
0   250   500 Kilometers

In which two states did most of the civil rights encounters take place?

3 BLACK POWER

▼ How did the goals of the Black Power movement differ from those of Martin Luther King?

On June 5, 1966, James Meredith decided to march from Tennessee through his native Mississippi to encourage the state's nearly 450,000 African Americans to vote. He planned to walk 220 miles from Memphis to Jackson. That Sunday, a handful of people started the walk.

On the second day of the march, a white man armed with a 16-gauge shotgun fired a round of birdshot into Meredith. Other marchers hit the ground. As Meredith lay bleeding, he cried out: "Oh, my God, is anyone going to help me?"

March Against Fear. Help arrived in the form of Martin Luther King. Joining him were Stokely Carmichael, the newly elected leader of SNCC, and Floyd Mc-

Kissick of CORE. The three leaders decided to finish Meredith's march.

The new "Meredith March Against Fear" set out June 7. King tried to rally crowds with the traditional cry of "Freedom Now." Carmichael, however, used a new language of protest. "We've been saying freedom for six years," he told one crowd in Canton, "and we ain't got nothin'." He then used a new phrase: "What we're gonna start saying now is Black Power!" At this point, SNCC worker Willie Ricks jumped up on the stage next to Carmichael. He yelled out to the crowd: "What do you want?" The crowd yelled back: "Black Power!" "What you want?" he called out again. The crowd exploded. "Black Power! Black Power! Black Power!"

Carmichael defined **Black Power** as:

a call for black people . . . to unite, to recognize their heritage, to build a sense of community. It is a call for black people to begin to define their own goals, to lead their own organizations and to support these organizations.

Some African American leaders urged Carmichael to stop using the phrase. They felt it would frighten whites whose support they needed to get civil rights measures through Congress. Carmichael refused, and the split between SNCC and more conservative organizations, such as the NAACP, widened.

"Black Is Beautiful." Carmichael urged SNCC to stop recruiting whites into its ranks. He argued that African Americans did not want to be assimilated, or merged, into white society. They wanted to stand apart as their own people. A slogan took hold, "Black is beautiful," that went back to Marcus Garvey.

Carmichael's tough talk found an audience among many of the nation's African Americans. Frustrated by poverty and police brutality, these people embraced Carmichael's outspoken racial pride.

In October 1966, in Los Angeles, Bobby Seale and Huey Newton, founded a new militant political party—the **Black Panthers**. The Panthers demanded the right of African Americans to control their own communities. They asked the federal government to rebuild the ghettoes in repayment for the years African Americans had spent in slavery. They wanted African Americans freed from jail and re-tried by African American juries.

Not everyone knew about the Panthers' political platform. But nearly all recognized their dress: black trousers, black leather jackets, blue shirts, and black berets.

Groups of Panthers soon formed in other cities around the country. A white

backlash set in against all civil-rights groups, including the moderate SCLC.

King's Death. By 1967, Martin Luther King had come to believe that the nation's main enemy was economic injustice. Poverty, he said, bred violence. To end the violence, the nation needed to wipe out poverty. King therefore began building what he called the Poor People's Campaign.

King planned to start his campaign in April 1968 with a huge march on Washington. That spring, he traveled about the nation drumming up support. He visited Memphis, Tennessee, to lend support to a strike by the city's garbage workers.

On April 3, King addressed a Memphis crowd. "I've been to the mountaintop," said King, "[and] I've seen the glory." He then described his vision of a world free of poverty. "I may not get there with you," he continued, "but I want you to know that we as a people will get to the promised land."

The next afternoon, King stood on the balcony of his motel room, joking with members of his staff. Suddenly, a shot

Black Panther leader Huey Newton brings his militant message to thousands of young people in Philadelphia.

rang out from a high-powered rifle. King fell, a bullet through his jaw. An hour later, the leader who dared dream of interracial peace lay dead.

King's assassin, James Earl Ray, was a white man. That fact alone set off a burst of fury among African Americans. President Johnson tried to calm passions. He addressed the nation, saying: "I ask every American citizen to reject the blind violence that has struck down Dr. King, who lived by nonviolence." Despite his plea, African American rage led to riots in 125 cities, leaving 45 people dead.

King was buried in an African American cemetery in Atlanta. His tombstone read: "Free at last, free at last, thank God almighty I'm free at last." The world that King left behind, however, was anything but free.

Taking Another Look

1. How did the Meredith March Against Fear reveal splits in the Civil Rights Movement?

Two African American winners at the 1968 Olympic games give the black power salute in a gesture of protest.

2. How did the aims of the Black Power movement differ from King's?

3. **Critical Thinking** Imagine it is April 1968. You work on a major city newspaper. How would you word the obituary for Martin Luther King, Jr.?

4 NO TURNING BACK
▼ What did the Civil Rights Movement accomplish?

"Our nation is moving toward two societies, one black, one white—separate and unequal." That was the conclusion drawn by the Kerner Commission in 1968. At the request of President Johnson, the 11-member panel spent seven months looking into the causes of the riots of the 1960s. In a 200,000-word document, the commission pinned the riots on one main cause—prejudice.

Painful Legacies. The Kerner Commission report described a society with deep-rooted social and economic differences between African Americans and whites. These differences fueled the anger of the Black Power movement, which continued into the 1970s.

As the 1970s unfolded, the average income for African American families still lagged more than 50 percent behind that of white families. In 1975, unemployment among African Americans was 13.7 percent, while unemployment among whites stood at 7.6 percent.

African American activists in the late 1960s increasingly focused on improving conditions for what they called the nation's **underclass**—the group of people with incomes below subsistence level. This class included a large number of African Americans—particularly rural sharecroppers and urban ghetto dwellers. In 1970, only about 13 percent of all African

Americans belonged to the nation's middle class.

The Promise of Change. Although inequities existed in the 1970s, the Civil Rights Movement had achieved lasting advances. Supreme Court decisions had ended legal segregation and thrown open educational and public facilities to all. The Civil Rights Act of 1964 was the most sweeping civil rights legislation since Reconstruction. The Voting Rights Act of 1965 and the registration drives gave African Americans the political power to take part in shaping their futures.

Most important, the Civil Rights Movement exposed flaws within U.S. society. No longer could people pretend that the blessings of liberty fell equally on all citizens. Because of the Civil Rights Movement, people learned how to force political and social change. So successful was the movement that other groups adopted its tactics—women, the aged, the handicapped, and other ethnic groups.

As African Americans took greater control over their affairs, the number of African American elected officials increased. Between 1970 and 1975 alone, their numbers grew by 88 percent. For the first time, African American mayors took office in large cities, such as Atlanta, Detroit, Los Angeles, and Newark, New Jersey.

Building on these gains, African Americans broke new cultural ground in the United States. Students demanded—and won—courses in African American studies. African Americans adopted styles of dress or took names that expressed pride in their heritage. In the 1920s, Marcus Garvey had preached of the beauty of blackness. In the 1960s and 1970s, many African Americans came to share his idea, proudly proclaiming "Black is beautiful."

Taking Another Look

1. What obstacles faced African Americans as the 1970s began?

2. What did the Civil Rights Movement achieve?

3. **Critical Thinking** What do you consider the greatest achievement of the Civil Rights Movement?

LOOKING AHEAD

Toward the end of the 1960s, turmoil surrounding the Vietnam War increased in U.S. society. Stories of the war and the protests against it often pushed news of the Civil Rights Movement off the front pages. Yet, the importance of that movement to U.S. society cannot be overstated. In the words of African American politician Barbara Jordan:

> The civil rights movement called America to look at itself in a giant mirror. . . . Do the black people who were born on this soil, who are American citizens, do they really feel this is the land of opportunity, the land of the free. . . . America had to say no.

The demand for African American studies in schools and colleges spread during the Civil Rights Movement.

BLACK STUDIES

FOCUS ON

SINGING FOR FREEDOM

During the Civil Rights movement of the 1960s, African American and white demonstrators sang songs to inspire and unite them. One freedom song summed up the hopes of demonstrators — "We Shall Overcome." The promise of the title was repeated in the final stanza:

We shall overcome
We shall overcome
We shall overcome someday.
If in our hearts we do believe
We shall overcome someday.

Freedom songs grew out of the African American musical heritage. The songs echoed the spirituals sung by slaves, the gospels and hymns of African American churches, and even a little Motown—the sound of African American pop singers of the 1960s. The melody of "We Shall Overcome" is based on the spiritual "I'll Be Alright." The words are based on a hymn, "I'll Overcome Someday." "We Shall Overcome" became the theme song of the Civil Rights Movement of the 1960s.

Both African American slaves and the demonstrators of the 1960s sang about emancipation. Spirituals promised freedom from slavery, and freedom songs demanded an end to racial inequality.

The Who, What, Where of History

1. **What** was COFO?
2. **What** was the MFDP?
3. **Who** was Fannie Lou Hamer?
4. **Who** was Malcolm X?
5. **What** is the Nation of Islam?
6. **Who** was Stokely Carmichael?
7. **Where** did SNCC want to focus its voter registration drives in 1965?
8. **Who** founded the Black Panthers?
9. **What** is the underclass?
10. **What** was the Kerner Commission?

Making the Connection

1. What was the connection between the riots in Harlem in 1964 and Lyndon Johnson's War on Poverty?
2. What was the connection between the events in Selma, Alabama, in 1965 and the Voting Rights Act?
3. What was the connection between African American activists and the underclass?

Time Check

1. In what year was Martin Luther King assassinated?
2. In what year did the Kerner Commission report come out?
3. In what year was the Black Panther party formed?

What Would You Have Done?

Imagine that you are living in Los Angeles in fall 1966. A good friend announces he is thinking of joining the Black Panthers. He asks your opinion. How do you respond?

Thinking and Writing About History

Write a paragraph explaining which African American leader discussed in this chapter you think was the most effective spokesperson for the African American community.

Building Skills: Analyzing Oral History

Which would you rather do? Read a history book or a scholarly article about Malcolm X or talk to someone who knew him personally and heard him speak? By reading or listening to oral history, you can actually capture the experiences of people who lived through a historical period.

Oral history gives the atmosphere and mood of an event in much the same way that fiction does. Oral history is immediate and down-to-earth.

When you read or listen to oral history, however, you must remember that you are hearing one person's version of an event, sometimes years after it occurred. Look for generalizations and opinions. Take the point of view into consideration as you decide whether you accept everything or not.

Below are two quotations from a book of oral history called *Voices of Freedom*, edited by Henry Hampton and Steve Fayer. The quotations are both about Malcolm X. Read the quotations and on a separate sheet of paper, answer the questions that follow.

When [Malcolm X] talked that night . . . he was absolutely mesmerizing. He was brilliant. He was funny. He expressed the rage that all of us continued to feel at the slow pace of change in the country, but he did it in just the cleverest and funniest way you could imagine. I just remember laughing uncontrollably at some of the ways in which Malcolm would answer questions and put down whites who were trying to trick him at that point. So, he was a new outlet for the anger and the frustration. But he sure was smart.

—Marian Wright Edelman

Nowadays you might hear a lot of people talking about how they followed [Malcolm X] and so forth, but my perception at the time was that the large majority were frightened by the things Malcolm said. They were so extreme, it seemed, and so radical by comparison with what others were saying. But there were those who were . . . feeling that Malcolm was having the courage to say aloud, publicly, things which they had felt or which they wished somebody would say.

—Alex Haley

1. Does the quotation from Edelman give facts or opinions?

2. What quality of Malcolm X did Edelman find most appealing?

3. Does the quote from Haley give facts or opinions about the response to Malcolm X?

4. Write the phrase from Edelman's quotation and the one from Haley's quotation that express the same thought about Malcolm X.

5. Do you think that Edelman and Haley share the same opinion of Malcolm X? Explain.

John Wilkins at right and buddies in Vietnam

Marching Off to Vietnam

(1963–1982)

THINKING ABOUT THE CHAPTER

How did the Civil Rights Movement affect African Americans serving in Vietnam?

On the night of April 4, 1968, John Wilkins climbed into an army truck at Fort Sill, Oklahoma. Fresh out of basic training, the young African American from Beacon, New York, had expected to be shipped off to Vietnam. Instead, it looked as if his first tour of duty might be on U.S. soil. Wilkins and other members of the 82nd Airborne stood on alert, waiting for orders to put down the riots that broke out after the assassination of Martin Luther King. But the orders never came.

Later that April, Wilkins flew off to Fort Lewis, Washington. There, Wilkins and a couple of his buddies decided to see *The Green Berets,* a movie about the Vietnam War starring John Wayne. The film showed lots of heroics. But what Wilkins and his friends saw were the casualties. The teenagers knew that they would soon be facing real battles in a real war.

Still shaken by the movie, Wilkins left for Vietnam. He wore a heavy field jacket against the chilly Washington weather. Hours later, he stepped off the plane into the hot, humid air of Vietnam. Soon another flight carried him to a base deep in the country.

The next time Wilkins touched down, a wave of rocket fire greeted him. Someone barked out for the recruits to take cover. When the attack ended, Wilkins stared back at the plane. He saw troops loading the cargo bay with aluminum coffins. Battle-tested soldiers shouted out to the still-green troops, "Mr. Charlie's waiting for you." Mr. Charlie was the nickname for the Vietcong—the enemy Wilkins had come to fight. This chapter tells the story of what it was like for African Americans, such as Wilkins, to fight in Vietnam.

1 UNDER FIRE
▼ What role did African Americans play in Vietnam?

The war that Wilkins and other African Americans found themselves fighting in Vietnam demonstrated some of the changes the United States had undergone since World War II. Through the end of World War II, the vast majority of African Americans who fought in the nation's wars did so in segregated units. Toward the end of World War II, the number of integrated units slowly increased.

Korea. In 1948, President Truman issued an executive order to integrate the armed services. A commission that he had appointed recommended increased integration in all the armed forces. By 1949, the various branches of the service had begun to take action toward implementing that goal.

The move toward an integrated military got another boost in 1950. In that year, Communist North Korea invaded neighboring South Korea. The United States quickly entered the conflict on the side of South Korea. When the first U.S. combat troops arrived, fewer than 9 percent of the units were integrated. U.S. troops and their allies won early success, but late in 1950, the Communists launched a major attack.

Army commanders, desperate for men to hold back the enemy, began to integrate their fighting units rapidly. By August 1951, 30 percent of the fighting units in Korea were integrated. The enemy advance was stopped, and a later report concluded that the integration of African Americans into units had greatly aided U.S. efforts.

The Korean War ended in 1953. By the following year, the process of integration in the armed forces was complete. How this fully integrated military force would perform in combat would not be known until ten years later in another war in Asia, this time in Vietnam.

African Americans in Vietnam. Vietnam had been divided after World War II. By the early 1960s, rebels supported by the Communist government in North Vietnam were seeking to overthrow the U.S.-backed government of South Vietnam. The United States began to send military advisers to aid South Vietnam. By 1965, it was sending combat troops, large numbers of which were African Americans.

One U.S. magazine reporter studied the involvement of African Americans in

1965	First U.S. combat troops arrive in Vietnam.
1967	Muhammad Ali resists draft on religious grounds.
	Martin Luther King speaks out against Vietnam War.
1969	Vietnam Moratorium day
1973	Last U.S. troops leave Vietnam.
1975	Vietnam falls to Communists.
1982	Vietnam Veterans Memorial is dedicated.

the war. He offered the following evaluation:

> For the first time in the nation's military history, its Negro fighting men are fully integrated in combat. . . . In the unpredictable search-and-destroy missions, . . . on the carrier decks and in the gun mounts of the Seventh Fleet offshore, in the cockpits of helicopters and fighter-bombers, . . . the American Negro is winning—indeed has won—a black badge of courage that his nation must forever honor.

The acts of many individual African Americans helped the reporter reach this conclusion. Army nurse 1st Lieutenant Dorothy Johnson cared for the wounded while pinned down under mortar fire. Air Force Major James T. Boddie, Jr., flew more than 153 missions over North and South Vietnam in seven months. Milton Olive threw his body over a live grenade to save his squad-mates.

Back in the United States, dissent over the Vietnam War was tearing the nation apart. But in Vietnam, many African Americans supported the war. In 1967, African Americans reenlisted at three times the rate of whites. Some reenlisted to avoid high unemployment back home, but others saw Vietnam as a chance to build a career in the integrated military. Still others viewed military service as a patriotic duty.

Such soldiers looked down on African Americans and whites who resisted the draft for whatever reason. The most controversial **conscientious objector** case involved boxer Muhammad Ali.

Muhammad Ali was born Cassius Marcellus Clay in 1942 in Louisville, Kentucky. As a teenager, Clay won the light heavyweight boxing title at the 1960 Olympics. He turned professional and took the world heavyweight championship from Sonny Liston in 1964. That same year, Clay converted to Islam, joined the Nation of Islam, and changed his name to Muhammad Ali.

In 1967, Ali was drafted, but he refused to serve. The war, said Ali, violated his Muslim faith. He said that the real enemy was in U.S. society. Ali's decision cost him a $10,000 fine, a five-year jail sentence, and his boxing title. In 1971, the Supreme Court overturned the conviction, and Ali went on to win the heavyweight title two more times.

In Vietnam, some soldiers criticized Ali's decision. "He gave up being a man when he decided against getting inducted," said one. However, many African Americans applauded Ali's courage. The debate over Ali revealed a widening split among African Americans, and the nation in general, over the war.

Taking Another Look

1. How did African American involvement in Vietnam differ from that in earlier wars?

2. Why did Muhammad Ali refuse to fight in Vietnam?

3. **Critical Thinking** One African American veteran said of his experience in Vietnam, "Why should I come over here when some of the South Vietnamese live better than my people in the world?" Explain.

2 WAR AND PROTEST

▼ Why did many African Americans oppose the Vietnam War in the late 1960s?

In 1967, Martin Luther King, Jr., spoke out to protest the Vietnam War. "The Great Society has been shot down on the battlefields of Vietnam," exclaimed King. "It would be very inconsistent for me to teach and preach nonviolence in this situation [the Civil Rights Movement] and then applaud violence . . . in this war."

Growing Opposition. Leaders of CORE and SNCC joined King in opposing the war. They pointed out that although African Americans made up only about 10 percent of the nation's population, they accounted for 20 percent of the draftees fighting in Vietnam. African Americans there represented only 5 percent of the commanding officers. Moreover, in the first 11 months of 1966 alone, African Americans accounted for nearly 22.4 percent of combat deaths.

Some African Americans used these figures to argue against the war. "I don't trust a black dude who stays in the Army," said one supporter of Black Power. "I don't see why a brother would live with this prejudice for more than two or three years."

The war had other costs for African Americans as well. By 1967, the federal government was spending $24 billion a year on the war. Many African Americans believed that such sums would be better

An integrated artillery unit in Vietnam bombards the enemy. Why did many African Americans turn against the Vietnam war?

spent on improving conditions in the cities. King complained:

> I watched the [Great Society] poverty program broken . . . and I knew that America would never invest the necessary funds or energies in rehabilitation of its poor. So long as adventures like Vietnam continued to draw men and skills and money.

Racial Turmoil Overseas.

According to a Gallup Poll in late 1968, some 70 percent of African Americans on the home front opposed the war. A growing number of African Americans drafted after the 1968 riots opposed it, too. Many of these draftees carried the Black Power movement with them to Vietnam. Local draft boards sometimes unintentionally aided the growth of the Black Power movement among troops in Vietnam. They often drafted African Americans who were active in the Civil Rights Movement as a way of removing them from their communities.

Stirrings of racial discontent soon appeared in Vietnam. Many African Americans wore their hair Afro-style and greeted each other with the Black Power handshake or a closed-fist salute. The gestures silently sent a message of unity.

By late 1968, many African American soldiers preferred to spend their free time apart from white enlistees. They took their passes in the area called Soulsville—the self-segregated section of Saigon, capital of South Vietnam. In "soul kitchens" there, soldiers ate turnip greens, barbecued ribs, chitlins, or other food that reminded them of home, while jukeboxes played Motown songs.

Racial tensions grew. In spring 1968, Staff Sergeant Clide Brown woke up one night to find Confederate flags and burning crosses outside his tent. By 1969, hate-filled racial graffiti written by both African Americans and whites became a common sight. Fights broke out at military bases throughout Vietnam.

Holding Ranks.

The Vietcong tried to take advantage of the racial tensions. Leaflets pinned to bodies read: "Black GIs in the U.S. Army. Twenty million of your fellow countrymen in the U.S.A. are being abused, oppressed, exploited, manhandled, murdered by racist authorities." Radio stations in Hanoi, capital of North Vietnam, boomed out a similar message: Defect to our side.

But the Vietcong plan didn't work. African American GIs refused to buy into the propaganda. "I've seen enough of their brutality," explained one medic, "to know that the V.C. [Vietcong] draws no color line in their killing . . . of American soldiers—black or white." By the end of the 1960s, not a single African American had crossed over to the enemy.

Taking Another Look

1. Why did some civil rights leaders feel African Americans carried an unfair burden in the Vietnam War?

2. What effect did the war have on African Americans at home?

3. **Critical Thinking** Study the table on page 353. What generalizations can you form about African American involvement in the nation's wars?

3 COMING HOME
▼ What difficulties faced African American veterans after Vietnam?

In late summer 1969, John Wilkins was going home. He walked straight off his base and onto a plane, still wearing his raggedy infantry fatigues. Wilkins flew to New Jersey, where he and other returning veterans got new uniforms and any medals they had earned.

Wilkins then took a 30-day leave and headed home to his native Beacon, New York. Everything seemed different now. Wilkins felt out of touch with his once-familiar world.

Moratorium Day. When his leave ended, the Army assigned Wilkins to Fort Meade, Maryland, with the 6th Armored Cavalry. That October, Wilkins pulled riot duty in Washington, D.C. Armed with gas masks, rifles, and bayonets, his unit headed into the nation's capital to stand guard over a peace demonstration. One of the leaders of the march, Coretta Scott King, demanded that President Johnson "bring the boys home and bring them home now."

The march formed part of a nationwide Vietnam Moratorium—a day of reflection and protest over the war. Some protesters spat on the soldiers. Others shook their hands and gave them peace medals. Home little more than a month, Wilkins felt conflicting emotions about the demonstration:

> There I was in Vietnam with weapons turned against one people. Then I come home, and I watch weapons turned against my own people. It was all so confusing. I was angry because I couldn't figure it all out.

The Vietnam Syndrome. A lot of returning veterans felt as Wilkins did. With civil rights leaders and students loudly protesting the war, they grew silent. Yet, privately, they supported the troops still in Vietnam. "I knew what those guys were going through," said Wil-

kins. "Like me, most didn't care about politics. Their thing was getting home—getting home alive."

The silence, the anger, the confusion—some people called this widespread reac-

There were many African Americans among those Americans who wanted the United States to pull out of the Vietnam War. Here they take part in a Moratorium Day protest in 1969 in Washington, D.C.

tion among veterans the Vietnam Syndrome. Many had marched off to war expecting to fight clear-cut battles. Instead, they slogged through steamy jungles and flooded rice paddies searching for an enemy that could easily fade into the general population.

Relatively few GIs fought in hand-to-hand combat with the Vietcong. But some 76 percent came under enemy rocket fire, and about 56 percent were wounded.

Many soldiers expected to return home heroes. They had honored their country's call to duty and had fought to stop the spread of communism. But the country was not yet prepared to honor their sacrifices. Debate raged over the war even after the last United States troops left Vietnam on March 29, 1973.

The Long Process of Healing.
South Vietnam fell to the Communists in 1975. According to a 1980 poll by the Veterans Administration, more than 71 percent of all veterans—African American and white—still expressed pride over their service. But some 82 percent felt their government had let them down by not fighting an all-out war. They also felt let down by the lack of recognition by their country. It took until November 11, 1982, and the dedication of the Vietnam Veterans Memorial in Washington, D.C., for the nation to honor its Vietnam veterans formally.

Public recognition of their service did not solve the problems Vietnam vets faced. Many suffered from depression. Some battled with drug and alcohol abuse. One of the Vietcong's not-so-secret weapons had been a ready supply of cheap drugs to undermine GIs' fighting ability. Unlike the soldiers who fought in World War II, Vietnam vets had a hard time find-

The names of over 58,000 Americans who died in the war are carved on the granite walls of the Vietnam Veterans Memorial in Washington, D.C.

AFRICAN AMERICANS IN U.S. WARS

War (years)	Numbers Who Served	Other Information
American Revolution (1775-1781)	5,000 in the Continental Army	fought in integrated units
Civil War (1861-1865)	386,000 (Union Army)	38,000 died
World War I (1917-1918)	367,000	100,000 served in France
World War II (1941-1945)	1,000,000	6,000 officers; 4,000 women
Vietnam War (1965-1974)	274,937	5,681 killed in combat
Gulf War (1990-1991)	132,300	24.5% of total troops

Source: Figures for the Gulf War from the Directorate of Defense Information, U.S. Secretary of Defense; for other wars, *World Almanac,* 1991

What percentage of those who fought in Vietnam were African American?

ing their own way back into school or the job market.

A Changed Military. Despite the problems many African American veterans faced after the war, their service during the war brought far-reaching changes to the U.S. military. African American enrollment at all the service academies increased. In 1973, 79 African Americans entered West Point, up from the 9 who attended in 1968. In 1973, 46 African American cadets joined the first-year class at the Air Force Academy, compared with none in 1963. Also in 1973, the Naval Academy counted 150 African Americans among its students.

African Americans broke into the top ranks of the military in significant num-

bers, too. In 1969, the army promoted 27 African Americans to colonel. By 1971, the army claimed 12 African American generals. In 1971, the navy made Samuel L. Gravely, Jr., the first African American admiral in U.S. naval history.

The scope of these changes became clear when the nation entered its next major war, against Iraq in 1991. At that time, the highest position in the nation's armed forces, Chairman of the Joint Chiefs of Staff, was held by General Colin Powell, an African American.

Taking Another Look

1. What difficulties did African American veterans face when they came home?

2. How did African American service in Vietnam reshape the United States military?

3. **Critical Thinking** Some African Americans have said Vietnam was the second front of the war for civil rights. Do you agree? Explain.

LOOKING AHEAD

African Americans have performed military service for their nation since the American Revolution. But the African Americans who came home from Vietnam arrived in the midst of a civil rights revolution. "I don't know whether I would march if I became a civilian again," one soldier said in 1967. "But nobody is going to shove me around." This was the attitude that many African American veterans brought home with them. Together with the civil rights leaders of the 1960s, they helped produce a new United States— one that would never again be the same for African Americans or whites.

FOCUS On

REMEMBERING VIETNAM

> *When we got to the memorial, I grabbed his hand. Like brothers do. . . . We looked for one name on the memorial. Louis. We found it, and I called his mother. I told her it was nice, and she said she might be able to come see it one day.*

This is how one African American ex-soldier described his reaction to visiting "the Wall"—the Vietnam Veterans Memorial in Washington, D.C.

Like the war itself, the Vietnam Veterans Memorial generated controversy. First, people argued over its funding, and then they argued over its design. In the end, some 650,000 people contributed to the cost of creating the Wall, which was designed by Asian American Maya Ying Lin.

Lin's design was selected from among many submitted in a contest. Some thought her plan for a black granite wall was too stark, too cold. However, the memorial committee foresaw that the Wall—with the names of the more than 58,000 who died in Vietnam inscribed on it—would be a powerful monument.

Over 5,600 African Americans were killed in Vietnam. Their names are among those inscribed on the Wall. Many who visit the Wall find a chance to remember and to heal.

CLOSE UP: Chapter 32

The Who, What, Where of History

1. **Who** were the Vietcong?
2. **Where** was Soulsville?
3. **Where** is Hanoi?
4. **Who** is Muhammad Ali?
5. **Who** is Samuel L. Gravely, Jr.?
6. **Who** is Colin Powell?

Making the Connection

1. What was the connection between government spending on the Vietnam War and Great Society programs?
2. What was the connection between public protests over the Vietnam War and problems that many Vietnam veterans experienced after the war?

Time Check

1. In what years did the Korean War take place?
2. When did the first U.S. combat troops arrive in Vietnam?
3. In what year did South Vietnam fall to the Communists?
4. When was the Vietnam Veterans Memorial dedicated?

What Would You Have Done?

1. If you had been alive during the Vietnam years, would you have supported the U.S. government's actions in Vietnam, or would you have joined the protesters against the war? Explain.
2. If you had been a 19-year-old African American in 1967, would you have enlisted in the army? Explain.

Thinking and Writing About History

Imagine it is the year 1967. Write a newspaper editorial either supporting or criticizing Muhammad Ali's refusal to fight in the Vietnam War.

Building Skills: Interpreting a Newspaper Article

On a day-to-day basis, newspaper articles and radio and television newscasts and news bulletins provide most of us with all we know about current events. Newspaper articles provide a great supply of primary source material for the historian. However, there are a few things to keep in mind when you refer to newspaper material. Most newspaper reporters write to a strict style. They stick to the basic facts of the story without analyzing them, comparing the story to events of the past, interpreting the story, or stating an opinion about it.

Read the following article that appeared on the front page of the *New York Times* on April 6, 1968. Then answer the questions that follow.

Khesanh, South Vietnam—The 76-day North Vietnamese siege of the Marine base at Khesanh was officially declared lifted today.

United States marines and helicopter-borne Army troops today pushed toward what was described as North Vietnamese regimental headquarters south of the base.

The 20,000-man relief column reached the base and then fanned out on three sides in search of the vanishing enemy soldiers. Army helicopter units entered the base.

The sweep could take the Americans all the way to the Laotian border, less than 10 miles away, in the effort to root out the 7,000 men said to remain in the enemy force once estimated at 20,000. North Vietnam uses Laos as a staging area for attacks along South Vietnam's borders.

The United States command said that helicopter gunships of the First Cavalry Division (Airmobile), criss-crossing the skies ahead of the ground troops, killed 50 North Vietnamese late yesterday near the town of Khesanh, which is two miles south of the base.

Earlier, United States troops fought about 150 enemy soldiers four miles east of the town. Nine enemy soldiers and one American were reported killed.

1. Write one sentence explaining what the article says happened at Khesanh on April 6, 1968.

2. What does the reporter presume the reader already knows about the conflict in Vietnam?

3. Does the article tell you anything about the opinions of the journalist who wrote it? Explain.

4. a. What is one source for some of the information contained in the article?
   b. Might that source be biased in any way? Explain.

5. What would you like to know about the siege at Khesanh that is not in the article?

355

UNIT 10

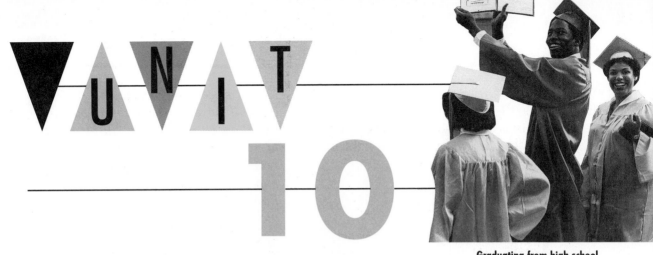

Graduating from high school

CROSSCURRENTS IN TODAY'S WORLD

(1972–Present)

Mural painted as part of an antigang violence program, Philadelphia

An African American Speaks

If America's role was to lead the world toward peace and international understanding, Negro Americans had a special function to perform in carrying forward the struggle for freedom at home, for the sake of America's role, and abroad, for the sake of the survival of the world.

—John Hope Franklin and Alfred A. Moss, Jr.
Historians

Unit 10 traces developments in the United States during the 1970s and 1980s and into the last decade of the 20th century. The Civil Rights Movement of the 1950s and 1960s left the United States permanently changed. No longer would African Americans be required to eat in separate restaurants, sleep in separate hotels, or ride in separate sections of buses and trains.

Even more important, African Americans would no longer be prevented from voting. With the right to vote came the power to elect public officials. By 1991, there were 27 African American members of Congress. African Americans served as the mayors of 30 U.S. cities, including the three largest, New York, Los Angeles, and Chicago. For the first time, an African American had been elected governor of a state. Thousands of other African Americans had been elected to offices in state and local governments.

Gradually, some barriers fell in the world of work. In business after business, industry after industry, African Americans held jobs that once only white people would have held. To qualify for these jobs, increasing numbers of African Americans were graduating from high school, college, and professional schools.

Changing Attitudes Toward Civil Rights. As the 1960s gave way to the 1970s, there were disagreements about what the federal government should or should not do in the area of civil rights. Most African Americans and many whites felt that more government action needed to be taken, particularly in the cities, where many African Americans lived. Some whites, however, came to feel that the Civil Rights Movement had gone far enough. Government, they thought, had other matters to attend to.

This reaction against the Civil Rights Movement was partly due to the turmoil of the 1960s. The Vietnam War, the demonstrations against it, and the riots in the cities combined in many people's minds to form a picture of a society that was coming apart. To many of those who thought this way, the Civil Rights Movement was part of the turmoil. They saw the federal government as a captive of radical elements. They felt that quiet, law-abiding people like themselves had been forgotten.

The Nixon Years. In his 1968 campaign, Richard Nixon, a Republican, appealed to those people who disliked the way society was developing but were not inclined to raise their voices in disagreement. Nixon called them the Silent Majority. He talked also of a "New Federalism," which would return power in many areas of government to state and local levels, and thus to the people.

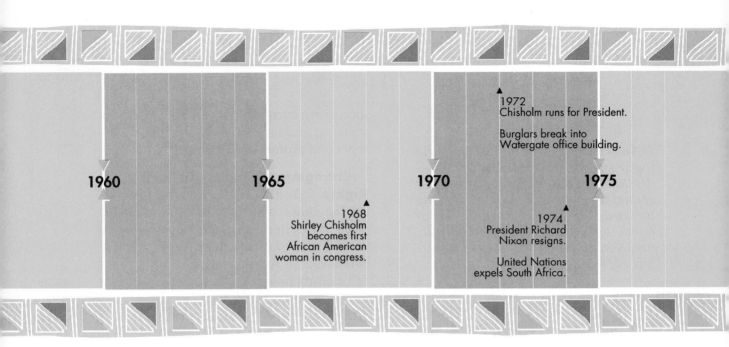

1972
Chisholm runs for President.

Burglars break into
Watergate office building.

1960   1965   1970   1975

1968
Shirley Chisholm
becomes first
African American
woman in congress.

1974
President Richard
Nixon resigns.

United Nations
expels South Africa.

Some of the steps taken by Nixon had the result of slowing down progress on civil rights. For example, he kept government officials from taking action against school districts that had not desegregated. He also cut back on the money for some of Johnson's Great Society programs. Other programs he turned over to the states, which could continue them or not. Much of his influence, however, came through the strong statements he issued against war protesters, rioters, and others.

Despite Nixon's intentions, the power of the federal government increased while he was President. Although he began to change the way people thought about the federal government, he did not really change what the government did.

In 1973 and 1974, a series of investigations by Congress revealed that many of Nixon's associates had been involved in planning and then in covering up a break-in at the Democratic National Committee office, during the 1972 election campaign. Nixon had been involved in the cover-up. As a result of the Watergate scandal, named for the building where the burglary occurred, Richard Nixon resigned from the presidency in 1974.

Nixon was succeeded by Gerald Ford, who continued Nixon's policies. From 1977 to 1981, Jimmy Carter, a Democrat, was President. Carter was more sympathetic to African American goals of equal rights than Nixon, but his presidency was largely taken up with economic problems and foreign affairs.

Changes in the Supreme Court. One of Nixon's campaign promises had been to change the Supreme Court. To many in the Silent Majority, it seemed that over the years the Court had favored the poor, the nonwhite, and disadvantaged over middle-class people like themselves. Nixon promised to appoint people to the Court whose views were more rep-

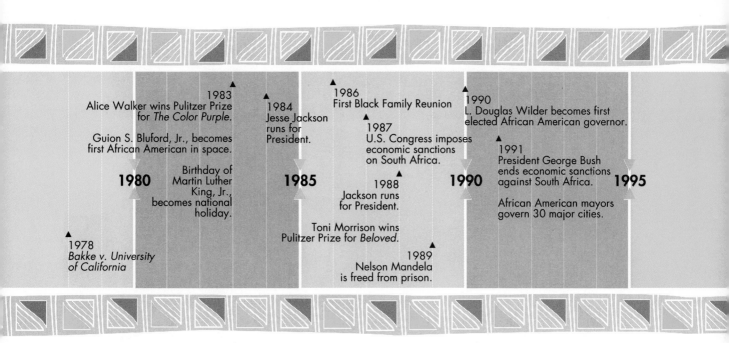

1983
Alice Walker wins Pulitzer Prize for *The Color Purple*.

Guion S. Bluford, Jr., becomes first African American in space.

Birthday of Martin Luther King, Jr., becomes national holiday.

1980

1978
Bakke v. University of California

1984
Jesse Jackson runs for President.

1985

Toni Morrison wins Pulitzer Prize for *Beloved*.

1986
First Black Family Reunion

1987
U.S. Congress imposes economic sanctions on South Africa.

1988
Jackson runs for President.

1989
Nelson Mandela is freed from prison.

1990
L. Douglas Wilder becomes first elected African American governor.

1991
President George Bush ends economic sanctions against South Africa.

African American mayors govern 30 major cities.

1990

1995

resentative of the "Silent Majority."

By the time Nixon left office, he had appointed four of the nine members of the Supreme Court. As a result, the Court's decisions in some types of cases began to change. Its decision in *Bakke* v. *University of California,* in 1978, is an example.

The Bakke case had to do with **affirmative action**, which means giving preference in hiring and similar situations to groups who have suffered in the past from discrimination. Bakke, a white man, sued the University of California because of reverse discrimination. He claimed he had been kept out of medical school in order to admit a less well qualified African American man. In its decision, the court upheld the principle of affirmative action. At the same time, though, it issued new and more limited guidelines for applying the principle in the future. Even so, thousands of people, not only African Americans, were able to find employment because of the policy of affirmative action.

Economic Downturn. Meanwhile, a series of events made jobs, with or without affirmative action, harder to find for all Americans. In 1973 and again in 1979, developments in the Middle East caused sharp rises in the cost of petroleum. The resulting increased costs of gasoline, diesel fuel, and heating oil speeded up **inflation**. Inflation is a general increase in prices over a period of time. At the same time, foreign industries, particularly in Germany and Japan, were becoming strong competitors with U.S. industries in world markets.

The result was a **recession**, or decline in production and employment. Plants closed, people lost their jobs, and greater competition existed for the jobs that there were. African Americans of both sexes, as well as white women, were now seeking jobs that once had been held mainly by white males. Meanwhile, Hispanic immigrants, who were entering the United States in large numbers, competed for

359

Robots are used in automobile and truck assembly plants like this one in Tennessee. What effect do you think the use of robots has on the employment of factory workers?

those jobs that required less education and training. But fewer such jobs were available as the economy shifted from factory to service-related industries. The result was increasing unemployment among African Americans, particularly teenagers and men in large cities. By the late 1970s, the number of African Americans living below the **poverty level** had increased significantly.

The Reagan Years. Ronald Reagan, a former movie actor and a past governor of California, was elected President in 1980. Reagan, a Republican, promised in his campaign to make major changes in the government. Because of his great popularity and the resulting influence on

Congress, he was able to bring about many of those changes.

One of Reagan's major goals was to cut both taxes and government spending. Cutting taxes turned out to be easier than cutting spending. Tax reductions under Reagan cut the income of the federal government significantly. However, steep increases in the military budget caused spending to go up so much that the government had to borrow billions of dollars to pay its bills. At the same time, the cuts in federal spending for social programs reduced the benefits available to the poor and the ill, and particularly to children in these groups. Many African Americans were affected by these policies.

Meanwhile, life improved for the middle class, including a large number of middle-class African Americans. Inflation was brought under control, and in many industries, the number of jobs increased. But the benefits of society were by no means evenly distributed.

The Reverend Jesse Jackson kept the issues of social, political, and economic inequities before the public with his 1984 and 1988 presidential campaigns. Jackson was an African American minister from Chicago, who had earlier worked with Martin Luther King, Jr. As a presidential candidate in 1984 and again in 1988, he spoke of a **Rainbow Coalition**—people of all colors working together for the good of all people.

In both years, Jackson won enough votes in primary elections across the country to be a major force at the Democratic party's national convention. Although he failed to win his party's nomination, his candidacies kept alive issues that might otherwise have been overlooked, such as the needs of the cities, nonwhites, farmers, and the unemployed.

I Have a Dream. In some ways, the dream held out by Martin Luther King in 1963 has come true. Today, African Americans can be found in every walk of life—as doctors, nurses, lawyers, teachers, business executives, scientists, astronauts, and so on. In 1991, when the United States fought the Persian Gulf War, African American and white soldiers were led by African American General Colin Powell, Chairman of the Joint Chiefs of Staff.

Yet, in some ways, the dream remains sadly unfulfilled. Cities teem with tension. Too few African Americans sit in the top offices of major corporations. Too many teenagers drop out of school and are unemployable. The nation has yet to see an African American President or Vice-

These soldiers are putting on protective suits in anticipation of germ warfare in the 1991 Persian Gulf War.

President. To be sure, much remains to be done before all African Americans achieve Martin Luther King's dream. Still, all Americans can take pride in the achievements of African Americans today.

Taking Another Look

1. What policies did Richard Nixon adopt to appeal to the Silent Majority?

2. How did changes in the U.S. economy affect African Americans in the 1970s?

3. **a.** Why did Jesse Jackson call his movement the Rainbow Coalition?
   b. In what important way did his ideas differ from Ronald Reagan's?

4. **Critical Thinking** List two policies important to African Americans that you think should be part of a presidential candidate's platform in the next election. Explain.

Civil Rights Memorial, Montgomery, Alabama

Agenda for Change

(1972—Present)

THINKING ABOUT THE CHAPTER

What are some of the biggest challenges facing African Americans in the 1990s?

In May 1991, 51-year-old John Lewis strolled through the parking lot of the Greyhound Bus Station in Montgomery, Alabama. Lewis, the son of an Alabama sharecropper, was now a U.S. Representative from Georgia. He paused as memories flooded back. "Some of us almost died here 30 years ago," he told a reporter. "I saw men and women carrying baseball bats, chains. It was not a pleasant sight."

Lewis was one of the former freedom riders who returned to Montgomery to celebrate the 30th anniversary of the freedom rides. Reverend Joseph Lowery, the 67-year-old president of the SCLC, joined Lewis. So did James Farmer, the 71-year-old founder of CORE and the person who started the rides. The three civil rights veterans proudly recalled their struggle.

Said Lewis, "To come back all these years later, it's good to see whites and blacks boarding the bus together."

Lewis grew silent as he stopped by the national Civil Rights Memorial in the center of Montgomery. The black stone monument carries the names of those who died during the movement.

But the former freedom riders did more than remember the past. At a series of meetings called "A Look Back—A Leap Forward," they set an agenda for change. Topics included "The Role of Economics in the Struggle for Equality," "Rebuilding Our Extended Family," "A Call to Save Our Children," and "Direct Action 30 Years Later."

1 AFRICAN AMERICANS TODAY

▼ How has life changed for African Americans since the Civil Rights Movement?

African Americans are returning South. So said the 1990 Census. For the first time in this century, the percentage of all African Americans living in the South had increased. Since 1980, over 100,000 more African Americans headed into the South than left it. Some experts predict that this trend will continue throughout the 1990s. This is part of the **demographics**, or population statistics, that help describe the African American people today. Other demographics are shown on pages 364–365.

A Changing South. In 1990, African Americans accounted for 12.1 percent of the population. Nearly 56 percent of them lived in the South, up from 52 percent in 1980. Today, many African Americans find that the South has fewer barriers based on skin color than does the North.

Andrew Young, an African American who is a former mayor of Atlanta, Georgia, credits this change to gains made during the Civil Rights Movement. Says Young: "We dealt with race overtly [openly]. I don't think they had to in the North. I mean, we really had to *struggle*."

Statistics seem to support Young. As the 1990s began, more than two-thirds of all African American elected officials— 67.5 percent—were found in the South. This change reflects the far-reaching effects of the voter registration drives of the 1960s. Today, African Americans can freely vote in a region where racism once kept nearly 97 percent of African Americans off the voting rolls.

Today, almost half of all African Americans in the South own their own homes, compared to only 31 percent in the Northeast. Still, as in the rest of the nation, there exist wide economic gaps between African Americans and whites. In 1988, African American families in the South earned an average annual income of $17,545, compared to $31,475 for whites. Also, in 1990, some 25 percent of African American students in the South attended schools that were more than 90 percent African American. But the percentage was twice as high for African American students in the Northeast.

The African American Population

		Percent of Total
Total U.S. Population	248,709,873	
African American Population	29,986,060	12

Source: U.S. Department of Commerce, Bureau of the Census, from the 1990 Census of Population and Housing

Income of African Americans

Family* Income (yearly)	Percent
Under $10,000	25.4
$10,000–24,999	32.1
$25,000 and over	41.9

Median Family Income: $20,209/Year

*Family is defined as two or more persons related by blood, marriage, or adoption.

Source: U.S. Department of Commerce, Bureau of the Census, "Money Income and Poverty Status in the United States, 1989," *Current Population Report*

Leading African American Businesses

Business	Percent
Auto Dealers	37.07
Food/Beverage	30.48
Media	6.40
Manufacturing	5.67
Computer/Office Supplies	5.43
Construction	4.94
Health and Beauty Aids	2.53
Entertainment	2.20
Transportation	1.60
Telecommunications	1.35

Source: "1990 Black Enterprise 100s Companies by Industry," *Black Enterprise*, Copyright June 1991, The Earl G. Graves Publishing Co., Inc., 130 Fifth Avenue, New York, NY 10011. All rights reserved. (Ranking based on millions of dollars to the nearest thousand; prepared by BE Research; reviewed by Mitchell/Titus & Co.)

Regional Distribution of African Americans

Region	Percent
South	55.9
Midwest	19.1
Northeast	16.5
West	8.5

Source: U.S. Department of Commerce, Bureau of the Census, "Black Population, by Region: 1988," *The Black Population of the United States,* March 1988, p. 3

Ages of African Americans

Age	Percent
under 25	39.6
25–49	39.5
50–74	17.4
75 and over	3.5

Source: U.S. Department of Commerce, Bureau of the Census, "Projections of the Population of the United States, Age, Sex, Race, 1988-2080" (P-25 #1018), *1991 Current Population Survey*

Education of African Americans*

Education Completed	Young Adults	Percent
1–3 Years High School	444,000	16.4
High School Graduate	1,279,000	47.4
1–3 Years College	573,000	21.2
4 Years College	254,000	9.4
5 or More Years College	78,000	2.9

*25–29 year olds in 1988

Source: U.S. Department of Education, "Years of School Completed, Aged 18 and Over by Age, Sex, Race, Ethnicity: 1988" in *1990 Digest of Education Statistics* (based on 1988 *Current Population Survey*, Bureau of the Census)

Occupations of African Americans*

Occupation	Percent Total	Percent Men	Percent Women
Managerial and Professional Specialty	16.1	13.4	18.8
Technical, Sales, and Administrative Support	28.9	18.5	39.2
Service Occupations	22.9	18.6	27.2
Precision Production, Craft, and Repair	9.0	15.8	2.3
Operators, Fabricators, and Laborers	21.7	31.1	12.4
Farming, Forestry, and Fishing	1.4	2.6	.2

*Employed, 16 years and older

Source: U.S. Department of Labor, Bureau of Labor Statistics, *Employment and Earnings,* vol. 38, No. 1, Jan. 1991, p. 38

As the U.S. economy has changed, more office jobs have been created, opening up new careers.

Nationwide: Gains and Lingering Problems. The Civil Rights Movement made tremendous progress possible for African Americans throughout the nation. Since 1970, the number of African American households earning over $50,000 more than doubled. The number of African American college graduates soared from 281,000 in 1960 to more than 2 million in the early 1990s. The drop-out rate among African American high school students fell from 31 percent in 1970 to 18 percent in 1988.

But troubles still persist. African Americans as a whole earn only about 59 cents for every dollar earned by whites. A larger percentage of African Americans also fall below the poverty level. In 1990, 33.1 percent of African American households earned less than $10,000 a year, compared to 13.6 percent of white households.

In addition to an income gap, a "health gap" exists between African Americans and whites. "Economics is definitely a factor," said Dr. Neil Shulman, an expert on minority health care. "[It affects] access to care, access to medication, access to preventive services." An African American child born in 1989 could expect to live 69.7 years. A white child born that same year might expect to live 79.9 years.

These are some of the disturbing figures that have helped African Americans chart a course of action for the future. In the 1950s and 1960s, African Americans battled for political equality. Today, they are fighting for economic equality and equal access to the American dream.

Taking Another Look

1. How has the size of the African American population in the South changed since the Civil Rights Movement?

2. What advances in education have African Americans made since the 1960s?

3. **Critical Thinking** Based on the tables on pages 364–365, what generalizations can you form about African Americans today?

2 OVERCOMING ECONOMIC BARRIERS

What economic difficulties did African Americans face in the post–civil rights era?

"A lot of people like to talk about "post civil rights," commented the Reverend Joseph Lowery at the 1991 reunion of freedom riders. "We won some important battles," Lowery conceded, "but the war never did end, particularly in the economic area. We won the right to check into the Hyatts and the Hiltons [hotels].

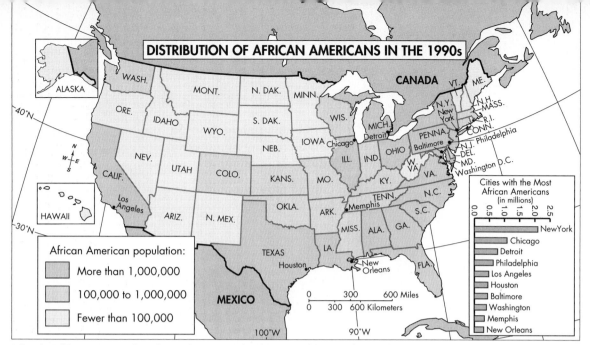

DISTRIBUTION OF AFRICAN AMERICANS IN THE 1990s

African American population:
- More than 1,000,000
- 100,000 to 1,000,000
- Fewer than 100,000

Cities with the Most African Americans (in millions)
- New York
- Chicago
- Detroit
- Philadelphia
- Los Angeles
- Houston
- Baltimore
- Washington
- Memphis
- New Orleans

What do California, New York, and Texas have in common? How do Idaho and Illinois differ?

But too few of us have the means [money] for checking out."

The Civil Rights Movement opened most occupations to African Americans. But it did not end economic inequalities. Wages for African Americans still lag behind those for whites, while unemployment runs ahead. Even college-educated African Americans earn 85 percent of what their white counterparts earn. Those without a college education can expect to work at low-paying jobs in far greater numbers than whites with similar schooling. As one African American surgeon put it, "being black in America is harder than being white."

Pockets of Rural Poverty. When Senator Robert Kennedy visited the Mississippi Delta region in 1967, he exclaimed: "My God! I didn't know this kind of thing existed. How can a country like this allow it?"

Kennedy was talking about the rural poor—the mostly African American farm workers who lived in the Deep South. Many teetered on the edge of starvation.

They lived in tin-roofed shacks without heat or indoor plumbing. They were former sharecroppers put out of work by huge farm machines.

A quarter-century after Kennedy's visit, conditions for the rural poor remained grim. By the mid-1980s, only about 148,000 out of 28 million African Americans worked at farming. Of this number, 99 percent lived in the South. Most small-scale independent African American farmers barely scratched out a living. Sharecroppers rarely had work.

By 1991, unemployment among African Americans—and poor whites—in rural Mississippi towns such as Tunica, Jonesville, and Greenwood neared 20 percent. "I do not think this area has the capability of righting what is wrong on its own," said an editor in Greenwood. "There is too much poverty, too few jobs, too little education."

The Urban Underclass. An equally bleak future faced African Americans living in cities outside the South. In the 1980s, some ghetto dwellers returned to

367

Job applicants, including many African Americans, wait in line to take a test for the federal civil service. The civil service is now one of the major employers of African Americans.

hometowns in the South, creating what one Greenwood official called "inner rural cities." But most remained trapped in decaying projects and tenements in run-down sections of cities, such as New York's South Bronx or East Harlem and Chicago's Southside.

The flight of middle-class white families into the suburbs in the last half of the 20th century left many cities impoverished. City governments lost taxes. Urban businesses lost people with incomes to support them. In ghettoes, housing decayed further and conditions worsened.

African American families who could fight their way out of the ghettoes moved, too. African Americans who remained behind formed part of an underclass of urban poor. Douglas Glasgow defined this group in his 1981 book *The Black Underclass*. He described the underclass as "a permanently entrapped population of poor persons, unused and unwanted, . . . unemployed, welfare dependent, and without sufficient income to secure a decent quality of life."

The conditions that created an underclass, argued Glasgow, also created the potential for violence and crime. Drug and alcohol abuse, random violence, poverty, and teenage pregnancy increased among whites and other groups as well in the 1970s and 1980s. But the burden of poverty and fear fell heaviest on African American youth.

Growing Up in the Towers. In November 1990, a 20-year-old African American named Bernard Richardson went out into his Harlem neighborhood to get a late-night snack. Two of his friends walked with him. One wore a black sheepskin coat. An African American teenager approached the trio and demanded the coat. When the young men refused, the teenager pulled a gun and fired. A bullet hit Richardson in the back and killed him.

Such scenes have become all too common in U.S. cities. Richardson, like his two friends, grew up in a public housing project called Martin Luther King, Jr. Towers. The ten rust-colored buildings

368

cover three city blocks and house some 3,600 people.

The Towers are similar to other projects in other large cities across the nation. Most people in the Towers are working-class men and women. Only about one third of the families receive welfare. Most moved into the low-rent housing so that they could save money to move up into the middle class. That was the dream held out by city planners when they first built the Towers in the 1950s. Some African Americans realized the dream. Others did not. Many fell victim to government cutbacks and economic recessions in the 1970s and 1980s.

Today, drug dealers, crack addicts, and unemployed teenagers wander the streets around the Towers. Parents often send their children to school with the warning "Be safe." But children face tremendous pressure on the streets. With unemployment running as high as 50 percent among African American youth, some teenagers deal drugs to earn fast money. Others use drugs to escape misery. But a drug habit often leads to crime and more misery.

Teenagers in the Towers and surrounding tenements often experience parenthood all too soon. Some girls have their first babies as early as age 13 or 14, fathered by boys the same age. They seldom marry, and the young single mothers try to juggle child-raising with homework. Many never finish school at all. They often become single heads of households—the most poverty-stricken group in the underclass.

Making It. "Raising a family, especially in this project, is not easy," said Ernest Youngblood to a reporter for the *New York Times* in 1991. "You have to

Why is education so important in today's economy?

stay on your kids all the time. If you let up, they're gone astray."

But Youngblood, an auto mechanic, and his wife, a nurse's aide, are successfully raising four children in the Towers. The Youngbloods' 18-year-old daughter Schwanna attends Manhattan's John Jay College. Schwanna has lost friends to drugs and seen 13-year-old neighbors bear children. But Schwanna plans to become a corporate lawyer. Her 17-year-old boyfriend also dreams of law school.

The news about the crime and poverty of the cities masks some good news concerning African Americans. The high school drop-out rate has declined among African Americans since 1970. In 1991, about 86.2 percent of African Americans who entered high school graduated— about the same as the 87.6 percent of whites who graduated.

The young people who have come of age in the decades since the Civil Rights Movement have a chance to realize the dreams of their parents. Many hope to join the African American middle class—a group that has steadily grown since the

1960s. Today, some 25 percent of African American families earn between $25,000 and $49,000. Nearly 11 percent earn between $50,000 and $99,000.

African American middle-class parents, like white middle-class parents, inspire their children to reach for success, too. But some leaders worry about the wide gap between middle-class and poor African Americans. "The middle-class blacks of the future," concluded one government report, "may feel little in common with poor blacks because their experiences will have been so dramatically different in so many ways."

How do middle-class African Americans react to such reports? Many agree with an African American social worker who said, "Those of us who have made it must come back and give back to the community." Giving back, for many African Americans, means helping the youth and rebuilding the family—two traditional sources of hope and strength for African Americans over the centuries.

Taking Another Look

1. What economic gaps exist between African Americans and whites?

2. What factors have contributed to the decay of the nation's cities?

3. **Critical Thinking** Imagine you are a U.S. Representative in Congress. What proposals would you submit for easing poverty in the African American underclass? Explain your reasons for each proposal.

3 LENDING A HELPING HAND

▼ How are African Americans continuing a tradition of self-help?

In the early morning hours, most people in Harlem are asleep. But Clara McBride Hale walks back and forth across a darkened bedroom. She cradles a sobbing infant in her arms. The baby, only a few weeks old, is withdrawing from drugs taken by its mother during pregnancy. The painful process will last from 12 to 18 months. The woman known as Mother Hale has helped hundreds of such infants to health.

Clara Hale was 63 when she took in her first drug-addicted baby in 1969. Within months, she had 22 drug-addicted babies in her five-room apartment. Her three children worked to raise money to help care for the infants. In recalling these first babies, Hale said, "We would hold them

Clara McBride Hale, known as Mother Hale, cradles an infant. Why has she been honored?

and rock them. They love you to tell them how great they are." Hale's love helped all 22 recover. Hale's love also convinced the babies' mothers to enter drug rehabilitation programs. She thus opened the door to reuniting drug-free mothers and their children.

In the early 1970s, New York City began funding Hale's work. Private donations from people such as former Beatle John Lennon helped buy what became known as Hale House. Hale's daughter Lorraine earned a degree in medicine and took over administration of the project. But her mother remained the program's heart and soul.

In 1985, President Reagan honored Mother Hale in his State of the Union address. He called her "an American hero." Clara and Lorraine Hale continue their work today in New York City. They are an inspiring example of how African Americans are seeking to solve difficult problems themselves.

Strengthening the Family. In 1986, Dorothy I. Height, president of the National Council of Negro Women (NCNW), watched a TV program about African American families. It painted a picture of despair—teenage pregnancies, high unemployment, poor households headed by women. Height decided to show the nation another side of African American life. That year, she organized the first Black Family Reunion—a festival that drew over 200,000 people to the Mall in Washington, D.C. Height said of that first reunion,

> One of the things I hoped the Black Family Reunion Celebration would do is to stimulate the sense that we're an African American people, and that we are not alone, no matter how isolated.

The event triggered a movement to celebrate the bonds of kinship among all African American people. In 1990, the festival traveled to six cities and drew more than a million people. The festival emphasized self-help and African American pride. Teenagers could visit booths to get tips on applying to college or to learn how to make an African mask. Some of the most successful African Americans in each city rubbed elbows with some of the most disadvantaged.

The festival, which has been an annual event since 1986, inspires what Height calls "our African tradition . . . of sharing." It was kinship that helped African Americans survive slavery, says Height. She believes it is kinship that will help them solve their problems today.

A Tradition of Self-Help. Individuals such as Hale and Height are part of a long tradition of self-help among African Americans. As Earl G. Graves, editor of *Black Enterprise*, explained:

> One of the untold stories of the black American community has been its history of generosity. Kind words and healing hands from our families, neighbors, and the clergy have always embraced us in times of sorrow or need.

Today, as more and more African Americans are entering the middle class or becoming successful entrepreneurs, they are continuing this tradition. Entertainer Bill Cosby and Camille Cosby, his wife, have donated millions of dollars to such African American colleges and universities as Fisk and Spelman. Mel Blount, former star of the Pittsburgh Steelers, has set up several farms to help troubled children. Vincent Lane put aside a multi-million-dollar real estate career to become head of the Chicago Housing Authority (CHA).

Vincent Lane's family moved to Chicago from Mississippi when he was an infant. As a child, he watched his neighborhood become a crime-ridden ghetto ruled by street gangs. Lane's family escaped the city, but Lane never forgot where he came from. Since he took over the CHA in 1988, Lane has used his considerable energy and talents to make the grim housing projects on Chicago's South and West sides livable. His work earned him a place in *U.S. News and World Report's* 1991 list of "The Best of America."

African American Churches. Many African Americans who want to save youth in the nation's cities are turning to one of their oldest resources—the African American church. Explained the Reverend Alicia Byrd of the Congress of National Black Churches, "If you want to deal effectively with the black community, you have to deal with the churches."

Across the nation, African American churches are reaching out to the community. "We've been watching the neighborhood crumble all around us. We couldn't stand by and do nothing," said Linda Perkins of Detroit's Greater Christ Baptist Church.

Because education is often the ticket out of the ghetto, many African American churches have begun teaching the children. "Reach one, teach one, we'll make a difference." That's how the Reverend Willie Gable describes the educational programs offered by his New Orleans Progressive Baptist Church.

With the help of donations from individuals, foundations, and some government agencies, African American churches are offering a whole range of educational services. They provide tutorial programs, computer-literacy projects, science learning centers, and much more. The success of these programs was perhaps best described by 10-year-old Michael Dameron as he rushed into a church school in Chicago. "I can't wait to get to school," he told a reporter, "so I can get A's." So far, the church schools are also receiving A's from many of the nation's top educators.

Taking Another Look

1. How have African Americans reached out to children in the cities?

2. Why have African Americans such as Dorothy Height emphasized kinship ties so strongly?

3. **Critical Thinking** Why have African Americans traditionally looked to their churches for help?

LOOKING AHEAD

The Civil Rights Movement inspired African Americans to take charge of their lives—to make a difference. In the closing years of this century, African Americans have been crossing new frontiers. These pioneers are changing the face of the nation—introducing more and more African American culture and influence into mainstream U.S. society.

African American churches continue their historic involvement in self-help efforts such as this after-school education program in Chicago (top) and a community outreach program in New York City (bottom).

CLOSE-UP: Chapter 33

"I want to go someplace different. I want to go to a prestigious black college," one high school senior said recently. Many talented African American students today are choosing African American colleges over Ivy League schools. In the late 1980s, Virginia's Hampton Institute received more than 8,300 applications for 900 slots in the freshman class—a ratio that rivals that of Dartmouth.

Students are drawn to African American universities like historic Bethune-Cookman, Fisk University, Howard University, and Spelman College, the first African American women's college, because of their vitality, distinguished heritage, and academic traditions.

Students study for undergraduate or advanced degrees at schools like Clark College in Atlanta, Georgia; Meharry Medical College in Nashville, Tennessee; and Xavier University of Louisiana in New Orleans. Grambling State University in Louisiana was originally patterned on the Tuskegee Institute model. Today, it not only provides extensive educational opportunities, but has also produced more professional football players than any other African American university in the nation.

The Who, What, Where of History

1. **What** was the Silent Majority?
2. **What** was *Bakke* v. *University of California?*
3. **What** is affirmative action?
4. **What** is inflation?
5. **Who** is Jesse Jackson?
6. **Who** is Joseph Lowery?
7. **Where** is the Civil Rights Memorial?
8. **What** are demographics?
9. **What** is a health gap?
10. **What** actions by Mother Hale continued African American traditions of self-help?
11. **What** is the Black Family Reunion celebration?

Making the Connection

1. What was the connection between the Civil Rights Movement of the 1960s and the increase in the percentage of African Americans living in the South?
2. Explain the connection between the "income gap" and the "health gap."
3. What is the connection between the flight of white families to the suburbs and the growing financial difficulties of big cities?

Time Check

1. When did Jesse Jackson first run for President?
2. In what year did the first Black Family Reunion take place?
3. When was the 30th anniversary of the freedom rides?

What Would You Have Done?

1. Imagine that you are an African American adult who can afford to take a year off. If you wanted to spend the year being useful to other African Americans, what would you choose to do? Explain your choice, and tell how you would go about doing it.

2. Suppose that you are on a committee in charge of setting up a booth at a Black Family Reunion. What do you think the booth should offer to the people at the reunion? Explain the purpose behind your idea and tell how you think the booth could be set up.

Thinking and Writing About History

1. Write a letter to an African American friend who lives in another part of the country. Suggest either (a) that you think your friend should move to where you live, or (b) that you are thinking of moving to where your friend lives. Compare the good and bad aspects of each area, and give reasons for your preference.

2. Write a magazine article titled "The Role of Economics in the Struggle for Equality." Tell what the present situation is. Give examples. Then give your ideas on how the situation might be improved.

3. An organization that you belong to is giving its "Woman of the Year" award to Mother Hale. You have been selected to present the award. Write a brief speech that tells the audience what Mother Hale has done and what that means to you.

Building Skills: Comparing and Contrasting

Often when you are asked to write for a class or on a test, you must compare and contrast. In other words, you have to demonstrate the similarities and differences between two subjects. One technique that will help you organize information for a compare-and-contrast essay is a Venn diagram. A Venn diagram has two intersecting circles. You write things that your subjects have in common in the overlapping section, and you put the differences in the outer sections.

Look at the Venn diagram below. The writer has started to organize facts that compare the situation of African Americans in the North and in the South after the 1960s. Use information from the text to complete the diagram on a separate piece of paper. Add facts about family life, politics and government, business and employment, housing, education, self-help, and major social problems.

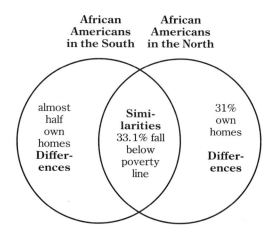

African Americans in the South — African Americans in the North

almost half own homes
Differences

Similarities
33.1% fall below poverty line

31% own homes
Differences

Astronaut Guion S. Bluford, Jr.

Crossing New Frontiers

(1972–Present)

THINKING ABOUT THE CHAPTER

How have African Americans helped remake the culture of the United States in the last part of the 20th century?

In 1967, the weekly TV show "Star Trek" blazed across the nation's television screens. The crew of the starship *Enterprise* was drawn from many peoples—and even a few other planets. African American actress Nichelle Nichols played the part of Lieutenant Uhura.

Nichols believed the show promoted her dream of equality. So when scriptwriters cut back on Uhura's part in late 1967, she decided to quit. At this time, Nichols met Martin Luther King, Jr. She told King of her decision, expecting his full support. But King startled her. "You must not [leave]," said King. "You must stay. You don't understand the effect you're having not only on black people, not only on young women—but on everybody. Everybody's mind and attitude is changed immeasurably simply because you are there."

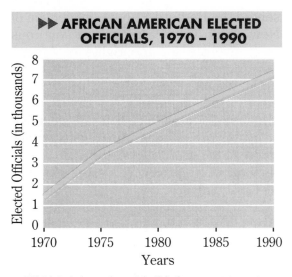

▶▶ AFRICAN AMERICAN ELECTED OFFICIALS, 1970 – 1990

Officials include members of the U.S. Congress; state senators and representatives; county commissioners and supervisors; city mayors, council members, and alderpersons; judges, magistrates, justices of the peace and constables; and members of college and local school boards.

Source: Joint Center for Political & Economic Studies, "Black Elected Officials" (Washington, D.C.)

Who are some African American officials in your state?

Nichols stayed. In 1977, the National Aeronautics and Space Administration (NASA) asked her to help recruit women and minorities for the space program. Nichols appeared on television to tell audiences that NASA needed recruits to help launch a real starship *Enterprise*—a spaceship piloted by men and women of every race. Explained Nichols: "So that's why I'm speaking to the whole family of humankind—minorities and women alike. If you qualify and would like to be an astronaut, now is the time. "

Applications poured into NASA. From the applicants came the nation's first three African American astronauts. Others soon followed. Colonel Guion S. Bluford, Jr., became the first African American in space. Ronald E. McNair was aboard the ill-fated shuttle *Challenger* when it exploded after launch in January

1986. In 1991, Mae C. Jamison, physician, chemist, and expert in African American studies, became the first African can American woman astronaut in space.

Although few in number, the African Americans in the space program are nevertheless symbols of the new worlds that African Americans are conquering at the end of the 20th century. More than ever before, African American pioneers are leaving their marks on all aspects of U.S. society—science, politics, culture, international affairs, and much more.

1 A GREATER VOICE IN POLITICS

▼ How have African Americans increased their influence at all levels of government?

The 1968 elections marked a turning point in U.S. history. That year, African Americans won ten seats in Congress—the highest number since Reconstruction. New faces included Shirley Chisholm, the first African American woman ever elected to Congress. Chisholm repre-

In 1972, Shirley Chisholm became the first African American woman to seek a major party's nomination for President.

1968 Shirley Chisholm becomes first African American woman elected to Congress.

1972 Chisholm runs for President.

More than 200 African Americans elected to state assemblies

1976 *Roots* is published.

1983 Martin Luther King's birthday is made a national holiday.

1984 Jesse Jackson runs for President.

1988 Jackson runs for President.

1989 Nelson Mandela is freed in South Africa.

1990 Douglas Wilder becomes first elected African American governor.

David Dinkins becomes mayor of New York City, the nation's largest city.

Nelson Mandela visits United States.

1991 First African American Summit

Why did the Rev. Jesse Jackson, shown here in a march protesting President Reagan's civil rights policies, organize the Rainbow Coalition?

sented the Bedford-Stuyvesant section of New York City. She was a vigorous spokeswoman for the rights of African Americans and of all women.

On January 25, 1972, Chisholm announced her candidacy for President of the United States. Chisholm won enough delegates in the state primaries to put her name on the first ballot at the Democratic National Convention. The votes received by Chisholm fell far short of the number needed for nomination. But her campaign raised a new question in the minds of many: Why not an African American or a woman for President?

A Time of Mixed Gains. The Civil Rights Movement had helped transform the role of African Americans in the nation's politics. In 1966, whites had controlled all major city governments. By 1973, there were African American mayors in a number of Southern towns and cities and in major cities across the nation, such as New Orleans, Detroit, Los Angeles, Cleveland, and Newark.

By 1973, African Americans had risen to higher levels of government, as well. That year, more than 200 African Americans sat in 37 state assemblies. Sixteen held seats in Congress—nearly double the number in 1968. In 1971, African Americans in the House formed the **Congressional Black Caucus** to address minority concerns.

Despite such gains, African Americans still faced an uphill battle to win their fair share of government posts. By mid-1975, they held only 3,503 of the more than 500,000 elective offices in the nation.

The Rainbow Coalition. A new willingness and ability of African Americans to do battle in national politics could be seen during the 1980s. The decade had opened with a stepped-up campaign to make the birthday of Martin Luther King, Jr., January 15, a national holiday. President Ronald Reagan was lukewarm to the idea, but he finally bowed to pressure. On November 2, 1983, he signed a bill approving the holiday.

Reagan's act came too late to win many African Americans over to his side. He had favored sharp cutbacks in too many social welfare programs that benefited minorities to win their support. African Americans searched for a candidate more to their liking. In 1983, they found their candidate in the Reverend Jesse Jackson.

Jesse Jackson was born in Greenville, South Carolina, in 1941. He studied at North Carolina Agricultural and Technical University and later attended Chicago Theological Seminary. In 1966, Jackson became a Baptist minister and a close aide to Martin Luther King, Jr., in SCLC. Under King's direction, Jackson organized Operation Breadbasket 1966, a program in Chicago to help expand educational and job opportunities for African Americans. In 1971, Jackson left SCLC and founded People United to Save Humanity (PUSH). He served as its president until 1983. Operation PUSH soon claimed 80,000 members, thrusting Jackson into the national spotlight. By the 1980s, Jackson had pressured a number of major businesses into opening their doors to African Americans.

Jackson used his great popularity among African Americans to make a run for the presidency. He told African Americans that they had the political power to make a difference in the United States. "Hands that picked cotton in 1884," said Jackson, "will pick the President in 1984."

Jackson's political appeal was not limited to African Americans. He called his followers the Rainbow Coalition. Explained Jackson:

> Our flag is red, white, and blue, but our nation is a rainbow—red, yellow, brown, black, and white. . . . America is not like a blanket—one piece of unbroken cloth, the same color, the same texture, the same size. America is more like a quilt— many patches, many pieces, many colors, many sizes, all woven and held together by a common thread.

Jackson entered the Democratic National Convention in 1984 with 300 delegates. But like Chisholm, Jackson lacked the votes to gain the nomination. Even so, Jackson's candidacy that year, and again in 1988, electrified African Americans. They marched to the polls in record numbers and showed that their power would have to be reckoned with in the not so distant future.

Toward a New Century. For the rest of the 1980s, African Americans led the battle against huge budget cuts by Presidents Reagan and Bush and a political climate in the country that threatened some of the gains of the Civil Rights Movement. They also pressured President Bush to declare a national war against drugs—one of the leading enemies of African American youth.

African Americans kept up their efforts to win elective office. In 1990, L. Douglas Wilder became the nation's first elected

In 1991, L. Douglas Wilder, governor of Virginia, announced his candidacy for the Democratic nomination for President.

African American governor. He won his victory in Virginia, a state with a white population of 81.2 percent. In 1991, African American mayors governed 30 major cities, 16 of which had white majorities. One of these African American mayors was David N. Dinkins, whose election in New York City in 1990 made him head of the nation's largest city.

Tensions and Divisions. Racial tensions between African Americans and whites remained, however. Clashes also occurred between African American and Hispanic leaders as each group struggled to win a greater voice in political affairs. As a result, the Rainbow Coalition forged by Jackson began to crumble.

Meanwhile, divisions occurred among African Americans themselves over several issues. One of those issues was affirmative action. As you have read, affirmative action programs gave preferences in hiring to members of groups that had been victims of discrimination in the past. Under such programs, thousands of African Americans entered colleges and universities or got jobs in government or in business. Many African American leaders strongly supported these affirmative action programs.

POINTS OF

Is racism the main problem that African Americans face? Not all African Americans agree on the answer to that question. Here are two points of view that were expressed on a 1991 TV news show. The first speaker is Robert Woodson of the National Center for Neighborhood Enterprise. The second is the Reverend Joseph Lowery of the Southern Christian Leadership Conference.

Woodson's View

We need to embrace the problems within the black community [that] have nothing to do with racism, but instead we should be looking at what is the crisis within ourselves. Why is it that prior to 1959, 78 percent of all black families had a man and a woman raising them, when we were facing racism in its most intense form? Why now do we have the decline? . . . Now I heard [that] racism is the big problem and that we need a more sensitive government. The destiny of black America has never been determined by what white people would allow us to do. . . . I think [people] do the community a tremendous disservice by saying somehow . . . that white people are responsible for what we do.

Lowery's View

You said racism was not a factor. . . . What we've got to do is develop the will to achieve.

. . . , a will first in the hearts and minds and determination of black people. . . . Then we've got to develop a national will so that we provide opportunities for employment, . . . job training. We have not developed that national will. We are more concerned about the well-being of the rich in Kuwait than we are about the poor in the United States of America. It's an elitist [attitude of superiority] and insensitive posture that says that everybody . . . can be a self-starter. [People] have to be motivated . . . and there have to be opportunities . . . for them to . . . grab hold of once they're motivated. . . . They do need help, as all of us had help who made it. . . . I just think we have to provide the environment where their opportunities of making it are maximized [made the most of].

In 1991, Clarence Thomas became the second African American to become a Supreme Court justice.

Other African Americans found problems with affirmative action. They felt such programs were part of a cycle of dependency that had been created among the poor. They called instead for self-help programs, as Booker T. Washington had, and self-determination, in the tradition of Malcolm X.

In the early 1990s, debate over the issue of affirmative action continued. The representatives elected by African American voters would play a major role in resolving it. "Black politicians are the quintessential [ultimate] pioneers," explained Charles V. Hamilton of Columbia University. "As such, whatever they do—successfully or unsuccessfully—American politics will never again be the same."

Taking Another Look

1. What is the "crisis within ourselves" that Woodson refers to?

2. **a.** What is the disservice that Woodson says people do to the African American community? **b.** Why do you think he believes it is a disservice?

3. What kinds of "will" does Lowery say need to be developed?

4. **Critical Thinking** Is there anything that you think Woodson and Lowery might agree on? Explain.

Taking Another Look

1. What political gains have African Americans made in the last three decades of this century?

2. **a.** Why did some African Americans favor affirmative action programs? **b.** Why did others oppose them?

3. **Critical Thinking** Do you agree with Hamilton's description of African American politicians? Explain.

2 THE CHANGING FACE OF THE NATION

How have African Americans brought about a quiet revolution in U.S. society and culture?

In June 1991, one high-fashion designer told models: "Wear these clothes the way they're worn on the subway—the look is, 'I don't care what's going on around me, nothing's gonna disturb my world.' It's the ultimate cool."

Lights dimmed on the runway, and the audience held its breath as a rap song shook the room. This was the first glimpse of the latest fall fashions. Some models strutted down the runway wrapped in fabrics inspired by West African kente cloth. Other models wore gold baseball caps and vinyl coats inspired by the styles worn by African American teenagers.

In the August 1991 issue of *Ebony*, publisher John Johnson commented on the growing influence of African Americans. He wrote, "Never before have so many White Americans paid Black Americans that sincerest form of flattery— imitation." African Americans, said Johnson, were changing the look of the nation.

The African Influence. Many African Americans refer to Africa as Mother Africa—the continent that gave birth to their culture. That culture has been deeply affected by the experience of African Americans on this continent. But ties to Africa remain strong.

The spirit of Africa can be seen in clothing styles worn by some African Americans today—kente-cloth crowns, robe-like dashikis, or T-shirts emblazoned with the word *Africa*. Some parents give their children African names. Twins, for example, might be Taiwo (first born) and Kehinde (second born). Women tightly braid their hair in beaded cornrows, similar to hairstyles worn in West Africa. Young men wear dreadlocks similar to those worn in the Caribbean, another area of African culture.

The outpouring of black pride during the 1970s boosted the African spirit to new heights. Historian Robert Weisbord described the period as "Afro-America's African Renaissance." This rebirth of African culture cut across color lines. Larger numbers of whites than ever before became keenly aware of African American creativity.

An African American family and friends celebrate Kwanzaa, an African-inspired harvest festival. The candles, fruit, and wine mark the seven principles of thought.

Dancing to an African Beat.

African American dance caught the public attention as a new generation of choreographers came of age. They built on the work of African American pioneers in modern dance, such as Katherine Dunham. African American dance troupes, such as the Alvin Ailey American Dance Theater and Arthur Mitchell's Dance Theater of Harlem, performed classical ballet. But they also introduced serious African American choreography to the public. Mitchell called it "ballet with soul."

Across the nation today, people dance to an African beat as they did in the 1890s with the cakewalk and the 1920s with jazz. In the 1950s, white Americans gave up the two-step in favor of Chubby Checker's Twist. They learned to Moonwalk with Michael Jackson. They picked up high-energy Hip Hop moves from the rappers. "To put it very simply," says Arthur Mitchell, "Black dance got everybody dancing." Katherine Dunham agreed. Observed Dunham:

> The influence continues to be seen in videos and TV award shows, which are using Black dance, whether they know it or not. . . . Black dance is coming to the fore [becoming strong] in the night clubs, and TV through people such as Michael Jackson and his sister, Janet, and Prince.

Artists and Writers.

The explosion of African American culture in the 1970s and 1980s brought well-deserved attention to African American artists. Many of their works had been exhibited in Latin America, Europe, and Africa. Now white Americans began to notice home-grown African American talent. Galleries across the nation showed the works of painters

What is there about this college student that reflects her interest in her African heritage?

such as Jacob Lawrence, Romare Bearden, and Lois Mailou Jones. The photographs of Gordon Parks and the sculptures of Elizabeth Catlett-Mora went on tour, too.

What do you think Arthur Mitchell meant by the phrase "ballet with soul"?

Ntozake Shange is a poet, novelist, and actress. Her novel *Betsy Brown* has been turned into a musical.

What are some of the themes that Alice Walker, above, Ntozake Shange, and Toni Morrison write about?

▶▶ SOME AFRICAN AMERICAN PULITZER PRIZE WINNERS IN LITERATURE

Winner (year)	Type of Work and Title
Gwendolyn Brooks (1950)	poetry, *Annie Allen*
Charles Gordone (1970)	drama, *No Place to Be Somebody*
Alex Haley (1977)	special category, *Roots*
Charles Fuller (1982)	drama, *A Soldier's Story*
Alice Walker (1983)	fiction, *The Color Purple*
Rita Dove (1987)	poetry, *Thomas and Beulah*
Toni Morrison (1988)	fiction, *Beloved*
August Wilson (1987; 1990)	drama, *Fences;* drama, *The Piano Lesson*

The names of African American writers also became familiar to the American public. Alex Haley published *Roots,* the story of his search for his ancestors both in this country and in Africa. Appearing in 1976, the year of the U.S. bicentennial, it was what Haley called "a birthday offering to my country." Because of *Roots,* both African Americans and whites took a fresh look at their history. African Americans saw reason to be proud of their culture; whites saw reason to respect it.

African American writers and poets climbed to the top of the bestseller lists.

Once an editor of school textbooks, Toni Morrison has become one of the nation's most popular novelists.

When the TV version of Alex Haley's *Roots*, left, was aired in 1977, it attracted record audiences. Bill Cosby's series about the Huxtable family regularly topped the TV ratings.

The Color Purple, by Alice Walker, inspired a popular movie by the same name. It also won Walker a Pulitzer Prize in 1983. She and Gwendolyn Brooks, the Pulitzer Prize winner for poetry in 1950, were joined in 1988 by Toni Morrison for her novel *Beloved.*

Popular Entertainment. In 1990, more than half the parents surveyed in a study of prime-time TV said they relaxed when their children switched on the Huxtables. The Huxtables, said respondents, projected the values they most wanted their children to see. The Huxtables are African Americans, and their lives are the subject of "The Cosby Show," produced by popular entertainer Bill Cosby. The results of the survey led *U.S. News and World Report* to name "The Cosby Show" to its 1990 list "The Best of America."

The magazine also put filmmaker Spike Lee on its list with the title "Artist who best captured the ethnic experience in America." What Lee showed was a glimpse into the African American world. He also depicted the racial tensions between African Americans and whites with a force that sometimes caused audiences to flinch.

Other African American directors and actors have joined Lee as box-office hits. Directors such as Matty Rich, John Singleton, and Euzhan Palcy have earned

Movie directors Spike Lee, left, and John Singleton, right, made audiences aware of the creative talents of African Americans. What themes do they use in their movies?

places in Hollywood. So have stars such as Eddie Murphy, Whoopi Goldberg, and Denzel Washington.

African American influence in popular music has never been stronger. Great stars of the earlier days of rhythm and blues and rock remain popular—Tina Turner, James Brown, and Aretha Franklin. Older jazz legends, like Miles Davis, have been joined by newer ones like Wynton Marsalis. Rap artists like Queen Latifah, Ice Cube, and Hammer deliver blistering social commentary, while C + C Music Factory and De La Soul produce new dance music. The forms may vary, but the message is the same—African American culture is popular everywhere, including foreign countries.

Taking Another Look

1. What influence does Africa have on the culture of today's African Americans?

2. How has African American culture touched white Americans?

3. **Critical Thinking**   What important changes do you think African Americans will experience in their lives and culture during the first decades of the 21st century?

3 BRIDGING THE CONTINENTS

▼ How have African Americans become involved with events on the African continent in recent years?

In June 1990, New York City took Nelson Mandela, leader of the **African National Congress (ANC),** to its heart. Thousands of New Yorkers turned out for a parade honoring this man, who had spent nearly 27 years in South African prisons. His crime had been opposition to **apartheid** (uh-PAHR-tayt), the white South African government's policy of rigidly segregating its people in almost every part of their lives. Finally free at age 71, Mandela had come to the United States to thank Americans for supporting the struggle to end apartheid.

Later that day, Mandela addressed a crowd of some 100,000 in Harlem. The

Flanked by David Dinkins, New York City's first African American mayor, and the governors of New York and New Jersey, Nelson Mandela speaks to thousands in Harlem who welcomed him on his 1990 visit.

years spent behind bars had not dampened his fiery spirit. He called out the names of African Americans whose words had rung out in Harlem in years past—Marcus Garvey, Paul Robeson, Malcolm X, Martin Luther King, Jr. With each name, the roars of the crowd grew louder. Mandela stilled the audience with a wave of his hand. He declared:

I have come here to claim you because . . . you have claimed our struggle. Harlem signifies the glory of resistance. We are on the verge of victory. . . . Death to racism!

Mandela, bitter foe of apartheid, symbolized for many African Americans their own struggle for civil rights. The response he received on his visit demonstrated, too, the ties that many African Americans felt to the land where their ancestors had lived.

Fighting Against Apartheid. The struggle of black Africans to end the crushing system of segregation that oppressed their lives had drawn support from many U.S. citizens. African Americans, especially, urged their government to take action that would help bring apartheid to an end.

The roots of South African apartheid went deep into that nation's history. Dutch settlers had colonized South Africa in the 1600s. Although the British took over and ruled South Africa from the 1800s to 1931, descendants of the Dutch settlers, known as Afrikaners, controlled the government.

Whites made up only about 17 percent of South Africa's population. To ensure their continued control over the nation, the whites set up the system of apartheid as the official policy of the government in 1948. Under apartheid, blacks were ef-

fectively denied any say in the country's political affairs. This was similar to the experience of African Americans in the South during the era of Jim Crow after Reconstruction.

The ANC had been organized in 1912 to seek greater political and economic rights for South African blacks. After apartheid became the law in 1948, the ANC focused its energies on overthrowing that system. The ANC used boycotts, strikes, and demonstrations in its efforts. Often, its protests were met with violence by the South African government. Nelson Mandela had joined the ANC in 1944 and quickly rose to a position of leadership in the organization.

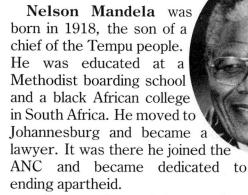

Nelson Mandela was born in 1918, the son of a chief of the Tempu people. He was educated at a Methodist boarding school and a black African college in South Africa. He moved to Johannesburg and became a lawyer. It was there he joined the ANC and became dedicated to ending apartheid.

As part of a crackdown against the ANC, the South African government branded Mandela a traitor. He was arrested in 1962 and imprisoned for the next 27 years. Nevertheless, even in prison, Mandela's words and ideas continued to reach and inspire South Africa's blacks. That they did owed much to the efforts of his wife, Winnie Mandela. She remained active in the ANC and helped ensure that the world would not forget the cause that Nelson Mandela was fighting for.

Like these New Yorkers, African Americans throughout the nation kept up a constant cry for South Africa to end apartheid.

Ending Apartheid. The world did not forget. As the South African government's effort to keep apartheid in place bred more and more violence, protests began to build around the globe. Recently independent nations in Africa were among the most vocal critics of apartheid. They were joined by other nations that put increasing pressure on South Africa to change its policies. Some nations imposed **economic sanctions**—put limits on trade with South Africa. South Africa was barred from taking part in the Olympics and other international events. In 1974, the UN voted to expel South Africa until it ended apartheid.

In the United States, civil rights groups became active in pushing for an end to apartheid. They urged corporations to end business dealings with South Africa. They also pushed the U.S. government to impose economic sanctions. Local people did their part, too. African American dockworkers in Oakland, California, re-fused to unload ships from South Africa. In 1987, Congress did vote for such sanctions, barring the importation of foods and consumer products from South Africa.

The combination of international economic pressure and continuing protests from black groups within South Africa finally succeeded. In 1989, the South African government resumed talks with the once-banned ANC and freed Mandela. Over the next several years, it moved to dismantle the system of apartheid.

In 1991, President Bush ended economic sanctions against South Africa. Nelson Mandela objected strongly to this move. African American civil rights leaders joined his protest. They knew from bitter experience that the ending of an official system of oppression was no guarantee that people would be granted equal rights. These leaders vowed to monitor U.S. policy toward South Africa carefully to ensure that pressure for equal rights for black Africans was kept up.

A New Pan-Africanism. African Americans had worked at home for an end to apartheid. Many also wanted to become more actively involved in the affairs of the African continent. Some 3,000 miles to the northwest of South Africa, a jumbo jet touched down in Abidjan, the capital of Côte d'Ivoire, in 1991. On board were more than 300 African American leaders from all walks of life. As the wheels hit the runway, these educators, politicians, business people, and religious and civil rights leaders burst into cheers. They had returned to West Africa, the homeland of many of their ancestors, to renew ties between African Americans and black Africans.

They had come to attend what one organizer called the "first African/African American Summit." That organizer, civil rights leader the Reverend Leon H. Sullivan, set out the purpose of the meeting: "Let us build a bridge together that will help move Africa forward as it has never moved before."

The meeting was part of the tradition of Pan-Africanism that went back to Martin R. Delany (see page 166), W.E.B. Du Bois (see page 250), and Marcus Garvey (see page 269). Those earlier Pan-Africanists had drawn their inspiration from black Africans and their history. Now black Africans were being inspired by the struggles and successes of African Americans. The president of Côte d'Ivoire, Felix Houphouet-Boigny (oo-FWAY bwah-NYEE), expressed this feeling: "We have looked to [African Americans] and your fight against racism and have been proud."

The summit delegates hammered out programs to expand cooperation between the United States and Africa. Ideas included fairer prices for African exports,

cancellation of $100 billion in debts owed by African nations to the United States, and support for dual citizenship for African Americans in the United States and some African nations.

Organizer Sullivan saw these plans as "a launching pad for the future." He hoped to encourage "the best and brightest" among African Americans to work with Africa. This would be yet another way of ensuring that the African American heritage remained vital and strong.

Taking Another Look

1. How did African Americans try to force an end to South Africa's policy of apartheid?

2. How did the 1991 meeting in Côte d'Ivoire represent a continuation of the tradition of Pan-Africanism?

3. **Critical Thinking** Do you agree with President Bush's decision to end sanctions against South Africa? Explain.

LOOKING AHEAD

This chapter has followed African Americans on many different journeys. Some have ventured into the reaches of outer space. Others have explored the machinery of politics on local, state, and national levels. Still others have charted new paths in the arts and in entertainment. For some, their journeys have led back to Africa. All the people discussed in this chapter have been, in different ways, pioneers.

There is still new ground to be broken, new journeys to be taken. The pioneers of the future are you, the readers of this book.

CLOSE UP: Chapter 34

"A child's behavior and personality resemble so much his name-bearer," declares an African proverb. In keeping with this saying, most West African peoples had special naming ceremonies for their children. A Hausa child, for example, received two names—a secret, real name whispered by his or her mother and a public name for daily use. Other West African peoples also gave their children two names: one for good times, one for bad; or one temporary, one permanent.

As a result of the Civil Rights Movement of the 1960s, some African Americans are reclaiming their heritage by taking African names for themselves and their children. Some of these names include:

Female

Ainka	The cherished one
Menjiwe	The trustworthy
Sowo	Medicine woman
Mirembe	Peace
Wamuiru	The beautiful black one
Yakiri	Truth, certainty
Baraka	Blessing, prosperity

Male

Oba	King
Seve	Hawk, aggressive person
Ola	Noble man
Mwangi	One who conquers
Chiri	One with a lot of money
Manani	The beneficent one
Uwezo	Power

The Who, What, Where of History

1. **Who** is Guion S. Bluford, Jr.?
2. **Who** is Shirley Chisholm?
3. **What** was the Rainbow Coalition?
4. **Who** is L. Douglas Wilder?
5. **Who** is Clarence Thomas?
6. **Who** is Katherine Dunham?
7. **What** is *Roots?*
8. **Who** is Alice Walker?
9. **Who** is Nelson Mandela?
10. **What** was *apartheid?*
11. **What** are economic sanctions?

Making the Connection

1. Explain the connection between the Civil Rights Movement of the 1960s and the growth in the number of African American elected officials in the 1970s.

2. Explain the connection between U.S. economic policies toward South Africa and that nation's system of official segregation.

Time Check

1. In what year was the first African American woman elected to Congress?

2. Explain the importance of each of these dates in the history of South Africa and the life of Nelson Mandela: 1962, 1989, 1991.

What Would You Have Done?

1. Imagine that it is the early 1980s. You are part of a committee trying to per-

suade President Reagan to make Martin Luther King's birthday a national holiday. What arguments would you use to convince him?

2. Suppose that you are a member of the ANC with Nelson Mandela in the 1960s. You have a difficult choice to make. If you stay in South Africa, you are certain to go to jail, probably for many years. If you leave the country, you will be free to do what you believe in, but you will be far from where the action is. Would you stay or leave? Explain your choice.

Thinking and Writing About History

1. Write a one-minute radio commercial supporting the presidential campaign of either Shirley Chisholm or Jesse Jackson.

2. Suppose that you could interview any one of the dancers, artists, writers, or musicians mentioned in the chapter. Decide which one you would choose to interview. Then write three questions you would like to ask that person.

Building Skills: Summarizing

Suppose you are walking down the street, minding your own business, when you meet a friend. Your friend seems very excited.

"What are you so excited about?" you ask.

"Well," says the friend, "I just saw a *great* movie. You want to hear about it?"

"Sure," you answer.

"Well," your friend begins, "it's about these two cowhands. One of them is African American and one of them is white.

When the movie opens, they're riding together behind a herd of cattle. The African American is on one of those tan horses with a white tail. What do you call those horses? They have a special name. Well, never mind what they call it. But the color of the horse is going to be important later on, because, see—"

"Hold on a minute," you interrupt. "Can't you just give me a summary?"

"A what?"

"A *summary*," you answer. "You know. The main points. The main ideas. Brief. Also saves time."

Here is a summary of the opening section of this chapter:

In 1967, Martin Luther King, Jr., persuaded African American actress Nichelle Nichols not to leave her role in "Star Trek." Ten years later, Nichols appeared on television to recruit women and minorities for the U.S. space program. Many applications were received. African American astronauts are now an important part of the space program. African Americans have also filled important roles in many other aspects of U.S. society.

Notice that the summary gives only the main points of the section. It leaves out all the details, even though the details may be very interesting.

On a separate piece of paper, write a summary of one of the main sections of this chapter: "A Greater Voice in Politics," "The Changing Face of the Nation," or "Bridging the Continents." Write the main ideas of the section, without any details. *Hint:* Look for main ideas in the first sentence of the paragraphs.

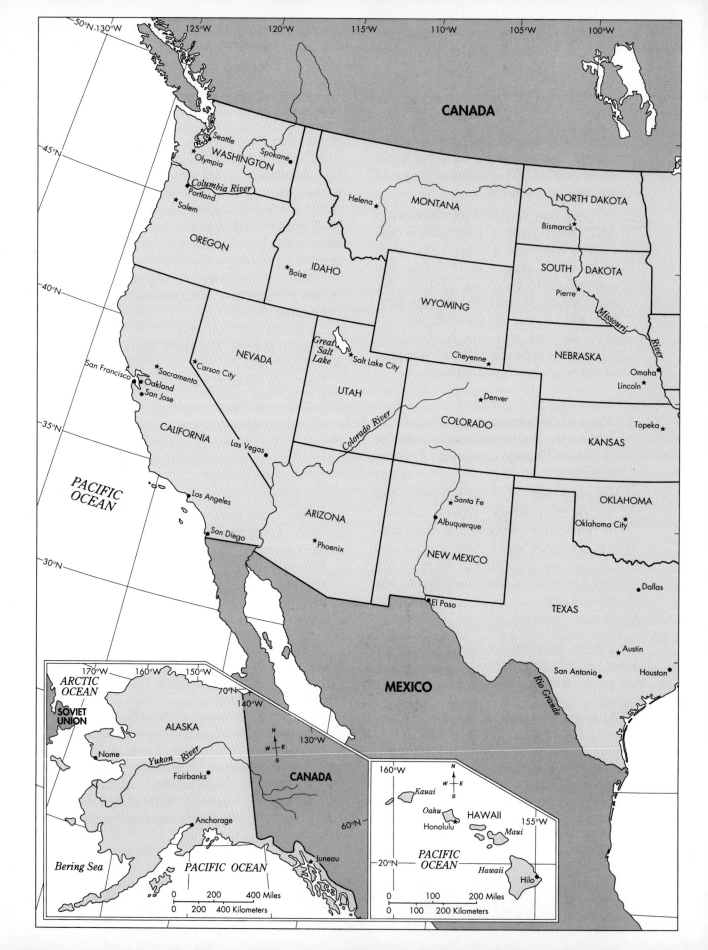

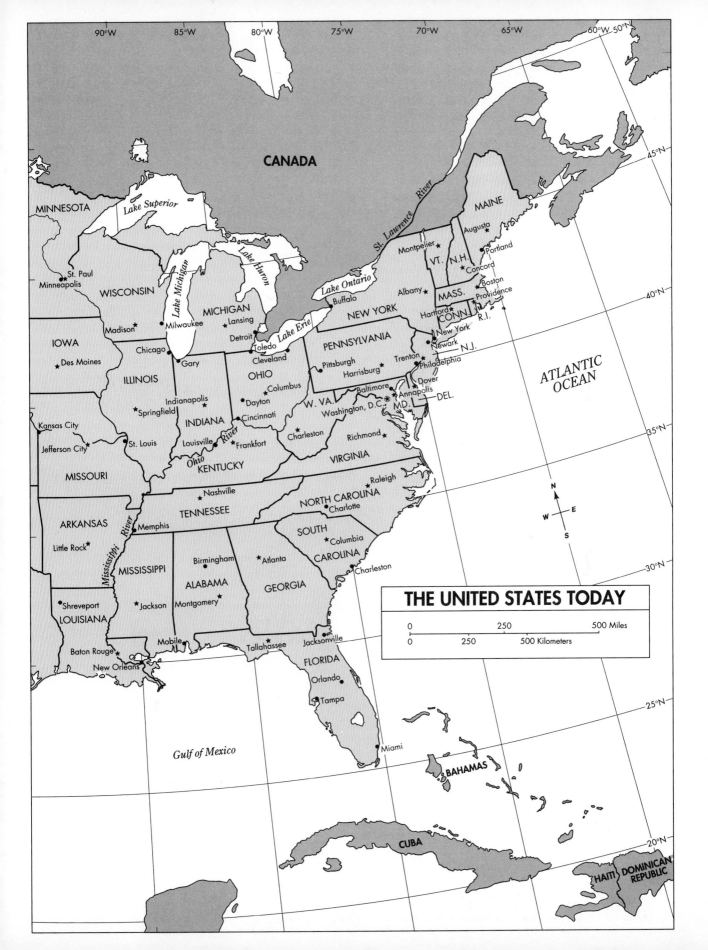

THE UNITED STATES TODAY

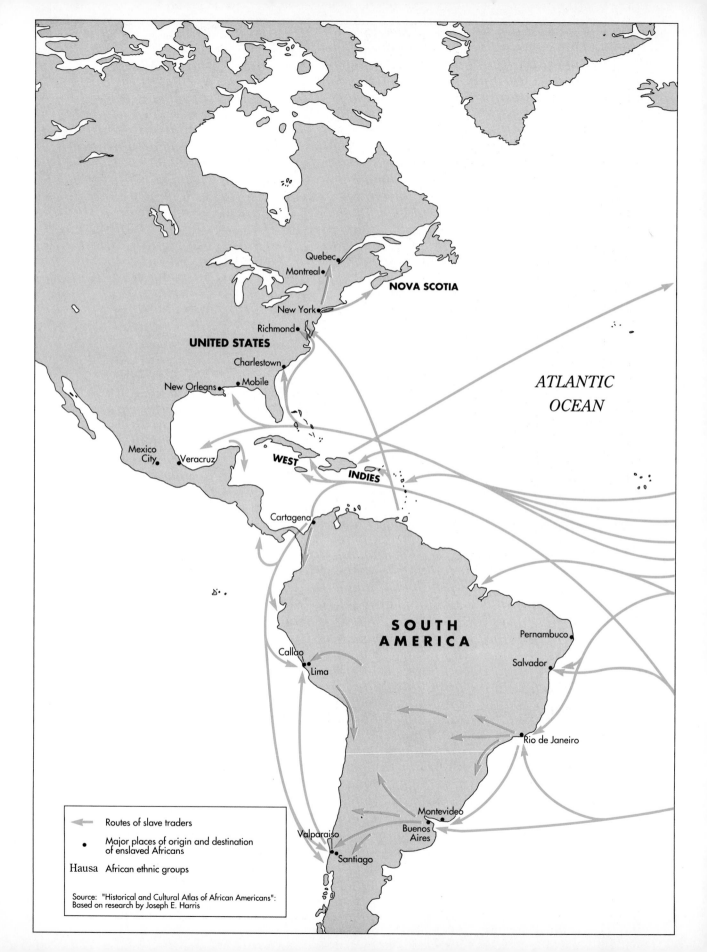

Quebec

Montreal

NOVA SCOTIA

New York

Richmond

UNITED STATES

Charlestown

New Orleans

Mobile

Mexico City

Veracruz

WEST

INDIES

ATLANTIC OCEAN

Cartagena

SOUTH AMERICA

Pernambuco

Salvador

Callao

Lima

Rio de Janeiro

Montevideo

Valparaiso

Buenos Aires

Santiago

Routes of slave traders

Major places of origin and destination of enslaved Africans

Hausa   African ethnic groups

Source: "Historical and Cultural Atlas of African Americans": Based on research by Joseph E. Harris

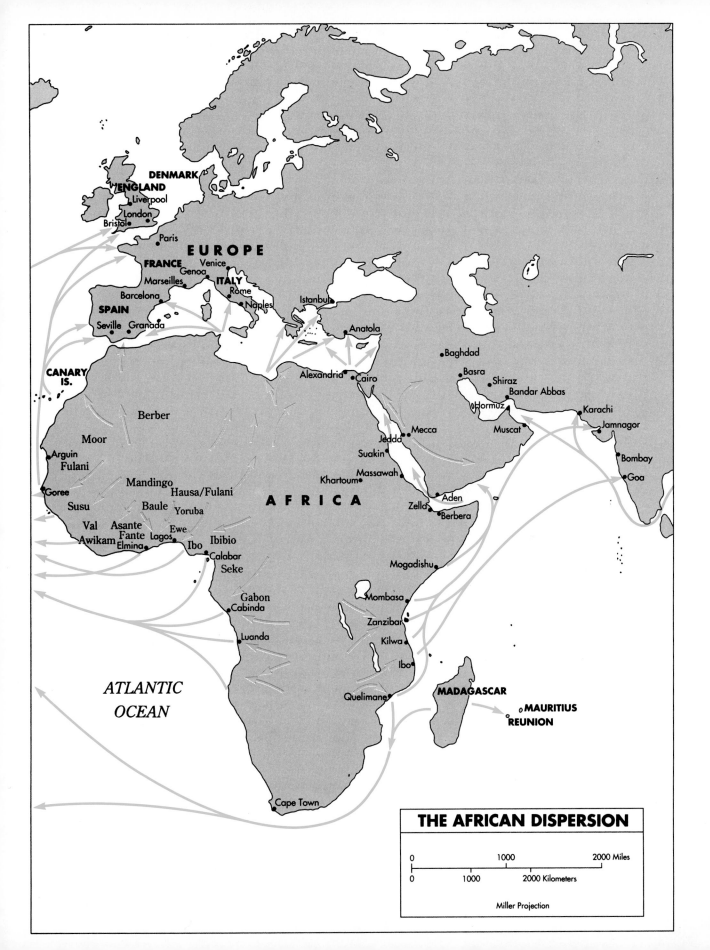

DENMARK

ENGLAND
Liverpool
London
Bristol
Paris
EUROPE
FRANCE
Venice
Genoa
Marseilles
ITALY
Rome
Barcelona
Naples
SPAIN
Istanbul
Seville Granada
Anatola
CANARY
IS.
Baghdad
Alexandria Cairo
Basra
Shiraz
Bandar Abbas
Berber
Hormuz
Karachi
Moor
Jamnagor
Arguin
Jedda Mecca
Muscat
Fulani
Bombay
Goree
Suakin
Goa
Mandingo
Massawah
Susu
Hausa/Fulani
Khartoum
AFRICA
Zella Aden
Baule
Yoruba
Berbera
Val
Asante
Ewe
Awikam
Fante
Lagos
Elmina
Ibo
Ibibio
Calabar
Seke
Mogadishu
Gabon
Cabinda
Mombasa
Luanda
Zanzibar
Kilwa
Ibo
ATLANTIC
OCEAN
Quelimane
MADAGASCAR
MAURITIUS
REUNION

Cape Town

THE AFRICAN DISPERSION

| 0 | | 1000 | | 2000 Miles |

| 0 | 1000 | | 2000 Kilometers | |

Miller Projection

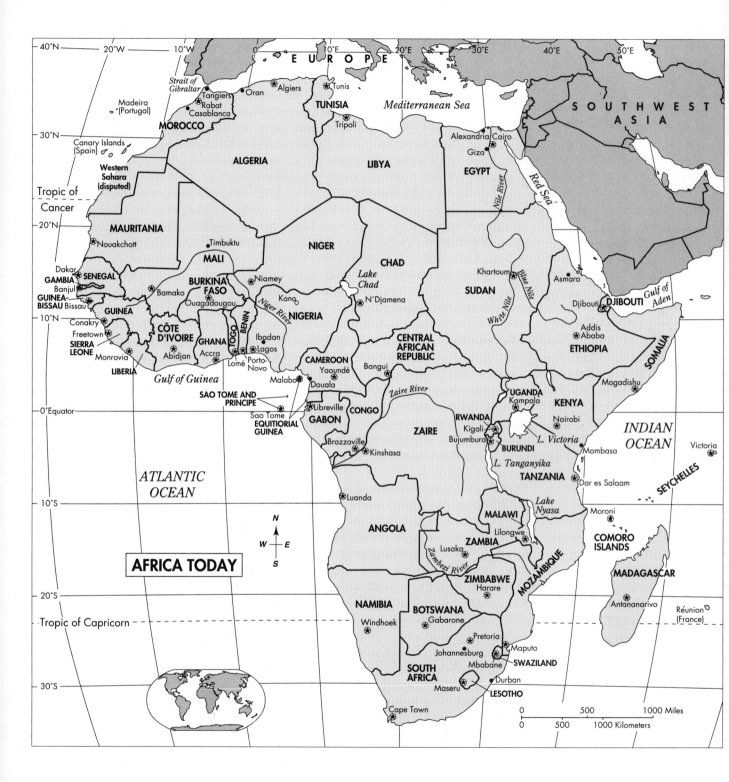

AFRICA TODAY

40°N · 20°W · 10°W · 0° · 10°E · 20°E · 30°E · 40°E · 50°E

E U R O P E

Strait of
Gibraltar
Madeira
(Portugal)

Tangiers ⊛
Rabat
Casablanca

⊛ Oran ⊛ Algiers

⊛ Tunis

Mediterranean Sea

S O U T H W E S T
A S I A

MOROCCO

TUNISIA

Tripoli ⊛

Canary Islands
(Spain)

**Western
Sahara
(disputed)**

Tropic of
Cancer

20°N

ALGERIA

LIBYA

Alexandria ⊛ Cairo
Giza ⊛

EGYPT

Nile River

Red Sea

MAURITANIA

⊛ Nouakchott

⊛ Timbuktu

NIGER

CHAD

*Lake
Chad*

Khartoum ⊛

SUDAN

⊛ Asmara

Blue Nile

Djibouti ⊛ **DJIBOUTI**

*Gulf of
Aden*

Dakar ⊛
GAMBIA ⊛ **SENEGAL**
Banjul

MALI

**BURKINA
FASO**

⊛ Niamey

Kano ⊛

White Nile

Addis
Ababa ⊛

**GUINEA-
BISSAU** Bissau

Bamako ⊛

Ouagadougou ⊛

N'Djamena ⊛

SOMALIA

GUINEA

Conakry ⊛

Niger River

NIGERIA

**CENTRAL
AFRICAN
REPUBLIC**

ETHIOPIA

Freetown ⊛
**SIERRA
LEONE**

**CÔTE
D'IVOIRE**

GHANA

Ibadan ⊛
⊛ Lagos

Monrovia ⊛

Abidjan ⊛

Accra ⊛
Lomé

Porto-
Novo

CAMEROON

Yaoundé ⊛

Bangui ⊛

Mogadishu ⊛

LIBERIA

Gulf of Guinea

Malabo ⊛

Douala ⊛

UGANDA
Kampala ⊛

KENYA

**SAO TOME AND
PRINCIPE**

**EQUITORIAL
GUINEA**

⊛ Libreville

CONGO

Zaire River

RWANDA
Kigali ⊛

Nairobi ⊛

*INDIAN
OCEAN*

0° Equator

Sao Tome ⊛

GABON

ZAIRE

L. Victoria

Brazzaville ⊛

⊛ Kinshasa

Bujumbura ⊛
BURUNDI

L. Tanganyika

TANZANIA

Mombasa ⊛

Victoria ⊛

SEYCHELLES

Dar es Salaam ⊛

*ATLANTIC
OCEAN*

10°S

⊛ Luanda

N
W ✦ **E**
S

ANGOLA

*Lake
Nyasa*

Moroni ⊛

**COMORO
ISLANDS**

MALAWI

Lilongwe ⊛

ZAMBIA

Lusaka ⊛

Zambezi River

MOZAMBIQUE

MADAGASCAR

ZIMBABWE

Harare ⊛

Antananarivo ⊛

Réunion
(France)

Tropic of Capricorn

NAMIBIA

BOTSWANA

Windhoek ⊛

Gaborone ⊛

Pretoria ⊛

⊛ Maputo
Mbabane ⊛

SWAZILAND

Johannesburg ⊛

30°S

**SOUTH
AFRICA**

Maseru ⊛

Durban ⊛

LESOTHO

Cape Town ⊛

0 · 500 · 1000 Miles
0 · 500 · 1000 Kilometers

GLOSSARY

This glossary defines important terms used in this book. The page on which a term first appears is given in parentheses at the end of the definition.

abolition   act of ending something, such as slavery (65)

abolitionist   person who worked for an end to slavery in the United States in the 1800s (124)

affirmative action   policy designed to compensate for past discrimination in hiring practices and education and to increase opportunities for minorities and women (359)

African National Congress (ANC)   major antiapartheid organization in South Africa (386)

almanac   book that contains weather forecasts and astronomical information (79)

amendment   change made in the U.S. Constitution, or in a bill or law (68)

ancestor worship   belief that one's ancestors survived death and can be reached through prayers and offerings (27)

annex   (uh-NEKS) to take over territory of another country or state (88)

apartheid   (uh-PAHR-tayt) South African policy of strict segregation of, and discrimination against, nonwhites (386)

Articles of Confederation   plan of government drawn up during Revolutionary War (80)

Atlanta Compromise   name given to speech made by Booker T. Washington in Atlanta, Georgia, in 1895 (225)

Black Cabinet   African American advisers in Franklin D. Roosevelt's administration (293)

Black Codes   laws passed by Southern states after the Civil War to limit the rights of African Americans (164)

Black Muslim   informal term for a member of the Nation of Islam (336)

black nationalism   belief that people of African descent have had a common experience, share a common culture and world view, and have a common destiny (269)

Black Panther party   radical political party of the 1960s and 1970s, stressing self-defense by African Americans and, later, violent revolution (341)

Black Power   movement beginning in the 1960s emphasizing control of their communities by African Americans according to their own values (340)

Bleeding Kansas   nickname given to Kansas territory in 1856 because there was so much violence there over slavery (162)

blues   form of music that developed in the United States probably from African American work songs; uses call-and-response pattern; often expresses loneliness or sorrow, but sometimes reflects with humor on life's problems (238)

border states   four slave states—Missouri, Kentucky, Maryland, Delaware—that remained loyal to the Union during the Civil War (177)

Boston Massacre   Patriots' name for incident in which British soldiers killed five people, including Crispus Attucks (72)

Boston Tea Party   act of defiance in which Patriots dumped hundreds of pounds of tea into Boston Harbor in 1773 (72)

boycott   organized refusal to buy or use a certain product or service, in order to achieve certain aims (66)

bridewealth   gifts of money or goods made by a groom to the family of his bride (25)

cakewalk   high-stepping promenade, begun by African American slaves as a way to poke fun at the manners of plantation owners (238)

call-and-response   music pattern from West Africa in which leader sings a short bit and people sing it back, accompanied by percussion instruments (28)

cash crop   crop raised for sale rather than for a farmer's personal use (36)

cataract   strong rapids along a river (6)

checks and balances   system by which each of the three branches of government (executive, legislative, judicial) checks the power of the other branches to ensure that no one branch has too much power (80)

Christianity   religion based on teachings of Jesus (13)

civilization   total way of life of a people and period; also, a high level of social organization (3)

civil rights   those rights given to all citizens of the United States by the Constitution and its amendments, such as the right to vote and the right to equal treatment under the law (218)

Civil Rights Movement   movement of the 1950s and 1960s to win equal rights for all African Americans (303)

Civil War   war between the United States of America and secessionist Confederate States of America to restore the Union and free African American slaves (161)

Cold War   conflict between the United States and the Soviet Union, stopping short of actual warfare, which lasted from the end of World War II to 1990 (301)

collective bargaining   negotiation between union workers and management to reach an agreement on wages, hours, and working conditions (246)

colony   settlement of people living in a land outside their home country, but under the power of the home country (36)

compromise   agreement in which each side agrees to give up some demands in order to reach a settlement (68)

Compromise of 1850   agreement under which Congress admitted California to the Union as a free state, left the slavery question in other former Mexican lands up to the settlers, and passed the Fugitive Slave Law (162)

Confederacy   Confederate States of America, states that withdrew from the Union, or the United States, in the 1860s (163)

congregation   group of people gathered together for religious worship (154)

Congressional Black Caucus   informal organization of African American members of Congress (378)

conquistadors   (kahn-KEES-tuh-dawrs) Spanish conquerors sent to the Americas in the 16th century (35)

conscientious objector   someone who, because of moral or religious objections, refuses to fight in wars (348)

constitution   basic laws and principles of a nation (65)

Constitutional Convention   meeting called in 1787 to revise Articles of Confederation, at which delegates decided to create a new constitution instead (68)

Continental Army   the colonists' military force (67)

contraband   used during the Civil War to describe a runaway African American slave behind Union lines whom the North refused to return to a Southern owner (181)

convict-lease system   hiring out of convicts to private employers (214)

Cotton Belt   band of cotton-growing states that stretched from Georgia to Texas (96)

cotton gin   machine for separating cotton fibers from the seeds of the plant (96)

credit   promise to pay in the future for goods or borrowed money (192)

culture   skills, beliefs, customs, and arts of a given people (6)

Declaration of Sentiments   statement of liberation for the 2 million African Americans living under slavery; issued by the American Anti-Slavery Society (135)

de facto segregation   separation of people by racial groups that results from customs and economic conditioning rather than from laws (316)

demographics   population statistics (363)

denomination   religious group called by the same name, such as Baptists (153)

depression   period marked by a drastic decline in production and sale of goods and services and a severe increase in unemployment (246)

dialect   form of language spoken in a particular region or community (99)

discrimination   unjust treatment based on race, religion, or sex (121)

disfranchise   to deny people their rights of citizenship, especially the right to vote (215)

dynasty   series of rulers who are members of the same family (6)

economic sanctions   refusal to trade or do business with another country until that country changes certain policies (388)

economy   system of producing, distributing, and using goods and services (37)

Emancipation Proclamation   declaration freeing all African American slaves in those parts of the South that were still in rebellion against the Union on January 1, 1863 (164)

entrepreneur   person who risks money organizing a business to earn a profit (123)

escarpment   steep cliff (4)

ethnic group   people who share a culture and, often, a geographical location (261)

Exodusters   African Americans who fled the South in large groups in 1879 and 1880, heading west (200)

extended family   family that includes other relatives as well as parents and children (25)

federal system   system of government that divides power between the national government and state governments (80)

folk hero   an admired person, a legendary figure (203)

folktale   traditional story handed down from generation to generation (29)

Free African Society   civic and religious organization founded in Philadelphia in the 1790s by Richard Allen (79)

Freedmen's Bureau   federal agency set up in 1865 to help freed African American slaves in the

South by providing food and medicine, helping with jobs and housing, and starting schools (164)

freedom ride any of a series of trips taken by groups to test and defy segregation of trains, buses, and bus stations in the South during the 1960s (329)

Free-Soil party pre–Civil War antislavery political party (132)

free state state of the United States in which slavery was not permitted (161)

fugitive runaway (112)

Fugitive Slave Law an 1850 law that required runaway slaves to be returned to their owners (162)

ghetto section of a city in which many members of the same ethnic group live (261)

grandfather clause device in some Southern states designed to exclude African American men from voting; it exempted from literacy and property tests men whose grandfathers had voted before 1867 (215)

Great Migration movement of African Americans in large numbers from the rural South to industrial cities of the Northeast and Midwest, during and after World War I (245)

Great Rift Valley deep cut in earth's surface in Africa, which extends more than 6,000 miles, from Red Sea south to Mozambique (4)

Great Society social and economic policies and programs of President Lyndon B. Johnson in the 1960s (304)

griot (GREE-oh) in West Africa, a person who memorizes and recites the important cultural and historical events of a society so that they can be passed down through the generations (19)

gross national product the total value of all goods and services produced in a country (207)

hajj pilgrimage to the Muslim holy city of Mecca (16)

Harlem Renaissance period in the 1920s when literature and arts by African Americans flourished in Harlem, a section of New York City (246)

hieroglyphics (hy-ruh-GLIF-iks) an ancient system of writing that uses symbols and pictures to represent words (6)

immigrant person who comes to a new country, usually to settle there (36)

indentured servant person in colonial times who worked for someone for a specific amount of time in return for passage to the colonies (37)

industrialization development of an economy based on large industries and machine production (207)

inflation a general increase in prices over time (359)

integrate to abolish separation of groups so that people of all races and ethnic groups can associate freely (190)

Islam religion based on the teachings of Muhammad (13) *see also* Nation of Islam

jazz highly rhythmic music, often using improvisation that was originated by African Americans in the late 1800s (266)

jihad a holy war waged to spread the religion of Islam (18)

Jim Crow system of laws put into effect in the South after 1877 that discriminated against African Americans and provided for segregated public facilities (213)

Kansas-Nebraska Act law that organized Kansas and Nebraska as territories, repealing the Missouri Compromise and letting settlers there decide whether or not to allow slavery (162)

kente (KEN-tee) brilliantly colored woven cotton cloth, originally produced by the Asante of what is now Ghana (29)

labor union an association of workers formed to protect their rights (209)

levy to impose a tax or fine (65)

Liberty party first antislavery political organization formed in the United States (132)

Louisiana Purchase French territory, stretching from Mississippi River to Rocky Mountains, purchased from Napoleon by Thomas Jefferson in 1803 (69)

lynch to hang or otherwise murder by mob action for supposed crimes (165)

Maroon in Jamaica, a runaway African slave or a descendant of such (46)

Middle Passage passage across the Atlantic Ocean from West Africa to the Americas that was the route of the African American slave trade (33)

migrant person forced to move in search of work (261)

migration act of moving from one country or region to another (often in a group) (9)

militant aggressively active in support of a cause (135)

Minuteman Patriot who was ready to fight at a minute's notice (66)

Missouri Compromise agreement made in 1820 by which Missouri was admitted to the Union as a slave state, Maine was admitted as a free state, and Louisiana Territory was divided into slave and free parts (161)

monopoly the complete or nearly complete control of an industry by one company (208)

Mountain Man one of the rough-and-tumble fur trappers who helped open the lands beyond the Mississippi in the early 1800s (89)

Muslim believer in the religion of Islam (16)

NAACP National Association for the Advancement of Colored People (244)

nation grouping of people with a common culture in a single political and economic unit (65)

National Urban League organization, founded in 1910, that works to increase the economic and political power of African Americans and to end racial discrimination (262)

Nation of Islam organization of African Americans, led by Elijah Muhammad, who followed the religious principles of Islam and emphasized separation from white people; now, a group that split from the preceding, retaining the original name and principles of racial separation (262)

New Deal political, economic, and social policies and practices of President Franklin D. Roosevelt in the 1930s (246)

Niagara Movement group that called for equality for African Americans, first met at Niagara Falls in 1905 (251)

nonviolence policy of not using violence or any physical force when protesting unjust laws (327)

Northwest Ordinance (AWRD-en-uhns) law passed in 1787 barring slavery in Northwest Territory (69)

overseer person who supervised the work of slaves on a plantation (105)

Pan-Africanism belief that people of African descent have common interests and should join in a common struggle for freedom, at home and abroad (270)

papyrus writing material made from the papyrus plant, used in ancient Egypt (7)

Patriot colonist who favored independence (66)

personal liberty laws laws passed by some Northern states forbidding anyone from helping to

enforce the Fugitive Slave Law; some laws tried to guarantee a fair trial for runaways who were caught (169)

pharaoh (FAIR-oh) title of the rulers of ancient Egypt (6)

plantation large farm in the Caribbean, and later in the South, that grew cash crops and was worked by African American slaves (35)

planter plantation owner (47)

plateau an elevated piece of level land (4)

poll tax fee that a person had to pay in order to vote; instituted in the South to prevent African Americans from voting (215)

polygyny (puh-LIJ-uh-nee) practice of having more than one wife at the same time (25)

popular sovereignty principle that the people who lived in a territory should decide whether or not to allow slavery there (162)

poverty level an officially defined level of income below which a family cannot afford its basic needs (360)

prejudice (PREJ-oo-dis) suspicion or intolerance of racial or ethnic groups other than one's own (79)

Progressivism reform movement of the early 20th century (243)

public opinion collective beliefs of the people in a given community or nation (129)

pyramid huge structure with square base and four triangular sides used as a royal tomb during Egyptian civilization (5)

racism the unjust treatment of a people by others who falsely believe that their race is by nature superior and who have the political, economic, and military ability to enforce their attitude (49)

ragtime type of music that uses a strongly accented melody (238)

Rainbow Coalition political organization, formed by Jesse Jackson, that reaches out to all minority groups (361)

rain forest thick evergreen forest that grows in hot, wet climates near the equator (3)

recession general decrease in business activity, including production and employment (359)

Reconstruction period, after the Civil War, from 1865 to 1877, during which former Confederate states rejoined the Union (161)

Redcoat name for a British soldier during the Revolutionary War (71)

savanna flat grassland with scattered trees (3)

secede to withdraw officially from a country or organization (163)

segregation separation by law or custom of racial

groups on public transportation and in public facilities and residential areas (216)

sharecropping system of farm labor under which a person farms another's land, in return for a share of the crop (192)

silent trade exchange of goods conducted without the traders' speaking (17)

sit-in form of protest during the Civil Rights Movement of the 1950s and 1960s, in which African Americans tried to integrate segregated public facilities such as lunch counters by occupying the premises and refusing to leave until they were served (328)

slave a human being owned by or subject to another as a result of capture, purchase, or birth (7)

slave codes harsh restrictive laws designed to limit the activities of African American slaves (61)

slave driver a person, often a slave, who directed the work of slaves (105)

slave factory name for one of the slave-trading centers built by Europeans along the West African coast (40)

slave raider person who raided villages in Africa for people to sell as slaves (34)

slavery practice of owning human beings as property, or the condition of being a slave (18)

slave state state in which slavery was legal before the Civil War (161)

slum poor, overcrowded area of a city (243)

sodbusters name given to farmers on the Great Plains (201)

spiritual type of song that originated among African American slaves, usually dealing with Biblical themes (107)

strike an organized refusal by employees to do work, in an attempt to gain better pay and working conditions (214)

sub-Saharan Africa the part of Africa that lies south of the Sahara (3)

subsistence farmer farmer who produces crops for personal use only (26)

surname family name or last name (189)

Talented Tenth the well-educated upper 10 percent of the African American population, who, according to W.E.B. Du Bois, have a duty to become leaders "among their people" (250)

triangular trades name for a number of three-legged routes that were part of the sugar-slave trade of the 1600s and 1700s (48)

unconstitutional (un-kon-stuh-TOO-shuhn-uhl) not permitted by the Constitution (171)

underclass group of people with incomes below poverty level (342)

Underground Railroad system set up by opponents of slavery to help African American slaves escape to the free states of the North and to Canada (146)

Union United States of America (161); the Northern and border states in the Civil War (163)

women's rights equal rights for women (129)

SOURCES

Sources for quotations are given by page number (in parentheses) and in the order in which the quotations appear on each page.

UNIT 1

THE BIG PICTURE

(3) Lerone Bennett Jr., *Before the Mayflower: A History of the Negro in America 1619–1964* (New York: Penguin, 1982), p. 5. (5) W.E.B. Du Bois, quoted in Maulana Karenga, *Introduction to Black Studies* (Los Angeles: Kawaida Publications, 1982), p. 57. (9) Herkhuf, quoted in Basil Davidson, *The African Past* (Boston: Little Brown, 1964), pp. 47–48.

CHAPTER 1

(10) Kashta, quoted in Davidson, p. 51. (12) Ezana, quoted in A. Adu Boahen *et al.*, *The Horizon History of Africa* (New York: American Heritage, 1971), p. 80. (14) French explorer, quoted in Davidson, p. 277. (15) Pharaoh, quoted in Lionel Casson, *Ancient Egypt* (New York: Time, Inc., 1965), p. 95.

CHAPTER 2

(19) West African griot, quoted in E. Jefferson Murphy, *History of African Civilization* (New York: Dell, 1972), p. 115. (21) Scholar, quoted in Daniel Chu and Elliot Skinner, *A Glorious Age in Africa* (Trenton: Africa World Press, Inc., 1990), p. 112.

CHAPTER 3

(25) Yoruba praise song, quoted in Boahen *et al.*, p. 206; Olaudah Equiano, quoted in Henry L. Gates, Jr., ed., *The Classic Slave Narratives* (New York: Penguin, 1987), p. 25. (26) Olaudah Equiano, *Ibid.*, p. 19. (27) R.H. Stone, quoted in Robert Farris Thompson, *Flash of the Spirit* (New York: Random House, 1983), p. 3. (28) Olaudah Equiano, quoted in Gates, p. 14. (29) Yoruba Proverbs, quoted in Boahen *et al.*, p. 207.

UNIT 2

THE BIG PICTURE

(33) Slave, quoted in Julius Lester, *To Be A Slave* (New York: Scholastic, 1968), p. 24. (37) British critic, quoted in Gary Nash, *Red, White, and Black: The Peoples of Early America* (Englewood Cliffs: Prentice Hall, 1982), p. 151.

CHAPTER 4

(39) Bartolomé de las Casas, quoted in Daniel J. Boorstin, *The Discoverers* (New York: Random House, 1983), p. 631 (40) African survivor of the Middle Passage, quoted in Lester, p. 25. (42) Sailor, quoted in William Loren Katz, *Eyewitness: The Negro in American History* (New York: Pitman, 1967), p. 6. (43) Lord Chesterfield, quoted in E. Jefferson Murphy, *History of African Civilization* (New York: Dell, 1972), p. 294.

CHAPTER 5

(48) Olaudah Equiano, quoted in Henry Louis Gates, Jr., ed., *The Classic Slave Narratives* (New York: Mentor, 1987), p. 37. (49) Olaudah Equiano, *Ibid.*, pp. 37–38. (51) Benjamin Quarles, *The Negro in the Making of America*, Revised Edition (New York: Collier Books, 1969), p. 28.

CHAPTER 6

(54) 1667 law, quoted in Lerone Bennett, Jr., *Before the Mayflower: A History of the Negro in America 1619–1964* (New York: Penguin, 1982), p. 46. (55) African farmer, quoted in Robert A. Devine, *America Past and Present* (Illinois: Foresman, 1984) (57) Georgian leader, quoted in Katz (1967 ed.), p. 21. (58) Council of New Netherlands, quoted in Bennett, p. 442; Colony's Director, quoted in George Williams, *History of the Negro Race in America, 1619–1880* (New York: Arno Press, 1968), p. 135. (59) German Quakers, quoted in Katz (1967 ed.), p. 35. (62) Alex Haley, quoted in "Why Roots Hit Home" *Time*, Feb. 14, 1977.

UNIT 3

THE BIG PICTURE

(65) Jupiter Hammon, quoted in Benjamin Quarles, *The Negro in the American Revolution* (New York: Norton, 1961), p. 27. (67) Lord Dunmore, quoted in John Hope Franklin and Alfred A. Moss, Jr., *From Slavery to Freedom: A History of Negro Americans* 6th ed. (New York: Knopf, 1988), p. 69; Petition to New Hampshire assembly, quoted in Mary Beth Norton *et al.*, *A People and a Nation* 2d ed. (Boston: Houghton Mifflin, 1986), p. 161; Thomas Jefferson, quoted in Franklin and Moss, p. 67; (68) White soldier, quoted in William C. Nell, *The American Negro: His History and Literature, Volume I, The Colored Patriots of the American Revolution* (New York: Arno Press, 1968), p. 130.

CHAPTER 7

(71) Prince Whipple, quoted in Benjamin Quarles, *Black Mosaic* (Amherst: University of Massachusetts Press, 1988), p. 48; Passersby, quoted in Quarles, *The Negro in the American Revolution*, p. 3; Boston Massacre participants and witnesses, quoted in Nell, p. 15; Crispus Attucks, quoted in Lerone Bennett, Jr., *Before the Mayflower: A History of the Negro in America 1619–1964* (New York: Penguin, 1982), p. 61; Andrew (an African American slave), quoted in William Loren Katz, *Eyewitness: The Negro in American History* (New York: Pitman, 1967), p. 56. (73) Major Pitcairn and white officers, quoted in Franklin and Moss, p. 68; Slave owner, quoted in Quarles, *The Negro in the American Revolution*, p. 57. (74) White soldier, quoted in Bennett, p. 67. (75) British official and slave-ship owner, quoted in Quarles, *The Negro in the American Revolution*, p. 165; Slave-ship owner, quoted in Nell, p. 244; George Washington, quoted in Robert Goldston, *The Negro Revolution* (New York: Macmillan, 1968), p. 53.

CHAPTER 8

(79) Benjamin Banneker, quoted in Milton Meltzer, ed. *In Their Own Words: A History of the American Negro 1619–1865* (New York: Crowell, 1965), pp. 14–15; Free African Society, quoted in August Meier and Elliot Rudwick, *From Plantation to Ghetto*, 3rd ed. (New York: Hill and Wang, 1976), p. 106. (81) Mr. Ellsworth, quoted in George Williams, *History of the Negro Race in America 1619–1880*, (New York: Arno Press, 1968), p. 418; Free African Society, quoted in Quarles, *Black Mosaic*, p. 63. (82) Lord Chief Justice Mansfield, quoted in Josephine Kamm, *The Slave Trade* (London: Bell & Hyman, 1983), p. 25.

CHAPTER 9

(87) John Johnson and ship captain, quoted in Williams, p. 30; Commodore Chauncey, quoted in Katz (1967 ed.), p. 53; Oliver Hazard Perry, quoted in Franklin and Moss, p. 100. (88) Andrew Jackson, quoted in Bennett, p. 452.

UNIT 4

THE BIG PICTURE

(93) Ralph Ellison, quoted in Herbert George Gutman, *The Black Family in Slavery and Freedom* (New York: Pantheon, 1976), p. 360.

CHAPTER 10

(98) Harriet Jacobs, quoted in Henry L. Gates, Jr., *The Classic Slave Narratives* (New York: Mentor, 1987) pp. 353, 354. (99) White New England minister, quoted in George Williams, *History of the Negro Race in America 1619–1880* (New York: Arno Press, 1968), p. 193; Georgia newspaper, John W. Blassingame, *The Slave Community: Plantation Life in the Ante-Bellum South* (New York: Oxford University Press, 1972), p. 207. (100) South Carolina law, quoted in William Loren Katz, *Eyewitness: The Negro in American History*, 3rd ed., (Belmont, CA: David S. Lake, 1974), p. 34. (101) Song, Millie Williams, former African American slave, quoted in George P. Rawick, ed., *The American Slave: A Composite Autobiography* (Westport, Connecticut: Greenwood Press, 1972), p. 172. (102) Uncle Silas, quoted in Saunders Redding, *They Came in Chains* (New York/Philadelphia: Lippincott, 1973), pp. 35–36. (103) Stephen (an African American child) quoted in James Mellon, ed., *Bullwhip Days* (New York: Avon, 1988), p. 290; Roberta Manson, quoted in Julius Lester, *To Be a Slave* (New York: Scholastic, 1968), p. 33. (105) Solomon Northup, quoted in Milton Meltzer, ed., *In Their Own Words: A History of the American Negro 1619–1983* (New York: Crowell, 1984), p. 24, 25. (107) Harriet Jacobs, quoted in Gates, p. xviii; Henry "Box" Brown, quoted in Charles Stearns, *Narrative of Henry Box Brown* (Boston: Brown and Stearns, 1849), p. 57; song, quoted in William Francis Allen, *Slave Songs of the United States* (New York: Nation Press, 1871), p. 112. (108) One American on slave literature, quoted in, R.J.M. Blackett, *Building an Antislavery Wall: Black Americans in the Atlantic Abolitionist Movement, 1830–1860* (Ithaca: Cornell University Press, 1989), p. 25.

CHAPTER 11

(110) David Walker, quoted in Lerone Bennett, Jr., *Before the Mayflower: A History of the Negro in America 1619–1964* (New York: Penguin, 1982), p. 148. (111) David

Walker, quoted in Milton Meltzer, ed. *The Black Americans: A History in Their Own Words 1619–1983* (New York: Harper and Row, 1984), p. 16. (112) Observer of Stono uprising, Nat Turner, quoted in Herbert Aptheker, *Nat Turner's Slave Rebellion* (New York: Humanities Press, 1966), p. 136. (114) Gabriel Prosser, quoted in Bennett, p. 126. (115) Frederick Douglass, *Ibid.*, p. 170. (116) Nat Turner, quoted in Blassingame (1979 ed.), p. 219. (117) Nat Turner, quoted in Katz (1974 ed.), p. 121; judge, quoted in Bennett, p. 139. (118) Grave marker, quoted in Milton C. McFarlane, *Cudjoe the Maroon* (England: Alison and Busby, 1987).

CHAPTER 12

(120) Nancy Gardner Prince, quoted in Mary Frances Berry and John W. Blassingame, *Long Memory: The Black Experience in America* (New York/Oxford: Oxford U. Press, 1982), p. 50. (121) Nancy Gardner Prince, *Ibid.* (123) Frederick Douglass, quoted in Bennett, p. 180. (125) Free African American statement, quoted in Bennett, p. 147. (142) Sojourner Truth, quoted in Diane Ravitch, *The American Reader: Words That Moved a Nation* (New York: HarperCollins, 1990), p. 86.

UNIT 5

THE BIG PICTURE

(129) Frederick Douglass, quoted in Lerone Bennett, Jr., *Before the Mayflower, A History of the Negro in America 1619–1964* (New York: Penguin, 1982), p. 160. (131) William Lloyd Garrison, *Ibid.*, p. 153.

CHAPTER 13

(135) Women abolitionists' statement, quoted in Dorothy Sterling, ed., *We Are Your Sisters* (New York: Norton, 1984), p. 115. (137) Frederick Douglass, quoted in Benjamin Quarles, *Black Abolitionists* (New York: Da Capo Press, 1969), p. 63; Henry Highland Garnet, quoted in Bennett, p. 155. (138) Henry Highland Garnet, quoted in Mary Frances Berry and John W. Blassingame, *Long Memory: The Black Experience in America* (New York/Oxford: Oxford University Press, 1982), p. 62; Frederick Douglass, quoted in Quarles, p. 66. (139) Frederick Douglass, quoted in Edgar Toppin, *Black Americans in United States History* (Needham, MA: Allyn and Bacon, 1973), p. 121; Frederick Douglass, quoted in William Loren Katz, *Eyewitness: The Negro in American History* (Belmont, CA: David S. Lake, 1974) pp. 162–163. (140) F.E.W. Harper, quoted in Berry and Blassingame, p. 66. (142) Sojourner Truth, quoted in Diane Ravitch, *The American Reader: Words That Moved a Nation* (New York: HarperCollins, 1990), p. 86; Frederick Douglass and Elizabeth Cady Stanton, quoted in Sarah M. Evans, *Born for Liberty* (New York: Free Press, 1989), p. 122. (143) Merchant, quoted in Katz (1974 ed.), p. 173.

CHAPTER 14

(145) William Still, quoted in Quarles, p. 156. (146) Edward Lycurgas, quoted in James Mellon, ed., *Bullwhip Days* (New York: Avon, 1988), p. 302. (148) Thomas Cole, *Ibid.*, p. 65; Harriet Tubman, quoted in Sterling, p. 66. (149) Harriet Tubman, quoted in Bennett, p. 166; Harriet Tubman, quoted in Sterling, p. 69; Harriet Tubman, quoted in Linden, *et al., Legacy of Freedom: A History of the*

United States, (River Forest, IL: Laidlaw, 1986), p. 298; Harriet Tubman, quoted in Bennett, p. 184; Frederick Douglass, quoted in Katz (1974 ed.), p. 185. (150) Reporter, quoted in Sterling, p. 71. (151) John Hope Franklin and Alfred A. Moss, *From Slavery to Freedom,* 6th ed. (New York: Knopf, 1988), pp. 168–69; Charles Blockson, "The Underground Railroad," *National Geographic,* July, 1984, p. 9.

CHAPTER 15

(152) Thomas James, quoted in William S. McFeeley, *Frederick Douglass* (New York: W.W. Norton, 1991), p. 82. (153) Richard Allen, quoted in Katz, p. 59. (154) New York, *Colored American,* quoted in August Meier and Elliot Rudwick, *From Plantation to Ghetto,* 3rd ed., (New York: Hill and Wang, 1976), p. 105. (156) Samuel Ringgold Ward, quoted in Quarles, p. 72. (157) Samuel Ringgold Ward, quoted in Bennett, p. 183.

UNIT 6

THE BIG PICTURE

(161) Frederick Douglass, quoted in Milton Meltzer, ed., *A History in Their Own Words 1619–1983* (New York: Harper and Row, 1984), p. 73. (163) Abraham Lincoln, quoted in Daniel J. Boorstin and Brooks Mather Kelley, *A History of the United States* (Lexington, MA: Ginn and Co., 1981), p. 289.

CHAPTER 16

(166) Frederick Douglass, quoted in Lerone Bennett, Jr., *Before the Mayflower: A History of the Negro in America 1619–1964* (Baltimore: Penguin, 1964), p. 149; (167) Martin Robison Delaney, quoted in William Loren Katz, *Eyewitness: The Negro in American History* (New York: Pitman, 1967), p. 189. (168) African Americans, white abolitionists, and President Franklin Pierce, quoted in James McPherson, *Battle Cry of Freedom* (New York: Oxford, 1988), p. 119. (169) Anthony Burns, quoted in Herbert Aptheker, ed. *A Documentary History of the Negro People in the United States, Vol. I* (New York: Citadel, 1951), p. 371. (171) Newspaper, quoted in McPherson, *Battle Cry,* p. 176; Frederick Douglass, quoted in John Hope Franklin, *From Slavery to Freedom: A History of Negro Americans,* 3rd ed. (New York: McGraw-Hill, 1988), p. 179; John Brown and Frederick Douglass, quoted in McPherson, *Battle Cry,* p. 203. (172) John Brown and Frederick Douglass, *Ibid.,* p. 205. (173) African American women in Brooklyn, quoted in Herbert Aptheker, ed., *A Documentary History of the Negro People in the United States* (New York: Citadel, 1968), p. 441; Baltimore newspaper, quoted in McPherson, *Battle Cry,* p. 211.

CHAPTER 17

(177) *Atlantic Monthly,* quoted in McPherson, *Battle Cry,* p. 686; Frederick Douglass, quoted in James McPherson, *The Negro's Civil War* (New York: Ballantine, 1991), pp. 39–40; Abraham Lincoln, quoted in Boorstin and Kelley, eds, p. 281. (178) Frederick Douglass, quoted in McPherson, *Battle Cry,* p. 558; Henry M. Turner, quoted in McPherson, *Civil War,* p. 50. (179) Linton Stephens, (Southern leader) quoted in Peter J. Parish, *Slavery: History and Historians* (New York: HarperCollins, 1989),

p. 153. (180) Susie King Taylor, quoted in McPherson, *Civil War,* p. 57; Planter, quoted in Franklin, *Slavery to Freedom,* p. 192. (181) Frederick Douglass, quoted in McPherson, *Civil War,* p. 164; Cincinnati whites, quoted in Jack Fincher, "I Felt Freedom in My Bones," *The Smithsonian,* October 1990, p. 48. (182) Abraham Lincoln, *Ibid.,* p. 49; Militia Act, quoted in McPherson, *Civil War,* p. 167; Elijah Marrs, quoted in Fincher, p. 52. (184) African American soldier, *Ibid.;* Lorenzo Thomas (Adjutant general), quoted in Franklin, p. 197. James A. Seddon, quoted in McPherson, *Battle Cry,* p. 793. (186) Peter Burchard, "Heroes of 'Glory' Fought Bigotry Before All Else," quoted in *New York Times,* December 17, 1989. (187) Edwin Stanton, quoted in Benjamin Quarles, *The Negro in the Making of America, Revised Edition* (New York: Collier Books, 1969), p. 119.

CHAPTER 18

(188) Freed African American, quoted in Milton Meltzer, ed., *In Their Own Words: A History of the American Negro 1865–1916* (New York: Crowell, 1965), p. 3. (190) Northern white woman, quoted in Gerda Lerner, *Black Women in White America* (New York: Vintage, 1972), pp. 102–103; Resident of Selma, quoted in Eric Foner, *Reconstruction: America's Unfinished Revolution 1863–1877* (New York: Harper and Row, 1988), p. 98. (191) Former African American slaves, quoted in J.W. Davidson, *et al., Nation of Nations: A Narrative History of the American Republic, Volume II, Since 1865.* (New York: McGraw-Hill, 1990), pp. 621, 624. (192) John Solomon Lewis, quoted in Nell Irvin Painter, *Exodusters* (New York: Knopf, 1977), p. 3. (194) Blanche K. Bruce and white Democrat, quoted in *American Adventures, Vol. 2, Old Hate-New Hope,* (New York: Scholastic, 1970), p. 65. (195) Former African American slave, quoted in Meltzer, (1965 ed.), pp. 34–35. (196) W.E.B. Du Bois, quoted in Foner, p. 602.

CHAPTER 19

(198) John Solomon Lewis (African American sharecropper), quoted in Painter, p. 3. (201) Henry Adams, *Ibid.,* p. 87. (203) Nat Love, quoted in William Loren Katz, *The Black West,* (Seattle: Open Hand, 1987), p. 152.

UNIT 7

THE BIG PICTURE

(207) Thomas E. Miller, quoted in William Loren Katz, *Eyewitness: The Negro in American History* (Belmont, CA: David S. Lake, 1974), p. 334.

CHAPTER 20

(212) "Jim Crow" song, quoted in Lerone Bennett, Jr., *Before the Mayflower: A History of the Negro in America* (New York: Penguin, 1982), p. 255. (213) T. Thomas Fortune, *Black and White* (New York: Arno Press, 1968), p. 29. (214) African American fireman, quoted in Katz (1974 ed.), p. 305. (217) Editor of white newspaper, quoted in C. Vann Woodward, *The Strange Career of Jim Crow* (New York: Oxford University Press, 1974), p. 68. (218) T. Thomas Fortune, quoted in Katz (1974 ed.), p. 343; *Savannah Tribune,* quoted in Katz (1969 ed.), p. 378. (219) Ida B. Wells, quoted in Dorothy Sterling, *Black Foremothers* (New York: Feminist Press/McGraw-

Hill, 1979), p. 79. (220) Delegate and George White, quoted in Katz (1974 ed.), p. 318.

CHAPTER 21

(222) New York *World*, quoted in Bennett, p. 204. (224) Booker T. Washington, *Up From Slavery* (New York: Dodd, Mead, 1965), p. 80. (225) Booker T. Washington, quoted in Emma Lou Thornbrough, ed., *Booker T. Washington* (Englewood Cliffs, NJ: Prentice Hall, 1969), pp. 34, 35. (226) T. Thomas Fortune, *Ibid.*, p. 113; William Monroe Trotter, *Ibid.*, p. 118; Charles W. Chesnutt, *Ibid.*, p. 117; Ida B. Wells-Barnett, *Ibid.*, p. 121; Booker T. Washington, *Ibid.*, p. 35; Andrew Carnegie and Theodore Roosevelt, *Ibid.*, p. 17. (230) Booker T. Washington, courtesy of Tuskegee University.

CHAPTER 22

(240) George Washington Carver, quoted in Gene Adair, *George Washington Carver* (New York: Chelsea House, 1989), p. 83. (241) Paul Laurence Dunbar, *Lyrics of Lowly Life: The Poetry of Paul Laurence Dunbar* (New York: Citadel Press, 1984), p. 167.

UNIT 8

THE BIG PICTURE

(243) W.E.B. Du Bois, quoted in William Loren Katz, *Eyewitness: The Negro in American History*, (Belmont, CA: David S. Lake, 1974), p. 421.

CHAPTER 23

(249) Samuel Courtney (Washington supporter), quoted in Stephen R. Fox, *The Guardian of Boston: William Monroe Trotter* (New York: Atheneum, 1970), p. 52. (250) W.E.B. Du Bois, quoted in August Meier, Elliott Rudwick and Francis L. Broderick, *Black Protest Thought in the Twentieth Century* (New York: Macmillan, 1971), pp. 67–68; W.E.B. Du Bois, quoted in Howard Brotz, ed., *Negro Social and Political Thought 1850–1920* (New York: Basic Books, 1966), p. 518; W.E.B. Du Bois, quoted in Arvarh Strickland and Jerome Reich, *The Black American Experience: From Reconstruction to the Present* (New York: Harcourt Brace Jovanovich, 1974), p. 52. **Points of View:** Booker T. Washington, quoted in *American Reader: Words that Moved a Nation* (New York: HarperCollins, 1990), p. 187; W.E.B. Du Bois, *The Souls of Black Folk* (New York: Bantam, 1989), p. 42. (251) W.E.B. Du Bois, quoted in Herbert Aptheker, ed. *A Documentary History of the United States, Volume II* (New York: Citadel, 1968), pp. 907, 909. (252) William English Walling, quoted in Lerone Bennett, Jr., *Before the Mayflower: A History of the Negro in America* (New York: Penguin, 1984), p. 337. (253) W.E.B. Du Bois, quoted in Bennett, p. 383; National Negro Committee, quoted in Patricia W. Romero, ed., *I, Too, Am America: Documents from 1619 to the Present* (New York: Publishers Company, 1969), p. 182; NAACP, *Ibid.*, p. 183; Deputy, quoted in Katz (1974 ed.), p. 350. (254) NAACP, quoted in Meier, Rudwick and Broderick, p. 66. (255) W.E.B. Du Bois, quoted in Katz (1974 ed.), p. 420–421. (256) Benjamin Hooks, quoted in "Called Complacent, NAACP Looks to Future," *New York Times,* June 10, 1991. (257) W.E.B. Du Bois, quoted in *The Souls of Black Folk*, p. 37.

CHAPTER 24

(258) Hattiesburg, Mississippi man, quoted in Leslie H. Fishel, Jr. and Benjamin Quarles, *The Negro American* (New York: William Morrow & Co., 1967), p. 399. (260) Lonely voice, quoted in Milton Meltzer, ed., *In Their Own Words: A History of the American Negro 1916–1965,* (New York: Crowell, 1967), pp. 4–5; African American newspapers, quoted in Emmet J. Scott, *Negro Migration During the War* (New York: Arno Press and the *New York Times,* 1969), p. 31. (265) W.E.B. Du Bois, quoted in Meltzer, *(1916–1965),* p. 27.

CHAPTER 25

(269) Marcus Mosiah Garvey, quoted in E. David Cronon, *Marcus Garvey* (Englewood Cliffs, NJ: Prentice Hall, 1973), p. 8; Hugh Mulzac (meeting participant), quoted in David L. Lewis, *When Harlem Was in Vogue* (New York: Oxford University Press, 1981), p. 39; W.E.B. Du Bois, *Ibid.*, p. 15. (270) *Kansas City Call, Ibid.*, p. 24; Claude McKay, quoted in Mary Ellison, *The Black Experience: American Blacks Since 1865* (New York: Barnes & Noble, 1974), p. 106. (271) Marcus Garvey, quoted in E. David Cronon, *Black Moses: The Story of Marcus Garvey and the Universal Negro Improvement Association* (Madison: The University of Wisconsin Press, 1969), p. 189; Marcus Garvey, quoted in John H. Bracey, Jr., August Meier, Elliot Rudwick, *Black Nationalism in America* (New York: Bobbs-Merrill, 1970), p. 191. (272) Marcus Garvey, quoted in Maulana Karenga, *Introduction to Black Studies,* (Los Angeles: Kawaida Press, 1982), p. 118; Marcus Garvey, quoted in Cronon, *Marcus Garvey,* p. 29; Mary White Ovington (Garvey observer), quoted in Lewis, p. 39. (273) *New York Amsterdam News,* quoted in Ellison, p. 102; Marcus Garvey, quoted in Cronon, *Black Moses,* p. 207. (274) Kwame Nkrumah, quoted in David Lamb, *The Africans* (New York: Vintage Books, 1987), p. 286. (275) Cronon, *Black Moses.*

CHAPTER 26

(277) African American newspaper, quoted in Lewis, p. 24; African American poet, quoted in Milton Meltzer, ed., *The Black Americans: A History in Their Own Words 1619–1983* (New York: Harper and Row, 1984), p. 202; African American writer, quoted in Lewis, p. 96. (283) Sargent Johnson, quoted in *The Negro Almanac* (New York: Bell-Weather, 1976), p. 765. (287) Langston Hughes, reprinted in *The American Experience* (Englewood Cliffs, NJ: Prentice Hall, 1989), p. 965.

CHAPTER 27

(288) Crowd member, quoted in Meltzer, *In Their Own Words* (New York: Crowell, 1967), p. 98. (289) Langston Hughes, *The Big Sea* (New York: Thunder's Mouth Press, 1986); Arnold Y. Hill, (Urban League member), quoted in Howard Sitkoff, *A New Deal for Blacks: The Emergence of Civil Rights as a National Issue, Volume I: The Depression Decade* (New York: Oxford University Press, 1978), p. 35. (291) Robert Vann, quoted in Strickland and Reich, p. 74; Man, quoted in Studs Terkel, *Hard Times: An Oral History of the Great Depression* (New York: Pantheon, 1970), p. 499. (292) Franklin D. Roosevelt, quoted in "The Negro and the New Deal Era," *Wisconsin Magazine of History* (Winter 1964–5); African American woman, quoted in

Katz, (1969 ed.), p. 435; Franklin D. Roosevelt, quoted in Sitkoff, p. 44; NAACP member, *Ibid.*, p. 55. (293) African American newspaper, *Ibid.*, p. 65; Eleanor Roosevelt, *Ibid.*, p. 63; Mary McLeod Bethune, quoted in Paula Giddings, *When and Where I Enter: The Impact of Black Women on Race and Sex in America* (New York: Bantam, 1984), p. 222. (294) New Deal program, quoted in Sitkoff, p. 69; Paul Robeson, *Ibid.*, p. 328. (295) Frances Perkins, quoted in Katz, (1974 ed.), p. 430; Union organizer, *Ibid.*, p. 423. (296) Thurgood Marshall, quoted in Bracey, Meier, and Rudwick; A. Philip Randolph, quoted in Edgar Toppin, *The Black American in U.S. History* (Boston: Allyn and Bacon, 1973), p. 233. (298) Ernest Critchlow, quoted in Katz (1974 ed.), p. 428.

UNIT 9

THE BIG PICTURE

(301) Martin Luther King, Jr., quoted in Diane Ravitch, ed. *The American Reader: Words That Moved a Nation* (New York: HarperCollins, 1990), p. 333.

CHAPTER 28

(307) Leslie Lee, quoted in "World War II's Black Pilots Fought on Two Fronts," *New York Times*, April 21, 1991. (308) African American soldier, quoted in William Loren Katz, *Eyewitness: The Negro in American History* (Belmont, CA: David S. Lake, 1974), p. 466. (309) Sybil Lewis, quoted in Mark Jonathan Harris, Franklin D. Mitchell, and Steven J. Schechter, *The Homefront: America During World War II* (New York: Putnam, 1984), p. 119. (313) Geoffrey Perrett, *Days of Sadness, Years of Triumph* (New York: Coward, McCann, and Geoghegan, Inc., 1973), p. 323; James Baldwin, quoted in J. Milton Yinger, *A Minority Group in American Society*, (New York: McGraw-Hill, 1965), p. 52.

CHAPTER 29

(318) John Birks "Dizzy" Gillespie, quoted in Studs Terkel, *Giant of Jazz* (New York: Crowell, 1957), p. 192. (320) John H. Johnson, "Publishers Statement" *Ebony*, Nov. 1990. (321) Ralph Ellison, "Flying Home", quoted in Edgar V. Roberts and Henry E. Jacobs, *Literature: An Introduction to Reading and Writing* (Englewood Cliffs: Prentice Hall, 1986), pp. 357–358.

CHAPTER 30

(323) Thurgood Marshall, quoted in William H. Chaffe, *The Unfinished Journey* (New York: Oxford University Press, 1986), p. 149. (325) Earl Warren, quoted in Chaffe, p. 152. (326) Rosa Parks and white bus driver, quoted in Henry Hampton and Steve Fayer, *Voices of Freedom: An Oral History of the Civil Rights Movement From the 1950s Through the 1960s* (New York: Bantam, 1990), p. 20; Leaflet, quoted in Anna Kosoff, *The Civil Rights Movement and Its Legacy* (New York: Franklin Watts, 1989), pp. 31, 33. (327) Elderly African American woman, quoted in Robert Weisbrot, *Freedom Bound* (New York: Plume, 1990), p. 17; Martin Luther King, Jr., quoted in J.W. Davidson, *et al.*, *Nation of Nations: A Narrative History* (New York: McGraw-Hill), p. 1167. (328) Ezell Blair, Jr., quoted in Chaffe, p. 168; A&T student, quoted in "Negroes in South in Store Sit-down," the *New York Times*, Feb. 3,

1960; Martin Luther King, Jr., quoted in Stephen B. Oates, "Trumpet of Conscience," *American History Illustrated*, April 1988. (329) James Farmer and Diane Nash, quoted in Pete Seeger and Bob Reiser, *Everybody Says Freedom* (New York: Norton, 1989), p. 52. Freedom Rider's song, *Ibid.*, p. 61. (330) Martin Luther King, Jr., quoted in Lerone Bennett Jr., *Before the Mayflower: A History of the Negro in America 1619–1964* (New York: Penguin, 1982), p. 388; "Bull" Connor, quoted in Katz, p. 484; Martin Luther King, Jr., quoted in Seeger and Reiser, p. 109. (331) John F. Kennedy, Jr., quoted in Chaffe, p. 214; Martin Luther King, Jr., quoted in Ravitch, *The American Reader*, p. 332. (332) School board member, quoted in "Historic Battleground, Old Battle: School Bias," *New York Times*, December 22, 1989.

CHAPTER 31

(335) Martin Luther King, Jr., quoted in Paul Sann, *The Angry Decade: The Sixties* (New York: Crown, 1979), p. 140. (336) Fannie Lou Hamer, quoted in Hampton and Fayer, p. 178; Fannie Lou Hamer, quoted in Chaffe, *The Unfinished Journey* (New York: Oxford, 1986), pp. 312–313. (337) Malcolm X, quoted in Meier, Bracey, and Rudwick, p. 41. (338) Malcolm X, quoted in Seeger and Reiser, p. 190. (339) Commentator, quoted in Rhoda Lois Blumberg, *Civil Rights: The 1960s Freedom Struggle* (Boston: G.K. Hall, 1991), p. 41. (340) James Meredith, quoted in Sann, p. 181; Stokely Carmichael and Willie Ricks, quoted in Seeger and Reiser, p. 218; Stokely Carmichael, quoted in Blumberg, p. 431. (341) Martin Luther King, Jr., quoted in Chaffe, p. 367. (342) Lyndon B. Johnson, quoted in Sann, p. 229; Martin Luther King, Jr., *Ibid.*, p. 231; Kerner Commission report, quoted in Anna Kosof, *The Civil Rights Movement and Its Legacy* (New York: Franklin Watts, 1989), p. 91. (343) Barbara Jordan, quoted in Kosof, p. 91. (344) C. Eric Lincoln and Lawrence Mamiya, *The Black Church in the African American Experience* (Durham: Duke University Press, 1990), p. 369. (345) Marian Wright Edelman, quoted in Hampton and Fayer, p. 244; Alex Haley, *Ibid.*, p. 250.

CHAPTER 32

(348) Robin Mannock (reporter) and Clide Brown (soldier), quoted in "The Negro in Vietnam," *Time*, May 26, 1967, p. 15. (349) Martin Luther King, Jr., quoted in Weisbrot, p. 247; African American soldier, quoted in Mary Frances Berry and John W. Blassingame, *Long Memory: The Black Experience in America* (New York: Oxford University Press, 1982), p. 333. (350) Martin Luther King, Jr., quoted in Weisbrot, p. 247; Viet Cong leaflets and African American medic, quoted in *Time*, Jan. 19, 1968, p. 21. (351) From an interview with John Wilkins, Aug. 1991. (353) African American soldier, quoted in "The Negro in Vietnam," *Time*, May 26, 1967, p. 18. (354) Visitor to "the Wall," quoted in Wallace Terry, *Bloods* (New York: Ballantine Books, 1984), p. 331. (355) "Siege of Khesahn Lifted; Troops Hunt Foe," *New York Times*, April 6, 1968.

UNIT 10

THE BIG PICTURE

(357) John Hope Franklin and Alfred A. Moss, Jr., *From Slavery to Freedom: A History of Negro Americans* (New York: McGraw Hill, 1988), p. 494.

CHAPTER 33

(362) John Lewis, quoted in "For Freedom Riders the Journey Continues," *USA Today*, May 3, 1991. (363) Andrew Young, quoted in "Race and the South," *U.S. News and World Report*, July 23, 1990. (366) Dr. Neil Shulman, quoted in "Gap Widens Between Blacks', Whites' Life Expectancies," *Poughkeepsie Journal*, July 26, 1991; Reverend Joseph Lowery, quoted in *USA Today*, May 3, 1991. (367) Lee Woods (African American surgeon), quoted in "Success Divides Blacks," *USA Today*, Aug. 1991; Robert F. Kennedy and John Emmerich, (Greenwood editor), quoted in "Sad Song of the Delta," *Time* magazine, June 24, 1991. (368) Bern Keating, (Greenwood official), *Ibid.*; Douglas Glasgow, *The Black Underclass* (New York: Vintage Books, 1981), p. 274. (369) Ernest Youngblood, quoted in "Holding on to Dreams Amid Harlem's Reality," the *New York Times*, Feb. 1991. (370) Population Reference Bureau study, quoted in "Blacks Gaining, Receding," the *Baltimore Sun;* African American social worker, quoted in "As Many Fall, Projects' Survivors Struggle On," the *New York Times*, February 5, 1991; Clara McBride Hale, quoted in "I Dream a World," *National Geographic*, August 1989. (371) Dorothy I. Height, quoted in "Celebrating the Black Family," *Ebony*, Oct. 1990; Earl G. Graves, quoted in "Giving Until It Helps," *Black Enterprise*, July 1990. (372) Reverend Alicia Byrd, Linda Perkins, Reverend Willie Gable and Michael Dameron, quoted in "Black Churches Turn to Teaching their Young," the *New York Times*, Aug. 17, 1991. (374) High School senior, quoted in *Time* Magazine, Mar. 20, 1989.

CHAPTER 34

(376) Martin Luther King, Jr., quoted in *Black Stars in Orbit*, a film by Williams Miles; Miles Educational Film Productions, Inc., in association with WNET/13, produced in 1990. Nichelle Nichols, *Ibid.* (379) Jesse Jackson, quoted in Franklin and Moss, p. 478; Jesse Jackson, quoted in Diane Ravitch, ed. *The American Reader: Words that Moved a Nation.* (New York: HarperCollins, 1990), p. 368. (380) **Points of View:** Robert Woodson and Reverend Joseph Lowery, courtesy of MacNeil/Lehrer News Hour, May 27, 1991. (381) Charles V. Hamilton, quoted in "How Black Politicians Changed America," *Ebony*, Aug. 1991. (382) Charlotte Neuville, quoted in "Where the Home Girls Are," *Newsweek*, June 17, 1991; John Johnson, "Publisher's Statement," *Ebony*, Aug. 1991; Robert Weisbord, quoted in Benjamin Quarles, *The Negro in the Making of America*, (New York: Collier Books, 1969). (383) Arthur Mitchell and Katherine Dunham, quoted in "There's No Business Like Black Show Business," *Ebony*, August 1991. (384) Alex Haley, quoted in "Why Roots Hit Home," *Time*, February 14, 1977. (385) "Hitting the Hot Button" *US News & World Report*, July 9, 1990. (387) Nelson Mandela, quoted in "Mandela," *Newsweek*, July 2, 1990. (389) Leon H. Sullivan, quoted in "A Meeting Place for Africans and U.S. Blacks," the *New York Times*, April 18, 1991; Leon H. Sullivan and Felix Houphouet-Boigny, quoted in "First African/African-American Summit," *Ebony*, Aug. 1991; Leon H. Sullivan, quoted in "Meeting Place for Africans," the *New York Times*, April 18, 1991. (390) African proverb, quoted in Kamuyu-wa-Kangethe and Maina-wa-Kinyatti, *What Is Your African Name?* (Jamaica, New York: Pan African Students' Organization), unpaged leaflet.

INDEX

Note: Pages in **boldface** indicate photographs, maps, charts, and graphs; pages in *italics* indicate incorporated biographies and galleries.

A

Aaron, Hank, 323
Abbott, Robert S., 262, *263*
Abeokuta, Yoruba city of, 27–28
Abernathy, Ralph, 328
abolitionism, 80, 124, 129, 131–32, 134–43, 150
 differences among abolitionists, 136
 in 1840s, 156–57
 former slaves in, 137–39
 John Brown's raid and, 171–73, 251
 reactions to, 136
 tactics of, 140–41
 women's movement and, 132–33, 135, 139, 142
Abu Bakr, 18
Accra (Ghana), 44
actors, 319, **385**–86
Adams, Henry, 200, 201
Adams, Lewis, 230
Addams, Jane, 243, 253
Adulis, 13
affirmative action, 359, 381
Africa
 African American involvement in events of, 386–89
 ancient kingdoms of, 5–7, **9**–13
 birthplace of humans in, 4–5
 contemporary, 44, 386–89
 cultures of, 9–11, 382
 physical features and climates of, **3**–4
 religion in, 13, 18, 19, 20, 26–27, 44
African American studies, 343
African dialects, 44, 99
African Methodist Episcopal (AME) Church, 154, 158
African Methodist Episcopal Zion (AMEZ) Church, 152, 153, 248
African National Congress (ANC), 386, 387
Afro-American League of the United States, 251
Afro-Caribbean culture, 50
agenda for change (1972–present), 362–73
ages of African Americans, 365
Air Force Academy, 353
Akhenaton, 7
Alexander the Great, 7
Ali, Muhammad, *348*–49
Allen, Richard, **78**, 79, 87, 153–54, 157, 158
Allies, World War I and II, 244, 301
almanac, 79
Almoravids, 18, 19
Alvin Ailey American Dance Theater, 383

American Anti-Slavery Society, 131–32, 134–35, 136. *See also* abolitionism
American Colonization Society, 125
American Federation of Labor (AFL), 209, 295
American Revolution, 61, 65–68, 70–77
 African American participation in, 66–67, 73–74, **353**
 battles of, 72–74
 British promises of freedom to slaves in, 67, 74
 debate over slavery and, 67–68
 seeds of conflict, 65, 66, 71–72
American Society for the Promotion of Temperance, 129
Americas, spread of slavery to, 35–37. *See also* colonial America
Amsterdam News, 273
Anansi the Spider, 30
ancestor worship, 27
Anderson, Aaron, **182**
Anderson, Elijah, 147
Anderson, Marion, **292**
Anderson, Osborne Perry, 173
Antietam, Battle of (1862), 178
Antislavery efforts, early, 130–31. *See also* abolitionism
antislavery newspapers, 140–41
apartheid, 386–88
armed forces. *See also* enlistment in armed forces, African American
 African American officers in, 308, 312
 integration of, 302, 303, 347
 segregation in, 263–64, 297, 301, 307–309, 308
 after Vietnam War, 353
 women in, 312
 in World War II, 307–309, 311, 312, **353**
Armistead, James, **74**
Armstrong, Louis "Satchmo," *280,* 285, 317
Armstrong, Samuel Chapman, 223
Army, U.S., 263–64. *See also* armed forces
Articles of Confederation, 80
artists, 234, 235, 238, 277, **282**–83, 298, 319, 383–84
arts, the, A1–A16
 contemporary, 382–386
 in 1800s, 234–35, 238
 Harlem Renaissance and, 276–85
 post–World War II, 317–19
 West African artistic styles, 28–29
Asante, 29, 30, A2
Ashworth, Aaron, 123
Askia Muhammad, 21
Aspelta, King, **12**
assimilation, 341
Assyrians, 10–11

Atlanta Compromise, 225, 239, 250
Atlanta Constitution, 211
Atlantic Monthly, 177
Atlantic slave trade. *See* slave trade
Attucks, Crispus, **71**–72
Axis powers, World War II, 301
Axum, kingdom of, 7, **9**, 12–13
Ayllon, Luis Vasquez de, 52–53
Aztec empire, 52

B

Bailey, Frederick Augustus Washington. *See* Douglass, Frederick
Bailey, Xenobia, A13
Baker, Henry E., 239
Bakke v. *University of California,* 359
Balboa, Vasco Nuñez de, 35
Baldwin, James, 316, 317
banks, African American, 228
Banneker, Benjamin, 64, 78–79
Baptist church, 154
Baraka, Imamu Amiri (LeRoi Jones), 317–18
Barbadoes, James G., 135
Barnett, Ferdinand L., 219
Barthé, Richmond, *282*
baseball, major league, 322–23
Basie, Count, 317
Baumfree, Isabella. *See* Truth, Sojourner
Bearden, Romare, *282,* 383, **A16**
Beaty, Powhatan, **182**
bebop, 318
Beckwourth, James P., *89*
Belafonte, Harry, 319
Bell, Alexander Graham, 207
Beloved (Morrison), 384, 385
Benin, people of, 26, 29, A4
Berry, Chuck, 286, 318
Bessemer, Henry, and Bessemer process, 207
Bethel Church. *See* Mother Bethel African Methodist Episcopal Church
Bethune, Mary McLeod, *293,* 312
Bibb, Mary, 139
Biddle, Nicholas, **182**
big business, 103, 207–208
Biggers, John, A14
Birmingham, Alabama, King's civil rights march in, 330–31
Birney, James G., 136
birthplace of humans, 4–5
Black Cabinet, 293
Black Codes, 164, 193
Black Eagles, **307**, 308
Black Eagles (play), 307
Black Enterprise, 371
Black Family Reunion (festival), 371
Blackman, Pomp, 73
Black Muslims, 336–37, 338, 348

education (*continued*)
African Americans colleges and universities, 124, 223–25, 229-**30, 233,** 238, 374
after Civil War, thirst for, 190
desegregation of, 323–25
drop-out rate, 366, 369
of free African Americans, 124, **125**
industrial, 224–25, 226
in Mali empire, 19–20
post-World War II, 316
public, 129–30, 190, 233
reform of, 129–30
today, **365,** 366
Washington's belief in advancement through, 223, 225
Egypt, ancient, 5–**7,** 9–11
Eisenhower, Dwight, 302–303, 325
elections
of 1932, 291
of 1936, 291–92
of 1964, 335
of 1968, 305, 377–78
electricity, invention of, 207
Elementary and Secondary School Act (1965), 305
Ellington, Duke, 276, *280,* **285,**
Ellison, Ralph, 93, 298, 317, 321
Emancipation Proclamation (1863), 163–64, 177, 178-**79,** 329, 330
employment. *See also* labor; working conditions
affirmative action and, 359
during World War II, 310
English, William, 256
English colonies, 36–37, 47, 48, 52–63
enlistment in armed forces, African American
in American Revolution, 66–67, 73–74, **353**
in Civil War, 176–77, 181–85, **353**
in Vietnam War, 347–49, **353,** 354
in World War I, 263–64, **265,** 353
in World War II, 307–309, **311,** 312, **353**
entertainment, 246, 385–86
entrepreneurs, African American, 123–24
equator, 3
Equiano, Olaudah, **25,** 26, 27, 28, 48
escaping from slavery, 141, 144–51
Underground Railroad and, 121, 145, 146–49, **147,** 150, 157, 158, 166, 252
Estabrook, Prince, 73
Estevanico, 53
Ethiopia, 7, **13**
Europe, expanding horizons of, 33–34
Europe, James, 266
European immigrants, arrival of, 95
Evers, Medgar, 331
Executive Order 8802, 297
Exodusters, 200–202

extended families, 25, 106–107
Ezana, King, 12–13

F

face vessel, A7
factories, 94–95, 243
Fairbanks, Calvin, 146–47
Fair Employment Practices Committee (FEPC), 297, 310
family life, 25–26, 99, 101, 102–103, 106–107, 189, 371
Farmer, James, 328–29, 362
farmers, subsistence, 26, 36
farming, invention of, 5
Farm Security Administration (FSA), 293
Faubus, Orval, 325
Fauset, Jessie R., *278*
federal system, 80
Female Anti-Slavery Society of Philadelphia, 135
15th Amendment, 142, **165,** 215
51st Fighter Interceptor Wing, 308
54th Massachusetts Infantry, 176–77, 186
Fire!! (Thurman), 279
First Battalion of the 367th Infantry Regiment of the 92nd Division, 265
Fisk Jubilee Singers, **232**
Fisk University, 219, 232, 374
Flora, William, **88**
Florida, fugitive slaves in, 88, 112
"Flying Home" (Ellison), 321
folk heroes, 203
folktales, 29, 30, 101
Foote, Shelby, 186
Ford, Gerald, 358
Forneret, Charles, **88**
Forrest, Nathan B., 185
Forten, Charlotte, 253
Forten, Harriett, Sarah, and Margarette, 135
Forten, James, 123, 124, 126, 134, 135
Fort Pillow, massacre at (1864), 184-**85**
Fort Sumter, bombardment of (1861), 163, **164**
Fortune, T. Thomas, 213, 218, **226,** 251
Fort Wagner, Battle of (1863), 176–77
450th Anti-Aircraft Artillery Battalion, 311
14th Amendment, 142, 164, **165,** 216, 325
14th U.S. Colored Infantry, 160
France, 65, 264
Franklin, Aretha, 386
Franklin, Benjamin, 65
free African Americans, 120–127, 130–31
Free African Society, 79–80, 81, 153

Freedmen's Bureau, 164, 189, 190, **191**
freedom laws, 169
freedom rides, 328-**29,** 362, 363
Freedom's Journal, 110, 141
freedom songs, 344
Free Soil party, 132
Free Speech (newspaper), 219
French and Indian War, 65
Frye, Marquette, 339
fugitive slave laws, 137
of 1793, 146
of 1850, 150, 157, 162, 167–69, 171, 173
Fuller, Meta Vaux Warrick, *282*
Fulton, Robert, 93
fund-raising, antislavery, 141
fur trade, 89

G

Gable, Willie, 372
Gandhi, Mohandas, 327
Garnet, Henry Highland, *137–38,* 148, 156
Garrison, William Lloyd, 124, 131–32, 134, 136
Garvey, Marcus Mosiah, **268**–69, *271,* 274, 277, 336, 343, 387, 389
black nationalist message of, 269, 271–73
gens de couleur, 90
Georgia, colony of, 57
German immigrants, 95
Ghana, 30, 44, 274
Ghana, empire of, 7, **17**–18, 19
ghettoes, 261, 339, 369–71
GI Bill, 311
Gillespie, Dizzy, 318
Glasgow, Douglas, 368
Glory (movie), 186
gold, trade in, 17–18, 19, 20
Goldberg, Whoopi, 386
Gold Rush of 1849, 165, 199–200
gospel music, 318
government(s)
Constitution and formation of, 80
policies on discrimination, 295–97
Reconstruction, 190, 192–94
governors, African American, 193, 379–80
gradualists, 131
Grady, Henry, 211
Grambling State University, 374
grandfather clause, **215**
Grand United Order of True Reformers, 228
Grant, Ulysses S., 164
Gravely, Samuel L., Jr., 353
Graves, Earl G., 371
Great Britain, 65, 68, 82, 87–88, 130. *See also* American Revolution
Great Depression of 1930s, 288–97
New Deal and, 246–47, 291–95
Great Migration (1915–1930), 245, 258–65, 277

413

PHOTO CREDITS

UNIT 1

2: (top) Art Resource; (bottom left) Art Resource; (bottom right) International Film Foundation. 6: Russell Thompson/Omni Photos. 8: Russell Thompson/Omni Photos. 10: British Museum/Michael Holford. 11: Museum of Fine Arts, Boston. 12: American Museum of Natural History. 13: Photo Researchers. 16: Granger Collection. 19: American Museum of Natural History. 20: Granger Collection. 21: Tom Hollyman/Photo Researchers. 24: UNICEF Photos. 25: The Schomberg Center for Research in Black Culture/New York Public Library/Astor, Lennox & Tilden Foundation. 26: American Museum of Natural History. 27: Art Resource. 28: George Gerster/Comstock. 29: National Museum of African Art, Smithsonian Institution.

UNIT 2

32: (top) Granger Collection; (bottom left) American Museum of Natural History; (bottom right) Granger Collection. 36: Granger Collection. 38: National Maritime Museum. 39: Granger Collection. 41: The Schomberg Center. 43: The Schomberg Center. 46: Granger Collection. 49: The Schomberg Center. 52: Colonial Williamsburg. 56: The Schomberg Center. 57: The American Antiquarian Society. 59: Granger Collection.

UNIT 3

64: (top) Maryland Historical Society; (bottom left) The Schomberg Center; (bottom right) Bettmann Archive. 68: Courtesy of the Valley Forge Historical Society. 70: Library of Congress. 71: Bettmann Archive. 72: Library of Congress. 74: The Valentine Museum, Richmond, VA. 78: (left) Granger Collection; (right) The Delaware Art Museum. 84: Bettmann Archive. 87: Courtesy of the Historic New Orleans Society. 89: State Historical Society of Colorado.

UNIT 4

92: (top) Granger Collection; (bottom left) Oberlin College Archives; (bottom right) The Schomberg Center. 96: National Archive. 97: Historical Picture Service. 98: Granger Collection. 101: Granger Collection. 102: Culver Pictures, Inc. 104: (top) Courtesy of the Historic New Orleans Collection, Museum/Research Center; (bottom) The Schomberg Center. 105: Courtesy of the Historic New Orleans Collection. 106: The Schomberg Center. 110: The Library of Congress. 111: Granger Collection. 112: Culver Pictures, Inc. 116: Granger Collection. 117: Culver Pictures, Inc. 120: Granger Collection. 122: State Department of Cultural Resources, Division of Archives and History, Raleigh, NC. 123: Granger Collection. 124: The Schomberg Center. 125: The Schomberg Center.

UNIT 5

128: (top) Granger Collection; (bottom left) The American Antiquarian Society; (bottom right) Bettmann Archive. 132: Granger Collection. 133: Granger Collection. 134: Three Lions, Inc. 137: (top) Granger Collection; (bottom) The Schomberg Center. 138: Granger Collection. 139: (left) Granger Collection; (right) The Schomberg Center. 140: (top) Granger Collection; (bottom) Bettmann Archive. 141: Granger Collection. 144: The Sophia Smith Collection. 145: Bettmann Archive. 147: The Schomberg Center. 148: (left) The Schomberg Center; (right) Granger Collection. 152: Mother Church of African Methodism. 155: Museum of Art, Rhode Island School of Design, Gift of Miss Lucy T. Aldrich. 156: The Schomberg Center.

UNIT 6

160: (top) Granger Collection; (bottom left) Granger Collection; (bottom right) Alan Scherr. 164: Granger Collection. 166: Granger Collection. 167: Granger Collection. 168: Granger Collection. 170: Granger Collection. 172: Granger Collection. 173: Granger Collection. 176: Culver Pictures, Inc. 180: Granger Collection. 181: Granger Collection. 182: Culver Pictures, Inc. 183: Chicago Historical Society. 184: Granger Collection. 185: Granger Collection. 188: Morris Museum of Art, Augusta, GA. 191: Bettmann Archive. 192: Culver Pictures, Inc. 193: (top) Bettmann Archive; (bottom) Culver Pictures, Inc. 194: Granger Collection. 195: The Rutherford B. Hayes Presidential Center. 198: Nebraska State Historical Society. 199: The Schomberg Collection. 200: Denver Public Library. 201: Bettmann Archive. 203: The Schomberg Center.

UNIT 7

206: (top) Granger Collection; (bottom) Tougaloo College Archives. 210: Museum of the City of New York. 211: Brown Brothers. 212: (top) ME Warren Collection/Photo Researchers; (bottom) Culver Pictures, Inc. 214: Granger Collection. 217: Bettmann Archive. 219: The Schomberg Center. 222: Library of Congress. 223: State Historical Society of Iowa, Museum Bureau. 224: Bettmann Archive. 225: Granger Collection. 227: Granger Collection. 228: Granger Collection. 229: Bettmann Archive. 232:Culver Pictures, Inc. 234: (top) Brown Brothers; (bottom) Ohio Historical Society. 235: (top to bottom) Brown Brothers; Smithsonian Institution; Schomberg Center; Granger Collection. 236: (top to bottom) Granger Collection; Bettmann Archive; U.S. Department of the Interior, National Park Service, Edison National Historic Site; Granger Collection. 237: (top to bottom) Granger Collection; The Schomberg Center; Granger Collection; The Schomberg Center. 238: Schomberg Center.

UNIT 8

242: (top) The Schomberg Center; (bottom left) Bettmann Archive; (bottom right) Bettmann Archive. 246: Brown Brothers. 247: Culver Pictures, Inc. 248: Courtesy of NAACP Public Relations. 249: Bettmann Archive. 252: Granger Collection. 255: Courtesy of NAACP Public Relations. 258: Bettmann Archive. 260: Bettmann Archive. 262: Brown Brothers. 263: The Schomberg Center. 264: Bettmann Archive. 265: Bettmann Archive. 268: UPI Bettmann. 269: The Schomberg Center. 270: Brown Brothers. 271: Culver Pictures, Inc. 272: The Schomberg Center. 276: The Schomberg Center. 278: (top to bottom) Granger Collection; Courtesy of the National Portrait Gallery; Granger Collection; Granger Collection. 279: (top to bottom) Brown Brothers; Brown Brothers; National Portrait Gallery; 280: (top to bottom) Photofest; Granger Collection; Culver Pictures; Bettmann Archive. 281: (top to bottom) Granger Collection; Granger Collection; Granger Collection; Photofest. 282: Courtesy of the National Portrait Gallery. 283: Courtesy of the National Portrait Gallery; Bettmann Archive. 284: Culver Pictures. 285: Duke Ellington, Inc. 288: Bettmann Archive. 290: Bettmann Archive. 292: Bettmann Archive. 293: Bettmann Archive. 294: Bettmann Archive. 295: Bettmann Archive. 296: Culver Pictures, Inc. 297: Wide World Photos.

UNIT 9

300: (top) Burton Berinsky/Omni; (bottom left) Carl Iwasaki/Life Magazine © Time Inc.; (bottom right) Culver Pictures, Inc. 304: UPI Bettmann. 306: The Schomberg Center. 307: Culver Pictures, Inc. 308: Bettmann Archive. 310: Wide World Photos. 311: Bettmann Archive. 314: Courtesy of the National Cotton

Council. 315: Courtesy of the Chicago Housing Department. 317: Bettmann Archive. 318: Bettmann Archive. 319: Bettmann Archive. 322: Bettmann Archive. 323: Library of Congress. 325: Bettmann Archive. 326: Bettmann Archive. 327: Bettmann Archive. 328: Wide World Photos. 329: Bettmann Archive. 331: Bettmann Archive. 334: Magnum Photos. 336: Bettmann Archive. 337: Bettmann Archive. 339: Bettmann Archive. 341: Wide World Photos. 342: Bettmann Archive. 343: Magnum Photos. 346: John Wilkins. 348: Bettmann Archive. 349: Granger Collection. 351: Wide World Photos. 352: Wide World Photos.

UNIT 10

356: (top) Stock Boston; (bottom) Omni. 360: Stock Boston. 361: Bettmann Archive. 362: Wide World Photos. 364: Photo Researchers. 365: Stock Boston. 366: Ken Karp/Omni. 368: Wide World Photos. 369: Stock Boston. 370: Wide World Photos. 372: Wide World Photos. 373: (top) Steve Kagan/NYT Pictures; (bottom) Photo Researchers. Archive. 376: Bettmann Archive. 377: Wide World Photos. 378: Bettmann Archive. 379: Stock Boston. 380: Bettmann Archive. 381: Wide World Photos. 382: Photo Researchers. 383: (top) Bettmann Archive; (bottom) Martha Swope. 384: (top left) Bettmann Archive; (top right) Wide World Photos; (bottom) Bettmann Archive. 385: (top left) Photofest; (top right) Photofest; (bottom left) Photofest; (bottom right) Wide World Photos. 386: Gamma Liaison. 387: Bettmann Archive. 388: Photo Researchers.

ACKNOWLEDGMENTS

Grateful acknowledgment is made to the following for permission to reprint copyrighted material:

AYER COMPANY—p. 99: from *History of the Negro Race in America 1619–1880*, by George Washington Williams. Reprinted by permission of Ayer Company Publishers, Box 958, Salem, N.H. 03102.

BANTAM DOUBLEDAY DELL PUBLISHING GROUP INC.—pp. 251, 257: from *The Souls of Black Folk*, by W. E. B. Du Bois. Courtesy of Bantam Doubleday Dell Publishing Group Inc.—pp. 326, 336, 345: from *Voices of Freedom: An Oral History of the Civil Rights Movement from the 1950s Through the 1980s*, by Henry Hampton and Steve Fayer. Copyright (c) 1990. Reprinted by permission of Bantam Books.

THE JOAN DAVES AGENCY—p. 330: from "Letter from Birmingham Jail," Copyright 1963 by Martin Luther King, Jr., copyright renewed 1991 by Coretta Scott King. Reprinted by permission of The Joan Daves Agency.—p.335: from "Nobel Acceptance Speech," Copyright, 1964, 1965, The Nobel Foundation. Reprinted by permission of The Joan Daves Agency.— p. 341: from "I've Been to the Mountaintop," Copyright 1968, the Estate of Martin Luther King, Jr. Reprinted by permission of The Joan Daves Agency.—pp. 301, 330: from "I Have a Dream," Copyright 1963 by Martin Luther King, Jr., copyright renewed 1991 by Coretta Scott King. Reprinted by permission of The Joan Daves Agency.—"

JOHNSON PUBLISHING COMPANY—pp. 3, 54, 58, 71, 74, 88, 110–111, 114, 117, 123, 125, 129, 131, 137, 149, 157, 166, 252, 253: from *Before the Mayflower: A History of Black America*, Fifth Edition, by Lerone Bennett Jr. Copyright (c) Johnson Publishing Company, Inc. 1961, 1962, 1964, 1969, 1982.

WILLIAM MORRIS AGENCY INC.—p. 321: from "Flying Home" by Ralph Ellison. Copyright (c) 1944 (renewed) by Ralph Ellison. Reprinted by permission of the William Morris Agency, Inc.

OXFORD UNIVERSITY PRESS, INC.—pp. 168, 171, 172, 173, 177, 178, 184: from *Battle Cry of Freedom: The Civil War Era* by James M. McPherson. Copyright (c) 1988 by Oxford University Press, Inc. pp. 120–121, 138, 140: from *Long Memory: The Black Experience* in America by Mary Frances Berry and John W. Blassingame. Copyright (c) 1982 by Oxford University Press, Inc. Reprinted by permission.—pp. 137, 138, 145, 156: from *Black Abolitionists* by Benjamin Quarles. Copyright (c) 1969 by Oxford University Press, Inc. Reprinted by permission.

PENGUIN USA—pp. 25–26, 48, 49, 98–99, 107: from *The Classic Slave Narratives*, edited by Henry Louis Gates, Jr. Courtesy of Penguin USA.

PRENTICE HALL—pp. 225–226: from the book, *Booker T. Washington*, by E.L. Thornbrough, Copyright (c) 1969. Used by permission of the publisher, Prentice Hall/a Division of Simon & Schuster, Englewood Cliffs, NJ.

RANDOM HOUSE, INC./ALFRED A. KNOPF, INC.—pp. 177, 178, 180, 181, 182: from *The Negro's Civil War*, by James McPherson. Copyright (c) 1965 by James McPherson. Reprinted by permission of Pantheon Books, a division of Random House, Inc.— pp. 68, 73, 87, 171, 180, 184, 357, 379: from *From Slavery to Freedom* by John Hope Franklin. Copyright (c) 1980 by Alfred A. Knopf, Inc. Reprinted by permission of the publisher.

UNIVERSITY OF NORTH CAROLINA PRESS—pp. 65, 73, 75: from *The Negro and the American Revolution*, by Benjamin Quarles. Copyright (c) 1961 by The University of North Carolina Press. Reprinted by permission of The University of North Carolina Press.

UNIVERSITY OF WISCONSIN PRESS—pp. 269, 271, 272, 273: from *Black Moses: Marcus Garvey and the Universal Negro Improvement Association*, by E. David Cronon. Copyright (c) 1969, The University of Wisconsin Press. Reprinted by permission of The University of Wisconsin Press.